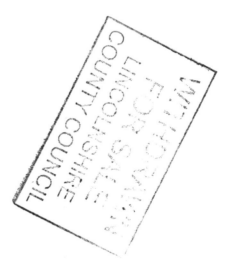

HELLO: THE AUTOBIOGRAPHY

A host of friends and colleagues recalled with wit and perceptiveness...

For more than seventy years, Leslie Phillips has been a working actor, appearing with Dame Anna Neagle in the 1930s and John Malkovich in the twenty-first century, and just about every star in between. It was in the 1950s that the predatory charm and knowing leer of his screen persona became recognised, and he made the word 'Hello' uniquely his own! With hundreds of film and theatrical roles to his credit, he can truly be described as 'a star of stage and screen', whilst remaining a father at the centre of a large, loving family, sometimes against severe personal odds.

HELLO: THE AUTOBIOGRAPHY

Hello:
The Autobiography

by

Leslie Phillips

Magna Large Print Books
Long Preston, North Yorkshire,
BD23 4ND, England.

British Library Cataloguing in Publication Data.

Phillips, Leslie
    Hello: the autobiography.

    A catalogue record of this book is
    available from the British Library

    ISBN   978-0-7505-2716-3

First published in Great Britain 2006 by Orion Books,
an imprint of the Orion Publishing Group Ltd.

Copyright © Leslie Phillips 2006

Cover illustration © Rex Features

Published in Large Print 2007 by arrangement with
Orion Publishing Group

Magna Large Print is an imprint of Library Magna Books Ltd.

Printed and bound in Great Britain by
T.J. (International) Ltd., Cornwall, PL28 8RW

For my children, grandchildren and great grand-children, whom I have often neglected as the workaholic that I am. Before I even had a chance to realise, my family of four children – Caroline, Claudia, Andrew and Roger – had grown to gigantic proportions. Caroline has had four children – Claudia, Gemma, Hannah and James – as has Claudia – Joanna, Emily, Thomas and Ben. With Andrew's four – Clifford, Matthew, Amelia and Henry – and Roger's three – Charlotte, Rebecca and Robert – to add to the number, my hands are beginning to become quite full. Then there's my stepson, Dan, and step-grandchildren, Bridget and Georgia, not to mention all of my great grandchildren. There's Joanna's son, Fred, and Emily's son, Felix, and Gemma and Thomas are both due to increase the number still further very shortly, making a grand total of twenty-six. So, far from me neglecting them, it's now me who is being neglected, and I think I may have to retire very soon to keep up with that number! And it's not likely to stop at twenty-six, is it?

Acknowledgements

A big thank you also to my editor Ian Marshall, his assistant Lorraine Baxter and all at Orion Books, as well as to Morris Bright of Pinewood Studios for his invaluable help with the photographs.

I would also like to thank my wonderful wife, Angela (Scoular) Phillips – how she copes with me I really don't know! I can't forget my brother, Fred Phillips, for his contribution to this book. My admiration for his bravery when he was so badly wounded at the Anzio Beachhead serving as a staff sergeant for the Middlesex Regiment during the Second World War is boundless. Then there's my adorable sister, Doris, who looked after me beautifully as a child and devoted herself to Mum till the day she died. And lastly to my darling mother, whose idea it was for me to become an actor, and who encouraged me always. My memories could fill another book!

Contents

Prologue • London 1944

Picture, for a moment, a young man in his twenties: slim, a little pale and recovering from war. A few blond curls show below the back of his cap as he pauses indecisively outside the tall, brass-handled door through which he has just emerged from a late nineteenth-century building near Victoria Station. He has been visiting an organisation set up to find jobs for ex-army officers who, like him, have been downgraded in health and demobilised while war still rages in Europe. Despite this, he is wearing his khaki uniform, spotless and neatly pressed, carrying the flashes of the Durham Light Infantry, 151 Brigade, 50th Northumbrian Division – Montgomery's own.

In the winter sun, the young officer's Sam Browne gleams, offering him for a while some protection from the uncertainties that life outside the army will now bring. Despite the disappointment and bleak uncertainty in his sea-blue eyes, there remains a jauntiness in his demeanour. He felt better just for being out of hospital.

In his heart, on this bright winter's day, he is still a soldier and devastated that the army doesn't want him any more. But he is now in the last stages of his final leave, still entitled to the style of a serving officer until the leave expires. He has come that morning to the Ex-Officers'

13

Association to continue discussions about suitable gentlemanly employment in Civvy Street.

Import–export in Basra was on offer, overseeing the flow of goods, he imagines, up and down the Shatt-al-Arab canal. Washing machines and telephones in; exotic feathers, dates and carpets out. He relished the idea of late-Empire – solar topees, gin slings at sundown in the Planters' Club; the dewy-eyed daughters and bored young wives of the diplomatic corps. All fanciful nonense, of course – a result of seeing too many Maugham plays – and anyway, as it turns out, not an option.

A grey-faced, middle-aged major in the office has just told him:

'I'm sorry, Lieutenant, but you'll have to rule out this job in Iraq. I'm afraid you've failed the medical. Tell me, what were you doing before you were called up?'

'I was in the theatre, sir – an actor.'

'Why don't you go back to that? I don't doubt there's a shortage.'

'Oh no, sir, I've finished with all that. If I've got to leave the army, I want a proper job.'

The major shook his head. 'I don't have anything else for you at the moment, and frankly I'm worried about your health. You must have had a bad time...'

But the young officer was already gone.

Outside the building now, the young man lifts his head and inhales a lungful of cold morning air and tells himself that, somehow, he must get a grip on his life.

His burnished brown shoes shimmy down the smooth-worn steps of York stone. No staff car with deferential driver is waiting at the kerb for him, as it would have been a few months before. With an inward sigh, he turns right and strides smartly down the street towards the station, to make his way back to his mother's home.

When she heard he was leaving the army, she had welcomed him back with tears of happiness and thanked God her younger son hadn't been sent to Normandy. He, conversely, cursed fate for not being allowed to go.

In the two and a half years since his call-up, he had been exposed to a continuous onslaught of live ammunition on army training grounds. The damage he suffered was so severe that when the time came for him actually to fight the enemy on the beaches of Normandy, army doctors had other ideas.

His loved and trusted friends in the Durham Light Infantry went; too many were killed. He knows he should have been there and would rather have died with them. Now he's racked with shame and the guilt of survival, while his brother is still in Italy, alive, at least, but confined to hospital, recovering from a chunk of shrapnel in his guts.

Picture the young former officer of the DLI, floundering at the lowest point of his life – a failure, as he saw it – with no idea of how to handle the shattering loss of his friends, with no inkling of where life will now lead.

At a time of profound self-doubt, this is Lieutenant Leslie Samuel Phillips.

A number 38 bus is waiting outside Victoria Station. This will take me all the way back to Chingford, where I'm living with my mother – to her unalloyed delight, and my stifling frustration.

I climb the stairs and settle on the back seat to nurse my disappointment at being turned down for the job. The bus heads up to Hyde Park Corner and turns right into Piccadilly, crawling through the stagnant traffic towards Eros. It swings around the little bronze bowman into Shaftesbury Avenue, moves on a few yards before shuddering to a halt in a solid jam of cars, buses, vans and taxis.

I look through the grimy window beside me. The bus is right outside the Lyric Theatre. I look at the road ahead. It's static at least as far as Cambridge Circus. On an impulse, surprising myself, I clatter down the stairs, leap off the open platform, dodge a taxi sneaking up the nearside of the bus and make landfall on the pavement right outside the Lyric. My eyes turn up to the billboard, which tells me Lynne Fontaine and her husband, Alfred Lunt, are playing in *Love in Idleness*. I glance up the road at the Apollo, the Globe and the Queen's and suddenly I'm awash with memories of my former life, for in the Lyric I appeared in *The Nutmeg Tree* with Yvonne Arnaud, in the Queen's with Dame Marie Tempest in *Dear Octopus*. In the Globe, I used to scuttle up the stairs or cram into the tiny two-man lift to reach the top floor to see Mr Binkie Beaumont, supremo of the London theatre and my employer for several happy, youthful years.

16

Submitting for a while to the seductive grasp of nostalgia, I saunter up Shaftesbury Avenue and into Soho, where the tawdry streets, bruised and battered by German bombs, are still as familiar to me as my mother's face. There was a time in this raffish place, even while the Blitz raged, when I felt at home, secure, and in control of my destiny.

Amid the smell of spices and elderly cabbage, and the scruffy bustle around Berwick Street Market, I step gingerly over rubbish-filled gutters and discarded crates in cobbled alleys. In my pristine officer's uniform, I can't help feeling I don't belong in this world any more, and don't ever want to belong again, but out of old habit I return a twinkling grin as the red-mouthed women call out, 'Hello, dearie!' and leather-skinned traders wink with friendly nods of recognition.

Before I was called up, I think, *this* was my bloody world – theatre folk and dancing girls, stallholders and tarts, all plying their trade side by side. Since then, I've turned from a junior theatrical dogsbody into an officer in His Majesty's Armed Forces – at least, until now – and, at the same time, from a working-class Cockney kid into an English gentleman, more or less.

My life was here, working behind the scenes and on the stage in the Queen's, the Lyric and the Haymarket, until I became a soldier. At nights I hung around, fed up and cold, high on the roofs over Charing Cross Road, watching for firebombs, ready to extinguish them and full of wheezes for dealing with the boredom. Down below, I laughed and drank with my friends from theatreland in the pubs in Old Compton and

Greek Street, or in the SF Grill in Denman Street and the bar of the Regent Palace.

Spurred on by the memory, I set off down Archer Street, through a gaggle of musicians clustered by the entrance to their all-powerful Union, and past the stage door of the Windmill, where the manager was a friend and the girls used to tease me.

The SF Grill is bustling like it always did and I spot a few familiar faces. I nod a greeting, but find a quiet corner to sit alone. When the coffee arrives, I look around, suddenly reminded of one of the best days of my life. I've just realised I'm in the very seat where I first met Odette.

Before I know it, my mind is panning back three years, to the spring of 1942.

I wasn't quite eighteen and call-up was six months in the future when I received an urgent summons to go up and see my boss, Binkie Beaumont. To reach the offices of H.M. Tennent Ltd in the Globe (now the Gielgud) I took the tiny lift, in which the wags advised me never to travel alone with Binkie. In truth, although everyone knew he was gay, he was very discreet – he had to be, in those days – and certainly never propositioned me; perhaps he didn't prefer blonds. Perhaps, if he had, he might have given my early career a boost – thank God he didn't!

On the way up on this occasion, I bumped into Lily Taylor who'd been my lovely chaperone on *Dear Octopus* and who was now Tennent's chief wardrobe designer.

She gave me a great welcome. 'Hello, Leslie,

darling, how are you? Been up to mischief again?'

'I don't think so, but Mr Beaumont wants to see me. I hope I'm not in trouble.'

Mrs Taylor laughed. 'No, of course you're not, darling. They love you up there.'

Grateful for her reassurance, although still a little sceptical, I carried on up in the lift to Binkie's very elegant and theatrical office, where I found him with his trusted lieutenant, Elsie Beyer, still wearing her tinted spectacles.

'Hello, Leslie, dear,' Binkie greeted me with his legendary, camp charm. 'Lovely to see you. We've got a bit of a problem, but I'm sure you'll do a good job for us, won't you? Elsie will tell you all about it,' he added and, with a flip of his hand, left us together.

Tennent's had been caught out with an unexpected hitch in a play running at the Lyric. *The Nutmeg Tree*, starring the great French actress, Yvonne Arnaud, was a comedy which included a short but significant scene with a troop of three acrobats, all professional tumblers. Two of these were foreigners of a type perceived as a potential security risk, and the government were taking no chances. 'If in doubt, lock 'em up,' was the policy. Only one, a Pole, was allowed to stay (he was on our side). This posed a problem for the management since professional tumblers were in short supply in wartime, like bananas.

Elsie assured me that I was doing a fine job as ASM at the Haymarket Theatre and they wanted me to carry on with it, while also taking over the part of the one tumbler who had dialogue, without having to do much by way of acrobatics.

19

Jacob Kreiger, the Pole, would do the tumbling, while Bert Bone, a huge, muscled creature who was fireman at the Lyric, would do all the lifting. Actors were also in short supply. I was delighted with my part – a third job, and salary, to add to my others.

I became good friends with Jacob and we often went out together after the show for a drink at the SF Grill, where I'm sitting right now.

There would always be a crowd of actors and crew from the various West End shows and a big, bubbling, busy crowd they were, high on the adrenaline of performance, and creating a heady atmosphere, despite the blackout and regular visits by the Luftwaffe. Jacob had done a lot of living as he'd tumbled his way around the world before settling in London, and we would often run into beautiful girls he'd met on his travels. I drank it all in and my ganglions quivered in response to the sexual energy that always seemed to flow through theatreland, while I was painfully conscious of my own teenage virginity.

One night we were in the SF Grill when several actors from other theatres turned up, among them a girl so lovely that there was a slight dim-inution in volume in the room when she walked in, despite the air raid going on at the time. She sat at our table and I managed to manoeuvre myself around it until I was sitting right next to her.

'Hello,' I murmured, with only a little of the clarity and confidence I brought to that same word in later years.

She rested a pair of dark, sparkling eyes on me

while she spread her luscious lips in a slow, confident smile to reveal a set of perfect teeth. She didn't seem to have any of the self-conscious coyness of the London working girl, nor the superciliousness of the well-bred English rose. There was something more sophisticated about this girl and, I thought, a hint of Slav.

Jacob saw me ogling her. He grinned.

'Leslie, zis is Odette.'

I rose to the occasion, and taking a stab at her foreign origins, kissed her hand. This seemed to work and we got on well after that. She was as clever as she was beautiful and there was an amazingly erotic quality to her husky voice and foreign vowel sounds. It was getting late and I had to leave to do my fire-watching. I asked her if she would have a meal with me the following night. She nodded with a laugh and a bewitching twinkle in her eyes. The raid had quietened down by now, and I staggered up to my fire-watching post feeling as horny as a rhino.

The next evening was even better and we ended our date with a long, lingering kiss before I went up to my duties again with my pulse throbbing in anticipation of things to come; she'd asked me to tea the following afternoon at her flat on the Embankment.

Arriving at her block the next day, I gave my wavy blond hair a last comb, checked my tie in the glass in the door, rubbed the toe caps of my shoes on the back of my flannel trousers and gulped a couple of times before finally pushing the bell. She opened the door, a warm, knowing smile playing on her lips, and greeted me with a tantalising kiss and a hint of probing tongue.

She led me up and showed me into a beautifully decorated apartment. A loaded tea tray sat ready on a low table and she poured for us both. We settled back, side by side on a big, comfortable sofa. Despite the growing stiffness in my groin, I was completely relaxed in the company of this stunning girl with whom, only a few days before, I wouldn't have thought I had a chance.

When my cup was empty, I stood up to pour refills. As I was passing her, she stood too, putting herself in front of me. With a big smile, she took the cups from my hand, grasped my tie and gently tugged me back on to the sofa. She kissed me again, with her long, hot tongue twining towards my throat like a busy serpent. It was the first time anyone had done this to me; I was amazed how exciting it was as all my organs started to throb at once. She loosened my tie and dexterously unbuttoned first my shirt, then my flies, already threatening to burst apart.

Two minutes later, I was naked, in a state of obvious excitement. I could hardly believe what was happening as she guided me through the process of undressing her, and in no more than a minute she was standing in front of me, wearing nothing but a pair of high heels and a smouldering smile.

I was in heaven for the next two hours. She stroked me gently and pleasured me, showing me how to do the same for her, and how we could do it together. Then, with her lips, her hands, her tongue and the muscles of her magical pudendum, Odette did things to me and taught me things to do to her that I'd never imagined in my wettest dreams. After the first session, we gave an encore. Well... I was seventeen and a lot fitter than I am now; I think I'd have done it ten times over, if she'd asked.

She was a wonderful, patient teacher who didn't lose my attention for a nanosecond throughout the whole long lesson. Had there been an exam at the end of it, I feel sure I'd have scored an alpha plus.

But inevitably, as the time for my first call at the Haymarket Theatre drew closer, I hurriedly dressed, said a lingering goodbye and scurried off to work and reality, feeling like a man at last. A little tender, perhaps, but wearing one of the biggest smiles in London – if anyone could see it in the blackout. Before that incredible day, I would never have believed that sex could be so utterly joyous.

Odette and I met often over the weeks that followed and the intensity of the experience never failed. Although she was a few years older, and must have had more experienced boyfriends than me, perhaps she got a kick from my youthful exuberance and perhaps she thought I would soon be going off to fight, and we might never get the opportunity again. During the war, with death lurking around the corner for so many young men, I'm sure a lot of women must have thought that way, God bless them.

Having finished my coffee it's time to return to the present. I leave the SF Grill and wander back along Old Compton Street, acutely aware that all these memories spring from an earlier phase of my life – a former incarnation, as I see it. In a confused reverie, I'm crossing the road to walk down Dean Street when a close call with a taxi jerks me back to reality and I remember that I'm in my army officer's guise. I throw back my shoulders and break into what I hope is a convincing strut and turn down Shaftesbury Avenue, intent on escaping via the next 38 bus.

'Leslie? Leslie? Is that you under that cap? Gosh, Leslie, it is you!'

I know the voice – firm and soft, gentle and tough, source of my instructions while I worked for H.M. Tennent Ltd. It's Elsie Beyer.

'Elsie, how lovely to see you!' I feel my face light up as she stretches to give me an unexpected kiss. 'Leslie, how wonderful to see you. You're still in the army?'

I hope she doesn't see the flash of pain in my eyes – the pain and the shame that I'm not with my old unit and my friends, marching east through Holland towards Berlin.

'Yes, for a little longer, but I'm about to be demobbed.'

'When? Do you want a job? We must see what we can do to keep you off the streets, and we desperately need young men with experience – there aren't many around at the moment. When can you start?'

'I'm not sure exactly, Elsie,' I demur. 'You know how it is. I've got a few irons in the fire... Various things...'

Elsie brushes aside my prevarication. 'Now, just give me your phone number and I'll ring you the minute anything suitable turns up.'

On Shaftesbury Avenue, strangely buoyed by Elsie's infectious enthusiasm, I see another 38 bus approaching. I leap on and climb to the upper deck to continue the journey back to Chingford, but as we cross into Theobald's Road I'm jolted back in time again to my first journey here, to visit the Italia Conti stage school.

The bus slows to a stop. Abandoning all pretence at dignity, I leap from my seat and ricochet down the stairs, out on to the pavement. I watch the bus roll on before I turn into Lamb's Conduit Street and walk a few dozen yards up the road until I am outside the Italia Conti school, awash with memories of a day that was to change my life.

It was a Monday morning in 1936. I was eleven years old and it was exciting enough just to be missing a day from Chingford Senior Boys'; heading for the West End with Mum, a very big adventure indeed.

'What's this place like, Mum?' I asked as the school came in sight, curious but not at all anxious with her beside me.

'I'm sure you'll like it,' she smiled and gave my hand a squeeze. 'It's going to be real fun!'

Now it seems pretty extraordinary that my mother should have taken this initiative, although there was always a spark about her that allowed her to see well beyond the obvious boundaries of our lives. She was a romantic dreamer who once, on holiday in Ramsgate, had entered me – a blond, curly-haired boy – in a children's beauty contest. I never did discover how she heard about Miss Italia Conti's advertisement in the paper, inviting children to audition for an appearance in a professional Christmas play.

We went in, nervous but still excited, and were shown into an office where Miss Italia Conti and her assistant were seeing the aspiring young actors.

Miss Conti eyed me with flashing Mediterranean eyes and spoke to me in a very English accent, while her assistant looked on with a kindly smile. It was my first audition.

Looking back, I don't imagine it was the most impressive thing Miss Conti ever saw – a clean but threadbare lad spouting lines from *Julius Caesar* in undiluted Cockney – but I enjoyed myself, and apparently redeemed my shortcomings with a bit of imaginative business when I flung my little blue overcoat around my shoulders as a toga.

'I like his invention,' Miss Conti pronounced grandly, and I was in.

I went on to spend a few youthful years at the Conti school, performing every legitimate function the theatre had to offer. Besides acting, I was understudy, call-boy, ASM, devoted gofer to Vivien Leigh, in *The Doctor's Dilemma*, and to Rex Harrison's gorgeous lover, Lilli Palmer, in *No Time for Comedy*, both plays at the Haymarket.

After my short stroll down Lamb's Conduit Street, and Memory Lane, I return to Theobald's Road to continue my journey home to Chingford. I'm feeling a little lighter, but still wary of

26

any return to that phase of my life. After my youthful career in the theatre I entered a new phase – a third incarnation, you could say – the day I was commissioned a sub-lieutenant in His Majesty's Armed Forces, and the transformation from cheeky Cockney lad to fully-formed member of the salute-receiving, gin-drinking officer class was complete.

I hadn't set out to alter myself; I was no eager young social-climber with silly ambitions, but my brief theatrical career had inevitably brought about dramatic changes to the extent that my siblings, if not my mother, found it hard to recognise the youngest member of their family in the new me.

I had learned my lessons well, there's no doubt about that, and become a suave young man who could exchange pleasantries with Vivien Leigh and murmur sophisticated sweet nothings to the well-born girls who love a Sam-Browned soldier. In contrast, my elder brother, Fred, who was a working man at the Atlas Lamp Company in Edmonton, had become a staff sergeant in the Middlesex Regiment, while my mother remained a strong, cheerful Cockney with a working-class heart of gold.

It's enough – more than enough – to dis-orientate any young man. And I am thoroughly disoriented after a dozen years scuttling around the theatres and appearing in some of the earliest films made at Pinewood Studios. Now that my metamorphosis into pip-shouldered officer is complete, if I can only escape from the gloomy self-doubt that enwraps me, I think it's time to launch a new upward diagonal in the bizarre graph of my life so far.

Another number 38 rolls up and I carry on with my journey home, turning into Rosebery Avenue, past Sadler's Wells and up to the Angel, Islington, where the bus heads towards East London, by way of Balls Pond Road – a name I've always enjoyed – and Dalston Lane until it crosses the River Lea. To the south lies the flat expanse of Hackney Marsh and to the north the great Lea Valley reservoirs, which evoke another boyhood memory of the first of many, much-loved dogs in my life.

Spot was a smooth-haired terrier of frankly low caste and mixed parentage, of whom I was very fond. Like most terriers, he was a canny beast. He once saved my father from drowning – or at least from a good soaking – in somewhat ironic circumstances.

I was barely eight when Dad, who, like my mother, was never particularly fond of animals, decided that keeping a dog wasn't worth the bother or the cost, although I don't suppose it involved more than a shilling or two a week. With my uncles Tom and Bob, he conspired, not to kill the dog – which was big of them – but to 'lose' it when out walking one night. They ought to have considered that they were far more likely to get lost than Spot.

At that time, the Phillipses inhabited a small, plain, terraced house, long since demolished, near Tottenham Hale. The location for the dog's abandonment had been selected on the far reaches of the reservoir, beyond the River Lea, reached by crossing the Black Ditch, a stagnant waterway alongside the river. When they left the house, it was a cold, clear night, but down by the water conditions deteriorated until they were enveloped by an impenetrable blanket of mist and coal smoke, one of the dreaded 'pea-soupers', although this night, according to Uncle Tom, it was a kind of murky yellow; more of a 'carrot-and-coriander-souper'.

As they neared the river, Spot suddenly dug his paws into the muddy path and refused to budge another step. My father, still tugging the dog, thought it had guessed its fate. The next moment, blinded by the grimy fog, he almost stepped straight off the edge of the path into the still, deep waters of Black Ditch.

Dad, being no swimmer, admitted afterwards that the animal had probably saved his life. Not unreasonably, Spot was reprieved and I was mightily relieved. So, I imagine, was Spot. For me it would have been like losing a greatly loved friend.

Since then, innumerable dogs have snuffled, barked, stunk and farted their way through my life, along with a good many cats. It seems that I've always had a special affinity with animals and birds; I still have a certificate awarded by the RSPCA in 1932, when I was eight, highly commending me for my 'Knowledge of Care of Pets'.

Jerking myself back to the present, I find that the bus is turning left off the Lea Bridge Road, up Hoe Street, towards Walthamstow railway station, where I used to board the rattler up to Liverpool

Street. But the bus carries on into Old Church Road, past the turning to Middleton Avenue. It was to there, at the age of ten, that I had my first heartbreaking encounter with human death.

My father was just forty-four when dropsy finally got the better of his weakened heart and brought to an end all the frustrations and thwarted ambitions of his short life, the disease having been encouraged by the Gold Flake cigarettes he loved to smoke, and the filthy, sulphurous air of the factory where he worked. His death cut me up badly; I'd been used to him being ill but, like most kids, I was conscious only of his strengths and accepted his weaknesses as the norm.

Like most Cockney families, we followed the gruesome tradition of bringing the corpse back home. Dad was put on display, all besuited and with hair neatly brushed, in his coffin on a table in the front parlour. Relatives from Greenwich, Enfield and Tottenham came to take their leave in reverence and grief, while the neighbours didn't miss the chance to drop in for a gawp and, if they were lucky, a couple of drinks at the expense of the bereaved.

When I finally went in to the front room to see him, urged by my mother but dreading it, I found Dad with his head propped up on a mauve satin cushion and a white lace antimacassar. He'd been dead a few days and I recoiled at the sight of an orange fungus that had started to form in his ears and nostrils. I found it hard to believe that this cold, rigid, decaying form had so recently been my warm, lovely dad.

The image lingered in my head long after I'd left the room. At five the following morning, as I set off on my paper round, I could barely feel the weight of the sack of newsprint, so numbed was I by my grief and the horror of seeing Dad laid out in our front room. I don't know what my mother was thinking when she took me into the parlour; I've only ever recalled it since with a shudder of horror.

The number 38 trundles on, the long haul up Chingford Mount, past the cemetery where Dad was buried and Aunt Lil came over all hysterical at the graveside. Opposite is the thirteenth-century All Saints' Church, where I used to scrape a bit of pocket money (and, if I'm lucky, a little discount off my spell in purgatory) by adding my eager treble voice to the choir. A little further, on the right, is Wellington Avenue, where I attended Chingford Senior Boys' School and had my first taste of drama as third witch in the Scottish play and – to the merciless teasing of my school mates – Gianetta in *The Gondoliers.* In fact, I played females several times; no doubt on account of my blond locks, excellent legs and shapely bum. Mum didn't mind; she came to watch, goggle-eyed and thrilled by my performance.

'Look out Clark Gable!' she would say with the blindness of a doting mother, and it was there her dreams of my theatrical career were born, inspired, perhaps, by the increasingly desperate need for more money in the family.

Leaving Wellington Avenue and my memories of

school behind, the number 38 passes the Green Man. Soon it's rumbling up Station Road, where I get off. I watch for a moment as the bus carries on to the end of its journey at the Royal Forest Hotel, on the edge of Epping Forest.

As it disappears, I walk slowly back to my mother's house in Station Road, pondering my future. I can't just ignore Elsie Beyer's promise of work, for I had loved the stage, performing with absurd confidence and, I suppose, some skill. But I was no child star; my toe had barely reached the first rung on the ladder that leads to stardom. After a few years in the army, my aspirations have broadened, and I'm determined to remain immune to the allure of the seamy yet glamorous world I used to inhabit. Theatre was what I did as a child; now it's time to put away childish things and move on.

But where?

Whatever job Elsie may offer me, I must tell myself, I don't want it!

1 • An East London Boy

The house we'd left in Tottenham for the sake of my father's health was a small, late Victorian terraced house in the optimistically named Welbourne Road. I was born there on 20 April 1924. The sun was shining and no sooner was I out, blinking my eyes for a quick squint at the world around me when the home side scored a goal and – according to my mother – I yelled louder than the Spurs supporters in the stadium down the road.

I was the third and last child of Frederick Samuel Phillips and Cecelia, née Newlove, who'd been married at Edmonton Parish Church on 1 June 1914. Mum, I learned later, had carried other children, stillborn or dead soon after birth, which must have been hard to live with. We don't understand this tragedy so well these days, now infant mortality rates have plummeted. However, I was glad my mum persevered.

Our street, long since demolished to make way for a busy link road up to the great new M11, was just off High Cross, beyond the sonic reach of the Bow Bells but within the general footprint of Cockneydom. Not far from there, in a factory on a filthy, smelly industrial estate off Angel Road, Edmonton, my dad worked for Thomas Glover & Main, gas cooker manufacturers.

Sadly, although he was quick-witted, intelligent and industrious, Dad never really had a chance to make the most of himself. Any hope of promotion was scuppered by a chronic heart condition. He had previously suffered from rheumatic fever, which can only have been aggravated by the sur- roundings in which he spent his working days. Even now I can feel in my nostrils the acrid, pun- gent stink of gas, smoke and steam that hung about the place, long before words like 'ecology' had seeped into common use – or consciousness, for that matter.

This mean part of London was all I knew then, but I was always a sanguine child and just got on with extracting the most that life had to offer, pretty much as I've tried to do ever since. I wasn't unhappy; I loved my sickly dad and my down-to-earth, whimsical mum. And I adored my sister, Doris. Dolly, as we called her, was seven years older and used to cuddle me lovingly. Later, when I was seven or eight, and big soft breasts began to bulge beneath her blouse, she'd let me slip my hand in and gently fondle them, arousing a healthy fascination that's never completely left me. Of course, as we grew up, it didn't happen any more, but I had a special affection for her right up until she died, when thoughts of those moments leaped back into my head. I've never before told anyone of these prepubescent intimacies, and I never mentioned them to her, but they remain as warm and tender memories.

From when I was very young, I would tag along behind my brother Fred, three and a half years older, until he took to calling me his 'bloody shadow'. We were, physically at least, quite alike, although he always claims to have had the edge in the good looks department. Our lives could scarcely have turned out more differently, which ultimately created something of a barrier between us. I'm still very fond of the old sod though.

I think, in general, I must have been a very tactile boy. I vividly recall, after a session helping my dad in the garden, he would lather his hands to wash them, then take my muddy little mitts between his, still soapily soft, and gently cleanse them.

I'm sure, with hindsight, that there must have been great strains and stresses in the life of our working-class family at a time when there were no supplementary benefits or family tax credits. If you were poor, you were bloody poor, and tough shit. Despite that, life on the whole was peaceful, apart from the occasional explosion when I had to leap on my father's back to stop him taking out his frustrations on my long-suffering mum. My brother and sister always said that they never saw my parents fight, so it can't have happened too often, but poor old Dad must have felt like a rat in a trap at times, struggling with a debilitating condition and helpless to prevent the money running out.

To add to that, my brother and I were a pair of persistently naughty little boys. I learned years later from my charming and elderly cousin Gladys that, when her family heard my father was coming over, they'd say, 'I hope he doesn't bring them little buggers with him!'

Certainly his heavy leather belt was often removed from trouser loops to be wielded in a minatory way. Thankfully, it was never used on me, though I believe Fred felt it from time to time. But for the most part, Dad was a gentle man whom we all remembered fondly.

Mum, down-to-earth and resourceful, was also a bit of a romantic dreamer. I first experienced this quality when she entered me into that dreaded beauty competition in Ramsgate – the only place we ever went for our annual summer jaunt. I don't want to sound immodest, but I won the contest hands down. To my great embarrassment, the photos of my triumph clearly showed my unbuttoned flies, which I immediately inked over, feeling, perhaps, that it didn't pay to advertise at that age (though I made up for it later in life).

That same week, I was hauled from the beach and rushed off to hospital with serious sun burn. Curly blond hair, fair skin and strong sun don't mix. Of course, in those days there were no warnings about the dangers of the sun, nor sun blockers. Mum never learned; every year I burned and had to be smothered in calamine lotion after the visit to hospital.

Mum didn't swim either, so we children were never taught, and I developed a fear of water which I've found difficult to overcome. To this day the shallow end only is within my depth (a tad embarrassing when movie roles have required macho swimming performances; many's the time I've sunk).

Nor, when we got home in the evenings, did she read me bedtime stories. Either she was too busy or it didn't come easily to her. I regret that very much, even now, for in spite of being an actor for the last seventy years – give or take a few during the war – I've always found reading quite an effort, especially amid a relentless torrent of lines to learn.

I was six or seven when our parents decided to relocate to Chingford in 1931, in the hope of giving my father some respite from the foul air of Angel Road, and us children a hint of the joys of the countryside. This small Essex town on the fringes of Epping Forest was then growing like a rampant weed to meet the new suburban aspirations of East Londoners. Perhaps it is no surprise that its political associations include such conservative luminaries as Norman Tebbit, who was born there, and Iain Duncan Smith, the local MP.

Our house was a red-brick semi in Middleton Avenue, with a garden where my father loved to labour after a week's work in the factory. Sadly, he applied himself to the task of cultivating it with such vigour that his already weakened heart could not take the strain.

My cousin Peggy, a lively girl of curly hair, mischievous eyes and unusual upbringing, would come over to see us, and we played in the garden, with inevitable shenanigans in the shed. She lived with my Newlove grandparents, ostensibly as their daughter, in a prominent corner house on Ranelagh Road, Tottenham, surrounded by a wide garden with a massive lilac tree – a favourite destination.

When Spot the terrier eventually died – of natural causes, I'm pleased to say – he was replaced by Rosie, a fast, loveable whippet. She would roam with me through Epping Forest, where I used to collect grass snakes in the beech glades and take them home – to my mother's disgust when she found them in my bed.

I also wandered far and wide around East London with Fred. For a few pence we would get an all-day ticket on the tram and travel from Chingford to the Monument, walk over London Bridge across the Thames and take another tram across Bermondsey to Bellot Street in Greenwich, where my father's parents lived.

Granny Phillips loved Fred and me. She was an exuberant, special person, always pleased to see

37

us and, though just as poor as us, never failed to produce some edible treat out of nowhere when we turned up. We loved her, too, and being on the other side of the river our visits seemed to us a great adventure, almost like going abroad.

We saw less of Grandpa. He worked for the railway and loved it so much that, the day after he was forced to retire at the age of sixty-five, he hanged himself from the bedpost with his tie, leaving poor old Gran to fend for herself. That was one of two sadnesses that pervaded the house. A large photograph commemorated my father's brother, Arthur; while home on leave from the trenches in 1918, he drowned himself to avoid going back to the Somme. Had he waited a week or so, the war actually came to an end.

For all that, I have happy memories of Grandma's small, dun-brick house, one door and a window wide, with a worn and proudly scrubbed doorstep of York stone, probably worth more now than the whole house was then. When I last went to look at it, not long ago while visiting the theatre in Greenwich, I found the whole street transformed into desirable bijou residences for thrusting young professionals.

Soon after Grandpa's death, darling Grandma fell apart when, with no other option, she was moved to an old people's home near the tube station in Tooting Bec. I asked Mum to take me to visit her, and a nightmarish, Hogarthian place it turned out to be, with wire mesh between galleried landings. The staff in this uncompromisingly stern, glazed-brick institution had become brutalised by their work and flung their poor old charges around like sacks of flour. I took Gran some sweets and she immediately slipped them surreptitiously under her pillow; otherwise, she said, they'd be nicked.

One ancient couple, trying to find some solace in this hellhole, had decided to marry. He was deaf and she was blind. The other inmates teased her: 'Why do you want to marry him? You can't even see him.'

'No, but I can *feel* him,' she chortled toothlessly.

I shuddered. I couldn't wait to get out of the place, and resisted all further attempts to lure me back there.

The move to Chingford also brought about a change of school, to the New Road Primary, where I was introduced to drama and football, played with caution on a gravel pitch, but nevertheless resulting in permanently grazed knees. I was a speedy runner and a dangerous outside right (as well as a demon bowler on the cricket field, as I recall). On Saturdays, I loved my sport and became a devoted fan of Tottenham Hotspur, whom I still support, albeit more in sprit than physical presence these days. It's a great relief to see them back near the top of the league again after too many flat years.

The school stage productions – nativities and so on – I took in my stride, but they taught me the rudiments of performing. As did singing in the choir in a surplice and crisp white collar at All Saints' Church, though at the time it was just another way of earning some modest pocket-money.

Another earner, though, God knows, it must have yielded only pennies, was finding and dealing in stamps. I would diligently put together small, pathetic collections in packets which I was allowed to sell through the newsagents where I also did a paper-round, and later worked behind the counter, selling tobacco and snuff. The collecting habit has stayed with me, only now I never sell anything. Over the years I've become a compulsive buyer, accumulating hordes of *objets* of variable and eclectic beauty from around the world that my poor wife has to dust, but being a big spender herself she hasn't asked me to chuck the whole lot out. Naturally, the way things are today, I never see the more valuable items because those that haven't been stolen are tucked away in the bank – more's the pity. Potential burglars, take note! Those that have already pinched a number of my goodies, please bring them back.

In 1935 my father's health took a sudden turn for the worse and he was rushed to hospital. I remember waking up at night and wondering what life could be like without him. These fears were soon realised. But it was only when I saw my mother gazing into her empty purse as the last of the mourners left after Dad's funeral, that it hit me: it wasn't just Dad's presence we were going to miss.

Without his sporadic wages coming in, we were in dire straits. Fred and Doris were old enough to go out to work, which helped, but even at the age of eleven I knew I was going to have to do my bit to help with the family finances. We were reduced to a state of permanent penury; everything was geared to scraping together money to buy food and pay the rent. There was no money for presents or luxuries; nor were there parties at Christmas or on birthdays. If I wanted anything, I had to earn the money to pay for it. And by God I did! Try telling that to the average ten-year-old now. I know what it's like. Having been blessed with some twenty grandchildren and three great-grandchildren, I've become something of an expert on the demands of youth these days. I love them all, and do my best to tolerate some of their spouses, but I must confess I'm gradually finding it difficult to remember all their names and ages without stopping to think a bit.

2 • The Young Performer

It still amazes me, knowing my mother, that she ever took the initiative to get me into stage school. She was a warm but essentially humble creature, under-educated, with no certificates to her name and no great expectations – and no surplus cash. When Dad died, she had to sell the small house he'd so proudly bought. By the time all the loans had been paid off, she was left with the vast sum of £15. After that we moved from a rented house to a succession of rented flats, each a little lower down the scale than the last.

Mum earned what she could by taking in clothes for repair, but she wanted something better for us kids and was always on the lookout for ways we could have fun while making a bit of money for ourselves. One day she announced that she wanted me to come with her to meet a woman in the West End; it might as well have been Shangri-La, for all I knew back then.

'What for?' I asked.

'She's got a sort of school; they do theatricals,' she said.

'Theatricals? You mean plays and all that?'

'Yes, like you've done at school.'

Although I'd been picked for the school drama group and had made my first few appearances, I don't suppose I was much better or worse than any of the other kids. But the local paper had singled me out with a photo and a mention, and from that moment Mum was firmly convinced I had a great future in the theatre.

'The lady wants to see you Saturday morning,' she went on.

'I can't go on Saturday! I'm playing football – and I'm captain!'

'But it'd be fun, Leslie. You know how much you like doing the plays.'

'Not more than football, though.'

Mum sighed, knowing I wouldn't be budged. She got in touch with the school and told them we wouldn't be coming.

However, by Sunday I realised my mother was right; I'd always liked being in school plays and I was beginning to grow more curious about this lady with the mysterious theatrical academy.

'Why don't we go tomorrow?' I suggested, thinking I'd like a day off school, so next morning we set off for Central London on the number 38 bus.

Miss Conti was a clever old thing. After I passed my audition with that garbled chunk of *Julius Caesar*, recognising our inability to pay, she took my mother aside and said, 'When we see a child with promise, we look for other ways of providing their fees. We will take Leslie and, as soon as he is ready, we will find him work. We will act as his agents, and his fees will be paid from his earnings. Of course, as agents, we will take twenty per cent.'

It seemed, then, that Mum wouldn't have to worry about finding money for school fees, and we left in a glow. We didn't completely understand the arrangements Miss Conti had outlined, but we were left in no doubt that we wouldn't have to pay much. Mum's eyes were shining with excitement as we rumbled back to Chingford on the number 38. We were both thrilled by our first encounter with the world of professional theatre.

At home, Mum was bubbling over with pride, gleefully telling everyone in Chingford – or those who would listen – about her Leslie, the next great film star. By the time the story appeared in the *Walthamstow Guardian*, my future career was already on the move.

I had a nervous start at Conti's, though I settled fairly soon into the routine of going there three days a week after normal school to attend drama, dance and elocution lessons. In those days it was impossible to become an actor with what might now be called a 'regional' accent. Look at any

43

black-and-white movie of the thirties and forties, and you'll find that all the stars come across rather piss-elegant. That's all been reversed now to the point where Ray Winstone can deliver a fine performance as King Henry VIII in purest Plaistow, but it wasn't an option available to us then. So even though 'How, now, brown cow' without a Cockney accent sounded embarrassingly pretentious to me, I persevered.

Of course, to avert any sending up, I made sure I reverted to heavy Cockney when I came home to school in Chingford, but I couldn't escape the feeling that I was growing away from my old friends and even my own family. Fred – now working for the Atlas Lamp Company in smelly Edmonton – began to look a bit sideways at me. Mum tried to help by buying him a drum kit; he formed a dance band but never caused the stars of the day any lost sleep. She also paid for my sister to have piano lessons, of which I was rather envious. I've since made several attempts to learn the piano myself, and can now read a little music and pick out a tune quite happily by ear. But neither Dolly nor I were ever likely to rival Vladimir Horovitz.

Academically, I was doing well, even coming top of the class sometimes, but it wasn't enough to keep me entirely grounded or quell the resentment of some my school mates. I was careful not to boast about my stage work, and told them I was only doing it for the money, which at this stage was true.

There was, however, one awful occasion when I was subjected to the full, physical force of resentment. It happened as I made my way up Ching-ford Mount one morning with my friend Leslie Pressman, who often joined me on the walk to school. We had no idea that a gang of ruffians headed by an obnoxious leader called Harry were lurking in a narrow side road, waiting for us. When we drew level, they jumped out waving sticks and piled into us.

I had no idea why we were being attacked, but even though there were four of them Leslie and I fought back, landing a few kicks and punches, until we were both knocked to the ground, badly cut and bruised. Our attackers ran off when they saw a policeman approaching.

Leslie then turned to me and said, 'Sorry. That was my fault.'

'What are you talking about?'

'Didn't you hear what they said? It's because I'm Jewish. They're tied up with those Brown Shirts.'

Sir Oswald Mosley's British Union of Fascists had been recruiting in East London and the thugs who joined them were reflecting the vicious displays of anti-Semitism that were going on in Germany – Kristallnacht and the beginnings of the racial purge that Hitler had instigated.

It seemed absurd that this should be happening in Britain. It made no sense to attack Leslie Pressman. His father was a decorated First World War veteran who had lost a leg in the trenches and was now reduced to being the only official seller of pigeon feed in Trafalgar Square, a well-known London character.

I came to know the Pressmans well. Leslie's

mother, a big, cosy, generous Jewish momma, became a great friend of my mother's and many years later took her abroad for the first and only time in her life on a day-trip by boat to Calais.

Jack Watling, another schoolfriend, was already at Conti's and making a name for himself. Over the next thirty years, Jack and I saw each other and worked together often, although in the early days, I found myself as mere understudy to him. To some extent he prepared the way for me at Chingford Senior Boys. He even came back to star in our school plays, with the result that other boys didn't find the idea of a thespian class mate quite as strange as they might have.

It caused some envy that I was now mixing with sophisticated, stage-struck dancing girls at Conti's. There were a lot of them, all good-looking, busty, uninhibited and daring. They didn't care who saw their legs and knickers in a twirling dance, and if there was a quick change, they just stripped off in front of everyone. On one occasion I lost control completely and slipped a hand inside the back of a girl's frock and twanged her bra strap. I couldn't believe it when she sneaked, landing me with a severe bollocking. It taught me a lesson, though, about actresses; however inviting they may seem, beware: they may bite.

Back in Chingford, my first girlfriend, the angelic and submissive Jean Rowly, aged twelve, was less thrilled at the company I was keeping. I played down any talk of girls, but Jean needn't have worried; I wasn't getting up to anything –

yet. In those days adolescent sex meant kissing and, if you were incredibly lucky, a little groping in the bosom department. No one had real sex. But in the thirties the touching up was exciting enough, and teenage pregnancy was unheard of.

I travelled to Holborn to Conti's by myself, sometimes having to avoid the dirty old men who seemed to roam quite freely in those days. I learned to avoid sticky situations without telling grown-ups, who would only have told me not to be silly and to watch my manners.

There were a few beastly experiences on offer at Chingford Senior Boys' school, too. One of our teachers had all the outer trappings of a real role model. He was clever, athletic and good-looking, with a set of gleaming white Hampsteads (teeth); all very upper class and jolly, with a loud, manic laugh. He also liked to play a 'game' that involved grabbing a boy, holding him close from behind, and squeezing him tightly. Then he would invite each of us in turn to hold his rampant phallus through his trousers. We all had to comply. Soon the size of his cock became the talk of the school. I didn't tell my mother, and the other boys must have kept quiet about it, too. Finally someone must have blown the whistle because he disappeared abruptly in the middle of term, never to be seen again.

We heard rumours that he had gone a lot further with one or two of the other boys, but it was all hushed up. The last I heard of him, he'd refused his call-up as a conscientious objector. Probably just as well, though I'd love to have seen him in action in a barrack room full of raw recruits – they would have gelded him on the spot.

Given my stage career, it's ironic that this abuse should have occurred at my normal school, rather than at some seedy playhouse or digs on tour. Over the years that followed, I was certainly propositioned quite a few times by famous, widely revered actors, but never actually molested. As they say in the army, *No names, no pack drill.*

Towards the end of 1937, I was a confident – not to say cocky – thirteen-year-old. Miss Conti had been tremendously kind to me, as she was to nearly all the pupils. She would go to great lengths to keep her students happy and balanced, even inviting groups of half a dozen or so to her lovely seafront villa on the south coast for short summer holidays. It was great fun, of course, and involved a lot of groping.

One day, gazing at me with her customary circumspection, Miss Conti shook her head slightly and said, 'Leslie, you've changed since you started with us – your nose is getting too big. Still,' she shrugged, 'there are always other parts.'

I was horrified by this at the time, although I tried not to let it get me down. I'm very attached to my distinctive proboscis, so it's fortunate that she wasn't entirely right in her predictions. My face got bigger around the age of sixteen, making my nose seem smaller. Thank you God!

By the time Miss Conti's camp assistant got me my first film job, – a 'bit' in a movie being shot at Welwyn Studios – I'd already learned a great deal. The film was a romantic comedy called *Lassie from Lancashire*, and I played me. John Paddy Carstairs directed with bumbling good nature. He was very encouraging and a wonderful, multi-talented man – a fine painter in the style of Dufy, and a good writer, too.

He came from a great theatrical family, and his mother was often on the set. She liked me, for the strange reason that she was convinced I was an illegitimate son of her very errant husband, the comedian Nelson Keys. It was true that I did bear a strong resemblance to John Paddy's brother, Basil Keys, who became a successful producer.

But Mrs Keys was a loveable creature and full of pithy wisdom. She would tell everyone that she loved her children but they had completely ruined her marriage and she wished she'd never had them. I've never forgotten that!

Another of Paddy's endearing eccentricities while directing was his practice of wearing berets of varied hues, and changing them regularly as if to match his mood. A red beret showed he was in a good, approachable mood – that was the time to talk to him; a black beret meant avoid him; a blue beret indicated that he was feeling reflective, and a khaki one that he was in an organised, military frame of mind. And there was a white one he used only during Wimbledon or Test matches.

In the days when I started, all actors began their career in theatre. Hence to become an actor meant 'going on the stage', and that was where you learned your craft. Only later might you be considered for a movie. Television has completely changed all that, and now a lot of the biggest movie stars have never been near a real stage. I was thirteen when I first set foot on the stage of a West End theatre.

No doubt because it was the only way the Italia Conti school was going to be paid for my tuition, they found me a part in the next Christmas play, which turned out to be *Peter Pan* at the Palladium, with Anna Neagle in the title role. Thus, in December 1937, I signed my first theatre contract. The part – a Wolf – didn't require a great deal of acting skill (although it did require *some*, and perhaps set me up for the string of wolfish roles I played later).

As an ambitious child actor, I quickly discovered a strong affinity with the theatre world and the people in it. Anna Neagle, for instance, was very kind and considerate to us young actors, and we slavishly followed her every move, our awestruck gaze following her as she drove away after the matinee each evening with her husband, Herbert Wilcox, behind the elegant, long bonnet of her MG.

For the rest of my time at Italia Conti, and indeed for the next sixty years, I was seldom out of work for more than a few days, unless by choice. At the beginning I earned a weekly wage of twenty-five shillings – which was not to be sniffed at – and in the process I was gaining the kind of experience that's irreplaceable in an actor's career.

My mother was proud of what I was doing but, unlike some other Conti pupils' mums, she never interfered with my career or made herself obvious at my performances. I'm sure she felt that by taking me up to Conti's in the first place, she'd done all she could, but what a vital contribution it turned out to be. Even years later, when I was an established actor, she would buy her own ticket and sneak into the theatre without telling me she was coming. She only ever came backstage afterwards if I'd spotted her and sent someone out to grab her before she left to catch the bus home – the number 38, of course.

Not long after *Lassie from Lancashire* I worked in a few movies being shot at the distinctly superior Denham Studios. King Vidor, the big American director, was over here making a high-profile picture, *The Citadel,* which allowed me to study at close quarters the skills of Robert Donat, Ralph Richardson and, for me more interestingly, the young Rex Harrison, who for the next couple of decades made several entries into my life. I saw from the start that he was a man of spectacular sexual drive and apparently irresistible charm, which I immediately recognised as a formidable weapon for an actor.

On this picture, though, I don't think even Rex's charm was enough to pierce the defences of the film's beautiful American star, Rosalind Russell. She provided me with my first glimpse of true Hollywood glamour in the flesh and set my little knees trembling every time I saw her.

Poking around behind the set one day, I noticed smoke rising from a pile of props. As I crossed gingerly to investigate, knowing I was already out of bounds, I shivered with horror when a few tongues of flame began to lick up. I didn't hang around to weigh up the consequences. I rushed back on to the set in the middle of an important shot and shouted, *'FIRE!'* at the top of my voice.

Nothing – but nothing – and nobody in the studio should ever interrupt a shot, but now I – a humble 'bit' – had done just that. Suddenly everything stopped. King Vidor turned a pair of death rays on my shaking body.

'You better not be fooling, boy!' he roared. I quaked as the studio firemen raced off to check it, keeping my fingers so crossed they hurt, hoping I hadn't made a mistake.

Thank God, a real fire was beginning to take hold.

If I'd been wrong, I would have been chewed up and spat out by the director. As it was, King Vidor thanked me publicly and rewarded me with a second 'bit' part. Being a 'bit' may not sound much, but it was a whole lot higher up the pecking order than an 'extra'. Extras had only to stand and walk. 'Bits' were actors and did things – lifted cloaks, moved chairs, opened doors, reacted even, and were paid more. I was thrilled: more chances to ogle Miss Russell, and more guineas for Mum, and always twenty per cent for Miss Conti.

Denham Studio at the time was dominated by the Kordas, a family of Hungarian film makers. Alexander Korda had founded London Films and made a string of hits, both as producer and director. He was a spectacular deal-maker who earned a knighthood from King George VI for his impact on the British film industry. Under his brother, Zoltan, I was given the part of a lurking brat in *The Four Feathers* with a young John Clements and Ralph Richardson again – and if you haven't seen it, where have you been? It is without doubt one of the great British classics. It wasn't the last time I worked with Sir Ralph; thirty years later we appeared together in a BBC production of P.G. Wodehouse's *Blandings Castle* with my old mate Derek Nimmo.

After Denham, I worked on some of the first movies made at Pinewood Studios. J. Arthur Rank had built the place in 1936 with a consortium he'd formed to buy Heatherden Hall, a sumptuous country mansion not far from Denham. Over the years, I've made so many films at Pinewood, it's become a home from home. This year, 2006, it celebrates its seventieth anniversary, and I turn out to be one of the earliest actors to have worked there who's still alive and still working. I have great memories of the place.

The first Pinewood pictures I worked on were *The Mikado* – in which I was wonderfully miscast as a Chinese boy – and *Climbing High* for the fine director Carol Reed. *Climbing High* starred Jessie Matthews and Michael Redgrave – a light comedy actor at that stage in his career. I learned a lot from watching him and later took some encouragement from his transition to serious character actor when, thirty-five years later, I decided to make a similar move. By a strange twist of fate, almost seventy years on, I found myself working with his illustrious daughter, Vanessa, in the Hanif Kureishi-scripted film *Venus*, which will premiere around the time this book is published.

During these early forays into the wonderful world of movies, as a boy I was still living with my mother in Chingford, but feeling quite grown up as memories of Dad began to fade. I had also got myself a new friend – four-footed and furry. The cat's name was Smaxie, stolen from a character in a favourite Una Merkel movie. Poor Smaxie was bitten by the moggie from next door when I was fourteen and, having applied antiseptic ointment and bandages, I had to abandon him to go on tour. My mother didn't share my love of cats and took a lot of persuading to tend the animal when I wasn't there. But I've always loved their brave independence, and Smaxie, God bless him, was the first of many pussies I have loved and cherished over the years.

Reverting to my Cockney alter ego at home, I hung around with my brother Fred, and played footie – I was captain of the Senior Boys' XI – and joined in the various activities of the Cosmos Club as much as I could. The Cosmos was run by a pair of truly inspirational school masters, Mr Thomas and Mr Trafford. We played chess and went to the museums and on trips, including one to Cardiff. I remember finding Wales surprisingly foreign. Years later I made some great friends there through my brother and, to this day, I still own part of a business in West Glamorgan called Place for Homes.

With the hardening experience of *Peter Pan* at the Palladium behind me, in early 1938 I found myself performing in another of London's great auditoriums. I knew Covent Garden Market well enough – it was a favourite place to wander, especially in the early morning when the veg and flower traders got going – but I'd never entered the stage door of the Royal Opera House.

When finally I did, the first dressing room I saw was Eva Turner's. She was playing the title role in Puccini's *Turandot*. Just fourteen, I was still singing a good high treble, and on the basis of my church choir experience I'd been selected to be part of a small supporting group of children in the opera. I sang in Italian for the first time in my life – no doubt with a clearly discernible Cockney accent – but not so badly that I wasn't selected again.

I soon had a part in a second opera, Verdi's *Otello*, conducted by the great Constant Lambert. This was magically staged with sumptuous sets that cast reflections in the glittering chandeliers and the tiaras worn by women with breasts bursting from gorgeous dresses. Backstage it was almost better, as the huge cast waited, crushed together, nervous and sweaty, brilliantly choreographed to float on and off the stage, and all wrapped up in Verdi's glorious music. The effect on a romantic fourteen-year-old like me was overwhelming. It gave me a taste for classical music that has never left me; nor has my appreciation of gorgeous women in busty frocks – if anything it is stronger now that the fashion for bursting busty boobs has returned. I love it!

After such a high, it was quite a comedown to board the grimy train that would carry me home. One night, travelling alone as always, I had a frightening experience when a man got into my carriage and sat staring at me. As the train set off, he moved closer and asked me how far I was going; I lied and told him to the end of the line. He appeared to be playing with himself, and my mind leapt to my teacher with the big willy. Knowing that there was a tunnel coming soon and the carriage would be plunged into darkness, I decided to make a speedy exit. As the train drew level with Hoe Street Station I grabbed the door handle and leapt to the platform below, running along the train until I could haul myself through a door into a more populated carriage, sweating but safe.

In the summer of '38 my formal academic education came to an end, and my real education in life skills began, both on the stage and in the street. Most of my friends did as my brother had done and went straight off to work in the local factories, but I didn't envy them in the slightest. At the age of fourteen I was already earning a living and bringing in money to help my Mum, though nothing like enough, as the house was still filling up with more and more garments for repair. She seemed to spend her life wearing a thimble and pushing a needle through a horn button on yet another lady's tweed coat.

I was very keen to keep working and jumped at a chance to play a 'bit' at Ealing Studios along-side the magnificent Paul Robeson. He'd arrived from the States to make *Proud Valley*, a powerful movie about the harsh existence of the dis-gruntled Welsh miners. It was wonderful to see him, a truly elevating man of extraordinary and diverse talents – a Renaissance man, really, who was never able to realise his full potential as a result of the simple fact of being born black.

He had one of the finest singing voices I ever heard and gave an unforgettable performance in the brilliant film, *Sanders of the River*, which he made after *Proud Valley*.

After my first outing in *Peter Pan* as a wolf, I was promoted for the '38/'39 season to the role of John Napoleon Darling, this time to one of the greatest Peters of all, Jean Forbes-Robertson, with Sir Seymour Hicks as Captain Hook. It was a super part for me, made greater by the excitement of being back in the London Palladium.

I was petrified on the first night. A young chap in the cast, Ricky Highland, saw my nervousness and told me to walk out on to the stage and bellow to the back of the auditorium, as if I owned the place. It must have worked, because they told me later I could be heard from the back of the gallery. Poor Ricky was killed a few years later in the war, and I learned a lesson that stayed with me for life. I was never again fazed by large auditoriums like the Coliseum and Drury Lane, or the cavernous theatres I played touring Australia, many years later.

I also learned a lot about the great variety of people who walk the boards. On the one hand, there was the gentle Jean Forbes-Robertson; on the other there was Sir Seymour Hicks.

He was, to put it no more strongly than he deserves, an overbearing shit without a single redeeming feature that I ever came across. He was horrible to all of us, offstage and on. Once, during a matinee, he suddenly stopped speaking as he noticed one of the pirates – Cyril, I think his name was – was obscuring Sir Seymour from the patrons in the stage box. The great actor languidly stretched out an arm, poked his hook through Cyril's striped pirate jersey and glared at him. The audience wondered why on earth he had stopped. Ignoring them completely, he dragged the skinny lad behind the mast of his galleon, unhooked him and growled through clenched teeth, 'Now fucking well stay there!' Then, striding back to the group of bewildered pirates, he picked up the dialogue as if nothing had happened and carried on. We were all terrified of him – I can still hear him now, mimicking my rather squeaky voice – but, thank God, at the end of each performance he stalked off to his 'Star' dressing room and slammed the door behind him.

Sir Seymour had a horrendous reputation in the business and nobody could remember why he'd been knighted. He was the first of a number of bullies I was to meet on the stage and on movie sets, and to whom, over the years, I've tried to inure myself.

Jean Forbes-Robinson was a lovely lady, and a wonderful actress, not so surprising when you consider that her father, Sir Johnston Forbes-Robertson, was said to be the greatest Hamlet of his day. However, Jean always seemed rather unhappy. Each performance, after her energetic dance routine, she flew out of the Darlings' nursery window with Wendy, Michael and myself all dangling on the end of Kirby's Flying Ballet

58

apparatus, en route for Never Never Land – 'You turn right and go straight on till morning'. Jean always leaned on me, exhausted when we landed, and hugged me warmly.

'Thank you, my Darling,' she punned purrily, kissing me between gentle gasps of whisky flavour.

I suppose the stress of it all required the odd swig or two. I was to work with far more boozy actors over the next six decades and learned from an early age that drinking and acting are an unacceptable combination. I've come across many imbibers during my long theatrical life; it always brings problems.

As 1939 unfolded and we tried to ignore the rumble of approaching war, my theatrical career was beginning to burgeon. Doing any menial task the management required and understudying other junior actors, I got on well with everyone. I didn't challenge people as it was in my nature to be sunny. I learned about everything backstage in the theatre simply by having to do it or by poking my nose in and asking awkward questions. I was beginning to see this as a real job, where I could earn good money, but it was too early to consider it a career.

I pushed Conti's for more solid work, and was rewarded with a marvellous new job. At the impressive salary of three pounds ten shillings a week, I was engaged to understudy a 'cherub' in Dorothy L. Sayers' *The Zeal of Thy House*, starring Harcourt Williams. Soon after the play opened at the Garrick Theatre, I was lucky enough to take over the part – at five pounds a week – big money at fourteen, and my highest salary to that point.

Although the author was best known for her Lord Peter Wimsey stories, this play was a clever, religious piece based on a twelfth-century event in which a part of Canterbury Cathedral burned down and had to be rebuilt. My cherubic role was to stand together with four archangels, Rafael, Cassiel, Gabriel and Michael, and watch over the pilgrims, the clergy, the workers and their masters. The big angels had huge, gold, feathered wings sprouting from their shoulders, while I had little fledgling white ones, as worn by all Baroque cherubs.

Invisible to the peasants labouring on the building, we angels observed and reported to God on their doubtful activities and behaviour – always plenty of naughtiness going on between the men and women, on and off the stage. The architect, William of Sens, an older, bearded man given to spitting as he shouted, which so many actors do, indulged in sexual activity with the leading lady, played by Freda Gaye, that was quite outrageous – but then, of course, he was French and she did encourage him.

I stood on stage, swinging my thurible, for almost the entire play. When the peasants wandered off to get drunk and, one assumed, to copulate, the archangels and I went up to pray under an arch. It was then I would deliver my single line, a question to Michael:

'Why did God create mankind in two different sorts, if it makes so much trouble?'

'Why?' Michael replied, glaring at me. 'Why?

Angels never ask why!'

I cried and knelt down to pray. The lights dimmed and the curtain fell for the end of Act One.

I may have been getting a good wage for a cherub, but I had to work for it, and my performance earned me one of my best ever notices: *Leslie Phillips was the sweetest little cherub that ever came to life from a stained-glass window.*

However cherubic I may have appeared, my behaviour off stage was rather less than angelic. As a child actor, I was looked after by a chaperone, usually a female member of the cast. In this production, Jean Lind, a lovely young actress who was playing one of the pilgrims with necessary busty lustiness, was given the task of caring for me and a pilgrim boy called Jack Powney. Even though I was only fourteen, I fancied Jean tremendously; so did a number of others. After a London run lasting several months, the play toured all over Britain. In the close community of the cast and crew, I soon noticed the shenanigans that went on, and the buzz of sexual energy that pervaded the company. Jack and I spent a lot of time giggling and fantasising about the females and goings-on in the cast.

We were visited every week by Dorothy L. Sayers herself – a robust, kind lady who was wonderfully encouraging and generous to us all. On Saturdays she always invited the whole cast for drinks or lunch at whichever grand provincial hotel she was staying in, usually before the matinee. I admired her enormously and was amazed to learn, just recently, that as a young woman she'd had an illegitimate child – an act that must have been considered disgraceful at the time. Yet she'd managed to put that behind her, and was widely accepted as a genuinely good and spiritual person. Partly as a result of her influence, the company became a close and happy family. It was a lovely play to be in and I learned a great deal, perhaps more than I should, with this group of experienced and warm-hearted adults. My critical faculties, my English, my accent, my stage craft all benefited, as did my savings account.

There was horror when I returned home to find that Smaxie was dead. My mother said she had to have him put down when his wound became infected, but knowing how reluctant she had been to look after him, I found it hard to forgive and forget.

By the summer of '39 war the whole country seemed to be plastered with advertisements urging young men to join the Territorial Army, in case Mr Chamberlain's assessment of Hitler's trustworthiness turned out to be wrong. This call to arms and the macho uniforms appealed to a large number of young men with thoughts of glory. My brother, Fred, just eighteen, gleefully signed up to become a machine gunner in the 2/7th Middlesex Regiment, Territorials.

I was now fifteen – too young to be involved, and busy topping up my income between acting jobs by doing whatever work I could for the shopkeepers of Chingford. I delivered newspapers, helped out in the greengrocer's, served behind the counter in a newsagent's, delivered bread for the baker and milk for the milkman. On a good week, I made as much as three quid, the same as a bus conductor, and I'd already learned to be thrifty. Petrol was 1/3d a gallon, Players Cigarettes just 11d for twenty. I bought packs of three Crayols and smoked under the railway arches with my mates, secretly puffing and choking and thinking we were real men of the world.

Hitler ignored Chamberlain's ultimatums and, on 3 September 1939, war was declared. When it finally came upon us, it hit hard, especially when the air-raid sirens went off for the first time a few days later – a false alarm, thank God. My mother's memories of the Great War of 1914–18 were deeply alarming, but we were told this war would be over in a matter of months. I was three years away from call-up age myself. For my brother it was another matter.

Fred came home from work at the Atlas Lamp Company to find an OHMS package addressed to him lying on the mat. The letter inside ordered him to report to the Middlesex Regiment at 6 p.m. that evening. It was now 5 p.m. – no time to wait and tell Mum, who was out helping in a canteen somewhere, so he packed his belongings, wrote a note to say he'd been called up, and left it on the kitchen table.

It was a hell of a shock for Mum. I was away, touring with a play, so Mum was alone. Luckily for my mother, Doris was a devoted daughter and came back to be with Mum as often as she could. My sister was a saint to always devote so much time to Mum over the years that followed, though I was never sure how much my mother really appreciated it. My love for Doris never faltered. She was always cheerful and, when Fred and I had children, she became a super auntie. Her husband, Albert, was not an ambitious man. They didn't have children, though I dare say he tried, in between his nightly visits to the Green Man on Old Church Road. When he and Doris were courting, I would hang around in the sitting room until he was forced to slip me sixpence to leave them on their own – well, a boy has to live and one could buy quite a lot for a tanner in those days.

Soon after war was declared, I was back at Denham Studios working for the Kordas under Michael Powell in an early Technicolor swashbuckler, *The Thief of Baghdad*, starring Sabu, the Elephant Boy. I was miscast once again as a dusky urchin, along with the lovely Cleo Laine. The picture won three Oscars, but if you ever catch it on TV, you'll be pushed to spot me, or Cleo, for that matter.

At the same time, I was appearing at the Queen's Theatre in my first proper role in a full-blown, classy play: Dodie Smith's *Dear Octopus*. She was best known for writing *101 Dalmatians*, but was also a successful playwright. In *Dear Octopus* she'd created a cosy middle-class family saga, two and a half hours long and oozing feel-good, which in those uncertain times was just what people wanted.

'*The family, that Dear Octopus from whose*

tentacles we never quite escape, or really wish to.'

It was a wonderful production, created by Binkie Beaumont, directed by Glen Byam Shaw, and starring Leon Quartermaine, a youthful John Gielgud, and the amazing Dame Marie Tempest. Dame Marie was very particular about the pronunciation of her Christian name, insisting that it was 'Mary' as in Queen Mary, and correcting anyone who pronounced it differently. The director's wife, Angela Baddeley, was also in the cast.

After a short tour, the play opened at the Queen's to rave notices. I had originally been booked to understudy a young actor called Bobby Desmond, but it wasn't long before his balls descended and his voice broke. Once again I took over the part for the rest of the run – lucky Leslie! Yet another example of those pleasing, serendipitous occurrences that are so vital to an actor's career.

Playing a child in an upper-middle-class English family, I was worried that the remains of my Cockney accent – the odd dropped 'H' or dodgy vowel sound – might show through, and I worked hard to eradicate it. Socialising with other actors helped a lot with this, a critical learning stage in my life which brought about an irreversible change in my speech and the way people reacted to me.

Bobby Desmond was kept on as my understudy, which was fun as the two of us became the greatest of friends as we larked our way around the country. We were of course chaperoned, as the law required, by Mrs Lily Taylor, who was also Tennent's chief wardrobe mistress and later became a big cheese in the organisation. We were both very mischievous, constantly giving her the slip and misbehaving, although we were very fond of her, and we both kept up with her for years after, until she sadly died.

Bobby was a year or so older than me, and came from a theatrical family. His mother was an actress, Billy Hill, and his father, George Desmond, a top stage director. He had an advanced, dirty mind and was more daring then me. He loved to tease poor Muriel Pavlow, who played a child called Scrap. Muriel was a lovely, clever actress who went on to have a great career. At this time, though still amazingly good in child roles, she was in fact a young woman of eighteen or so.

On one occasion, in Norwich, just after we'd all been issued with our terrifying and utterly useless gas masks, Bobby and I were alone with Muriel, trying them on. Bobby took the opportunity to harass the young actress.

'I say, Muriel, do you know what "fuck" means? Oh, go on, do tell us, Muriel, please!'

The poor girl was deeply embarrassed, and didn't know how to deal with a cheeky young sixteen-year-old like Bobby. Of course, we learned nothing from her. However, in our digs in Leeds, we were sharing a room in which hung a print of a popular painting called 'Love Locked Out', depicting a naked girl outside a closed front door, which we thought tremendously sexy. We studied this minutely, considering all the possibilities, but then spent the afternoon, rather shamefully, taking pot shots with an air pistol at the unknown woman's private parts.

While we were playing at the Royal Court Theatre in Liverpool, I carried the mischief too far and almost got myself sacked from *Dear Octopus*. At one point in the play, there was a big entrance for the whole family into the nursery – about eight of us in all. Marie Tempest and Muriel Pavlow were ready on stage waiting to enter, while the rest of us were coming down in a lift from a few floors above. Once we were all in, as a prank, I pressed the wrong button. The lift stopped mid-floor, and wouldn't go up or down. We were stuck in the shaft.

Marie Tempest, with a curt nod at Muriel, strode on and they made their entrance without us. There was chaos on stage. Everyone was furious. I was blamed and given many lectures on the seriousness of my crime, the sanctity of drama, and the meaning of life in the theatre. If we'd been in London where replacements were easier to come by, I'd have been given the boot. In this case, I survived, mainly because Binkie Beaumont wasn't told, and I think Mrs Taylor pleaded for me, but the lesson was tucked firmly into my consciousness. Lucky Leslie, again.

Dear Octopus was for me the start of a long association with Mr Binkie Beaumont and H.M. Tennent, the production company that dominated London and New York theatre for a quarter of a century. He had first call on all the best directors and actors, and produced most of the top plays in London during the war.

The theatres, encouraged by the government,

were determined to keep going during wartime as best they could. The prospect of going into the army was still a very distant one for me; in the meantime, I was doing my bit in London, braving the bombs. By the middle of 1940, the Blitz was in full swing and the Germans were bombing indiscriminately all over London, although most theatres managed to stay open. Everyone knew that the performances might be interrupted at any moment. At the first toot of the air-raid sirens, whole audiences would evaporate and head for cellars or underground stations, all rigged out with metal-frame bunks where people would try to sleep until the 'All Clear' sounded. We kept thinking that, if it carried on like this, everything would ultimately have to close. But incredibly it didn't.

Life at home in north Chingford – living in Sunset Avenue now – could be quite hairy, too. Eschewing the moist charms of the useless government-issued Anderson shelters, Mum and I tended to take cover from the raids in our tiny cellar, beneath a trap door that I helped to make. A direct hit would have been curtains, anyway. Parachute bombs were extra lethal because they exploded as soon as they touched the ground. They caused far more devastation than normal bombs, which buried themselves, thus restricting their destructive power. We were lucky to escape when one dropped in our street one night. Watching the parachute bombs drifting down in the wind, we tried to guess their destination, as good a way of creating terror as anything thought up by Osama bin Laden and his cohorts. But somehow, being English, one learned to live with the fear and take it in one's stride.

I now had a nice steady girlfriend, Jane Greelish, who would come cycling through Epping Forest with me on a tandem I'd acquired, although it spent much of the time propped against the trunk of a tree while we practised teenage love in the undergrowth. Jane was also keen on classical music, and we enjoyed magical evenings at the Proms at the Albert Hall, developing my own taste for the music I'd originally enjoyed at the Opera House in Covent Garden.

When I left *Dear Octopus*, I went to play Bimbo in Ian Hay's *The Housemaster* at the People's Palace, a lovely little theatre in Mile End Road. Straight after that, Conti's got me an even better role, as Benji in *If Four Walls Told*, at the Connaught Theatre in Worthing, where I was to learn another important theatrical lesson.

Having just been paid my wages – eight quid for a week's work, princely by the standards of the day – I tucked the precious notes into the inside pocket of my jacket, which I then left hanging in my dressing room while I made my entrance. When I came back, the coat was still there, but the money had gone – a severe lesson which I took to heart, even though a kindly management did make it up to me. A few years later, playing one of the Selectors in the *Merchant of Venice*, a thief got into the theatre and did the rounds of the dressing rooms – everyone lost their money, except me; mine was hidden inside a pair of socks I was wearing on stage. In both cases I thought I knew who was responsible, but one can never be sure, so I kept silent.

By early 1941, it was obvious that the war – and the bombing – were on for the long term. Every night the Luftwaffe targeted the city with such regularity that you could set your clock by the air-raid sirens that heralded the latest wave of bombs and incendiaries. From Chingford we could see the sky lit bright red as London's docklands were bombed and burned. Fearing for our safety, Mum's brother, Jim, manager of the North Met Electricity Company and the most successful member of her family, invited us to move into his large Victorian house in the comparative safety of Stevenage at 19 Green Street.

Despite the dangers of staying in London, I was unwilling to leave. My reluctance grew even stronger when Elsie Beyer offered me a job on the West End stage; I was never one to turn down an opportunity to earn decent money. But, much as it upset me, I couldn't deny my mother's pleadings. Resigning myself to this hiccup in what I now saw as a future career, I turned down the job (which went instead to Bobby Desmond, who hung on to it for the next six months), and I moved to Stevenage with my mother.

Now missing the theatre, I got a full-time job at Woolworth's in Hitchin; I'd worked in the Walthamstow branch, and knew the ropes. Here, though, I was answerable to a beastly, beetroot-faced manager with a gut like a barrage balloon, who accused me of being cocky. I suppose that, thanks to my theatrical experience, outwardly I must have seemed supercilious for my age. Whatever the reasons, he took an instant dislike to me, which I duly reciprocated as he set about making my life hell. I would be ordered to stay behind after work to oil the vast parquet floor and, on several occasions, he even dragooned me into washing and waxing his bloody Vauxhall car. I stuck it out for the sake of the weekly pay packet.

To work off my frustration, I joined the local Home Guard and laboured all through the summer evenings on a hundred-foot allotment I'd dug behind Uncle Jim's house. I was doing my bit digging for victory, and flogging the surplus vegetables. My tomatoes were delicious and very popular. I expect I could have won prizes for them, though I never told people that I achieved such quality mainly through the regular night-time application of lashings of my own urine – a wonderful fertiliser, though I must make it clear I could not offer bottles of the precious liquid for sale, even to my most ardent friends or family.

After a few months of this new Stevenage routine, I thought my life as an actor, such as it had been, had reached retirement; my former life in the theatre seemed to belong to some distant past I'd sadly left behind.

Then, one Sunday morning, Bobby Desmond turned up in Stevenage out of the blue. He'd come up specially on the train and found his way to our house in Green Street to tell me that he'd had his call-up papers, being a year or so older than me, and was going to join the Royal Navy.

His job at the Haymarket Theatre would become vacant in three weeks' time. Would I like it?

Would I like it!

This was just the escape I needed. It was the act of a true friend!

But there was more! While he'd been working for H.M. Tennent, Bobby had wangled himself an extra night-time job as a fire-watcher, posted on top of a building in the Charing Cross Road. Though a bit on the scary side, it wasn't a demanding job, and it would be worth another four quid a week. I could take that on, too. Better still, this fire-watch job came with somewhere to sleep – in a building up an alley between the Sun Electric showrooms and the Phoenix Theatre in Flitcroft Street, off Charing Cross Road.

Poor Mum was upset when I told her I wanted to go; so was the commander of No.1 Platoon, Stevenage Home Guard, when I handed back my uniform. I went to Woolies to tell my manager and even he seemed sorry to be losing the butt of his bullying. Grudgingly he admitted that, if I played my cards right, I, too, could end up a Woolworth's manager. I wasn't tempted. Had it been Harrods, I suppose I might have been. As it was, I told him he could stick his Vauxhall up his Blackwall Tunnel.

Brushing aside all my mother's objections, I went straight up to London to see Elsie Beyer, who welcomed me with open arms. The fact was, the theatres were still very busy; it seemed they had a vital role to play in restoring the morale of forces on leave, as well as visitors and the war-weary inhabitants of London. Everyone needed an escape, from time to time, from the relentless German hammering. However, now that every able-bodied man over eighteen and a half had been snapped up by HM Forces, theatre managers were becoming desperate for anyone to help out. So began one of the most exciting and influential periods of my life.

I was back being a thespian again. *But I can't get too excited,* I told myself. *I'll soon be called up to fight in this bloody war – unless I'm killed in a London raid before I reach eighteen and a half!*

Heads or tails? Here goes! I didn't even look – I was on my way.

3 • Under Binkie's Wing

The production which Elsie had originally asked me to join before I went to Stevenage was *No Time for Comedy*, by American playwright Sam Behrman. Now I was to take on Bobby's job as ASM, understudy, call-boy and communal gofer in this play. It starred Diana Wynyard with the increasingly popular smoothie Rex Harrison, as well as his new lover (soon to be wife), Lilli Palmer, for whom I swiftly developed a tremendous crush, and Elizabeth Welch, a lovely black singer who was a big star at the time. She was also a great giggle and I loved her to bits.

I swiftly settled back into theatre routine as if I'd never been away or suffered under the ghastly manager in Woolies. I was very happy to continue my informal apprenticeship in theatre craft. It was not only the actors and producers I learned from. Joe Davis, the electrician, was one of the most skilled lighting men in the West End. He was never too busy to show me all his secrets of lighting. Jack Land, the carpenter, showed me the niftiest way to cleat flats and ingenious techniques for tricking the eye in a set. It was through Sam Gardener, Tennent's chief props man, that I understood the importance of props that actually did what they were supposed to.

If, for instance, there was phone which was supposed to ring at a crucial moment – to trigger a conversation, perhaps – it was vital before each performance to check that the bell worked and to have in place a back-up, in case it failed. There's nothing worse when you're on stage than waiting for a mechanical cue which never comes. You can't cup your ear to a deafening silence and declare, 'Ah, was that the phone?' – not in a way the audience won't twig and punish you for. Ask any actor how he feels when he's drawn a gun on stage and pulled the trigger to an inaudible click. It's worse for the prospective victim, who must decide if they should assume the shot has occurred and crumple up, only for a dilatory stagehand to realise he's missed a cue, and deliver the bang three or four seconds later, when the corpse is already slumped on the floor. Audiences will laugh and forgive it, but it doesn't help the play.

As the ASM, one is responsible for everything – it's a big job.

No Time for Comedy was doing well at the Haymarket, and even the fire-watching job wasn't too bad. After working in the theatre all evening, I would rush off along Old Compton Street to my next post. There would be several of us up on the roof to assist and keep each other company. The German bombers were still coming, though not delivering the same devastation as they did in the Blitz, and not always in the capital. Nevertheless, when they happened, incendiaries were dropping all over central London and it was pretty terrifying, exposed up there on the blacked-out rooftops. When a fire flared, we would rush over with our stirrup pumps and quell it. If there was a letup in the raids, I'd sneak down to my lair and get in a few hours' kip on my camp bed, and start the next day with a mug of thick tea.

I was getting on well with everyone in the play, adored Lilli Palmer from a distance and envied Rex when I found them in a passionate embrace, pinned up against the fly ropes, mouth to mouth, hip to hip. They had just made an exit from which he was supposed to return on stage almost at once, having said 'good bye' off stage. As the run of the play and his affair with Lilli progressed, the exit took longer and longer before he returned, leaving the stage empty, with nothing for the audience to look at. I would be sent round to get him back, tapping him gingerly on the shoulder.

'Mr Harrison, you're needed on stage!'

He removed his tongue from Lilli's mouth just long enough to growl, 'Go away, boy,' then put his tongue quickly back.

On the whole, though, Rex was quite charming to me, while I admired the way he handled Lilli, flirted with other women and brilliantly worked an audience. For many years he remained something of a role model for me, though I could never have reached anything like his heights in the philandering department.

Lilli Palmer was very sweet to me. She often asked me to run errands for her, and talked to me in her dressing room afterwards, while she finished her make up and casually stretched her lovely long legs in the air, one at a time, slowly slipping on her silk stockings. I could only stand there and gaze, captivated, as she chatted on.

Lucky old Rex, I thought, maybe one day my turn would come.

When *No Time For Comedy* came off, Elsie told me how well I'd done in my humble post, and I was very chuffed when she asked me to stay on with Tennents at the Theatre Royal in Haymarket and work on a production coming in from tour, Bernard Shaw's *The Doctor's Dilemma*, starring Vivien Leigh. I was to do more or less the same job as before – ASM, call-boy, working the Panotrobe and a bit of understudying.

At that stage, following the monumental success of *Gone with the Wind*, Vivien was the hottest female star in the world. In my eyes, she was unquestionably the most special actress I ever worked with and I felt incredibly lucky to be so near this goddess every day. As we all remember, she was beautiful. She was often likened to a piece of Dresden porcelain, a comparison which, I gathered, she didn't particularly like, but there was nevertheless something about her that was inescapably delicate and, as it were, staggeringly

76

beautiful but breakable. She was immensely kind to me, and spoke my name with a sensuous softness – a long, drawn out 'L..e..s..lie'. On her lips, I loved the name, although I'd always hated it before, and wished I'd been called by my father's second name, 'Sam'.

To crown all her charms, she tipped me five bob every week, and often gave me a hug and a kiss on the cheek.

I could only look on in utter awe the first time an immensely dashing man came backstage to see her; the uniform of a Fleet Air Arm officer seemed to emphasise the innate star quality of Laurence Olivier. Although he had nothing to do with the play or the company, as indisputably the most important actor of his generation, he was allowed to go wherever he wanted in the theatre, even into the wings, which no one – but no one – else would have been allowed to do. Laurence Olivier was an exception, like royalty; even at that stage in his career, although not yet a knight, he was treated like a king.

Through the work I did for Vivien, and my job as general dogsbody in the theatre, I came to see a lot of Laurence. I got to know him and, over the years that followed, as our lives crossed and re-crossed – in the theatre, on television and radio. As an actor he was in a category entirely of his own. He was always an inspiration and generous with his advice, giving me some of the most telling notes I've ever received.

Besides his passionate love for Vivien, whom he had married the year before, he had a special interest in this production, for it was he who had suggested to Binkie that he should put it on. Laurence and Vivien had been provisionally offered the two lead roles for a radio production of the play. But when the BBC decided they should do *Pygmalion* instead, Vivien declined, yielding to her doubts that she could produce Eliza's Cockney accent.

The rest of the *Doctor's Dilemma* cast was pretty spectacular, with some of the best character actors in London at the time, including the great Irish actor Cyril Cusack. Irene Henschel was the director and I was amazingly lucky to be involved in a piece of theatre of such quality.

In a nutshell, the play is about a beautiful woman, Jennifer (Vivien), married to an artist, Louis Dubedat, played by Cyril Cusack, who is dying from an incurable disease. She uses her beauty to persuade a diverse group of doctors to do everything in their power to cure him. Like most Shavian plays, it's beautifully balanced and subtly powerful. On our first night, 12 March 1942, Vivien took her solo call to one of the loudest and longest ovations ever heard at the Haymarket, and within days the play was booked for months ahead, in spite of the air raids.

A week into the run, on Saint Patrick's Day, Cyril Cusack had been out visiting one or two clubs with a few friends. He arrived at the theatre early to get ready in his dressing room. When I came in a little later the stage director told me to go straight to the front of house to fetch some strong black coffee for Mr Cusack.

Responding to the urgency of the request, I

went from the auditorium to the foyer through the pass door, which is normally absolutely taboo for stage staff. I ordered the coffee and was carrying it from the bar when I was stopped by the front-of-house manager, Charles La Trobe, one of the most respected and powerful theatre managers in London. He gave me a colossal bollocking for using the pass door and insisted that I should have gone out of the stage door and found the coffee in a snack bar. However, he allowed me to take the coffee to Mr Cusack's dressing room – a whole steaming pot – and Cyril thanked me with his customary Irish charm. I was curious, naturally; I'd heard there'd been some booze-related incident before I joined the company, while the play had been on tour. As far as I could see now, he was OK, though perhaps a trifle peaky.

He drank the coffee and revived a little – enough to make his first entrance in the Richmond scene. However, by his next important scene, the theatre had become hotter and stuffier. Cyril was obviously feeling unwell, and becoming noticeably unsteady.

During this scene, Dubedat is at his easel painting his wife, Jennifer; Cyril managed to busk his way through, though none too accurately. Vivien was not at all happy as she sat on her dais. She obviously had no idea how to cope with Cyril's condition and started angrily to tap the arm of her seat, while throwing increasingly desperate glances at the prompt corner.

The company manager, Frank Woolfe, saw what was going on from the wings, immediately panicked and ordered me to get the man who operated the curtain to bring it down at once. This was an incredible, drastic measure, but it wasn't my place to question it. I nearly fell down the iron staircase below stage as I dashed to relay the order. The curtain man, who was playing cards, gulped in astonishment, dropped the deck, then leapt up to do as I'd asked. I followed him back to the wings. He pulled the rope, and the curtain fell on a surprised and confused auditorium. A few people clapped, thinking it must be the interval, but most remained in stunned silence.

Dropping the curtain mid-scene – mid-dialogue, even – was almost unheard of in the West End theatre.

Vivien walked straight off the stage and went to her dressing room, slamming the door behind her.

Cyril Cusack stayed where he was and buried his face in his hands. I went on stage and took his arm to lead him back towards his own dressing room. As we tottered off, Frank Woolfe grabbed me, and told me to go and find Cyril's understudy, Geoffrey Edwards, who had a small part as the newspaperman later in the play, as well as understudying the leading part of Dr Ridgeon.

I found Geoffrey in his dressing room, all ready for his appearance as the newspaperman. I told him that Mr Cusack had been taken ill and he had to go on as Dubedat right away. He nearly collapsed in horror.

'What!?' he yammered.

'Get into Dubedat's costume and go on, right

now,' I repeated.

'What are you talking about?'

'Cyril's come off; he's gone to his room – and you're his understudy.'

'I know that!' Geoffrey shouted. 'But I can't remember the bloody lines; I've been concentrating on Ridgeon.' As Ridgeon was being played by Frank Allenby, an elderly actor, this was understandable but not acceptable.

I thrust the open book into his hand and told him to read it.

Eyes wild, Geoffrey grabbed it and tried to hide the book under his dressing gown, while endeavouring to calm down.

Meanwhile, it was chaos. Cyril Cusack was in his room; the curtain was down; Frank Woolfe was hysterical, the audience were hushed in confusion.

Geoffrey took a deep breath and went on stage to play the scene where Dubedat dies, reading the part as his character expired. He died with the book still in his hand, and the final curtain came down. The audience clapped uncertainly, still stunned, but inclined to be kind and forgiving.

Binkie Beaumont, on the other hand, was not.

Shortly afterwards, he arrived with a chilly blast. He held a court of inquiry right away in the theatre. No one had never seen Binkie like this.

Cyril was white and silent, staring into space. This was a theatrical disaster and he knew it.

Binkie, it was well known, never really lost his temper. He started quietly. 'You do know I'm terribly angry with you, don't you, Cyril dear?' He proceeded then, with icy venom, to sack the

Irish actor. Geoffrey Edwards was blamed, too, for losing his bottle and not knowing the part. He was given little option but to resign.

If Binkie had been seeking vengeance for this disaster, he got it. Cyril went back to Ireland and I believe he didn't act again on a London stage for nearly two decades, although, a few years later, Geoffrey Edwards was to reward me with my first Shakespearean part (if you don't count a schoolboy Third Witch).

This production of *The Doctor's Dilemma* achieved notoriety in London theatre history. The story still fascinates people, and I've often been asked about it over the years. Naturally, it has become exaggerated, but my version is the true one – after all, I was there! I have since had the opportunity to tell one of Cyril's lovely children what happened that night, and they were sweet and grateful to learn the truth.

Peter Glenville took over the part of Dubedat at short notice, and did well to cope with playing opposite a star of Vivien's magnitude. Peter was never, in my view, a particularly great actor, and he was never able to roll his 'r's properly, which is a handicap in classical plays. However, he came into his own later as a top director in films and theatre, *Becket* and *Hotel Paradiso* among them. Like many in the profession, he was a camp individual, and quite overt about it, which inevitably drew some ribbing from his straight friends.

He would retort, hand on hip: 'My mother was a principal boy, and my father was a pantomime dame! What do you expect?'

Geoffrey Edwards' dual role of understudy and

newspaperman was taken on by a young actor and future friend of mine, Patrick Macnee, and the production soon settled down again, in spite of the war. It went so well that when Vivien took off for a short holiday with her beloved Larry, as she always called him, Celia Johnson was able to step into her shoes quite seamlessly. Celia, a supreme actress, handled the role with enormous skill. But in a plot where the principal woman's role relies on her intense beauty, she was always going to lose out in comparisons with Vivien.

Celia knew as much about stagecraft as anyone in the business. Many years later, she was with a group of actors, including my wife Angie, in a production of *Hamlet*. They were discussing a difficult director who refused to cut the play, with the result that the schools' matinee was running into the evening performance. Celia was asked who she thought was the best director she'd ever had.

'Best director?' she murmured thoughtfully, and seemed to be running through the dozens of fine theatre and film directors she had worked with over some thirty years. 'Let me see now ... best director...'

After a few more moments of humming and hawing and shaking her head, someone asked her, 'Well, tell us some of the good ones.'

Eventually, Celia shook her head again. 'Can't think of any,' she said, and she meant it.

It was soon after Cyril Cusack's debacle that I was summoned to Binkie Beaumont's office and given my role as a tumbler in *The Nutmeg Tree* with the great French actress, Yvonne Arnaud.

Working with Miss Arnaud was another lovely experience. She had been acting in England for thirty years by this time, and was very established on the British stage. Born, I believe, in Belgium, she'd been a child prodigy on the piano and won the Premier Prix at the Paris Conservatoire at the age of thirteen, before going on to tour as a concert pianist throughout Europe and America for the next six years. But in England, she'd built a career as an actress and singer in musicals. Since then she'd played in all the classics, and audiences adored her for her comedic skills and her distinctive, somewhat vulnerable voice, which had been damaged in earlier life during an operation. It still required soothing with regular libations of warm honey and syrup, which she built into her business in the play, if necessary.

I was mesmerised by the way she could hold an audience in her hand, and the subtlety of the business she would bring to a part to enhance the humour of it. On one occasion, she found she was getting more laughs than she expected – always disconcerting for a comedy actor when quite minute control of events can be critical. After a few moments, her instincts told her that their reaction was connected in some way with her underwear. By dint of a small unscripted movement she was able to ascertain that the elastic in her knickers had given out and they had descended to a point where they were showing below the hem of her dress.

Deftly turning the mishap to her advantage, she gave her behind a little wiggle and brought the knickers to the ground and her audience to tears of laughter as she stepped neatly out of them, picked them up, gave them an accusatory glare and stuffed them neatly into her handbag – a masterly piece of impromptu stagecraft and a fine example of how quick-witted comedy actors could turn a disaster to their advantage.

Despite her origins, Yvonne Arnaud was an honorary and much loved Englishwoman; was given a damehood and, having lived near Guildford for many years, the town paid tribute several years after her death by naming its busy and successful theatre after her.

My extra role in *The Nutmeg Tree* kept me very busy. Each evening, midway through the performance of *The Doctor's Dilemma* at the Haymarket, I literally had to run up to the Lyric in Shaftesbury Avenue to catch my cue as a tumbler, then run back to finish up at the Haymarket, before racing back along Old Compton Street to my fire-watching job, sometimes during an air-raid.

On the way, the tarts would call out from the shadows and doorways.

'Hello, Leslie. Time for a quickie?'

'You need a few lessons, darlin'.'

'Ooh, he's always in a hurry, that one.'

As long as they didn't call me Les, I didn't mind what they said, and I never stopped to take up their offers. I was far too busy. With all this activity and my call-boy's tips, on a good week I could make over £20 – considerable riches then. On a Sunday I was able to take the train to Stevenage to see Mum with my head high, and a decent wad of money for her, which cheered her up no end. It also gave me the chance to keep my allotment in order.

In the spring of '42, my brother Fred came back from Scotland, where he'd been posted as part of a large force mustered to repel the anticipated Nazi attack from Norway, which never came. My mother had by this time moved back to Chingford, despite the bombs, and Fred spent his home leave with her. When he came up to visit me in the West End, I was delighted to see him again, but it brought home to me how much I had changed since we last met.

The last few productions with H.M. Tennent, and my constantly mixing with sophisticated men and women of the theatre, had rubbed off on me more than a bit. I was a bright young man, on friendly terms with famous people like Rex Harrison and Vivien Leigh, two of the most sought-after personalities in our business. This was a long way from Fred's world and, apart from a similarity in our looks, nobody would ever have guessed we came from the same womb, let alone the close companions we had been during our childhood.

Fred came to the theatre and climbed up to my fire-watching post. With bombs falling all over London that night, he said it was worse than being in action in the army. After that he went on his way – to join the Middle East campaign – while I pushed all thoughts of my own pending call-up to the back of my mind and tried to extract as much fun as I could from my current occupation.

One aspect of my life in which I felt I wasn't making sufficient progress was sex, and I was looking around for the chance to put this right.

In fact, I was surrounded by sex. On reflection, I always have been. It was going on in the theatres where I worked, in the Soho clubs and streets I frequented; everyone was at it but me. In my search for the elusive apple, I used to pop in to watch the nude (though immobile) ladies at the Windmill – true to its much-vaunted claim, 'We never close,' performances continued throughout the air raids. I knew the manager and a lot of the girls, who were happy to flash, flirt and talk dirty but, obeying the house rules, would only allow me to look, not touch. From them and the men around, I started to pick up more about the seamier side of life. Since my early days at the Italia Conti School, I'd had a number of furtive fumbles with cooperative girls, but not the real thing.

Now I'd reached the age when that full initiation into sex was well overdue. And it was at this point that Jacob, my friend and fellow tumbler in *The Nutmeg Tree*, introduced me to Odette, whom I still dream about, and always will.

While all this was going on, I often thought about Bobby Desmond and wondered what he would have said about it. He'd always been more daring and advanced than me with girls. But with the bombs still falling on London almost every night, and Bobby somewhere deep under the ocean in his submarine, I could only hope that we'd both be around long enough for me to tell him all about my magical experience with Odette.

Sadly, that all came to an end when my own call to arms arrived on the mat. I was never to see Odette again. But the memory of her undoubtedly helped me through the first shock of the raw, lonely months of soldiering that followed.

I didn't tell anyone I'd received my marching orders – everyone had been pressing me to avoid it. My mother, already hurt by me leaving her in Stevenage, certainly didn't want me to go into the fray. Having lost her husband, and now faced with the very real prospect she'd lose Fred to the Germans in North Africa, she bitterly resented the prospect of losing me as well. She tried hard to talk me out of it, suggesting that I do what my dad had done in the First World War, due to his chronic ill-health, and become a Special Constable. I listened, but it went in one ear and out of the other.

My sister Doris, married now, joined in the chorus of dissuasion. She didn't want the responsibility of dealing with Mum on her own. Elsie Beyer, possibly out of compassion, and possibly because she didn't want to lose a useful all-rounder from the H.M. Tennent's team, worked hard to convince me that I had a good case for release from call-up on compassionate grounds.

It seemed there were innumerable ways to avoid being called up or, at least, doing any actual fighting. A lot of men, including my brother-in-law Albert, hadn't gone to war because they were in reserved occupations. There were advertisements in the papers for jobs in the coal mines. Musicians could elect to become bandsmen, doubling up as stretcher-bearers. In my own profession, there was the legitimate, and safer, option of entertaining the troops to boost morale in the field through the Entertainment's National Service Association, ENSA (known in the trade as Every Night Something Awful).

And, of course, those men who objected on grounds of conscience – known disparagingly as 'Conchies' – could act as medical orderlies or, if they had appropriate qualifications, do clerical, logistic work. I was canvassed by some of them – highly educated, well-read and articulate fellows, mostly, who knew how to put their case – but I was sure I could not calmly stand by and let a Nazi soldier walk into my mum's house with a gun in his hand and lust in his eyes.

Even if I had wanted to duck out of it, I hadn't made the necessary preparations. The fact was, I really didn't want to get out of it, even though I'm not by nature especially gung-ho. My patriotic senses were stirred. Deep down, I wasn't too worried about joining up. I'd been surrounded by war for over three years – the Home Guard in Stevenage, the Blitz and fire-watching in London. We had to protect our country and, as I told my mother, that included protecting her and my sister whatever the horrors.

The decision had been made – I told them all. I've got my call-up papers, so 'By the left, quick march!'

4 • An Officer and Almost a Gentleman

Now kitted out with my not very comfortable khaki uniform, the first ordeal to be endured was a very thorough medical examination – balls and all, as they say – to ascertain that an individual was worth training to kill other people. Every potential conscript was checked for both physical and mental disorders. One clever dodge for those who couldn't be bothered to go through the various options for avoidance was to attend the medical in a pair of their sister's or girlfriend's knickers, a practice which medical people in those days viewed askance. It was, in any case, a nerve-racking business waiting to be told your defects, and the chap in front of me was so nervous he knocked a bucket of urine all over the doctor, who didn't bat an eyelid, but smelled worse than the old people's home where poor old Granny Phillips had been incarcerated.

But I passed, Grade A, and in early November 1942 I said my emotional farewells to the companies at the Haymarket and the Lyric. I was given a tremendous and moving send-off by everyone, from Binkie and Vivien – who hugged me with tears in her beautiful eyes – to Bibby the stage-doorkeeper. At home, my sister was brilliant, distracting my mother so I could just slip away.

On Guy Fawkes' Day (how apt), a few days

after I'd reached the threshold of eighteen and a half, I became a member of His Majesty's Armed Forces and boarded the train from Liverpool Street to Brentwood and Warley Barracks for my induction course and rudimentary training in marching and weapons.

The barracks came as a hell of a shock, utterly confusing and disorientating after my life in London. I was intensely relieved to see Peter Graham-Scott, an old friend from my earliest theatre days. When I'd been playing a wolf in Anna Neagle's *Peter Pan*, I'd also understudied Peter, who'd been playing Curly. Since then, in that extraordinary cycle of life – 'the Dance to the Music of Time' that so exercised Anthony Powell – I would regularly bump into Peter for the rest of my life. I lost sight of him for the duration of the war, but when it was over he became an important TV and film director.

Nearly twenty years later Peter directed me, Ronnie Barker and James Robertson Justice in a comedy called *Father Came Too* for Rank. He even made me godfather to one of his children (a role in which, I'm ashamed to say, I've never excelled – frankly, I've got too many children of my own). I occasionally see him now, although he hung up his director's view-finder a long time ago and settled down to live within sliced-drive expletive-hearing distance of one of the tees at Wentworth.

One of my abiding memories of induction into the army was being used as a pincushion by a gang of hatchet-faced nurses for a series of vicious, arm-warping injections, followed by as many cups of bromide tea as a man could drink without being made totally impotent. Then we had to run round the barracks waving our arms in an attempt to distribute whatever substances those horrible injections had thrust into our systems.

The nurses turned out to be less intimidating than the sergeants who raucously drilled us on the parade ground, although I quite enjoyed drill, finding it not unlike stage choreography. My fellow conscripts at first sight were a motley crowd, with some uncouth habits. At tea-time, cakes would be set out on a plate for us; the greedy buggers would run in, seek out the best, lick them and put them back so that nobody else would take them. There was a lot of bullying, too, with obvious victims coming to the fore. One lad of eighteen who had married a woman old enough to be his mother was subjected to endless jibes about old ladies. I didn't join in, it was unbelievably unkind and pointlessly cruel.

Fortunately, I was used to looking after myself and mixing and soon got to know how the system worked. Life settled into a routine that was far quieter than London had been, which was just as well, as I had much less money to spend now. Over the last few years, I'd managed to save over £1,000 from my earnings; the money had been deposited in a Post Office, and I planned not to touch it until the war was over – if I lived to see the day. If I didn't, I left the money in my mother's name, just in case – all the conscripts made a will in their paybook. In the meantime, my salary had dropped from £21 per week to 21 shillings.

After six uncertain weeks in Warley Barracks, I was posted to the Royal Artillery (my first choice), which meant moving on to Deep Cut, near Camberley, for gunnery training. Part of the course covered the use of the Bofors gun – a light anti-aircraft weapon – and I soon got the hang of it. With my new upper-crust English accent, I found myself being placed in charge, and was swiftly promoted to Lance-Bombardier, complete with one stripe.

Even in those days, Deep Cut lent itself to some fairly unpleasant behaviour, although not as bad as the fatal treatment that has been meted out there in recent years. I remember one man, with the surname Rear, who was inevitably barracked as 'Gunner Rear'. The ceaseless jibes had the poor chap ready to go AWOL to get away from it. Such things sound utterly trivial, but if you felt you were alone and faced with a hostile majority, this kind of bullying could be intolerable. One needed a fantastic sense of humour to survive. Somehow, I managed to side-step any serious ragging, and emerged in good form. After only a few weeks I was recommended for a commission. I was sent along to be interviewed by a posse of po-faced moustaches on the WASBE (War Office Selection Board). I approached it much as I would an audition: I'd studied the role and I knew the lines; I was, through the variety of jobs I'd done in the theatre, used to telling people what to do in a crisis, even with a degree of authority. In my family, too, although I was the youngest, it seemed it was always me who was expected to sort out any problems that cropped up.

Above all, I suppose I looked right for the part and had theatrical confidence.

Even though I felt the interview had gone well, it still came as a surprise when the selection board informed me that I was indeed 'Officer Material' and suitable for enrolment at OCTU – Officer Cadet Training Unit.

Thus my billet for the next twelve weeks was a pre-OCTU in Wrotham, Kent. An officer cadet was an unfortunate beast, being neither Officer nor Other Rank. We were treated with disdain by the training sergeants, who were obliged to call their young pupils 'sir', but managed to imbue that short term of deference with the most withering contempt.

Quite a few of the entrants to pre-OCTU fell by the wayside, having been judged unsuitable to continue on the course. But I survived, and my stint in Kent was to be followed by nine months hard training in a Royal Artillery OCTU in Catterick, Yorkshire.

In between, I spent a few days at home. Fred turned up the same day, also on leave, weary from preparation for the campaign in the Middle East. The significance of my being in an OCTU wasn't lost on him. He was a staff-sergeant now, but I insisted that, as an NCO, he should call me 'sir', and reminded him that, when we next met, he should salute me, as required by army law. He swiftly retaliated by asking, 'Could you lend me some money, sir?' – a request which met a peremptory, 'Certainly not! You are earning more than me, so piss off, Sergeant!'

I was sorry to see him go, of course, and completely unaware that he was heading for the bloody desert war and then across the water to the foot of Italy, where he would be involved in the Anzio beachhead before moving on to Monte Cassino.

In Catterick I was put into a set of barracks which had until recently been occupied by a detachment of WRACs. At the start of the war, most women available for work were recruited into the so-called Land Army, labouring on farms all over Britain – and, if they happened to be near a barracks, ready to respond to the cry, 'Backs to the land, girls!' – but now they had started joining the forces and were being brought closer to the action in more ways than one. These women in khaki had left the barracks plastered with graffiti of quite startling, blush-making rudeness: mostly men's genitalia drawn with absolutely no sense of scale – either that or they'd had bigger men than Gunga Din. Even after my acquaintance with the working girls of Soho and the naked dancers in the Windmill, I never dreamed that women could be so coarse. Perhaps it was the first time they'd been free of men in this way – not answerable to fathers or brothers – and they were relishing it. In many ways, the war was a far more liberating time for women than the rise of feminism in the sixties. I found it fascinating that ordinary women could have such filthy minds, and was looking forward to making the acquaintance of some of them, but having seen their artwork, they might have been somewhat disappointed in me.

In Catterick we trained very hard, both physically and mentally. The Royal Artillery required a higher level of technical training than, for instance, the infantry, and I found I was being educated more than I had ever been at school. A firm grasp of maths was an absolutely crucial part of being a gunnery officer – logarithms, slide rules, and even calculus were needed to work out trajectories and lines of fire. I hadn't so much as licked a logarithm before and there were times when I felt this was worse than learning lines. Achieving a commission in HM's Army was a daunting task, but I threw myself into it, determined not to make a fool of myself and to fulfil the trust the selection board had placed in me. That may sound a bit goody-two-shoes, but what else could I do? I did understand one gets more pay and better food as an officer.

I shared my experiences of forced marches and assault courses with a very different bunch from the mixed intakes at Brentwood and Deep Cut. Here the Canadian and British gunners were generally well-educated, most had attended public school and some had good degrees. I was the odd man out, but my theatrical skills dealt well with that, and nobody would have guessed that I had never been at Radley, Harrow or Wellington. Of course, if they asked, I told them – Chingford Boys' School and Italia Conti – and if they then wanted to assume that I was the scion of some impoverished grand family of Phillipses, so be it. I could play that part very well indeed.

There was a potentially uncomfortable contrast between the English officer cadets and their Canadian counterparts. We Brits were only on three bob a day (15p), while they were on eighteen shillings (90p). It was unfair, and gave them a huge advantage in pursuing the local female talent, which was pretty scarce to begin with. I made several friends among the Canadians, but I didn't like them calling me 'Less'. It's too like 'Less we forget'. However, as we got to know each other better, we found they were very generous in the pubs.

I also attended a firing course on the Cornish coast with a group of newly arrived Americans. We practised trying to hit long red fabric 'sleeves' drawn through the air by small aircraft. The Brit gun crews were always smart and polished and went through a series of strict, staged movements, handling the shells and passing them carefully from one to another, sharp and to the beat. The Americans, on the other hand, would casually chuck the ammunition around without much regard for procedure. They thought our method was bullshit, but sometimes they paid the price for their casualness with friendly fire.

Some time after that I got my first taste of real warfare when I was posted to an active anti-aircraft battery near Southwold on the east coast where we had a steady flow of live targets to shoot at – German bomber squadrons heading for the Midlands. We didn't let many get by.

Then it was back to Yorkshire, where we moved on to heavier artillery. The training was physical as well as mental, becoming more intensive and gruelling in an effort to prepare us for the full onslaught of war. Failure or misdemeanour was punished with an order to run once round the drill square toting a twenty-five-pound shell – twice, if you were seriously in error. I earned one of these early on when my erratic maths led to an error of 180 degrees, which meant I fired on my own troops, but we were only rehearsing with blanks, thank God! Curiously, I discovered that I was a natural crack shot with a .38 revolver and a .303 Lee Enfield rifle. I've no idea how; I thought my eyesight was fairly crap. Perhaps I was just good at guessing and holding my hands steady. Using the bayonet on the end of the .303 was another matter. Sticking it into a stuffed model of a Nazi stormtrooper with a bloodcurdling yell was bad enough; the idea of doing it to a real, squishy human body – even a German one – made one feel very squeamish. Still, I thought, at least I could rely on my shooting prowess.

On an intensive training scheme in the Lake District, the harsh conditions were exacerbated by the man leading our unit: an individual of astonishing bitterness, perhaps explained by the fact his whole family had been wiped out in an air raid; he'd lost his house, wife and children – everything, except his dog. Now the loyal dog never left his side and he took out all his resentment on us. Aside from verging on the certifiable – God help any German who got in his way, for he was quite capable of killing at the click of a finger – he was also extremely fit. The forced marches he ordered were done at the double, carrying Bren guns (weighing 28 lb each) for miles, regardless of the sores on our feet or the live ammunition whizzing around our heads. It was hell, but one could be proud to have lasted the course.

I passed the OCTU course first time round, somewhat to my surprise. And so, on 8 November 1943, at the age of nineteen and a half, I took part in our Passing Out Parade, and proudly got my commission as a 2nd lieutenant in the Royal Artillery.

I knew I had entered another world when a tailor appeared and hovered, waiting to measure me for my new uniform, complete with a pip to be sewn on to each shoulder. I was also required to buy myself a new Sam Browne belt, which had to be kept burnished to gleaming magnificence. I'd always been paid in cash before, but now I had to open my first bank account with Messrs Cox & Kings to accept my monthly pay cheque – and I was no longer on the measly three shillings a day, plus all my rail travel would now be in a first-class compartment.

My first posting was to the 120th Field Artillery in Appledore, Kent. However, I had been granted two weeks' leave, and so I left Catterick for North Chingford. Privately, I was very proud of what I'd achieved and I couldn't wait to show off my new tailored uniform, my Sam Browne and single pip to a few of the local girls.

Mum took a moment to register that this well-groomed, belted officer was her son, then welcomed me home with great effusiveness, although I'm not sure that she took on board the significance of the transformation.

The euphoria of my new commission lasted a couple of days until the arrival of a telegram from the War Office, with the blunt message: *You have been transferred to the infantry. Have you any objection or reason to refuse?*

It was signed AG6 – Adjutant General 6, Hobart House, London.

Reeling with shock, I could think of plenty of objections. I had been looking forward to taking up my post with the RA and had no desire whatsoever to join a poor bloody infantry regiment. In a state of lofty dudgeon, I got straight on the phone and within twenty-four hours was facing AG6 himself across a highly polished table in his office overlooking the back wall of Buckingham Palace's garden.

AG6 was a large, archetypal senior English officer, sporting a moustache like a fence in the Grand National, a quantity of brass and red tabs, and exuding a kind of disingenuous charm that would brook no argument. He was a character, in fact, that I've gone on to play many times in movies – the Governor General of Kenya in *Out of Africa*, for example, although I didn't grow a big bush under my nose.

'You do, of course, have a choice of regiment, Lieutenant,' AG6 conceded generously. 'Any particular preferences at the moment?'

'Actually no, sir. I don't want to leave the Artillery.'

The ends of AG6's moustache twitched as he gave a light laugh. 'I should tell you,' he said, 'there are probably a couple of thousand other officers who feel exactly as you do, from all different units – tanks, gunners, cavalry – lieutenant-colonels down to your level, old chap, but I'm afraid we're rather short of infantry personnel; we've had some heavy losses in the Middle East. We don't have time to crank up new infantry OCTUs, and we need more officers right away.' He underlined all this with a bland, bogusly ingratiating smile.

I felt my hackles rise from my shoulders, as my cherub's wings had a few years before.

'I believe I have the right to resign my commission, sir.'

There followed a pause. I could tell by the way his moustache moved that he was pursing his lips as he looked me straight in the eye.

'What a pity,' he said without a trace of sympathy, 'after the immense amount of work you've put in, and the resources we've spent on your achieving it, Lieutenant.'

'Yes sir, but the Royal Artillery was what I wanted, not the infantry.'

I noticed that the smile had now completely disappeared, and the syrupy warmth had gone from his voice. 'If you resign, you'll be automatically and simultaneously conscripted as a private...' he paused, a brief glitter in his eye, '...in the infantry.'

His demeanour indicated clearly enough that there was nothing more to be said. As a chess player since my early youth, I recognised check mate when I saw it. I stood up, saluted, and slunk out of his office clutching a form on which to record my three choices of infantry regiments.

I filled it in right away. First choice: Middlesex Regiment, my brother's. Second choice: Essex, my county regiment, and third, any English regiment south of London, which I thought was fair and generous of me. As it subsequently turned out, I was posted to the Durham Light Infantry – so much for my three choices.

Thank you, AG6, I thought bitterly. Fifty years later, when I read that Hobart House, scene of bitter memory, had been demolished, I experienced a pleasing shiver of Schadenfreude as I pictured AG6 still sitting at his desk when the destruction boys moved in.

I returned home, miserable as hell, to contemplate my future. I was deeply resentful that all the hard work I'd put in learning the science of artillery – skills well beyond anything required of an infantry officer – would go to waste.

Still none the wiser as to my final destination, I was thrown into an arduous training course which had been devised for the two thousand unfortunate officers who, like me, were being transferred against their will into the infantry. There were two groups, each split into two courses of five hundred, which were scheduled to last six weeks.

The group I joined was sent to Dunbar in southeast Scotland, and a very grumpy lot they turned out to be. There were officers ranging from one-pippers, like me, right up to half-colonels, and, as AG6 had pointed out with his rictus smile, they came from a whole range of specialised units – tanks, artillery, engineers. They were all as bitter as I was about what had happened, and morale was extremely low. This disgruntlement gave rise to a lot of scheming to get out of the course we were on and the enforced transfer to the infantry which could only be construed as demotion. There was constant muttering about resignation, stifled only by the certainty that this would lead to being called up again as a private.

I was alarmed at first to find that I had been allocated 'hard lines' extra pay, due, apparently, to the paucity of my billet with a Mrs Shearlaw. I wondered how bad her accommodation in Dunbar could be to merit a reward for extra endurance and braced myself for further horrors.

Contrary to expectations, life at Mrs Shearlaw's turned out to be the only aspect of the course that *wasn't* hard lines. She was a Scottish princess, a beautiful woman of middle years on whose virtues and merits I could fill a chapter. She welcomed me and three of my colleagues with open arms. She wasn't supposed to give us anything to eat or drink, merely a bed (one each, of course!), but she simply didn't have it in her to treat her guests so cursorily. Her hospitality and baking were unbelievable, especially on a weekly ration of two ounces of butter and a cupful of sugar. I don't know how she did it. She was the only thing that made life worth living for the next six weeks, as we humped our Bren guns and packs over the trackless waste and soggy peat of the Lammermuir Hills, deafened by artillery and the relentless pounding of our own ammunition.

Since all training was carried out with live ammunition, a ten per cent casualty rate was officially permitted. It sometimes felt as if the course instructors were intent on using their full quota. Inevitably, with the intensity of the course, there were moments of trouble and anxiety, and no words of encouragement could compensate for the fact that I'd already spent over a year learning the Royal Artillery job.

One small treat in those bleak, craggy hills was the chance to catch brown trout to supplement our diet back at Mrs Shearlaw's. This wasn't done in a terribly sporting way – split cane rods were not wielded; dry flies were not tied or cast. A small charge of cordite emptied from some cartridges with a short fuse placed in a burn would bring to the surface every fish within twenty yards, ready to be scooped up, gutted and lightly grilled on a camp fire.

Another relief from this grim existence were the occasional dances given in the local hotels and big houses, to which many of us young officers would be invited. Inevitably the number of girls available was small and great beauty among those few was, frankly, elusive. However, after the rigours of the hills, I was happy enough to chuck myself into the vernacular revelry, in the form of the Highland Schottische – a kind of slow polka – and eight-some reels that were a tough, hairy version of the Dashing White Sergeants, as seen in so many of the BBC's Jane Austen assembly rooms. In this I was helped by a kind girl of considerable bulk and beetroot complexion whom I shall refer to as Agatha. She was very strong, and supremely well endowed in the breast region, where she didn't discourage exploration, though, personally, I had no urge for more adventurous forays. She had the strength of a dray horse and would fling me around the floor like a bag of King Edwards if I danced a bad step; I soon became something of an expert on Scottish dancing. Apparently I showed a quick grasp of setting and pointing – my

Italia Conti choreography coming in handy again. The activity was brought poignantly back to mind half a century later when I was working on the BBC's *Monarch of the Glen*. The big difference was that *Monarch* was made on the west coast in summer, which is very beautiful, but, as anyone who has been there will know, utterly ravaged by midges, whereas the one good thing (and it was the only one) about the Lammermuirs in winter was the lack of flies.

On the whole, we were quite well behaved in public in Dunbar, but we weren't allowed to drink there on Sundays – a result of arcane religious observance – so if we wanted any fun at weekends we had to drive or take the train to Edinburgh. We would book into one or other of the lovely old hotels on Princes Street and go berserk, occasionally with disastrous results. One of my fellow trainees was challenged to drink a whole bottle of scotch in a single hit. He stood on a table and started his attempt, only to collapse and land on his back, stone dead. The challenge was not issued again.

Despite that one ghastly incident, I went away from Edinburgh with fond memories, which were to be revived a few years ago when I was doing a one-man show at the Festival, written by the late Peter Tinniswood, and walked the full length of Princes Street every day on my way to the theatre, going over my monologue from start to finish, and arriving just in time for the half hour before curtain up.

We had arrived in Dunbar at the back end of

1943, staying on through Christmas and, more to the point, Hogmanay. On New Year's Eve, all five hundred officers on the course marched down the main street in Dunbar, before breaking into a kind of 'La Cucaracha' conga and a wild Brazilian dance routine, singing as if to rival Carmen Miranda. But we weren't wearing fruit on our heads; we were all togged out in the dress uniform of British Army officers. Disgruntlement at our imminent despatch to the PBI (Poor Bloody Infantry) was at its height, resignations were threatened, perhaps even tendered, albeit hurriedly withdrawn when sobriety brought sense in the morning. I could hardly believe it was happening.

Nobody was very surprised when, on New Year's Day, as we nursed vicious whisky hangovers, a gang of big brass from the war office descended on the town in a flotilla of khaki limousines. We were called into the main hall for a dressing down and a lecture about the value and importance of the infantry, and how it too was now a mechanised unit.

'What, the PIAT!!?' somebody shouted out, referring to the dreadful little anti-tank weapon.

The Hogmanay fiasco gave rise to a certain amount of bloodletting; heads rolled, and demotions were ordered. Not mine, thank God! The last thing I wanted to be was a private in the infantry.

The following week, the course finished and we all packed up to leave. The only thing that had kept me going through this purgatory was Mrs Shearlaw, her affection and her Scottish baking;

when we left Dunbar for the last time she shed genuine tears, and I joined in. I never saw her again, and have often wondered what happened to her. (If anyone who knows her should read this, please get in touch with me.)

After a brief spell of leave, I received a travel warrant to Haverhill in Suffolk and instructions to report to the 8th Battalion of the Durham Light Infantry (the DLI). Travelling south, in the usual blacked-out, stop-start-jerk-wait routine of a wartime train, I contemplated the last six weeks.

The Dunbar course had been a horrendous, miserable experience, perhaps as much as anything because there had been no real enemy on whom to vent our rage, yet we had suffered almost as much as if there had been. I wasn't sure that I was any fitter than before it started, although I was certainly tougher and, amazingly, still alive! At least I'd come through it, and been passed as capable for service in the infantry – a mixed blessing. Other men had dropped out, or failed. I can't imagine they had much fun wherever they ended up.

My arrival at the barracks in Haverhill (known locally as 'Aver'ill) was sobering, to say the least. Along with the other new officers, none of whom had been on my course in Dunbar, I was given a formal welcome by the adjutant of this battle-scarred battalion, which had recently returned from the murderous conditions of the Middle East much depleted. We were there to make up the numbers. I had been designated a platoon commander in 'C' Company, under the company commander, Major Leybourn.

Looking at the DLI men on parade, I couldn't miss the plethora of gongs – MCs and MMs, not to mention the odd DSO – that adorned the chests of the war-weary troops. Inside, I quaked – a nineteen-year-old uninitiated 2nd lieutenant, with the cradle marks of OCTU still etched on my arse, to command these heroes?

What the hell am I in for? I wondered.

I'd had barely six weeks to get used to the idea of being an infantry officer, and those in less than ideal conditions. Now I threw myself into the task. Eating in the mess provided a few lessons. The commanding officer would be sitting very grandly at the end of the table with his big moustache twitching, always on the look out for minor faux pas. I was not moustachioed myself at that time, but I began to grasp their purpose when, for some ill-advised reason, the colonel decided to shave his off. It had been a large wavy thing like a great hairy flag draped across his mouth, disguising it completely. Without it, his mouth was revealed as a weak pouting thing, and, like Samson, he seemed to lose all his power.

We ate asparagus and artichokes and things I'd never seen before, let alone eaten. I didn't know which tools to use, or how to use them, but my new colleagues became friends and gave me the wink on how to hold my knife and fork in approved officer fashion, and I was a quick learner. With the chameleon tendencies of a trained actor, I observed and quickly absorbed all the small mannerisms, even the attitudes of my fellow officers, who were for the most part men from privileged backgrounds.

I'd lost all trace of my Cockney accent through being in the theatre; now the army was finishing off the process. I hoped I would be a good officer, too, and although, within me, I often felt like the East London boy I was, I knew I had as much to offer as the others, even on this unequal battle-field.

I soon settled in and got to know the thirty men in my platoon. The older ones were indulgent and helpful. On occasions when I was supposed to take them through basic weapon training, I simply accepted that it would have been absurd for me, never having seen a battle, to instruct men who'd been in the thick of it for several years in the use of the rifle.

I told them I wouldn't insult them and asked them instead to recount their experiences in the Middle East to the newly recruited squaddies.

We were given some vague, deliberately un-specific indication of what lay in store for us when we received a sudden visit from General Montgomery – known universally, if not always affectionately, as 'Monty' – wearing his trade-mark beret. He was Commander of the 21st Army Group, of which our Division, the 50th Northumbrian, was a part. It was to be the only occasion on which I saw our three battalions on parade with glorious battle honours, now, with the help of our new intake, back up to full strength.

It was also to be the only time I saw Monty, although, some fifteen years later, I saw a lot of his extraordinary lookalike, Meyrick Clifton-James, when I played a member of the general's staff in the movie, *I Was Monty's Double*. Meyrick, an actor who during the war really had been Monty's double, played General Montgomery himself in this film.

After the real Monty's speech at Haverhill, the talk in the mess was all of invasion, although we could only speculate on where, when and how. But as the conviction grew that the Allies were planning imminently to open a new western front with an attack somewhere on mainland Europe, so the apprehension, along with the consumption of ale in the local pubs, increased – quite alarmingly, in fact. I soon learned that infantry officers took their beer seriously, and although not an especially keen drinker myself, I joined in, knocking back my quota of pints with frequent trips to the loo.

My position in the mess was becoming assured, and I was making friends there, too, among them, Johnny Mould. He had arrived in his new army uniform still wearing the wings he'd earned as an RAF fighter pilot. He'd flown dozens of missions before the medics found his sight defective and grounded him. If he couldn't fly, he said, he didn't want to stay in the Air Force. So he'd transferred to the army, where he now found himself, like me, making up numbers in the DLI, filling dead men's boots. He was a surplus officer in the regiment, without a platoon of his own at the time, and therefore designated, even on official lists, as a 'spare wank'. Johnny and I became close chums and spent many hours in the local pubs mulling over our prospects, trying to devise schemes whereby Johnny would get some men to command.

I was beginning to enjoy myself, and felt I was doing well. Any lingering resentment at being removed from the Royal Artillery was somewhat mollified by the thought that I would make captain pretty soon. But tales of war in the desert from the soldiers under my command brought home to me my lack of experience in real action, and I looked forward to showing my platoon what I could do. I was growing up fast and getting on well with them, and pleased that I could relate to them – working-class northerners, battle-hardened, mostly, with some raw recruits – telling them what to do, helping them out with their problems, writing their letters, advising on their love lives. It was crazy really – these men were five or ten years older than me, but they seemed to trust me.

Meanwhile, my twentieth birthday came and went. I'd always had a strong feeling that I wouldn't be around to see my twenty-first as the build-up to battle continued relentlessly, with more live-ammunition exercises and assault courses. It was tough, and breaks were few as leave was getting harder to come by; at best, we'd get a thirty-six hour pass. We rehearsed mass troop movements, coordinating with other units: the RAF, tank regiments and my old lot, the Gunners. Orders for battle positions in nebulous terrain were formulated. And we were given training in hand-to-hand combat in anticipation of what would face us when we established our new front. The only thing missing was a real live German on whom to vent our spleen, although we knew there were plenty of them waiting for us in Europe.

Johnny was growing envious that I had a platoon and he still didn't.

'Don't worry, old chap,' I laughed. 'I'm sure somebody'll buy it in action soon enough.'

I hoped it wouldn't be me.

The battalion carried on with its ceaseless training, with overnight manoeuvres on the flat heathland between Cambridge and Ely under heavy live artillery fire. Some shells and mortars fell far too close for comfort, and once again, the training took its toll. It crossed my mind more than once that life might have been a little easier in the Royal Artillery, and I suspected that Johnny Mould sometimes wished he hadn't exited the RAF quite so hastily. However, we survived – did well, even. My company, one of three in the 8th DLI, was picked to take a forward position. Our senior officers must have thought highly of us, I told myself proudly, though, of course, I was shit scared.

By the middle of May, it was clear that we were going to experience real war very soon, although we still had no idea where. I thought of my brother, now in North Africa, poised, we assumed, to make the leap across the southern Mediterranean into Italy. I was worried, too, about my

mother and my sister in London, where the new
V1 doodlebugs were causing panic and terror;
they were so unpredictable and unstoppable, making London once again the most dangerous place
in Britain. Of course, I couldn't tell Mum anything
about our position or activities, or my own views
on them. I was quite relieved that I didn't have a
particular girlfriend who needed to be comforted
and lied to. I made my army will, and was subjected to a routine examination by the regimental
Medical Officer, Captain Nigel Thornton, who
had become a good friend of mine.

A number of officers and men were suffering
from the effects of the heavy training bombard-
ments of the last few months. The previous days
had been the worst, and a rather strange, spas-
modic sensation of stiffness I'd been feeling in
recent weeks was becoming more persistent. I
hadn't thought it worth mentioning to anyone,
but when I saw Nigel, I sounded him out un-
officially on my condition.

He sat me in his make-shift surgery, ran a few
simple tests, and checked my limbs.

'Leslie, old man, I'm not sure exactly what the
trouble is, but I've seen a hell of a lot of it lately.
Actually, I'm amazed you've lasted this long
without coming to see me. I think the best thing
is for me to send you off for a few specialist tests.'

'What on earth for?' I gasped.

'Calm down, old man. It's probably nothing,
but I wouldn't be doing my job if I didn't at least
have you checked out.'

I respected Nigel's ability enough to submit to
his advice. Besides, it was an order. After that,

things moved fast. I was booked into a hospital in Chelmsford for a day and ordered to make my way there at once.

As my train approached Chelmsford, it showed no sign of slowing down. I asked a guard if it would stop there.

'No, not this one, mate,' he answered.

'But, look here,' I protested. 'I've got a date with the hospital. There'll be hell to pay if I miss it.'

'Sorry, carn' 'elp yer. You'll have to get orf the stop after and come back.'

'No, no. I haven't got time for that.'

'Well, we slows down a bit just past the station. There's an automatic mail pick up; we almost stops, sometimes. When you hear the whistle, be ready and you can jump off then. It's a big drop, so mind yourself. Good luck – and don't let anyone catch yer.'

And that was how I arrived. I leapt from the moving train on to a mercifully forgiving cinder bed, hopped, skipped and jumped over the rails of a small marshalling yard, tumbled down the embankment on the far side, picked myself up, dusted myself down and stuck out my thumb. In the war, every driver would stop for a soldier. Within minutes I was presenting myself at the hospital, early for my appointment.

It turned out that no one was expecting me. As with a lot of army efficiency, arrangements looked and sounded all tickety-boo at the time, but someone would forget to tell someone else, and then no one would be in a hurry to sort it out.

Sitting for two hours in the lobby of a huge, busy hospital, nervous about what I would be told, I was already missing my men and my friends in the mess; I even missed my mother. I found myself enveloped in a cloud of lonely depression. My papers had been taken off to be examined, since no one in the hospital seemed to know who I was. I felt abandoned, like a child who's not sure what he's done wrong, as I stared blearily at the cream and green of the hospital walls.

'Would you like a cup of tea, love?'

The offer jolted me out of my reverie. I looked up into the sparkling blue eyes of the cutest little nurse I'd ever seen.

'Thank you, nurse, just what I need.' Warm, sweet tea, poured by an angel. 'Oh, and a biscuit, too. Thanks so much.'

The nurse smiled at me as she poured. She was very young, and really lovely. 'You look a bit lost,' she said in a delicious, tinkling voice. 'Are you all right?'

'I'm fine, thanks,' I lied cheerfully.

'What are you doing here, then?'

'I wish I knew!' I said. 'Just waiting for orders.'

'Keep your chin up, and keep smiling, because you've got a lovely smile,' she laughed as she moved on to the next waiting patient.

After a while, the stern sister who had greeted me on my arrival reappeared. 'Lieutenant Phillips, I'm afraid the neurologist won't be able to see you until tomorrow. You'll have to stay here overnight.'

'But I've no kit,' I pointed out. 'I'm due back

with my unit tonight.'

'Don't you worry, Lieutenant, we'll fix you up,' she said. 'Bed, breakfast, even clean knickers! Come on; come with me.'

And so began a ghastly twenty-four hours.

Next day I faced the same tough nurse as she stripped me down, ready for the doctor. I wished my lovely young nurse with the blue eyes was doing it.

The doctor turned out to be a top specialist in neurological disorders. He perused my case history and examined me very thoroughly. He did the usual stuff with the mallet on the knee, cupped my balls in his hand – I'd sooner the lovely young nurse had done that, too – took specimens of blood and urine, gazed down my throat, shone a torch in my eyes, and held a freezing stethoscope to my thumping chest.

'All right, get dressed,' he said at last. 'I'm going to have to keep you here for more tests and further consultations.'

'But, Doctor,' I protested, 'I need to get back to my unit! I'm already a day late, and I think we might be moving out soon.'

'That's OK, old chap,' he soothed. 'We'll tell your unit.'

I couldn't just walk out, and with a heavy heart I accepted that I would be stuck here for another day. In the meantime, I thought I'd take a look around for the dishy nurse who'd brought me tea. Hopefully, finding her would cheer me up.

I didn't find her that evening, but it turned out that I was to have many more opportunities. One night in hospital had been bad enough; in the

116

end, I was there for ten interminable days. But my lovely little nurse came looking for me, thank God, and raised my flagging spirits wonderfully. She saw me several times, on the last occasion, over a light supper. Connie, she was called, and just what I needed. I still remember her clearly – the best medicine a man could have had in the circumstances – and I never even kissed her, though I certainly thought about it. She had a boyfriend, an RAF pilot heavily involved with constant raids over Germany, she told me, but I made her smile, and she kept me sane for those ten gloomy days.

Not even Connie, however, could have prepared me for the bombshell that hit me on my final day at the hospital – an explosion that changed my life, and whose reverberations I still feel today.

The senior neurologist came to see me.

'Well, Lieutenant, I'm sorry to have to tell you that your health has been downgraded from A to C – not fit for active service.'

'What?!' I gasped. 'But I'm fit; it's just a twinge of stiffness.'

'I can assure you, Lieutenant, it's a great deal more than a twinge, and you know it. There's a serious malfunction in your nervous system, and it'll be some time before it's cured – if ever. The simple truth is, you have a recurrent form of paralysis – it's not uncommon. Frankly, you've just got to try and accept that there will be casualties in preparation for battle, and you're one of them. It's bloody awful luck, but don't feel bad about it; you've done your bit.'

'But I can still rejoin my unit, can't I?'

'I don't think that's a good idea, Lieutenant.'

'But all my stuff's there.'

'It's here now. You'll find it all downstairs.'

Sure enough, my kit and most of my possessions were in a heap in the lobby of the hospital. With them was a letter from my company commander, brief and to the point. The whole unit was moving out – he didn't say where, of course – and my friend, Johnny Mould, had taken over my platoon.

Christ! I thought with growing despair.

But that wasn't all. A telegram was enclosed, informing me that my brother had been seriously wounded in southern Italy, near the Anzio beachhead. Few details were given, other than that he was in a field hospital in the region.

I immediately wrote my mother the warmest letter I could produce in the circumstances. I didn't tell her the truth about myself, just told her I was all right and in good form, and did my best to reassure her and dispel her anxiety over my brother.

At least he's alive, I wrote. *He'll pull through.*

Had she known the truth of my situation, she wouldn't have been able to handle it, coming on top of the news of Fred.

I went up to say goodbye to the nurses. I didn't let them twig my frustration and disappointment at letting down my regiment and my platoon. I thought bitterly of the irony of my banter with Johnny, when I'd said he would soon get a command of his own, only I hoped it wasn't mine. And now he was going to lead my men into action – any time now if the rumours were to be believed.

Feeling desolate, and without any other instructions, I wheedled permission to go back to Haverhill to look for a few of my things that hadn't been sent on to the hospital. My unit had gone; there was nothing of mine in the place, and no one would tell me where the 8th Durham Light Infantry had been sent. I never did find my missing gear.

The following day, 6 June 1944, along with the rest of Britain, I woke up to learn that D-Day had been launched. I could only guess what that meant for all my good friends in the 8th DLI. I thought they must be on their way to France for the early stages of the invasion, though, naturally there was a blanket on any information or communication about it. I could only fret and wait for news. It was one of the most unbearable periods of my life.

On my discharge from hospital, I'd been informed that not only had I been officially downgraded, I was now under medical supervision. My next destination was to be a special hospital in Banstead, Surrey.

I knew the minute I walked in that this was a mental institution.

What the hell am I doing here? I asked myself, feeling like a character in a Franz Kafka novel with no control over his own destiny. Was I really so bad, so mad, that I had to be in a place like this?

I was put into a ward overnight, and for twenty-four hours suffered the grimmest doubts I'd ever known about myself.

The following morning I was casually informed

that my being there was a mistake.

Another army cock-up. I'd been sent to the wrong place.

Visits to a couple more hospitals confirmed that I was suffering from a form of paralysis. Unwholesome doses of Luminol were prescribed, but no one seemed to know what to do with me. I was told to return home on leave until I received further orders. Two days later, I was informed by telegram that I'd been transferred from 50th Northumbrian Div to the 51st Highland Division. Och aye, I thought, let's hope Mrs Shearlaw is around.

Under this badge and, paradoxically, in my downgraded state of health, I was now given the most responsible job I'd held since being commissioned. I was put in charge of Chadacre Hall, a large Suffolk country estate in the village of Shimpling near Long Melford, which had been commandeered to create a transit camp. I was, effectively, to become the camp commandant (at least a major's job) coordinating the movement of thousands of officers and men of the 51st Highland Division – Black Watch, Argyle & Sutherland Highlanders and assorted other Scots – en route to France, where they would probably be reinforcing my old division, the 50th Northumbrian. It was an enormous responsibility for a twenty-year-old lieutenant.

Desperate for news of my unit, I set about tracking down the Home Detail Office of the 8th DLI. When a unit goes into action, a small staff is always set up to deal with communications and any problems that had been left behind. Within a few weeks of D-Day I hobbled up a dirty staircase near Paddington Station and pushed open the door into a dingy office, recognising at once a sergeant from the 8th Durhams who had been LOB'd – Left Out of Battle – and was now in charge of the 8th DLI Home Details.

He was very pleased to see me. After I'd shaken his hand, he silently passed me an up-to-date list of our casualties in France. To this day, I've not forgotten the shock of seeing in print the deaths and wounds of so many of my friends. I should have died with them.

Nigel Thornton, my friend the medic who'd first detected my condition, had been hammered with a piece of shrapnel that had lodged near his heart and couldn't be removed. He spent a long time holed up in a slit trench, pumping himself full of morphine to ease the agony, before he was finally gathered up.

The biggest blow was that Johnny Mould, the friend who replaced me, had been one of the first to be killed. Without a word, the sergeant shook my hand again, and I turned to leave. As I made my way back down that ghastly staircase, I knew I would never forget; it still haunts me, sixty-two years later.

Rather than go home, I went straight to Suffolk and threw myself into my new job. Chadacre Hall was a handsome house built by the Fiskes, big land-owners in the locality, in 1834. To run it, I had a small military unit of my own – a Scots batman called Lyndsay, a sergeant, and a group of men; like me, they were all under medical care, downgraded and unfit for active service, something which engendered a terrific empathy between us. I also had a large civilian staff to maintain the camp, managed by an enchanting old Suffolk man, known affectionately as 'Winkle' and answerable to me.

It was an unpredictable job. We could be on our own for days, sometimes weeks, at a time, then in a few hours, our numbers would increase by a thousand officers and men. Never knowing how long each intake would be staying before moving on to France, I was responsible for the finances, health, security, food, drink, transport, weapons, ammunition – everything, in fact. I was also in charge of the large NAAFI and mess facilities.

It was an emotional task, servicing these soldiers who were on their way to fight the Germans, possibly never to return. One had to strike a balance between discipline and understanding. On the whole, I was simply left to get on with this difficult job, though I never forgot my friends in the DLI. Once I'd settled, I began to enjoy the job and, naturally, started looking around for some female companionship. My search was soon rewarded by a chance meeting with the manageress of the NAAFI. She came under my jurisdiction, of course. Everybody did.

I had been called in to inspect the NAAFI premises. They were impeccable; as was she. She bore an uncanny resemblance to the famous Hollywood hoofer, Ginger Rogers, only younger.

This Suffolk Ginger was as wild as a mustang, but looked as docile as a kitten – an irresistible combination. Warm and cuddly, she even danced

122

divinely. And although her name escapes me now, I can remember everything else about her, and the wonderful rapport we found between the NAAFI sheets. My biggest problem was keeping the handsome Scottish kilts at a distance and making sure she had no chance to see what was hidden underneath! Women were in very short supply in this camp, and I wasn't about to yield up my own personal stock.

Liaison with local RAF and American units also came under my jurisdiction, which provided more fringe benefits. I made friends with several US Army and Air Force officers, which gave me, among other things, an entrée to their PX – their version of the NAAFI – which was far more exotically stocked than ours, and a considerable help in sourcing perks for Ginger.

I'd been at Chadacre a month or so before I received more detailed news of my brother. I was told that Fred had been hit by shrapnel which had lodged in his foot and calf, narrowly missing his genitals. His best friend, John Terry, whom I also knew from Chingford, had been killed out-right by the same shell.

Fred was still laid up in hospital, re-learning to walk, but there was no way of getting in touch with him. When this news reached my mother, she was ecstatic to hear that he was alive and recovering, just as she had been delighted to learn that I wouldn't be going to France. It was beginning to look as if she might still have two sons when this war came to an end.

I had some difficulty in persuading my mother

not to visit me in Suffolk. I thought that wasn't a good idea; she was still in the habit of treating me as if I were ten, and I really didn't want that in front of my team. Neither would she have approved of Ginger – or any woman, for that matter.

Facilities for entertainment were somewhat limited in the Suffolk countryside, so we had, on the whole, to make our own. When I discovered that the film star Jean Kent had a house nearby in Long Melford, I went round to see her. She remembered me and very graciously asked me in and, indeed, had me back several times – a pleasing reminder that I had once been an actor. The thought of going back to the theatre now seemed faintly ridiculous. I clung to the hope I would recover and return to active military service. I felt the army suited me, and I was capable of any amount of the work I was doing now. In a way, I felt I had found my true vocation – organising people, making sure they were properly housed and hosted. Perhaps I was destined, eventually, for the hotel trade. Well, one can dream!

I certainly enjoyed the task of keeping my guests entertained. Some of the visiting officers had plenty to offer: drinking games, bagpipes, gambling – anything to distract me from my defence of Ginger!

One of the Black Watch officers, a great big chap by the name of Captain McLean, became a good friend. His father was a bookie and he gave me several winners at Newmarket, as well as the Derby winner that year. Conveniently, he also brought his own supply of single malts. When he left, heading for France alone in his staff car, it was packed to the gunnels with whisky, smoked salmon, nylons, fruit, scent, maps, plenty of spare petrol, a gun and a box of grenades – what a character! He said he was going to join his unit in France, although he didn't seem at all sure how he was going to cross the Channel. It was as if he was conducting his own war under his own rules. One thing was certain, he would go short of nothing.

His was a great exit, toasted with some of his best malt scotch in beautiful antique tumblers, which he took with him. A piper played a lament as he drove away down the hill. Next stop France – and a battle somewhere.

Another piece of impromptu entertainment was provided during a church parade in a local hall – C of E, naturally. The sergeant on duty spotted a soldier sitting near the front still wearing his forage cap. With the service in full swing, the sergeant crept down, slid into the pew behind the offender, leaned over behind him and whispered raucously, ''Ere, don't you know where you are? You're in the 'ouse of the Lord. Take your 'at off – cunt!'

The vicar heard every word, but carried on regardless.

When this lot had moved on, I was able to grab nearly a week's leave and immediately headed to London to catch up with my friends and relations in Chingford. When I got home, Mum made a most extraordinary announcement.

'Fred's fiancée's coming down from Scotland.'

I was astonished. I'd had no idea Fred had a fiancée, and in any case, Mum never went in for any kind of entertaining, other than with her own family, and only then under sufferance. And this girl, whoever she was, certainly wasn't family yet.

Fred, as far as I knew, was still recovering in hospital in Italy.

'Why's she coming here when Fred's away?'

'She wrote and said he'd told her if she wanted to come to London, to let me know and she could stay. Well, I couldn't say "No", could I?'

'How does he know her?' I asked.

'From when he was stationed in Dumfries, before he went to the Middle East.'

'He never told me about her.'

'Well, as you're here, Leslie, you be nice to her. I certainly don't know what to do with her, and she's here for a fortnight.'

I resented the idea of having to look after one of Fred's girlfriends. I didn't think his taste in girls would be much like mine.

Never mind, I told myself, in an emergency, I can always say I've been called back to Chadacre.

The moment I saw Hannah, I couldn't believe my eyes; she was a lovely-looking girl. Lucky old Fred! I thought.

It was no hardship at all to take her out. The first thing I did was to take her up to Queen Elizabeth's Hunting Lodge, a palais de dance on the edge of Epping Forest, known affectionately as the 'Lizzie'. Then, one sunny day, we went to the swish new swimming pool at Larkswood, where we lay in the sun on the greensward around the edge and ate our picnic lunch. She had a great figure and she was very warm and relaxed with me. I fancied her like mad, and had to work hard to keep myself under control. She was my brother's fiancée, and he was lying wounded in some foreign place – I couldn't even think about poaching her.

But next time we went to Larkswood pool, we lay side by side and her delicate little hand crept across the grass. She knew where to put it; she wasn't hesitant or shy, and soon we started to kiss. It was delicious, but I couldn't help feeling very guilty about it, which made it even more exciting.

'We really shouldn't be doing this,' I whispered.

'You look so like your brother, it seems natural,' she said as she kissed me passionately.

'He might not think so,' I said.

We got up and walked along the side of the pool in an attempt to cool down a little. Hannah had obviously caught the eye of a couple of lads as she'd sat at the edge of the pool, and one of them crept up and pushed her in. She was no swimmer and was obviously very distressed as she splashed about in the deep end.

I was a lousy swimmer myself, but so gallant were my instincts that I jumped in and managed to get her to safety with some help from the crowd that gathered. The kids ran off and we lay down on the grass once more to dry off. But this time as we lay there, all warm and damp, we went a great deal further than before. Another session like this and I think we'd have been making love in some shady nook in the bushy wilderness around Larks Wood.

Perhaps it was lucky that, when we got home, I found I had really been summoned back to Chadacre to deal with an imminent new intake.

As I kissed Hannah goodbye – not in front of my mother – very mixed feelings churned in my guts. I was in half a mind to keep in touch, but we both seemed to feel it would be unfair. I left without her address, thinking it was probably just as well that way.

I'd fallen for her, no question, but although I often thought of her, even with Ginger to distract me back in Chadacre, I was glad I never betrayed my brother.

When Fred finally came back from the war, he made no mention of Hannah. Whatever there was between them must have fizzled out somewhere along the way. Eventually Fred met a girl called Joan, whom my sister's husband, Albert, had initially introduced to me. Indeed, I had taken her out, but, although I liked her, she wasn't for me. She was, however, great for Fred. They were married for over fifty years, until she died, and were very happy. Still, I often wondered what became of lovely Scottish Hannah.

It was only recently, in the autumn of 2005, as we were having tea at the Savoy to celebrate Fred's birthday, that I got around to asking him about Hannah.

'Fred, I hope you won't mind, but there's something I've always wanted to ask you. During the war when you were still in Italy, your girl, Hannah came down from Scotland to stay...'

Fred nodded. 'I remember Mum telling me, though I can hardly remember the girl.'

'And she was your fiancée?'

'No, she was just a girl I sort of took up with in Dumfries.'

'Sort of?' I gasped, thinking of the agonies of guilt and frustration I'd suffered for the sake of Fred's relationship with her. 'Was she or wasn't she your girlfriend?'

'Yes, but nothing serious.'

'Well, what happened to her?'

'Tell you the truth, Les, I can't remember. It was a long time ago.'

'You weren't engaged then?'

'Oh, no, nothing like that. She was just one of those girls I went around with while I was in Scotland.'

I leaned back in my chair and recalled about those guilty moments of passion that had almost reached boiling point, and what would have happened if I could have seen into the future and overheard the conversation that Fred and I were having now.

Ah well, I thought, a little self-restraint never hurt anybody, although it was a pity I didn't track her down. I was mad about her, and frankly never forgot her. These situations happened all too easily during the war.

When I got back to Chadacre after my encounter with Hannah, the Allied advance in France was going well, but not without terrible losses for the British and Americans. I tried to think of a better way of saying goodbye to my Scottish friends as they left for France. *'Au revoir'* didn't seem right somehow.

129

One day an Argyle officer I'd befriended grabbed me by the lapels with an urgent plea in his eye. I wondered what on earth he was going to ask me.

'Come outside a moment, Leslie. I want to show you something.'

He took me out into the park, and there, a hundred yards from the house, under one of the ancient spreading oaks in full summer foliage, stood a gleaming khaki Humber Snipe with a military number plate. He dangled a set of keys in front of me.

'Leslie, old man, I've got my movement order to France. This motor is now yours to use as often as you like, on one condition – you must never let it out of your hands. If you can't keep it and look after it, then you have to destroy it. Promise me you will do this.'

Mystified, but obviously unwilling to look a gift horse in the mouth, I said I would.

He dropped the keys into my hand. 'If you don't destroy it,' he went on, 'it's bound to end up back on my shoulders. I shouldn't really have it at all, but I brought it back from France when we got out after Dunkirk, and I've been using it ever since, quite illegally. The only way for me to avoid trouble now is to have it destroyed – without trace. I'd like you to do that and, in return, if you want to use it for a bit, that's fine – but you'll have to make up your own story if you're caught. You won't let me down, will you?'

I promised, we shook hands, and he walked away.

I never saw him again, but I now had a car that

130

didn't officially exist, and if inquired into, could cause tremendous trouble – a very bizarre situation.

Once the group had departed, I decided the time had come to take a run in the illicit Humber before consigning it to oblivion. Sadly, Ginger had also been moved on, so I rang Mum and told her I was coming home to North Chingford for a few days.

As I was about to set off, a large, split carton was delivered, marked *OFFICERS AND OTHER RANKS (MALE), FOR THE USE OF.* The contents were spilling out all over the place – thousands of army-issue condoms, arrived too late for the growing band of pregnant girls left in Suffolk. Great thick things that would have stopped an elephant's seed in its tracks, these prophylactics did little to improve the enjoyment of sex, other than providing reassurance that you wouldn't catch clap – or receive unwanted paternity orders. We used to call them overcoats; they were certainly heavy enough.

As we had no intake at the time, and I was in a hurry to get going, I threw the whole consignment of French letters into my tin trunk and heaved it into the back of the car. Feeling very pleased with myself, I filled up the Humber Snipe with petrol from my own pump, as if I were the Lord of the Manor, and set off down the London road.

Mum was thrilled to see me and was very impressed by the smart military Humber Snipe

131

outside the door.

I unloaded my gear, including the tin trunk. Months later, when I went back to open it, I discovered the thousands of condoms had all gone. Mum must have been poking around, and either thrown them away because she was worried I was a sex maniac or, thinking they were some kind of balloon, generously given them away. She never mentioned her find to me, I never asked, and the mystery was never solved.

Mum was always a little strange about any relationships I had with girls. She certainly had no idea about the encounter I'd enjoyed with Fred's 'fiancée' ... or at least I don't think she knew. I once asked her if any letters had arrived from Hannah, but she didn't respond. Though I wondered why Hannah hadn't written to me, I let the subject drop. Perhaps she did write, and Mum binned it. Later, when other girls began to appear on the scene, she was distinctly hostile towards them

As soon as I'd arrived back for this bit of leave, I'd gone out to renew old contacts. I knew that any of my friends who might be around would be dancing up at the 'Lizzie', and one of them introduced me to a lovely dark-haired beauty called Joy Herbert.

I spent the rest of the evening – and my remaining leave – with this dish. She was a very physical girl, and she obviously loved a man in uniform. I soon discovered that what she wanted most in the world was a well-turned out young army officer with prospects, money and sex galore. I fitted the bill and, as I fancied her enormously, I was happy to go along with her aspirational approach to our relationship.

I met her parents and family, too: a smashing group who lived in Chingford. They seemed to like me and certainly didn't mind their daughter going out with a well-groomed officer. In the privacy of their house, the soft rug in front of the fire in the living-room was in constant use, though visits to the upstairs bedroom were not encouraged. Joy's mother, also attractive and sexy, seemed to enjoy a cuddle with me when her daughter was otherwise engaged – very friendly indeed.

By the time I headed back to Suffolk, I was in love. It was the first time I'd been fully committed to a girl and I absolutely revelled in it. As with many young lovers at the time, a closer relationship was prompted by the insecurities of war.

Only a few weeks later, I dug into my savings and bought a solitaire diamond ring, and we became engaged. Everyone was delighted, except my mother – a common syndrome among widows, especially where their last-born are concerned. Mum's undisguised animosity towards Joy made it clear that she hated the idea of losing me to another woman. She was even spying on us, I discovered one night. Kissing Joy goodnight on the doorstep in the blackout, I saw my mother's little head pop up over the hedge in the front garden to see what we were doing. On guard!

I asked Doris to talk to her for me. She tried, but said there wasn't a lot she could do. Mum was a growing problem.

Back at Chadacre, another intake of Scots had arrived, the bagpipes were blowing, and plenty of problems were brewing. A few rather nasty court cases fell into my lap, as officer in charge, and some of the visiting troops ended up with prison sentences. I also had to contend with a few pregnant girls or, to be more accurate, their disgruntled mothers, who were turning up at the camp in a very militant frame of mind, all too inclined to blame me for the actions of some Jock squaddie who'd passed through a few months before, promising their daughter the earth but leaving only his sperm. Even if I could have identified the alleged father, it would have been quite out of order for me to pass on his details, although sometimes I was bullied into giving a hint. DNA testing would have been a boon in those days.

A more pleasant problem was the money that was being showered on me by local farmers. When it was fully occupied, the camp generated a great deal of edible waste, known in rural communities as 'swill', and it provided the best possible balanced diet to fatten pigs. I soon discovered that the farmers would pay handsomely for it – it was a seller's market – but I didn't know what to do with all the cash it generated. There simply wasn't a suitable category in the military accounting system to which it could be allocated, leaving me sitting on a rapidly mounting pile of cash, wondering where to put it.

In the meantime, though, I was having a lot of fun. Joy had replaced Ginger and was a regular visitor. Sticking to the instructions of its last keeper, I was using the Humber Snipe and intended to do so for as long as possible. Joy and I would drive around the countryside, visiting pubs and the Yanks' PX as well as seeking out obscure places to make love. What could be better than that?

That she was called 'Joy' generated some smutty mirth among my colleagues, though it was a common enough name then. At the entrance to German troops' recreation camps, were big signs proclaiming 'STRENGTH THROUGH JOY'. It was believed that, within these camps, Hitler's troops indulged in stress-relieving orgies with a supply of beautiful and willing girls. I've no idea if it was true, but my friends enjoyed ribbing me about it.

Towards the end of my tenure as Lord of Chadacre Manor, I had a brush with the theatre world when a group of entertainers came out from London to put on a play for the soldiers. I found that, if I offered free seats, no one wanted to come. However, when I started charging sixpence a seat, they flocked in. Such is human cynicism: 'If it's free it must be crap!'

The play was a murder mystery, and was going well until the leading man had just killed his victim, a rather lovely girl. She lay on the floor looking very dead while the murderer, breathing heavily from the effort and emotion, gazed down at her. He knelt to look at her more closely and make sure she was dead. Perhaps I'm being severely critical, but he rather overdid the heavy

135

breathing as the tension mounted. The audience were on tenterhooks, until a voice from the back of the makeshift auditorium shattered the silence with the old cry, 'Oi! Go on! Fuck her while she's still warm!'

The place erupted and the drama turned into a comedy – or should I say farce?

In France, the enemy were on the run. Although there was still some heavy fighting ahead as the Allies pressed through Holland into Germany, troop movements were a thing of the past. Chadacre had become surplus to requirements and, it seemed, so had I.

My medical mentors had by then sent through my next posting – to an observation and rehabilitation establishment for fresh tests. What they thought they were going to find, I had no idea. I was still on Luminol, and the medics wanted to check how much progress I'd made.

First I had to tidy up affairs at Chadacre as best I could, which included disposing of the Humber Snipe. With some sadness, I dismantled the vehicle, helped by Winkle and some of his staff. He hung on to the leather seats, which would be untraceable, and we buried the rest of it in the park. As far as I know, it's still there, unless some deep-furrow plough has snagged it by now and raised it to the surface. I had kept my promise!

I handed over the swill dosh to my superiors, not without a pang, but I made sure I got a signature for it. Probably they just stuck it in their trouser pockets; perhaps that's what I should have done. I said goodbye to my sergeant,

136

Lyndsay, and the rest of my unit, along with Winkle and his civilian staff, and Chadacre camp was effectively closed down. I was surprised I hadn't been promoted to captain or even major after the success I'd made of the job. It had been an incredible experience.

Nevertheless, I was still very much in the army and, with the war still going on, I was as anxious as ever to rejoin my DLI unit if possible. First I was sent to Woodside Hospital in Muswell Hill, hard by Highgate Wood, and still standing last time I passed. I arrived there optimistic that this place would bring me up to date with my medical position and my army future.

At this stage of the war, Woodside Hospital had used every known medical practice to help soldiers who had suffered shellshock and other war-induced nervous disorders, as well as those poor bastards who had been rescued from behind enemy lines and who now needed unravelling. Hypnosis, drugs, occupational therapy and psychiatry all formed part of the treatments on offer, and I had a bit of each. My official occupational therapy was weaving, which I enjoyed and can still do; I specialised in Turkish towelling. My unofficial therapy was snooker, which I was able to put to some use in my early, impecunious days in Civvy street, although I wasn't good enough to turn pro.

Woodside was a comfortable, quite cosy sort of place, housing about fifty officers. We each had a decent room, and plenty of space for recreation. It wasn't far for Mum to come to visit me, which she did quite often, but not at the same time as Joy – that wouldn't have been a good idea. Nevertheless Joy seemed as keen as ever and couldn't wait for me to be discharged so we could resume our busy sex-life and get married. This was a considerable incentive to get better, and I did everything I could to achieve the doctors' notion of fitness.

Some of the other inmates were in a very sorry state. Utterly screwed up, unable even to speak, they would sit in corners, staring around them like startled rabbits, wondering where they were and occasionally muttering to themselves. I realised how lucky I was and became quite hopeful that I would soon be passed fit to resume my military career.

I envied my brother, who had recovered sufficiently to rejoin his regiment on the push up from Monte Cassino, past Rome and eventually to Florence. He was still lame but, as he was with the brigade support group, backing up the troops, he wasn't so exposed to frontline activity. In his letters he explained how he had watched the retreating Germans blow up every bridge over the Arno in Florence, apart from the beautiful and historic Ponte Vecchio, and that survived only because the Jerries had to keep one bridge open for their own use.

I pleaded with the doctors at Woodside for another complete examination so they could assess and, I hoped, release me. With usual army efficiency, I was seen a few weeks later. The results of the tests were issued far more swiftly – with shattering consequences.

Far from being free to rejoin my colleagues in the DLI, I was told that I'd been downgraded to a health rating of 'E'; there was no point my remaining in the army – and I was free to leave Woodside forthwith.

Though deep down I'd known I wasn't fit, I was still desperately disappointed. The army had been my life for the past three years, and I was mortified that after all my intensive training I had lost the opportunity to return to my unit. It was a wrench; under the extreme conditions of battle-readiness, close bonds had been formed, and all along I'd felt I owed it to the Geordies to rejoin them.

But the medics were adamant. I was too badly damaged to join an active unit, so in due course I would be formally discharged. I was shattered.

5 • The Smell of the Grease Paint

Autumn 1944 found me demobilised, in an ill-fitting grey chalk-striped suit, with a limp trilby and a pension of 18/3d a week. I was feeling lost, inadequate and intensely depressed – until the morning Elsie Beyer phoned.

'Leslie, darling, I've found you a job! It's nothing terrific, but it'll keep you out of trouble until something else turns up.'

Since I'd left Woodside, I'd done all I could to avoid going back to my old life in the theatre. I was convinced that I'd left that world behind and, as an ex-officer, a whole new world of possibilities had opened up. When I ran into Elsie in Shaftesbury Avenue and she'd talked about my coming back to work for H. M. Tennent & Co, it was the last thing I wanted. But the days had stretched into weeks, the only other prospect had been stymied by my dodgy health, and I knew I had to consider every option. A job's a job, I thought, and at least I'd be among friends in familiar surroundings. Even so, I couldn't help thinking I should never have got off that 38 bus.

Elsie wasn't kidding when she'd said it wasn't much of a job: third assistant in the box office at the Lyric Theatre. I'd worked there three years before with Yvonne Arnaud in *The Nutmeg Tree*, so, of course, I knew it well and there was, I suppose, something of kismet about my return. But it was hell, being cooped up in a little office with two other men, Bobby Roberts, No. 1 and Fay Davies, No. 2. The theatre manager, an ursine fellow called Meyer Cook, would also cram into the tiny space with us, filling it beyond its natural capacity. For working all day at a boring job in these claustrophobic conditions, I was paid £5 a week – more than I was getting in the army, but still a pittance.

I wasn't ungrateful to Elsie, but as an ex-officer, for goodness sake, I'd been aiming a little higher than box-office clerk. I hated the job and would go off for a pee or coffee or use any other excuse to get out of the frightful little box and wander about. Nevertheless, I did have some good times with Bobby and Fay, and the experience was very valuable in my future career. I

140

learned all there is to know about the fiddles and practices that went on in theatres. Much later, when theatre managers tried to blind me with science over percentages I was due on the takings, I knew how it worked and where the leakages occurred – punters acquiring tickets by barter, for instance, which never showed up as takings, and theatre owners privately selling their personal perquisite seats, usually in prime positions, which didn't appear in the records.

Terence Rattigan had originally written *Love in Idleness*, the play running at the Lyric, for Gertrude Lawrence. Apparently, though, she'd forgotten she'd asked him to do it, or rather, when it came to it, didn't like the idea of playing a middle-aged woman when she was still getting away with thirty-year-old parts. That was the name of the game back then. Big names continued playing juvenile roles well into their thirties and forties, and in some cases even their fifties.

In this first production, Lynne Fontaine was starring with her husband, Alfred Lunt. The Lunts were stars whom Binkie Beaumont allowed to choose which plays they did. They'd made a big hit of *Love in Idleness* and the theatre was permanently busy.

Bobby Roberts, my No. 1 was like a performer dealing with the public from behind his box-office grille and could be rude but very witty about them. Knowing exactly how much could be heard inside and outside the box, he would insult the punters obscenely, just loud enough for me and Fay to hear, but not them. That side of life in the box office was a great laugh.

Life at home was less of a laugh. I was still living in Chingford with my mother. Doris was married and Fred was still in Italy, so Mum was on her own. She was thrilled I'd left the army and was back with her. However, she didn't like my having a fiancée and did nothing to hide it. She saw Joy, who was without doubt very easy on the eye, as a tremendous threat to her relationship with me.

Joy, on the other hand, was not at all pleased to see me out of the army. She was happy to be engaged to a smart young officer with prospects, but was less enthusiastic about a civilian in a demob suit earning a fiver a week, who wasn't at all sure what the hell he was going to do with his life. She was becoming disgruntled about our engagement and I'd been trying to think of some way to cheer her up – and myself, for that matter – so I was delighted when, out of the blue, my good old friend Bobby Desmond rang me.

'I'm on leave in London,' he said. 'Come up and meet me and we'll paint the town red!'

I was on for a bit of town-painting and told Joy the good news. I asked her to come with me and we set off for a great evening out.

It was Bobby, after all, who in 1941 had eased me into the job on *No Time for Comedy*, and the fire-watching and my long stint under Binkie Beaumont. Though he had stayed in touch, writing letters on telegraph paper from his submarine, I hadn't seen him since his call-up and it would be great to catch up. Inevitably we spent a while reminiscing about our time together on tour with *Dear Octopus*, Mrs Taylor and the lovely Muriel Pavlow. We drank more and more and fell about laughing at all the things we used to get up to. And, of course, I had to tell him about Odette. Joy didn't share our mirth.

He told me he'd been through a fair amount of hell as a submariner. How on earth he'd survived four years I couldn't imagine, but he was in great shape and full of stories. Though he had managed to evade being captured by the Germans, he'd done time in a Scottish jail. He and a group of mates, ashore on leave in Aberdeen, had got very drunk and gone to the cinema, where what had impressed them most was the enormous heater belting hot air into the auditorium – just what they needed on their freezing submarine, they thought, and set about pinching it. The police and the judge were not at all impressed and gave them three months each.

I should have spotted Joy's lips pursing at this stage, but I was too euphoric at seeing Bobby in one piece. As we made our way home, it was clear that Joy hadn't been as thrilled at seeing Bobby as I was. When I threw up, she took a seat further away up the bus.

'I hope you're not intending to associate with actors any more,' she said through tight lips.

'Good lord, no!' I declared, and almost threw up again.

Next morning I promised I would never go back on the stage again, though I still had no idea what else I could do.

Later that day, however, I had an experience

143

which, if I'd been superstitious, I might have taken as an omen.

I was down by the bus terminal at Chingford Mount when I heard the dreaded throb of a V1 flying bomb. When the engine cut out, I looked up and thought the terrifying object was heading straight for me. In complete agreement with the wag who said that discretion is the better part of valour, I scooted behind the nearest, most solid-looking wall I could see, and thanked my guardian angel when the thing exploded so close the wall trembled. It was a fantastically lucky escape, but I thought I'd been through more than my fair share of flash-bangs by then.

Despite Joy's disapproval, and much as I hated my job in the box office, I was making new friends through it. I was now quite glad to have put my toe back into the theatre pool and was growing confident that something better would turn up. One of my fellow tumblers in *The Nutmeg Tree*, Bert Bone, was still fireman at the Lyric. He'd always dabbled in the black market and regularly laid out his stall in the stage door-keeper's office. From him I could get anything I wanted, at a price – smoked salmon, bananas, nylon stockings, Scotch whisky, cigars. I asked him if he'd seen Jacob Kreiger or Odette, but he said they'd both gone and he didn't know where.

Slowly, though, a lot of my other theatre friends started to reappear. I hadn't been in the box office more than a few weeks when I heard through the grapevine that a company was looking for people to go up to the Dundee Repertory

Theatre to do *Hamlet*.

Once again I found myself exposed to the unpredictable rhythms of the Music of Time. I arrived at the audition to find that directing the play, and taking the role of the Danish prince, was Geoffrey Edwards.

Geoffrey, you may recall, played the newspaperman in *Doctor's Dilemma* at the Theatre Royal a few years before I joined the army, when I'd had the job of rather brusquely pushing him on stage with the book in his hand to take over Dubedat from the floundering Cyril Cusack. He gave me a great welcome as he was desperate for young actors, who were hard to find with the war still on, even though it was now in its final stages.

'How's your Shakespeare?' he asked, disguising any doubts he might have had.

This sort of question – like being asked if you can ride a horse – is always difficult for an actor, but I thought frankness the best policy. 'To be honest, I've never really done any,' I answered, 'unless you count Third Witch in the Scottish play at Chingford Boys' School when I was ten?'

Geoffrey struggled with his better judgement and gave me one of the larger parts: Guildenstern, who, with Rosenkrantz, is one of Hamlet's more influential chums. 'Would you like to do it?'

'I'd love to, Geoffrey,' I gushed, although the mere thought of playing a role like that made me want to lock myself in the lavatory. But I was desperate to escape from that box office.

I extracted some amusement from the irony of Geoffrey pushing me on to the stage having done the same to him some years ago. However, although I'd said 'yes', I was still doubtful and remembered the old joke among actors I'd known before the war, when they asked each other, 'What's your real job, when you're not acting?'

Joy reiterated her objections to my returning to the theatre. I knew what she meant: I had, after all, been an army officer, and I simply didn't feel like an actor any more. But it seemed there wasn't anything else for me, and I had to live. When I broke the news to Joy that I was 'considering' another job in the theatre, she took her cue and chucked in the sponge. No more 'STRENGTH THROUGH JOY' for me. She soon picked up a nice, clean-cut major and she eventually married him and went to Australia.

I arrived in Dundee where the snow on the ground and the cold clammy North Sea fog quickly dampened my already sagging spirits as I attempted to throw myself into rehearsals. Not only had I lost all my life supports – my uniform, my gun and my girl – but it had been years since I had acted, and even then I had never played a role like this. My inadequacies were made even more apparent by the impressive Rosencrantz: young Aubrey Morris, eighteen years old, fresh out of RADA and keen as mustard. He was, frankly, impressive and I wasn't. I overheard grumblings about me from the rest of the company on the other side of the flats. With great sensitivity, Geoffrey tried to ease the situation.

'Look, Leslie,' he would say, 'I've always

thought this line of Guildenstern's was much more Rosencrantz, don't you agree?' And he gave line after line to Aubrey. At least he was kind enough not to say, '...because you're so useless.' By the end, my part was severely truncated, while Rosencrantz became more of a leading role for clever young Aubrey.

I didn't blame Geoffrey; I was now having serious doubts about returning to acting, and the rest of the cast did nothing to reassure me; indeed, they were laughing at my efforts. Funnily, it was only Aubrey – who hadn't been at all beastly to me – who went on to make a name for himself, playing vivid, oddball roles in cult pictures of the seventies and eighties. The rest of the unkind company I never heard of again.

This was not a happy spell, and my memories of it are entirely tainted by a strong sense of failure. The only pleasing aspect of Dundee that comes to mind was that, unlike almost every other city in the British Isles in those bleak war years, you could buy fish'n'chips on a Sunday night – and if there's one thing an actor far away from home needs on a grey, wet Sunday evening, it's fish'n'chips.

I was ready to walk away from the theatre world right then. But just as *Hamlet* was about to close, Caven Watson – a Scottish actor I'd known before the war who was now an effective character player, on stage and in films – formed his own company and came backstage. He told me that he was reviving a play called *Hunky Dory,* and planned to take it on a short tour. Caven asked if

I would join him, right away. Thank God he didn't see *Hamlet*, so I put on hold my inclination to quit the stage, and said I'd love to.

Caven gave me the juvenile lead, as well as the job of stage manager. I suppose I should have been grateful, but I soon realised that *Hunky Dory* was an utter turkey, an out-and-out gobbler that only disappointed audiences on a tour of the murkiest, rat-infested, old playhouses and music halls in the North of England. Most of these seedy old theatres were demolished before the public woke up to their historic value. I'm aware, of course, that Bradford, Halifax and Huddersfield (for example) have since had their faces thoroughly scrubbed and are now referred to as 'the Naples of the North' or 'the Rome of the Ridings', but back then, they were jolly grim.

Nevertheless, the *Hunky Dory* tour yielded a few nuggets of experience. By that stage in my life, I was by no means a sexual ingenue, but neither was I a lecherous opportunist. The leading actress in *Hunky Dory* was a demure creature called Jean Blackshaw, who was pretty enough to stop a train in its tracks. She and I got on very well, but I hadn't attempted to progress this into a romantic relationship.

However, when one wet Sunday afternoon we arrived in Castleford, the next stop on our tour, we had no sooner stepped out of the train clutching our battered actors' bags than we were greeted by a buxom, warm Yorkshire woman who, before we knew it, picked up both our bags and we had to follow her through the rain-slicked streets beneath a lowering sky to her house. You can both stay with me, she ordered.

It was an old Victorian place in a more genteel part of town. With a flourish she flung open a door to reveal a large room festooned in story-book chintzes and a coal fire blazing in an open hearth, one large bed, and a small squashy sofa. It was, in contrast to the wet, bleak outdoors, and the prospect of another week of our hideous play, a vision of cosy tranquillity. Jean and I looked at each other, wondering what we should do until it dawned on both of us that the woman had assumed we were actually together – in modern language, an item.

With an encouraging smile she left us there and went off to make some tea. We looked at each other again, and I offered Jean the bed saying I would sleep on the sofa. She agreed and with that sorted out, we could relax. We didn't have a show until the following day so we went out for a bite of supper and we had a lovely evening.

When it came to bedtime, I prepared to settle down on the sofa, ruefully anticipating the cramp I'd have in the morning, when she told me not to be so silly, and share the bed with her. Both nervous, we slept on opposite sides of the bed with a large gap between us. Room for one more, we never touched each other all night. But the next night, as the fire died down and a cold, damp Yorkshire wind seeped into the room, we snuck a little closer to benefit from each other's body heat, and eventually cuddled up together. It was wonderful and the severest test of self-control I've ever undergone, as we were both so cosy and I seriously fancied her.

Jean had been brought up a Quaker and was still a virgin. She was certainly lovely, and I'm very proud that I didn't take advantage of her and try to seduce her. We stayed friends for a long time. I thought of her recently, when I was working in the Scramble voiceover studio near St Martin's Lane and a very pretty girl behind the reception desk told me a relation of hers had worked with me years and years before. It turned out that this beautiful creature was Jean Blackshaw's granddaughter. It gave me a lovely warm glow to be reminded of that cosy week in Castleford, more than half a century ago.

It was also in Castleford that I saw something that I'd learned all about during my stint in the Lyric box office. I'd come through to the front of house just in time to see the local butcher shoving two pounds of sausages and a leg of lamb through the hatch, in return for tickets to our dreadful play. I was pretty sure that our management wouldn't be seeing any percentage of that meat delivery, and I was right. In the end, I'd think the butcher would have wished he had hung on to his food.

The *Hunky Dory* tour took us quite close to York. Our play was far too shabby to appear in the twelve-hundred-seater palace of the Theatre Royal, but I'd been there before, touring with *Peter Pan*, *The Zeal of Thy House*, then *Dear Octopus* in 1939 with the legendary Dame Marie Tempest. I remembered the laugh I'd had with the staff there when Dame Marie, who had only to walk a few feet from her hotel entrance, insisted on her chauffeur picking her up in a Rolls Royce and driving her round the Bootham Bar to drop her at the stage door.

The theatre manager remembered me and introduced me to Alexander Scott, the new director, who told me they were on the lookout for a juvenile with some experience to join the repertory company. I asked if I could audition. To my utter amazement, they offered me the job, 'to play as cast'. After a slight deliberation, I signed up to York rep for a season.

Now, reviewing the bizarre course of my career, I know that this was the most significant move I ever made. To add to my pleasure at getting the job, they also signed up Jean Blackshaw for the first production, though we did not share digs again – perhaps a good thing as I know my resolve would have broken.

I started at the York rep at the beginning of March 1945. After *Hamlet* and *Hunky Dory* I had very little faith in my own abilities, but I was ready to give a fair trial to what I saw as my last chance. The Theatre Royal was a beautiful theatre whose history was deeply embedded in the city. It had been built by the widow of the great theatrical entrepreneur, Thomas Keregan, in the eighteenth century on the site of the medi-aeval hospital of St Leonard. The place oozed history and even boasted at least two regularly performing ghosts: the Grey Lady, a nursing nun who wafted around at the former levels of the hospital, and an actor who had been killed in a duel, whether over women or money is not known (with an actor, it was bound to have been one or the other).

The theatre's strong bond with its audience had been increased after it nearly went bankrupt in the 1930s and was formed into a charitable foundation – the York Citizens' Theatre Trust. It was adopted by York City Council, who bought the site and became its landlords, making it a source of civic pride and fierce local loyalty.

When I first arrived, I was sent by the management to live in digs run by Annie Lythe. Annie was an institution, a famous theatrical landlady with whom, apparently, every great performer who had ever passed through York had stayed. She would regularly drop their names with a leaden thud, cocking an eye to check that I'd registered them. She made me welcome and looked after me well as I settled in.

My first week in York, the company were performing Luigi Pirandello's *Six Characters in Search of an Author*. I didn't understand what on earth it was about and wondered if I'd bitten off a little too much by agreeing to join. A few days into the run, I turned twenty-one. I didn't let on that it was my birthday; that evening, once I had delivered my lines in the small part I had, I slipped out of the theatre while the rest of the company were on stage, thinking that I would celebrate my coming of age quietly alone. I couldn't help thinking of the previous year when, in the midst of some of the heaviest live ammunition training, I had wondered whether or not I would ever make it to this special day.

I walked around Bootham Bar, down to the spring-swollen Ouse and along the towpath to a riverside pub. I sat down at one of the outside tables, overlooking the river, and solemnly ordered twenty-one half-pints of beer. I placed them in a circle on the table and began to down them, one by one, drinking a silent toast to each of my absent army mates, starting with Johnny Mould. I drank six glasses to him, another six to my army doctor, Nigel Thornton, and so on. The last toast was to Jean Blackshaw.

By the sixteenth half-pint, I'd had enough and went off to have a pee and the tiny outside lavatory began to swirl around me. I came out and stood swaying for a moment as I persuaded myself to get back to my digs. Abandoning the remaining five half-pints, I tottered along the tow path, somehow failing to fall into the swift-flowing Ouse, which would surely have meant I would not have got beyond twenty-one. I half crawled up the stone steps of the embankment and got back to Annie Lythe's on auto-pilot. The last thing I can remember that evening was falling into my bed.

Next morning I was woken by a tapping on the door. Without lifting my eyelids, I croaked, 'Come in!'

I heard the door open and the rattle of breakfast crockery, immediately followed by an anguished shriek.

'Oh, oh! Oh no! Nasty, nasty!'

I blinked open my eyes to find myself swimming in what looked and felt like a sea of vomit. The bed and the floor all round was covered in sick.

Annie was gazing at the mess with quivering nostrils and purse-lipped disgust. 'Oh my God! In Phyllis Calvert's bed!'

It was a challenging moment. Annie tossed her head and left the room without a word. But amazingly she didn't throw me out – Yorkshire hospitality.

To begin with at York I was given only small parts, but they came thick and fast. We'd be playing in one show, rehearsing another and looking at a third, simultaneously. My very first appearance was in a clever comedy called *Give Me Yesterday*, in which I played the small part of a young lover opposite Jean Blackshaw, which was a bonus of a sort.

By my second month and fifth production, I was just about holding my own. I hadn't disgraced myself and the audiences were getting used to seeing me. The people of York were sophisticated enough to have high expectations, but they were also spontaneously kind, loyal and generous. Though I wasn't sure that I was going to get very far, settling into the routine of continuous rehearsal and production, I was beginning to enjoy it. This relentless stream of work made me feel as if I were back at stage school; all told, I appeared in nearly fifty productions during my eighteen months in York. With the high quality of directors and actors around me, I could have had no better training. At the same time, the sporadic paralysis that had afflicted me since the live-ammo manoeuvres was retreating slightly, and my confidence grew.

154

Early in the summer I moved to new digs in Fulford on the southern outskirts of York. Mrs Fisher and her daughter Hilary made me very comfortable, while at the back of the house, within hearing of my bedroom window, a carpenter busily carried on his trade as coffin-maker. They were a lovely family and I stayed in touch with them for a long time afterwards, always looking them up when on tours that took me back to Yorkshire.

In early May '45, Hitler shot himself and his generals surrendered unconditionally to the Allied armies. I could hardly believe the intensity of the relief we all felt, having been so wrapped up in the war for the past five years. On 8 May, VE Day celebrations were as massive in York as anywhere, and I felt that in my own small way I had made some contribution to our victory, and I was thrilled that Fred and all my friends who had survived would soon be home and hopefully out of danger.

Shortly after VE Day, while I was preparing for my next play in York, by happy mischance, I was given a part which was to define my future for years to come.

The playwright, Colin Morris, had already had some success with a serious war drama called *Desert Rats*. His new play, *Army of Preoccupation*, was a well-observed comedy, written from first-hand experience, about an assorted bunch of men adapting to military life. I was rehearsing the part of an enemy officer with a couple of lines, both in German, which I can still remember. However, the actor who'd been booked to play the much meatier role of Captain Percy, a young English officer, broke his leg and, with only three days' rehearsal before we opened, the director, Norman Hoult, called us all on stage.

'It looks as if Leslie's going to have to do it. There's no one else.' He looked at me forlornly.

I wasn't surprised. I'd done only minor roles in the weeks since I'd arrived. This one was far more demanding. It was an act of faith on Norman's part and I was determined not to let him down. Captain Percy was a character I found it easy to relate to; he was well-written and I learned the part very quickly. In the play he gives his troops a lecture, and I had a wonderful speech which reminded me of my own experiences in the Durham Light Infantry.

'Now, look here chaps and listen carefully. What I have to say is really very important...'

On the first night I realised something was going right as soon as I heard the audience howling with laughter at everything I said. It was my first experience of the enormous buzz one gets when you're really pleasing an audience. I've been lucky enough for it to have happened a few times since, and it still gives me as much of a rush now as it did then.

My feelings were confirmed as soon as the curtain came down and Norman, who was a cuddly, unequivocal homosexual, rushed across the stage, thrilled and flapping his arms to hug and kiss me.

'My God, Leslie, darling! You can play comedy!'

'Gosh, how marvellous! Can I really?' I was thrilled, too, loving the compliment, though less enthusiastic about the kiss.

'You can indeed, my dear. Your timing – perfection! That was wondrous!'

Timing, I was learning, is vital in comedy – just as it is in snooker or driving a bus, or crossing the road, for that matter – but it comes more naturally to some. I think I'd always known instinctively the importance of timing, and I knew I'd made good use of it that night.

At last, I felt I knew what I was doing; I felt like a real actor. I had found my natural métier, in comedy. And there I was to stay for the next thirty-five years.

After Captain Percy, I was given more leading roles, usually in the lighter comedies, but not always. I tackled several serious and challenging parts over the next fifteen months in York, working continuously except for the gaps between 'seasons'. The audiences began to look out for me, the notices in the York papers became more fulsome and my status in the company took a marked lurch in an upward direction.

I became great friends with one of the stage crew, Peter Letts, a young man of my own age. He was well-connected in the company. His uncle, Geoffrey Staines, was artistic director of York and Birmingham; his brother Barry Letts, had been a very successful and popular actor at York (and later a TV director and producer), while his sister, Pauline Letts, was already making her mark in London. Peter had the twin advantages of access to a good ration of petrol, thanks to his job with the theatre, and a 1931 Morris Cowley with a dicky seat, which did great service in carting us and female members of the company out into the fields and forests of North Yorkshire. It was this that inspired me to start looking around for a car of my own the following year when the government issued a small ration of petrol.

We had a break from the end of June until the middle of August, which meant that I could be in London for the rambunctious Election Night of 12 July, when the British people unexpectedly and, to my mind, inexplicably, decided to push out the victorious Churchill and replace him with the mouse-like Clement Attlee. I'd arranged to meet Bobby Desmond and we ended up in the West End, touring our old haunts and being invited to one party after another. I didn't get to bed that night – well, not my bed, anyway.

I was still in London on 6 August (my brother's birthday) when the Americans dropped an atom bomb on Hiroshima, bringing the war in the Far East to a close after a second bomb was dropped on Nagasaki. Once again we all went mad with relief, hardly daring to stop and wonder what a terrible, devastating waste of lives this whole pointless conflict had caused, or what our new world would be like with the atom bomb.

There were celebrations, too, back in York that autumn when the Citizens' Theatre Trust threw a party to celebrate their tenth anniversary. I was invited to attend, of course, along with a lovely girl called Enid Walsh, who was a classical singer.

In our production of *Trilby*, she had sung beautifully from the wings while Elizabeth Kentish, who was playing 'Madame Svengali', just mouthed the words of the song. Elizabeth was deeply embarrassed by all the plaudits she'd received for her 'singing', and was big enough to own up to the public.

Enid had an ethereal quality and a delicate prettiness that I found tantalising. Unfortunately, she'd been engaged only for the run of *Trilby* and I didn't get the chance to pursue my interest in her. It wasn't until the following year, when I was in London on a visit from York, that we bumped into one another again, and I immediately asked her out for dinner. We had a wonderful, spontaneous evening and followed it up by spending the entire weekend together – in bed. I discovered that not only did she have a beautiful voice but also, beneath the wide-eyed ingenuousness, was one of the most physical creatures I've ever met. I've never since come across a woman who had such profound serial orgasms – hugely exciting and a great boost to the ego. I never saw her again, but I've always felt it was one of those unforgettable opportunities that life offers from time to time and which, as long as no one gets hurt, should possibly always be taken.

At various York city functions, I also made friends with a lovely couple who ran one of the big riverside pubs in York, Ernie and Edie Atkinson. They owned a swish cabin cruiser which was fitted out like a cocktail bar and we trundled up and down the Ouse, laughter echoing off the banks. Peter Letts and I spent many happy, and sometimes profitable, hours playing snooker and cards in their pub or trying to pick winners at York races with them. As with so many of my friends from that time sixty years ago, I lost touch with them.

We rounded off the 1945 autumn season with a production of that hardy perennial *Charlie's Aunt*. Despite its age and familiarity, it always seemed to work and we played to ecstatic full houses for the week. I had a great time playing Charlie, although I would never have guessed the innumerable times over the next half-dozen years that I was to play the lead, Lord Fancourt Babberley, his cross-dressing 'Aunt'. York loved this production and it was a great note on which to hand over to the annual pantomime before I went home for Christmas to see my mother and the family.

Mum, as ever, was delighted to see me. I could never persuade her to come up to York. Through-out my life, an excess of modesty at her son's achievements made her reticent about showing too much interest in my career. I always found this a little strange, in view of the fact that it was her initiative that had started the whole thing.

While I was at home, I happily reviewed the past twelve months. Starting from the low point of *Hamlet* and *Hunky Dory* and my first lonely weeks in York, I had worked to establish myself as part of the community there – a stark contrast to the self-doubt and misery that had afflicted me in Dundee only a year before. I'd been made wonderfully welcome in York and I knew that the relentless production line of repertory theatre had taught me a great deal. I was looking forward to going back, and turned down a few tentative offers of work in London. In York, I was becoming one of the leading players, and I didn't feel like letting go of that just yet.

I quickly settled into the new season and other, unexpected, elements came into play to help me. Members of the company were often invited along to charity receptions to give events a bit of zing and provide a chance for the audience to meet some of the actors. After a big do one night, Peter Letts approached with a broad grin on his face; apparently I had an admirer who was very keen to meet me, and she'd given him a note to pass on. It was a flattering letter; I was susceptible then (I am still) and I arranged to meet her for a drink, with Peter in tow.

Freda was nice-looking, sophisticated, charming and about twice my age. She seemed to know a lot about the theatre and had been following my career at York. She invited Peter and me to dinner so that she could 'hold the book', to help me learn my lines for the next play. I was twenty-one and free as a bird. There was nothing to lose. I thanked her and said I'd love to.

Freda lived in a handsome villa on one of the leafy avenues near the race-course. Peter was unable to come, so I turned up on my own, hoping she wouldn't mind. When I got there I found she lived with her daughter, a pretty girl of twelve, with whom I quickly struck up a rapport. Her husband was no longer around, she said, although she did have a gentleman friend, a handsome clergyman from the evidence of a photograph on the mantlepiece.

She was sorry not to see Peter, whom she knew, but said it didn't matter at all as there'd be more dinner for me. I didn't complain; she was a sensational cook and I was given a delicious dinner. When we'd finished, her daughter was sent up to bed.

'Well, Leslie,' Freda asked, 'have you brought your play?'

'I certainly have,' I said, pulling the script from my pocket.

Her eyes lit up. 'Oh, good! I love doing this.'

She really was an enthusiast, it seemed, and it was a great help to have someone who knew what they were doing, able to listen and respond to one's lines. It soon became a regular thing. I would turn up at the house with a box of chocs or a bunch of blooms; she would cook a meal and we'd spend an hour or so on the script.

After dinner one evening, the little girl having retired to bed, we sat down in Freda's drawing-room in front of an enormous log fire. I'd been on the go all day, and was rather tired. I sank into an armchair, closed my eyes, and before I knew it, I'd nodded off.

Unbeknown to me, Freda had settled on the floor in front of me and the fire, lightly resting her hand on my outstretched leg. After a few minutes, her hand was on my thigh, gently undoing my buttons. The touch of her hand aroused me; I blinked my eyes open and discovered that Freda's skills were not limited to cooking and hearing my lines.

Seeing I was awake, she smiled, brought her head up and took my rigid erection gently between her soft lips. I could hardly believe what was going on; it was the most delicious thing that had ever happened to me. For the first time, I began to notice her lovely breasts and softly rounded body, and to realise what an attractive woman she was, so calm and so sensual.

Freda and I carried on this lovely relationship for several months with no commitment expected from me, and no pressure to do anything other than turn up for dinner every so often, and round off the evening with some exquisite physical pleasure. I certainly wasn't in love with Freda, but I was very appreciative of what she gave me. It was only when her daughter called me 'Daddy' one evening that I judged it time to ease off. In any case, I was coming to the end of my run at York. When I told Freda, to my surprise, she showed no obvious emotion, which made it a lot easier – one of the advantages of dealing with a more mature woman, I suppose.

Aside from regular liaisons with Freda, I spent a lot of time with other members of the company. They were a friendly bunch, some of whom had been at York for years and knew they would never move on. For a while I shared a dressing room with one of the older players who was also a watch repairer. When he wasn't on stage, he could be found in our room, hunched over a small vice and a cluster of watch parts, reminiscing about distant events in his love life.

'Many's the time I've charvered a young lady in the OP tit!' he would chortle obscurely. I never worked out what that meant!

163

Like a lot of us as we grow older, he had difficulty remembering lines, but he wasn't above
shunting the blame on to whichever poor sod was
playing opposite him. If he dried, he would
simply busk by asking a question – a non-existent
cue to which there was no reply – and the injured
party could only stand there stammering, looking
as if it were their fault. On the whole, though, the
senior actors were immensely kind and avuncular
towards me, and undoubtedly taught me a lot.

Some of the more transient members provided
amusement too. There was a girl called Primrose
who turned up as ASM for a few shows. She was
a very tall, gawky girl who made us laugh just by
looking at her, though we didn't mean to be
unkind. In fact, the one time she had to appear
on stage, she simply played herself and brought
the house down.

Primrose was ASM on a play called *Skipper
Next to God* in which I played the captain of a
ship transporting Jews from port to port, where
they are constantly refused entry. In a vividly
written scene of a violent storm, some of us go
out on deck – off stage – to take a look, coming
back on totally soaked. One of Primrose's jobs
was to stand in the wings and chuck buckets of
water at us so that we were completely drenched
before making our entrance from the storm.

She did this very efficiently on the first night,
but one of the wags in the cast said to her
afterwards, 'Primrose, darling, you gave us a
great soaking. But tell me, where did you get that
water?'

Primrose, who wasn't an idiot, blinked. 'From

the tap in the green room, of course. Why? What was wrong with it?'

'My dear girl, haven't you read the script? We're at sea, for God's sake. And the sea is full of salt. You should have used salt water.'

The next day she was seen pouring sackfuls of Cerebos into her three buckets. We chuckled to ourselves that she was so gullible, but she had the last laugh. She'd put such a lot of salt in the water that, when she chucked it straight into the face of the man who'd reprimanded her, his eyes were stinging so much he couldn't see a thing for the rest of the scene.

On another occasion, one of the cast asked the poor girl to go and find the key to the grid. The grid, dangling above the stage with all the apparatus to raise and lower various items of the set, was invariably the dustiest part of the whole theatre, and anyone crawling around on it would come back absolutely covered in filthy black dust, rat droppings, dead bats and God knows what else. No one warned poor Primrose. She came down looking like Liza Dolittle's dad, saying she couldn't find the key. When the cast fell about laughing, she realised she'd been had.

Towards the end of my run in York, petrol rationing eased a little and I became very excited when I saw an advertisement in the York paper for an Alvis car at what sounded like a bargain price. I went to see it and was greeted by a charming woman. The car had belonged to her husband who'd been killed in the war, she said. She took me through to the garage to show it to me.

But there was no car, only a cluster of boxes and old tea-chests, neatly labelled, apparently containing all the parts of a dismantled Alvis. Everything was clean and oiled, all ready to be reassembled in accordance with the instruction book that came with it. I could have the whole lot for £20.

Although I'd done a course in vehicle maintenance in the army, I knew my mechanical limitations, and putting this lot together was way beyond me. Disappointed, I said I'd think about it and left.

Despite the urgings of Peter Letts and Ernie Atkinson to buy it, my natural practicality prevailed and I settled instead for a more modest 1939 Standard 8, which cost me £6 – not a bad buy, really. I christened it George and it gave me several years' good service.

In September 1946 I played my last role at the York rep: Tom Pope in J.F. Wright's costume drama, *Tudor Twilight*. The management had released me from my contract to enable me to go back to London to take up a job with H.M. Tennent & Co – back with Binkie again.

I was given a marvellous send off by the company, making me wish I was staying. I had blossomed during my time at the Theatre Royal; having arrived there naïve and uncertain, I was leaving a confident, experienced and ambitious actor. Even then, I knew those eighteen months had been a pivotal period of my career – a journey from failure to success, without which my life would have taken a very different course.

Leaving wonderful memories of York behind me, I loaded up George and headed down the A1 to Chingford and my mother.

6 • On the Ladder

It should have been wonderful, being back at the Lyric in the first production of Terence Rattigan's *The Winslow Boy*. It was a fine play, about a boy wrongly accused of stealing from his school and his parents who fight the case. The boy is found innocent, but the family are financially ruined in the process. Emlyn Williams was masterly in the leading role, Sir Robert Moreton, counsel for the boy. I can still hear one particular line, delivered portentously as he ends his first meeting with the parents: 'I will accept the brief.'

I had worked with the director, Glen Byam Shaw, and his wife, Angela Baddeley, in *Dear Octopus*. Jack Watling, my old schoolfriend from Chingford, was playing Dickie Winslow; I was his understudy and also played Fred, the photographer, with two lines only; in addition, I was ASM and general dogsbody. In other words, pretty much back where I'd been the year before my call-up. At least I wasn't in the box office.

Although everyone was very friendly and pleased to see me, it was made obvious that, whatever I might have been in York – leading player, popular star, enthusiastically reviewed, admired by the fans – here, I was just young Leslie, the lowest of the low, and utterly dispensable. This hit me hard one day when I went up to see Jack, who was sharing a dressing room with one of the other major parts. The stage director, boss of the backstage area, found me there and beckoned me outside.

'Leslie – a quick word. Don't go pushing into the cast's rooms. It's not done for people in your position to go round visiting when you feel like it; you have to be invited.'

It was an absolute comedown after my success in York, and I missed the set-up there. Here, I wasn't simply in a bigger pond; I was so small a fish that I felt like a total nonentity.

Trying to pick up the threads of my former theatrical life, I sought out Bobby Desmond. He had landed a part in *Antony and Cleopatra* at the Piccadilly. At the Criterion Theatre, appearing in *The Guinea Pig*, was a young actor named Denholm Elliott. Though he had endured a hard spell in a PoW camp during the war, Denholm had retained his wicked sense of humour and I hit it off with him right from the start.

I carried on seeing a lot of Jack Watling, too, despite discouragement from the Lyric management. A year or two older than me, Jack had been more than a few jumps ahead ever since our schooldays. Now, he seemed well on the way to becoming a star after appearing in a well-regarded RAF movie, *Journey Together*, with Richard Attenborough, and taking the lead role in Rattigan's *Flare Path* in the West End. To some extent his career had been given a boost by his friendship with Rattigan's coterie of gay academics. Jack,

168

though not gay himself, was very good looking, but didn't let himself be drawn into the net.

Leonard Michel, stage manager on *The Winslow Boy*, asked me to help him in extricating Jack from an entanglement with a distinguished Oxford professor who had become obsessed with him – to the extent that he'd been to see Jack's performances in *Flare Path* and the current play night after night, sitting alone in a box. He even wrote a book about the experience.

We told Jack that he had to bite the bullet and tell this academic to get lost, and did not want him hanging around any more. Jack, of course, was reluctant to upset a close friend of Rattigan's, but in the end we worked out a plan which succeeded.

Not long after this, Jack asked me to join him on a double date with a couple of actresses. Apparently, it was the only way he could think of to persuade the girl he fancied to come out with him. She was playing a leading part in another West End play. The girl who was coming with her to partner me was her understudy.

We had a wonderfully entertaining dinner when everyone seemed on great form and, at the end of it, like a pair of gentlemen (which was unusual for us) we bade them a demure goodnight and the girls went off home. I didn't mind too much; I knew mine hadn't really gone for me, nice as she was. But I could see that Jack was bowled over by his, but didn't want to push his luck any further that night.

We were all set to head off back to Chingford when Jack caught my arm. 'Hang on, I've got a double room booked at the Cumberland. My girlfriend has gone home, so I'll have to pay for it anyway, so we might as well save the petrol and stay there tonight.'

With petrol rationing still severe, this made sense, especially as it was a horrid night, pouring with rain, so we duly made our way to Marble Arch. When Jack asked for the key to his room, the concierge checked the booking, then looked at the two of us standing there.

'Mr Watling?' he said, looking at Jack, and then, turning to me with a quizzically raised eyebrow, 'and Mrs Watling?'

We offered no explanation to dispel any thoughts that Jack and I might be up to something, and staggered up to the room. I asked Jack why he'd booked it.

'Well, I wanted somewhere to go in case it looked as if I might get lucky.'

'But she was all over you, Jack, and I know you really liked her. I'm sure she'd have come back if you'd asked her.'

'I know,' Jack said, 'but I'm potty about her already and I didn't want to spoil it by going too far too soon.'

This was quite exceptional behaviour in Jack and I was very impressed. Sure enough, it wasn't long before he proposed to his girl, Pat Hicks, and within months, married her (with me an usher at their wedding) and they lived happily together for the rest of his life.

My girl was Elspet Gray, who slipped through the net and ended up marrying Brian Rix. They are a super couple and great friends of mine.

Jack and I always kept in contact after that, both later joining the board of the actors' charity, the Royal Theatrical Fund, which was started by Charles Dickens and for which the Queen is the patron. He was eventually elected chairman and I am vice-president. During *The Winslow Boy*, people were hailing him as the new Laurence Olivier – he was such a good actor, and in later years earned himself a band of younger followers as Professor Maltravers in *Doctor Who*.

The Winslow Boy ran through Christmas '46 into the spring of '47. I was still Jack's understudy, so my efforts to find a better job would have been helped when I took over Jack's part at an hour's notice one night when he was held up in Oxford. Mind you, landing my hand on Angela Baddeley's ample bosom can't have scored me any points. When I had to dance the turkey trot with Angela I was very nervous. The paralysis that had finished off my army career was slowly diminishing in intensity, but I was still prone to occasional spasms. I got through it and my performance was well received, which boosted my morale. Binkie Beaumont gave no hint that greater things might be coming my way. In desperation, I surreptitiously transferred my card in the Tennent's filing system from the *Understudy* box to *Juvenile Lead* – to no avail. The next job Tennent's offered me turned out to be more of the same – understudy, ASM and errand boy in a new Noel Coward play at the Haymarket. I turned it down, as I didn't want to continue as an understudy.

On the advice of friends, I went to audition for

171

Anthony Hawtrey at the Embassy Theatre, Swiss Cottage. Tony was an actor/manager/entrepreneur who leased several theatres around the country. He was a charming, easy-going man with a great sense of humour and a natural instinct for popular theatre. His repertory companies toured new productions, taking them into the West End when they were right for it. He was currently casting for a summer season at the Playhouse in Buxton.

As I was waiting to audition, in walked one of the most beautiful women I had ever seen, looking around her like a lost faun. I manoeuvred to introduce myself and found that she was an actress called Penelope Bartley, who like me was hoping to be taken on by Tony Hawtrey for the same venue.

Both our auditions went well, and I took her for a drink afterwards to celebrate. In many ways she was an unstagey sort of person. She certainly didn't come from a theatrical background. Her father was a senior civil servant whose family lived in deepest Surrey. I rather liked that and was completely awe-struck by her delicate loveliness. With no longstanding girlfriend on the scene since Joy's departure a couple of years before, I was ripe for a new one. Our budding romance was almost brought to an abrupt end, however, when a tempting career opportunity unexpectedly came my way.

I had landed a bit part in the film of *Anna Karenina*, starring Vivien Leigh. While I was on the set at Elstree, I bumped into Austin Trevor, who was playing Colonel Vronsky. Austin was a renowned character actor and a very nice man whom I'd met when he was playing Bloomfield Bonnington in *The Doctor's Dilemma.*

'Leslie!' he called. 'You're back! How marvellous. How are you?' He was very warm and welcoming. 'Have you seen Vivien yet?'

'Lord, no!' I said, as if he'd inquired whether I'd had tea with the King.

'But you must come and see her! She'll be thrilled.'

'She won't even remember who I am. I can't possibly just go up to her and say "hello",' I demurred.

'Of course you can, dear boy! Leave it to me. She always loved you – we all did.'

He rushed off, and came back within minutes. 'She wants to see you!' he said, and led me to her as all the other bit players and extras looked on, amazed and envious.

Vivien kissed me warmly. 'Le..e..s..lie,' she cooed. 'How wonderful to see you! I'm so pleased you came through it all. What are you doing now?'

'I'm trying to get back into the business.'

Immediately, her eyes lit up. 'I know – you must come to Australia with us! Larry and I are taking the Old Vic company over there – *Richard II*, *School for Scandal* and *Skin of Our Teeth*. We can always use an experienced juvenile. Why don't you come for an audition for Larry, who's directing? Elsie Beyer is our manager, and you know her.'

A few days later, I was waiting in the wings at the Haymarket, trying to compose myself before going on to audition for the mighty Laurence

Olivier. Although I had carefully chosen what I was going to do, I was more nervous about this performance for an audience of one – and what a one! – than almost anything I've ever done.

I delivered a solo piece from *While Parents Sleep,* a very funny comedy which had made Irene Handl. With her extraordinary (and some actors might say, slightly irritating) talent for diverting the audience's eyes while others were speaking, she always stole the play. Irene had a strong line in malapropisms and misunderstandings, and was very good at getting laughs by mucking up cues, to the annoyance of whichever comedian she was stooging for.

With hindsight, it was a risky strategy to audition for a Shakespearean tour with a comic piece. However, at the end of my audition, the great man boomed from the middle of the auditorium: 'Very good, Leslie. I think we can find something for you to do. Would you like to come with us?'

What an offer!

'I'd love to, of course!

'The only thing is... Do you think you might have a job for a young actress, Penny Bartley. She's really lovely and ... you know...'

Larry started shaking his head before my words were out. It wasn't the first time an actor had asked to bring a girlfriend on a long tour. 'I'm sorry, Leslie, I'm afraid we've no room for any more girls.'

This was a blow and, not for the last time in my life, my heart clamoured louder than my ambition.

'Oh,' I said, and must have looked very crestfallen. 'I was hoping very much there might be something for her...'

'I'm so sorry, Leslie, but there's simply no more room. If you want to come, you come alone. That's it.'

Alone! Without Penny? But with Larry and Vivien!

It was a tricky conundrum.

I thought I should first see what Tony Hawtrey had to offer.

'My dear old chap,' Tony said, 'you don't want to go all the way to Australia just to carry spears for that tyrant. I'll give you a lovely time in Buxton and guarantee you plenty of work, and a tenner a week, on contract. And what's more, I've given your girlfriend a job, too.'

Thus it was he, not the illustrious and influential Binkie Beaumont, who launched me into the West End. As promised, he kept me in work for several years, but there never was a written contract. Tony's business methods were amazingly casual; he would often take me along to the box office at whatever theatre we were in, and just ask the cashier to give me ten pounds from the till as my salary, or he'd pull the notes out of his trouser pocket and stuff them into my hand – no tax, no agent's ten per cent. He could be a bit of a devil at times, but he never forgot to pay me that tenner.

The Playhouse was a wonderful place to work and Tony had assembled a top-notch repertory company. Buxton itself was a charming Georgian spa town, nestling in a valley amid the Derbyshire Peaks. I arrived in my new second-hand car to find Penny already installed in cosy digs on the edge of town.

The sun was bright, a gentle breeze stirred the leaves of the beeches in the elegant parks, and it seemed almost too good to be true that I would be working here, with this lovely girl, for the rest of the summer. The rest of the company showed every sign of getting on well together and several became good friends, like Gwen Watford, a fine actress who came with us on many forays into the golden vales and hills around Dovedale. It turned out to be an idyllic summer, and one of the happiest times of my life.

Our first production was *Claudia*, which opened to a lavish response from the local audience, despite a natural wariness of new faces in the company. We settled in quickly; in August Penny and I appeared opposite one another for the first time, in a Kenneth Horne comedy, *Fools Rush In*. It was a great success and Tony transferred it to give us our first taste of Croydon – a beautiful Victorian theatre, sadly now demolished – which became a familiar venue for me over the next four or five years. A string of good plays followed, much as they had in York, only this time we would run them on at one of Tony's other theatres.

It was in Buxton that Penny and I first appeared in a revival of Jean Webster's *Daddy Long Legs*, a loveable if sentimental comedy which we toured before taking it to the Comedy Theatre, which became my luckiest London theatre for the early part of my career. Jimmy McBride was my first good role in a West End play, and yielded a decent notice in the *Evening News*.

By the beginning of 1948, Penny and I were very much in love. As our thoughts turned to marriage and babies, I started to see more of her family in the laurel-leaved purlieus of their house in Horley.

The Bartleys were kind, thoughtful people, but they had never wanted Penny to go on the stage, let alone marry an actor. There was then a deeply ingrained English middle-class view that actors – and show-business people in general – were not *de trop* in polite society. Penny's father, Richard, was an erudite and garrulous man, but though he was always polite, even friendly, towards me, I was left in no doubt that he would have preferred his daughter to settle down with a nice young academic from a middle-class family.

Penny, however, wasn't about to be talked out of her career – or me. She was a good actress and the public never seemed to tire of her. Tony Hawtrey had us both shuttling ceaselessly between London, Croydon and Eastbourne. I played Dicky in *The Winslow Boy*, as well as appearing in early productions of such classics as *Arsenic and Old Lace*, Agatha Christie's *Ten Little Niggers* (now known as *And Then There Were None*) and *The Happiest Days of Your Life*, which started life as a Sunday try-out.

In the meantime, I remained an enthusiastic member of the Repertory Players, a group that provided a showcase for new plays, testing them on non-public audiences in theatres that were otherwise dark on a Sunday. It was quite normal for me to be learning lines for these one-off shows while occupied with one or two full-blown productions elsewhere. We all did Rep Player productions for no pay; it was a shop window, a way of letting people know what you were capable of – hard work, too, but always providing a pleasing coup when a play was sold and went on to great success. Our hits included *Happiest Days of Your Life*, *Subway in the Sky* and *The Happy Man*, by Norman Ginsbury, in which I played opposite a wonderful up-and-coming comedienne named Dora Bryan.

I was climbing up the ladder fairly fast myself, and my workload broadened to include the BBC – a relationship which has lasted over fifty years – when I was given the part of Stoker Snipe in *Morning Departure*, a TV play set in a wartime submarine. Like most early television, it was made at Alexandra Palace and broadcast live. It was a terrifying experience; with no retakes, if one messed up while the camera was on, the viewing public would witness it and any drying or fluffing in its full, unexpurgated glory.

The equipment often let us down, too. The cameras were enormous, unwieldy things that had a habit of going walkabout on their own across the studio floor. A card offering the BBC's apologies would hastily be held up by a shaky hand in front of one that was still working, while technicians raced around in a panic, trying to get us back on air. I always found live TV a great trial and was hugely relieved when they started recording and you got fifty goes at raising an eyebrow, just so.

Morning Departure had a distinguished cast, including Michael Hordern in one of his earliest TV appearances and, in one of the smaller parts, my good friend Nigel Arkwright. I'd originally met Nigel through Bobby Desmond. He was a good actor who always looked older than he was – one of those men who look forty at twenty, and much the same when he reached forty (which, sadly, he never did). Unlike Bobby and me, Nigel was never short of money. He would regularly inherit bundles of cash and the occasional property, which allowed him to be very easy-going. It was only years later that I discovered the source of his wealth was his ancestor, Sir Joseph Arkwright, the eighteenth-century textile tycoon and inventor.

In the early spring of 1948, Penny and I announced that we were going to be married. While our friends celebrated with champagne and a few plates of cheese straws, Richard Bartley took me to one side.

'Is everything as it should be?' he asked, somewhat cryptically.

I took it that he was trying to ask whether I'd slept with his daughter.

'Oh, yes,' I said. 'Everything is totally as it should be.'

He nodded, apparently reassured. It was only later that I realised his question had a different meaning entirely: being rather narrow minded, he expected his daughter to be a virgin on her wedding day, and might even have tried to stop the relationship had he known.

179

In any event, Penny's parents accepted her decision to marry me with reasonably good grace, and, on 30 May 1948, we were joined in Holy M by Rev Quintin Morris (aka the Radio Parson) at All Souls Church, St John's Wood, still standing but now unhappily closed and desolate.

It was a proud moment for me. Penny looked divine, and I don't know that I have ever been quite so in love – at twenty-four my optimism had not yet become tainted by the cynical world-weariness that tempers such moments in later life.

After a lavish reception at the Embassy Theatre, we took the sleeper train to Switzerland. We honeymooned at the Hotel Beau Rivage on Lake Lugano – the apogee of lavish living at the time, and a glittering contrast to the very real constraints of gloomy, post-war London. We wallowed in luxury, imagining what it would be like to be real film stars, not the jobbing rep players that we really were. Unfortunately our honeymoon was blighted somewhat by Penny's severe hay fever. In those ten days I learned what it was to be a caring, kind and tolerant husband.

On our return to London, I had plundered the savings I'd accumulated over the last ten years and paid £500 key money to secure an illegal lease on our first marital home: a flat at 107 Hereford Road, off the end of Westbourne Grove, at a weekly rent of one guinea (£1.05, for younger readers).

In no time, our honeymoon was a distant memory, thank God, as I again immersed myself in work. I was given a good part in another live

BBC TV broadcast drama and, shortly after that, appeared in my first radio production, as a character called Tom in *Mrs Dale's Diary*. Penny, who had been eager to start a family, was thrilled when she became pregnant. While I rounded off the year by appearing in the Embassy Christmas pantomime, Penny, who had stopped working when her pregnancy began to show, departed for Wiltshire to spend a weekend at her sister's.

That Saturday night as I arrived home after doing two shows, the phone rang. It was Penny's sister calling to tell me that things had taken a disastrous turn. Penny had gone into labour very prematurely; the baby had been born, and had died at birth. I didn't have to be told that Penny was utterly distraught. She had been looking forward to the baby's birth with all her being. I had no car and it was midnight, so I had to wait until first thing next morning to race down to see her. I was shattered by what I found.

The baby was very badly malformed and had died almost instantly, which was something of a mercy. But Penny's sister hadn't known what to do, and in her panic she had simply wrapped the tiny corpse in newspaper and stuffed it, covered in blood, under a chest of drawers. It was all I could do to stop myself going berserk. When I finally calmed down, thinking of the effect on Penny if she knew, I hid the ghastly package and later arranged for our tragic little Carolyn to be laid to rest.

The journey back to London was one of the most miserable journeys of our lives. Penny was racked with grief. All I could do was comfort her and try to tell her that she wasn't to blame. Back at home in Hereford Road, she continued to blame herself. Nothing I said or did seemed to pacify her. The doctor cautioned against her becoming pregnant again too soon, but seeing how desperate she was I began to doubt his advice. We talked it over quietly and decided to try for another baby. And thankfully we succeeded. Put the flags out – we're back on our way!

With Penny now content, in the early months of 1949 I was able to concentrate on the next big event in my career, the result – one of those convenient coincidences in the acting profession – of my part in *Daddy Long Legs* the previous Christmas. The play had been produced by Peter Dearing, and naturally his brother, Basil Dearden, had come to see it. (Born 'Dear', both brothers had decided to amend the name for professional reasons; Basil Dear and Peter Dear – not good.)

Basil was now an established film director with a dozen commercial pictures to his name, and on the strength of my performance in *Daddy Long Legs*, he offered me my first big movie role, in *Train of Events*. I played a steam-engine fireman to Jack Warner's engine driver, one of the few parts I've played that reflected my Cockney background. *Train*, filmed in black-and-white at Ealing studios, was the first of three pictures I made with Basil Dearden, and it launched my movie career amazingly speedily.

As usual, there were people on the set I'd worked with before, including Michael Hordern.

182

Also appearing was Peter Finch, in his first British movie since arriving from Australia. He'd been spotted by Laurence Olivier on one of his Antipodean tours and been encouraged by him to come to London and work in the theatre. But he suffered from intense stage fright and decided to work in movies. Already a boozer and womaniser of spectacular energy, Finch subsequently repaid Larry's kind and constructive attention by having a steamy and very public affair with his wife, the lovely Vivien.

I found I enjoyed the business of film-making, but I took it just as seriously as stage acting and tried to apply the same disciplines I'd learned during my apprenticeship in York. From the start, I made an effort to concentrate on the role, to prepare myself and my character thoroughly before I went on set – just as I do today. As a result, I've always been a little irritated by those actors who are still joking, drinking and arseing about before they go on. It's amazing how many people do this while on the job. It seems to me that we are usually being paid a lot of money for being there, and the least we can do is turn in the most professional, best-honed performance we can.

June 1949 saw me back at the Comedy in Philip King's *On Monday Next*. In the lead role was the veteran review player, Henry Kendall, who also directed. Henry – or Harry as he was always known – was a camp, flamboyant man with big, flashing eyes, wide, expressive nostrils and double-jointed wrists which allowed his hands to flail manically as he pushed his hair back over his head and struck angular poses. Life for him was one long, whirling party from whose vortex in his dressing room he held dominion and surveyed the world.

On Monday Next opened to almost universally favourable notices, although my own performance in the small part of 'Second Juvenile Lead' didn't greatly exercise the critics. They were, however, unstinting in their appreciation of the energetic performance of Harry Kendall as a doughty old trouper – a fine example of casting to type. Harry was in his element. For him the world outside the theatre did not exist. Unsurprisingly, he was not married, and neither were most of the actors with whom he'd surrounded himself in this production (there were only two who weren't gay – I was one of them).

It didn't worry me; I knew Harry of old. A few years earlier, he had invited me for lunch with a group of lads at the Ivy. I knew, of course, what object he had in mind, but my mother was adamant that I should go, as it might lead to a job. It would never have occurred to her that a distinguished old actor like Harry could possibly have any interest in male sexual adventure, let alone of an unconventional nature. In fact, my dear mother had no idea such things even went on. In any event, I didn't go. And now that I was married, I imagined I was of less interest to him and must therefore be in the cast out of merit.

Often, as I passed his dressing room, Harry would call, 'Hello, darling! What news of the *baby?*' Like most of the cast he was eager for regular updates on Penny's pregnancy, which was going well. As the birth drew closer, the excitement grew. At least one member of the male cast was knitting and others were busy making presents for the expected child.

On 31 October 1949, while *On Monday Next* was playing to packed houses, our first daughter, Caroline Elizabeth Phillips, a pretty little thing with blonde hair, was born in the Casterbridge Nursing Home near Reigate, conveniently close to Penny's parents' home in Surrey. When I came in to work the following evening, everyone was thrilled and clamouring to know how the baby was, its weight and gender. It was very touching, really, although a little bizarre to hear all Harry's cronies fussing about, oohing and cooing. When I told them it was a girl, they all did a very camp, 'Oh, what a pity!'

Penny was ecstatic about Caroline and seemed now to put all the ghastliness of the failed birth completely behind her. She made it clear she wanted several more little Phillipses, but when she expressed a wish to get out and work again, I took it as a positive sign and, to help her, I became at once a thoroughly modern, hands-on father. I did practically everything for our first child, bar breast-feed her – and she would even try that, grabbing at my less than ample breast and biting it. In order to make sure she wasn't being deprived of her fair share of Mother's Own Milk, I walked her in the pram every day from Hereford Road in Bayswater to the Embassy in Swiss Cottage, where Penny had started rehearsals for a new play. Once Penny had fed her in a

185

way that brought satisfaction to the hungry little creature, she would hand the baby back to me and carry on rehearsing, while I winded her and then pushed her home in the pram. When Penny got home, I would leave her with the baby while I set off to the Comedy Theatre for the evening performance of *On Monday Next*.

This play continued its run until 24 June 1950. It lived on for the next couple of years in various tours and sporadic productions at short notice. Because it had no set, it was remarkably easy to stage, provided cast could be found, and most of us were usually able to put in an appearance. I was in it two years later for a TV test at the Theatre Royal, Bromley, but it came to nothing. Instead, it was made as a film, *Curtain Up*, starring Robert Morley and Margaret Rutherford, as well as an emerging Kay Kendall. Of the original stage cast, only Charles Lamb and Liam Gaffney appeared in the film, which was a disappointment for me.

After a short break in the West Country with Penny and Caroline, it was off to Brighton for another play, and then a hasty return to London to start work on my second big picture. It's always special when a director asks you back. Either he must have missed all your mistakes last time, or he must really think you're good. Presumably Basil Dearden was happy with what I'd done on *Train of Events*, as he offered me a decent part in his next film, a big Ealing thriller called *Pool of London*. Once again, I enjoyed the process and made some new connections that lasted for years

– the most prominent of these was the unique and unmistakable James Robertson Justice.

James wasn't really an actor, but a great personality. He would have been the first to admit that he could never play a weak or doubtful man, but he was such a powerful and unforgettable character that he filled the screen, and audiences very quickly learned to recognise him. Nobody who has seen one of the *Doctor* films can have forgotten Sir Lancelot Spratt.

With theatre, television, film and radio work all coming in one after the other, I was learning to juggle the various aspects of my job. Often I would find myself working in film studios by day, racing up to the West End to act on stage of an evening. Sometimes this entailed having to be two, or even three, and in some extreme cases, four different people in one day (as well as being oneself, and often forgetting who the hell that was). But I loved to be busy – still do, as a matter of fact, although the stage work can be a bit of trial for an octogenarian. No matter what the schedule, I always turned up on time, I was seldom sick, I didn't get drunk on the set and I always remembered my lines. This made me a useful actor – if nothing more – and from then on the momentum of my film work gathered pace.

But the next few months of my career were dominated by *Charlie's Aunt*.

It was my intention when I started on this little book of memories not to light on every single play or film in which I have been lucky enough (and, sometimes, not so lucky) to participate.

I've already left out a lot, but there are certain key productions – plays, films, television series and, in one case, radio series – that form what could be described as the backbone of my career. The great Victorian hardy perennial *Charlie's Aunt* was one of these.

Walter Brandon Thomas' extraordinarily popular play, written in 1892, was first performed in a small theatre in Bury St Edmunds. Since then it must have played every theatre in the country. Our 1950 production was booked to open in London at the Saville Theatre on 21 December as a Christmas show, with wonderful costumes and a set designed by Cecil Beaton, but first we set off on tour to Bolton, Harrow, Reading and Birmingham in order to get this tricky play run in. Emile Littler and the author's son, Jevan Brandon Thomas, were producing and directing. Jevan was a sweetie; Emile was a controller who took himself very seriously, and always insisted on having his name on everything – even the furniture and all the contents of the wardrobe. A friend who had a brief fling with a girl in one of Emile's shows was frankly put off his stroke during a hot session when he took off her knickers – and found a label on them: 'Property of Emile Littler'. It was a killer for him.

I had played Charlie in a production in York four years before, so I knew the play, but this time I was cast in the leading role of Lord Fancourt Babberley, an Oxford student of comfortable means who has to impersonate his friend Charlie's female relative, putting me in drag for most of the play. *Charlie's Aunt* succeeds because it is such a well-constructed period comedy, but for it to work, the 'Aunt' has to be played very straight. I learned a great deal about the value of restraint during the times I played her all around the country in sporadic tours over the next two or three years.

I think perhaps it was this role that was the foundation of my early reputation as a farceur. I'm not ashamed of that either; farce may not have a good name among the intelligentsia, but, technically, it is one of the most difficult styles of drama to get right. It's very easy to overact, to push for the laughs too hard and to lose them completely by overplaying.

In the spring of 1951, while I was still tied up with the *Aunt*, I was thrilled to learn that Penny was pregnant again. However, the thought of another mouth to feed, and a pregnant or nursing wife who couldn't work, galvanised me into hunting out every job I could find. I wasn't discriminating; I would have a shot at anything, as long I got a good deal.

Luckily, on the whole, I was being offered reasonable parts. I was also gaining more experience in radio, both for the BBC and Harry Alan Towers' American Radio. Radio drama required special techniques. When your only visible audience is a large lozenge-shaped BBC microphone dangling from the studio ceiling, it's not easy to gauge the scale of the listening audience's reaction and an instinct for timing becomes even more crucial, especially in comedy.

Working in so many different mediums meant I

was always busy; the work I did in one format helped promote what I did in other areas. *Pool of London* was, by the standards of the time, a major British picture and had a suitably big premiere – an exciting event for me. Penny nudged me as we arrived at the premiere and pointed up at my name in huge letters above Leicester Square – as if I hadn't noticed! I can't pretend I wasn't chuffed to see it there.

Perhaps the excitement of all this work brought on the slightly early arrival of our second child, on 4 October 1950. Penny had been suddenly whisked away again to the Casterbridge Nursing Home. As soon as the curtain fell on that evening's performance of *Charlie's Aunt*, I raced to see our new daughter, another blue-eyed blonde whom we named Claudia after the play Penny and I had done together in Buxton when we'd first worked together. Mother and baby were both doing well, thank God.

Penny was a trifle disappointed not to have had a son, but there would be plenty more chances. Having two children was so much more fun than one, and I couldn't see why one shouldn't simply extrapolate this graph, though plenty of children meant plenty of work. At the same time, it was becoming pretty clear that we would need more space than the flat in Hereford Road offered, so I went to see our landlords, Harrow School, who owned vast tracts of land on the north-western approaches to London. Not far from our current flat, for a little more key money and a higher rent of 30 shillings a week, they could let us have a two-storey maisonette in a nineteenth-century

190

white stucco house in Westbourne Terrace Road, a stone's throw from the Regent's Canal basin at Little Venice. Penny liked the flat, and I loved being near the water and the bonhomie that seems to linger around the canal and its inhabitants. We moved in and it became home for the next four years.

In the summer of 1952, I landed my first lead in a television serial, *My Wife Jacqueline*. Each episode went out live from the BBC studios in Lime Grove. Though I had previous experience of live broadcasts, it remained terrifying, knowing the potential dangers of screwing up.

The series itself could best be described as experimental. The script was as light as a feather, with characters who appeared to live in a social, political and cultural vacuum that made *Mrs Dale's Diary* look like a profound study of social history. No one knew quite how to pitch it and, like a lot of early television drama, people still thought it was a stage play which happened to have TV cameras in the theatre. Undoubtedly lessons were learned from it, but we were all surprised how this production reached the public.

As always, I had other work on the go, mostly with the Salisbury Arts Theatre Company. It was there that I met a haughty young actor who took his calling very seriously. His name was Kenneth Williams.

There's no question that, at that stage in his career, Kenneth saw himself as a heavyweight actor, with plenty of intellectual gravitas. He was very widely read, impressively articulate and had already played the Dauphin in *St Joan*. As far as he was concerned, he was Stratford-bound and an artiste not to be taken lightly.

Off stage, despite his giant ego – which he was quick to poke fun at – he made friends with everyone. He was an incorrigible and outrageous clown who would describe, in salacious detail, his extensive repertoire of onanistic practices – stories of lavatory seats dislodged, cubicle walls pierced with apertures, washbasins cracked, God knows how! He could keep a bar full of relaxing actors howling with laughter for hours on end, for he loved an audience, as their response made him happy. I was never in a play with him at Salisbury, but we met up quite often over the next few years until, finally, we were to work together in the late '50s. By then it was apparent that his personality and power knew no limits.

After I'd done several plays with the Salisbury Arts company, the principal producer, Guy Verney, asked me if I'd like to direct a few, and take them up to Carlisle for our season there. I leapt at the chance; though only in my late twenties, I was becoming more interested in directing apart from acting. The plays he was offering were, frankly, the lighter stuff – *Charlie's Aunt* and *Harvey*, another very good comedy – but the cast was interesting and the later plays improved in quality. I began to suspect that directing might become more important in my future.

I enjoyed working in Carlisle. Her Majesty's Theatre was a beautiful building in a pleasant setting. Next door there was a good old pub beside an ancient bowling green. We would often have a few drinks and a game of bowls before going into rehearsals. It was a marvellous company to work with and we put on very few duds as a result. Rachel Roberts was there – several years later, she would marry Rex Harrison, which ended in disaster. George Baker, a very handsome young man, then in the early stages of his career, was also in the company. I was able to help him with a lot of advice about the job and we became good friends. It was not surprising when George rapidly shot up the ladder to fame on television.

I took to the creative process of directing and was delighted to be given a longer run with *To Dorothy, a Son*, a well-written comedy which went down well in Carlisle with me playing opposite Margaret Anderson. With a cast of only three, it was a comparatively easy play to put on, and we ended up taking it all over the country with a lot of success. I say 'we' because on our tour the role of Dorothy was played, rather conveniently, by my rather busy wife.

In the autumn of 1952 I had a call from John Counsell, who ran the Theatre Royal in Windsor, a cosy little place nestling beneath the vast ramparts of the Castle. He was putting on a new play by Arthur Watkyn, and although the lead had already been cast, John was doubtful that the actor he wanted might not be available to do it, and he wouldn't know for another three weeks. He offered to pay me for at least those three weeks if I made myself available on standby, and

I agreed. I think his excessive anxiety about the play may have had something to do with his fascination for the lovely Geraldine McEwan, who was to play the female lead; she had originally been working for him at Windsor as ASM and had an unusually high reputation already.

It turned out that the proposed male lead couldn't do it, and so I got the job opposite Geraldine and quickly acquainted myself with the play, *For Better, For Worse*. Watkyn was an experienced craftsman. The play was a charming, light piece about a chirpy young couple who get married and try to set up home on £5 a week with a lot of interference from incompetent tradesmen and her smart, fussy parents. There's not a lot more to it than that, but I can see that it must have been reassuring to the many young couples who were struggling with the same problem at the time, although I don't how they'd have afforded what the couple in the play managed on just a fiver a week. Geraldine was a delight as my vivacious bride. The *Daily Express* described her as 'a dinky little twenty-year-old with the charm of a surprised and urgent sparrow'. The same paper described me as having a 'Hulbertian chin' – after Jack Hulbert, no doubt – 'with a chirrupy kind of charm and a captivating plaintiveness'. The bossy char was played with lashings of sympathy and homespun wisdom by the inimitable Dandy Nichols.

Once the new play was up and running at Windsor, and getting some good notices, we were visited one matinee by George and Alfred Black, well-known London producers. They loved the

194

play and decided to take it into the West End. It was unfortunate for one of the cast who had decided that afternoon he was going to arse about giggling and take a few liberties with the script. He turned out to be the only element of the production the Blacks wouldn't take.

Thus, on 17 December 1952, *For Better, For Worse* came in from its introduction in the sticks to open as the Christmas show at the Comedy. This was a blessed relief for the theatre after a string of closures. In fact, it was to be their first success in three years, the last being my previous play there: *On Monday Next*.

For a couple of years, *For Better, For Worse* was to dominate my life. It was a fantastic success that kept on building and was featured, complete and in excerpts, on a string of radio shows. By May 1953, after well over a hundred performances, the Blacks were thinking about closing the play. Geraldine, who had just married Hugh Crutwell, the director at the Windsor Rep, was on the point of leaving for the post-nuptial jaunt when *For Better, For Worse* was shown on television, which packed out the Comedy all over again. The honeymoon had to be cancelled, and the momentum carried us right through the following autumn and beyond. Both Geraldine and I benefited enormously in our careers because of it, and it was great fun to work so long with such a special and enchanting colleague. Offers poured in for TV, films and theatre, which was thrilling in the light of my rapidly expanding family.

I was excited when my status as an established

West End lead was recognised by my being asked to introduce the guest star of the famously glittering cabaret at the Café de Paris, especially when it was the legendary Marlene Dietrich.

In return for dinner and a table for four, right in front of the stage, it was my job simply to come on and big her up before her entrance. I'd been told by the management specifically not to mention her age, or her children – or anything presumably that might give away her age. I thought it wise, too, not to mention the war.

I went along to her dressing-room the night before the show to meet her and have a chat. I reached her door and was about to knock when Ken Tynan opened it and walked out with a smile on his face. I nodded hello and went in to meet the legend.

'Vot are you going to say about me?' she purred huskily.

'I'm going to remind the audience of the Seven Wonders of the World, and invite them now to welcome the Eighth Wonder.'

'I like zat!' she cooed.

I went back, did my bit and she came on and wowed the house. It was a great evening to have been part of.

It was during that summer that I first came into contact with the Boulting brothers. Roy and John Boulting were identical twins, born into a respectable family in 1913. Entranced by movies from an early age, they had begun working in the industry in the 1930s, eventually starting their own company and producing their first film in

1938. Generally Roy directed and John produced, although they were fairly elastic in these roles. In 1940 they released *Pastor Hall*, which established their reputations as film makers. By the time I met them, they had made around ten pictures, some indifferent, some, like *Brighton Rock*, outstanding.

They were a notoriously strange pair; identical on the face of it, yet at the same time very dissimilar. Most people found if they liked one of them, they couldn't stand the other. Nevertheless, they worked together very closely. Like most people who worked with them, I soon saw that they were not terribly kind and, as a duo, they could be horrendous bullies. They thought their little games were amusing, but they were nothing more than control devices really. It was as if they wanted to demonstrate how much they owned the people whose time they'd bought – or, in my case, were trying to tempt.

They'd asked me to come for an interview about a part. The interview itself was all fine, polite and promising. When it was over, one of them asked me for a cigarette. I couldn't oblige – I didn't smoke cigarettes.

'Oh,' the other said, disappointed. Then his eyes lit up. 'Do you have a car nearby, Leslie?'

'Yes,' I answered.

'Oh, good. Could you give us a lift to Chelsea?'

'I can take you some of the way,' I replied, as we all got into the car. I knew they were having me on from the beginning of the interview.

'Thank you,' they said, with an edge. One of them opened the back door and they both climbed in, leaving me in the front like a chauffeur. 'Let's go, or we'll be late for our meeting.'

I drove them down Piccadilly as far as Hyde Park Corner, where I intended to turn right up Park Lane. As I pulled around the Triumphal Arch beneath Boudicea's quadrica, Roy leaned forward, and tapped me on the shoulder.

'Don't forget – we want to go to Chelsea.'

'I'm sorry, I'm heading up Park Lane here.'

'Oh, Roy, you can't expect Leslie to go out of his way for us,' John said. 'He's been very decent to bring us this far. We'll find a cab.'

'Don't be silly!' Roy snapped. 'Of course he'll take us where we want to go; he wants the bloody part, doesn't he!'

I reacted immediately and pulled up by the kerb, got out calmly and walked round to open the rear door on the pavement side and waited for them to get out.

They both emerged smiling and looking sheepish.

I didn't get the part, naturally, and for several years I never heard a word from them. What's more, although they continued to be influential, powerful producers, and my career blossomed, my agent John Redway couldn't sell me to them for years – I suggested he gave up trying.

As we entered 1954, I was on stage at the Comedy in *For Better, For Worse* – still going strong after thirteen months – when one night, just into the second scene, I passed out on the stage. I think it was probably sheer exhaustion from juggling three or four jobs at a time. It was the first time I had ever been too ill to go on stage, which had been a source of great frustration to my eager understudy, Nigel Hawthorne, who had been longing to get on and have a go himself as he'd been in that role for over a year. But as the curtain was lowered on my supine body, he thought, at last, his moment had come.

He'd got himself into costume and quickly made up for the part, when I saw Nigel passing my dressing room, smacking his lips with relish at the thought of getting on stage at last. Sadly for him, two hefty slugs of brandy sent kindly from the front bar had done the trick for me – only the second time in my career I'd ever had a drink during or before a performance – though I did later get a bill from the theatre.

'Sorry, Nigel. Not tonight,' I said, just in time to get back on stage before he did.

Poor Nigel – he never had another chance after that. Luckily, as subsequent events showed, he managed very well. He was a wonderful man and dear friend, and we did eventually work together later on.

The play had notched up five hundred performances by the beginning of March. It was also produced as a film with J. Lee Thompson directing Dirk Bogarde in my part. In a curious irony, Arthur Watkyn the writer was also A. T. Watkin, the chief film censor. In the stage version, Watkyn has the useless old plumber who comes round to fix something in the tiny flat remark, 'I'll laugh my bleeding head off!' For the tender sensibilities of the less sophisticated film-going public, A. T.

Watkin changed it to 'flipping head'. Of course, in 2006 it would be 'fucking head'.

With the success of *For Better, For Worse*, all the spin-offs and a steady stream of parts being offered in movies and television, I defied my normally cautious nature and decided to splash out on a house and mortgage to accommodate our existing family, plus the new baby Penny was expecting in the coming November.

Penny had grown up surrounded by greenery in the southern home counties, and she craved a return to rural tranquillity. I'd been brought up among the gas fumes and smog of Tottenham, and I certainly didn't fancy a return to that. So, by the simple expedient of taking a map of Greater London and placing a pin in the middle, where I tended to be working, with a pencil on a string, I drew a series of concentric circles until one of them included a good chunk of green. This turned out to be Mill Hill, which, as it happened, was very close to Elstree Studios, where I'd done a lot of work for MGM.

We jumped in the car and drove from our flat in Little Venice up the A1 to Mill Hill to start looking. It didn't take long to find an ideal place on Barnet Way: a big, handsome house with large grounds, quietly set between the golf course and the heath. The price was £6,000, a fortune then and more than I had, but Penny was thrilled with it and, for the first time in my life, I agreed to borrow money in order to buy it. It was a good move. We named it Perk House and the family lived in it for the next twenty-five years.

Though my film schedule was getting fuller, I jumped at the chance to work with the great Basil Dean on a stage production of *The Diary of a Nobody* which went into London to the Arts Theatre after opening at the Arts, Cambridge.

Basil Dean had the reputation for being a tremendous bully, and so he was, but only if he felt he'd been let down, or in the face of brazen incompetence or conceit. I'm glad to say he never bullied me and we became good friends. I think he is the best director in the theatre I've ever had. His direction of a play was minute; the depth and perceptiveness of his notes were testament to that, and he had a natural instinct for the telling metaphor.

I once asked him during rehearsals, 'Mr Dean, how do you feel it's going?'

'Well, Leslie, it's not quite right yet. But we'll put some scaffolding round it and get it right.'

On another occasion, he said to me, 'Leslie, you've got some very good coconuts in Lupin; don't try and take too much milk from them.'

He could register disapproval in an equally vivid fashion. At the end of a rehearsal he would go round the company, one by one, noting their performances and suggesting improvements they could make. A young man who had been employed as a pianist to provide incidental music would hang round these sessions like a dog panting for a bone. The fellow was obviously keen to be an actor, too, but as far as Basil was concerned, he was a functionary – not part of the play, as such – and therefore didn't merit a mention. Though he kept getting in Basil's way expectantly, Basil just pushed him aside and went on to the next actor.

It was blatant and quite cruel. Eventually, the chap couldn't contain himself and asked Mr Dean, 'How was I? Was I all right?'

All the cast put their hands over their eyes, waiting for Basil's predictable response.

'Oh, yes,' he said quietly. 'You were deliciously flat.'

Like many directors, Basil Dean had his idiosyncrasies, including one which was, as far as I know, unique among theatre directors. On the first night of a play he had directed, as the curtain began to rise, he would walk out through the front of house, into the street, and take himself for a long stroll around London, timing it precisely so that the moment the final curtain dropped, he would walk back in, having not seen any of the play to catch the audience's reaction from the applause that greeted him.

I loved working with him and when I was offered £40 a week to take over Dicky Attenborough's part in *The Mousetrap*, where he'd been for two years, I turned it down. The Lupin Pooter role may have paid peanuts, but integrity – and wisdom – prevailed. I stayed with Basil Dean.

Just as well – *The Mousetrap* is still running more than fifty years on. If you'd been engaged for 'Run of Play', it meant that you were contractually bound to it until it came off, which could mean that an actor might never work again in anything else. Equity has since put a limit of two years on these contracts, but, back then,

Peter Saunders, the first producer, wouldn't let anyone out of their contract. If an actor came in with a (usually specious) doctor's note, he would say, 'Of course I can let you go, if you're ill. But when you're better, you'll come back, won't you?' with a rictus grin. 'I'll keep your part open.' He would also check with the doctor to see how ill the actor was.

I was appearing at the Theatre Royal, Brighton, when Penny's third child was due. It was a damp November afternoon, and I had intended just to look in at the Casterbridge Nursing Home on my way to dress rehearsal, but Penny went into labour while I was there.

It is a golden rule of the theatre that nothing, not even death, gets in the way of a performance. Too many other people have a vested interest in every single show – not just the management, but the cast, the crew, the writer, and all the paying punters – and it is out of consideration to them that harsh decisions sometimes have to be made in one's private life. I stayed with Penny until the last possible moment, and then, feeling terrible about leaving her on the verge of bringing our third child into the world, I had to race off to Brighton for the dress rehearsal.

The stage doorkeeper at the Theatre Royal was a charming old cove, who seemed to know everything that was going on in the lives of 'his' actors. He also owned a fascinating dog, one of the few I've encountered who really could count – at least up to double figures. When you shouted a number at it, the dog would bark that number of times with surprising accuracy at the lower end. I wasted many happy hours trying to catch him out.

That evening the doorkeeper greeted me with a big, knowing smile, revelling in the fact that he was more up-to-date in my personal affairs than I was.

'Mr Phillips, sir, congratulations, you've got a son!'

Young Master Phillips had been born within the time it took me to drive from the nursing home to Brighton down the old A23 – which in those pre-limit days, I might say, wasn't too long. As soon as the dress rehearsal was over, I jumped into the car and headed north, where I was delighted to see that all was OK.

The character I was playing was called André, so we anglicised it to Andrew for our first son, although, as it turned out, he grew up to be bilingual in French after leaving Kent University. Andrew was a funny-looking fellow, and we were thrilled with him – our own little chap at last. At home, the girls looked down their noses at him for a while, but soon got into the swing of throwing him around and pretending he was a living, breathing, defecating doll. At the time they were being tended by a very large and jolly Swiss-German au pair called Ruth who looked a little like Arthur Mullard – my mother-in-law's dictum, that au pairs should not be too easy on the eye, held sway with Penny.

On the whole, domestic life was serene and enjoyable, when I had time to savour it. A dog lover since the days of Spot, I began looking around for an animal who might enjoy life with us in Mill Hill. A writer friend had a lovely golden Labrador bitch which I had often admired when she'd brought it to the studios. When she mentioned that she wanted to sell some of the latest litter, my ears pricked up. At the first opportunity, I drove down in our yellow Ford Consul we called Jaundice to inspect the pups.

I was left alone in a scullery with the litter to have a good look at them. I picked up each in turn; they were adorable and I wanted all of them. Eventually my friend came back into the room.

'Which one do you like?'

'They're all lovely, but I think I like that one most,' I said, pointing to the smallest of them, a tiny bitch pup. She had slightly in-growing eyelashes which gave her a charming, sad-eyed look, and she seemed to me to have an especially likeable demeanour.

'But that's the runt!'

'Well, it's the one I'd like.'

'Then you can have her for nothing. We didn't expect to sell her anyway.'

We called her Pippa and she was a delightful creature whose minor flaws we soon sorted out, though a couple of major ones were not so easily dealt with.

On the way back in the car, she sat next to me with her head on my knee, and as a result of this powerful early bonding, she was always very much my dog for as long as she lived. She became, as animals often have in my households, a major element of family life. The kids grew to love her too, and walking her through the leafy, wooded margins of Barnet golf course and beyond was a favourite outing for them.

While Penny focused on our growing family and her work grew more sporadic, I was now busier than ever. I had outings in Richard Greene's *Robin Hood*, various parlour games on television, as well as commercials on the recently founded ITV – all this on top of wall-to-wall theatre productions. There were also a constant number of movie parts, including a couple with John Gilling – *Gamma People*, an early Cold War thriller with Eva Bartok, and *High Flight*, filmed with the RAF near Lincoln, with Ray Milland in the lead.

In early 1956, I was thrilled to be offered a part in Sydney Franklin's *The Barretts of Wimpole Street*. The cast were a joy to work with. John Gielgud played Elizabeth Barrett's tyrannical father, with my great friend Bill Travers as Robert Browning, Virginia McKenna as Henrietta, and a charming cocker spaniel as Flush, Elizabeth Barrett's dog.

I had worked on a film and a play with John Gielgud when I was a child and I knew he was a charming, considerate and witty colleague, but making this film he demonstrated a generosity which is all too rare among the stars of our profession. He had finished his scenes for the day.

'It's half past four now, Mr Gielgud,' the assistant director said. 'I'm sure you'd like to go home while we do all the covering shots.'

'Covering shots' were an additional series of takes in which the camera would be trained on the other parts as they responded to the lead's lines. It was perfectly normal to have someone stand in for the principal, but the job of the supporting roles is made easier and their performances are probably better if the correct actor is feeding them the lines.

'My dear boy,' Gielgud fluted, 'of course I won't go home until you have all finished. I'll be happy to feed them their cues.'

Twelve shots were needed to cover the group, and he did them all. It was the act of a generous spirit which, over the years, I found to be a permanent characteristic of the man.

After *The Barretts* wrapped, I was finishing a TV show in the old Maida Vale studios, when, in the middle of the final evening, I had an urgent call from my agent, John Redway. Of all the agents I ever had (and I haven't been as fickle as some of my colleagues), I liked John the best. He lived near me in Mill Hill with his American wife, Hope, and became a close friend. I even allowed him to have one of the puppies from Pippa's only litter.

'Sorry to bother you, Leslie,' he boomed down the phone, 'but I've got a job for you. The only thing is, they want you tomorrow, early.'

'OK, what is it?' I asked.

'It's for the Boultings.'

'The Boultings?!' I was staggered, especially after three years of silence since refusing to provide a taxi service for them.

'I know. You've never worked for them, have you?'

'I certainly haven't,' I said, hardly believing that he could be right, even though I was aware my stock in the industry was rising.

207

'Well, they want you,' John repeated, having obviously forgotten the previous incident.

I was still doubtful. 'But what is it?'

'They're doing a film called *Brothers in Law*, and they've got a good cameo part for you. It's small, but worth doing because it could open a few doors.'

Although I hadn't seen a script or any outline of the part, something made me break one of my cardinal rules and I agreed provisionally to do it, unseen.

'They say they'll drop off a script at your house tonight. Roy Boulting's directing and he'll ring you in the morning about arrangements.'

Next day, the phone beside my bed rang at 5 a.m.

'Hello,' I whispered, trying not to wake Penny.

'Roy Boulting here.'

I looked at the clock, disoriented at having been woken so early. 'Oh... Hello?'

'I'm just ringing to let you know what we're doing today.'

'Fine,' I croaked.

'Are you all ready for it?'

'Well ... yes ... I've looked at the script.'

'Good. Now – wardrobe. What have you got in your wardrobe?'

'What do you want – a suit or something?'

'Yes. You're a shop assistant selling a barrister's brief bag to Ian Carmichael.'

'OK. What colour suit do you want?'

'Have you got a grey one?'

'Yes, but it's not terribly new, and not that good.'

'Oh, that won't do. What else have you got?'

'I've got a good navy blue suit.'

'No, no. That won't do at all – not navy blue.' He carried on, managing to rummage through my entire wardrobe down the telephone line like some demented bag-lady. After he'd quizzed me minutely on everything in my closet, bar my underwear, he said, 'Look, would you mind awfully bringing the whole lot in?'

This wasn't quite as shockingly presumptive as it sounds. The studios always have to clean or wash everything they use that belongs to the cast, so at least I'd save a large cleaner's bill.

However, this wasn't a request – it was a downright order, and I was beginning to feel put upon. I knew through Penny, from the time when she'd auditioned for *Brighton Rock*, that he liked to intimidate people, perhaps in order to control them more effectively. He'd certainly tried it on her. Now, it seemed, he was trying it on me – again.

Boulting wanted me at the studios early. 'Do you have a car?' he asked, and I wondered if he had the slightest recollection of our last meeting. 'Bring everything in it, and we'll see what we need. Have you learned your part?'

'I've looked at it,' I told him again, still quite groggy, though well aware he was needling me for some twisted purpose of his own.

I got up and packed all the suits I could find, barring the navy blue, into suitcases, knowing that it was almost certainly going to end badly. Then I loaded the car and set off for Elstree. When I drove up to the door where he'd told me to meet him – a few minutes early, as it happened

– he was standing on the doorstep waiting, glancing at his watch. I wound down my window and nodded.

'Oh, you got here,' he said, without any obvious pleasure. 'You can park over there...' He pointed at an adjacent space. 'But unload everything first and bring it in.'

As I heaved the cases out of the boot of my car and humped them into the building and into the wardrobe room, he stood by and watched without lifting a finger to help, or summoning someone to assist.

Once I'd parked the car, we went through all the suits, Boulting examining each of them with disdain. 'Fawn?' he muttered, 'No, I don't think so. I don't think we want pinstripe either...' discarding them in turn.

When he'd looked at the lot, he shook his head. 'I think what we really need is a nice navy blue.'

'You told me you didn't like navy blue,' I burst out.

'I said no such thing. I think navy blue will do very well.'

I was sweating with pent-up anger by this time, trying to work out what on earth the bloody man was trying to do. He, on the other hand, was now quite relaxed after all the fuss he'd made.

'Let's not worry about that. We'll get on into make-up.'

By this stage in my career, I was no new boy to directors and their idiosyncrasies, but I'd never come across anything like this. Penny had warned me that he was not a pleasant man, and I'd had my taxi encounter with him, but I could hardly credit the manic need to dominate that he was now displaying.

A make-up girl was waiting. I sat down and Roy sighed as if I presented a major problem. 'Oh, what are we going to do with him?'

'It should be pretty straightforward,' the make-up girl said.

'Agh!' Boulting gazed at me with exasperation, as if it were the first time he'd seen me. 'You're very blond, aren't you...' he said, as if I'd come out in a nasty rash.

Everything seemed to be a problem, but we finished eventually. Then it was on to wardrobe, where they found me another suit easily enough, and I made my way to the set.

On the way there I bumped into a cameraman I knew. He said to me quietly, 'Be careful with him. He's already given three people the sack for this.'

'What do you mean?'

'In the last two days, three young men have tried to play this part and they haven't been able to do it. They all got the boot.'

Another technician caught my eye and nodded discreetly at Boulting. 'He's in a very tricky mood on this picture,' he said. 'Terry-Thomas had to do thirty-five takes yesterday, then he printed take two.'

I was already sweating, but I heated up a little more. I couldn't understand what the problem was with my part. All I had to do was greet Ian Carmichael and present him with the brief bag that had been made for him with his name engraved on it in a fold of the material. We

211

started the scene.

Ian came in. I told him we had the bag ready and laid it flat on the table to show him. As soon as I'd put it down, Roy barked 'Cut! No, no, no, not like that. You've put it on the table so his name's covered by the fold.'

'I see, you want me to somehow expose the name? Fine,' I said.

We did it again, but this time I carefully pushed the folds apart to reveal the name, as he'd asked.

'Cut!' Roy barked. 'I don't want you to touch the bag once you've put it down.'

'What do you mean?'

'I don't want you to touch it. I just want you to lay the bag on the table.'

'But you won't be able to see the...'

'That is what I want,' Roy said with a steely glint in his eye.

I shrugged my shoulders, wondering what on earth he was trying to prove, and tried again, but, without any assistance from me, the folds covered the name. We did nine takes. It was, inevitably, the same every time.

After the tenth take, Boulting walked towards me sighing. 'No, no, no. You still haven't got it right at all. This is how to do it.' He came and stood behind me and put his arms around me. Placing the bag down, he rearranged the material with his hands to expose the name. 'Now, do it again,' he ordered sharply.

As I did it, he yanked my hand away from the bag. 'No, no, don't touch...' he started to say.

He stopped when I stretched my arm forward and then brought my elbow back into his guts as

212

hard as I could. He yelled with pain, let me go and leapt back like scalded cat. The watching Ian was speechless, and so was Roy. The crew, I noted with pleasure, gave a muffled cheer at seeing their director doubled up and gasping at the shock of being assaulted by an actor.

After that, we did one more take. I displayed the name on the bag by opening the folds with my hand. 'Fine,' Roy said, 'that'll do.' And that was the shot he used; it's still in the movie – after all that fuss!

I'd finished my one scene. I went to get my make-up off. It was a pleasure not to see Roy Boulting again for another forty years.

I told John Redway he was unlikely to receive any more requests from the Boultings for my services but, in that unlikely event, he had my full authority to turn down anything they offered.

John understood. He had a marvellous, laid-back sense of humour which often caught me out. Soon after I'd had my torture at the hands of Roy Boulting, I called him to check a few details of the terms he'd arranged for my next movie, *The Birthday Present*, which Pat Jackson was going make for British Lion. It was well written, with good leads for Tony Britton and Sylvia Syms and I was looking forward to it.

I was working on location at the time and rang him from a phone box on the corner of Hammersmith Broadway. We talked agreeably about all sorts of things, as we always did, until I had to get back to work and began to wind up the conversation.

'Oh, before you go,' he said, 'there was something else.'

'John, I've got to go now; they'll need me any minute. What is it?'

'It's not important – another small job that's come up.'

'Can we talk about it next time I ring?'

He ignored me. 'What was it now... Oh yes; I've had a cable from MGM. George Cukor wants you for a leading part in *Les Girls*, shooting starts in six weeks – in Hollywood.'

Now you can appreciate John Redway's sense of humour.

7 • Hollywood

By the time I reached my thirty-second birthday in 1956, I had lost count of the plays I'd appeared in. I also had about twenty films to my credit, but I still wasn't generally thought of as a 'star'. Of course, friends who weren't in the movie business would introduce me as 'Leslie Phillips... You know! The *film* star!' – which sort of makes my point.

Nevertheless, in the preceding year alone, I'd had leading roles in six feature films, and appeared in at least four separate stage productions. My reputation for consistent work, increasingly in comedy, was established and growing. I knew my craft and I liked the job, but I was well aware that on the greasy, treacherous ladder of fame, there were several rungs above me, not far out of reach, and, given the chance, I was ready to stretch up and grasp them without falling off.

When John Redway had told me about the offer from MGM, he knew that I'd just signed to make a film with British Lion Corporation, which could pose a few problems if the MGM deal went ahead. But the evening after John's call, MGM rang to confirm that George Cukor wanted me for one of the lead roles in *Les Girls*, with Kay Kendall, Mitzi Gaynor and Gene Kelly starring.

I could hardly believe my luck; I couldn't think how on earth Cukor had ever heard of me. As far as I was aware, he hadn't been to London in recent years, so he couldn't have seen any of my stage performances, and I doubted very much that he'd seen any of my movies either, unless he was specially looking for them. It occurred to me that he might have got the wrong chap – it sometimes happened in transatlantic deals – but the part of Sir Gerald Wren, a rich English banker, and playing opposite Miss Kendall appealed to me very much. Besides, I sensed that Cukor wasn't the sort of man to whom you might safely suggest he was mistaken.

In any event, MGM persisted, and agreed to buy me out of my contract for *The Birthday Present*, in which my part was taken, coincidentally, by my old school friend Jack Watling.

It may seem incredible, but the first time I stepped into an aeroplane was when I boarded a TWA Lockheed Super G Constellation to fly from London to Los Angeles. It had four massive propellers which produced a staggering racket and the flight took sixteen hours, apparently going over the top of the world rather than round it. I remember we stopped to refuel in Newfoundland. It was bitterly cold and the runway was covered in thick snow; massive bulldozers had carved a clear corridor in which our plane could land, with trench-like paths through to the airport buildings. I left that bleak corner of Canada with no strong urge to return.

For much of the flight, we lay trying to sleep in full-length bunks and, because fifty years ago airlines didn't have the equipment to show films, we were entertained by interminable word games with each other and the cabin staff, who in those days were all required to be elegant, beautiful and female. No chance of getting any of them to join me – not enough room in the bunk, except on top of each other, which would be too dangerous – though I smiled at the thought of the crazy idea.

I didn't sleep a lot. I admit I was very excited at the prospect of Hollywood, and of working with Gene Kelly, whom I'd always admired, not to mention Kay Kendall. At the time, Kay was as close as any English actress came to being a Hollywood star. She had all the attributes; her trumpeting scene in the big international hit *Genevieve* had placed her firmly at the top of the tree. I'd never met her, but I relished the thought of acting with her. Of course, I'd heard she was now the lover of the lusty and demanding Rex Harrison, who had recently abandoned my former great crush, Lilli Palmer. Rex had just opened on Broadway with *My Fair Lady*. Playing

Professor Higgins in the great Lerner and Loewe musical. Though he was utterly tone deaf, he had contrived to turn his principal solo into a sonorous monologue with musical backing. So successful was he in making the part his own that when George Cukor went on to make the movie version in 1964, he kept Rex in it. Let's face it, he couldn't have got anyone better to do it.

I suppose my first impression of Los Angeles was much the same as any other Englishman's in the fifties. The big cars, the ubiquitous 'diners' and the permanent sunshine were all familiar from the movies, but the reality was far more vivid and striking. At that time in England there was no such thing as a motorway and I was amazed by the abundance of smog, the scale and sheer volume of relentless traffic on the freeways that chequered the map of LA, the size of the great boat-like motors, the huge exotic palms, the sun, the glamour of Sunset Boulevard, and the snazzy gadgetry of the hotel where I'd been billeted by MGM.

But I was knackered – prop-lagged, you could say – after the journey in the noisy, throbbing plane, and disappointed that nobody from the studio had met me at the airport. I threw myself on the bed, feeling totally disoriented and very alone, and was just nodding off when the phone rang.

'Is that Mr Phillips?' an American voice asked. 'Are you settling in OK?'

'Thank you, yes. Everything's fine,' I answered politely.

'We may have something better for you. I'll have your bags brought down, and see you in the lobby.'

Mystified, but glad somebody cared about me after all, I grabbed my briefcase and went back down.

Who should I find, laughing his head off in the lobby, but my old chum Bill Travers, who was in LA with his girlfriend – virtual though not yet legal wife – Virginia McKenna. Bill was a lovely man, a year or two older than me, urbane and tremendously tall. He and I had worked together a couple of months before on *The Barretts of Wimpole Street* and, though I didn't know it at the time, we were to do another film later in the year.

'So,' he said, reverting to English, for it was he who had made the come-on-down call. 'What do you think of it here?'

'It's all right,' I said without much enthusiasm.

'Come back to our place and have a few drinks. Ginny's longing to see you.'

He drove me the few blocks to Horn Avenue, where he and Virginia McKenna had a beautiful fourth-floor apartment, full of light and somehow insulated from the hubbub of Sunset Strip, and overlooking some exotic jungle greenery which attracted a charming and tuneful bird life.

Champagne popped and we caught up on our news. Bill was making a picture here and Ginny had come along, not because she thought he'd have got up to mischief otherwise, but purely to keep him company.

'Wouldn't you rather be in a space like this?' Bill asked after a while, waving his arm around

218

the huge apartment.

'Yes, of course I would. I like my space and privacy.' Seeing Ginny, who looked and sounded very like Penny, made me think of home.

'Then come downstairs a moment.'

He led me out of their flat, down a flight of stairs and into another apartment, identical in size and décor. 'How about somewhere like this?' he asked.

'Well,' I laughed, scoffing a little at the remoteness of any possibility that I could afford a place like this. 'That would be really super, but the studios said...'

'Never mind what they said. You can't stay in that hotel, you'd go bonkers.'

'But...' I hesitated, never a profligate man. 'Isn't it rather expensive?'

'Not to you, Leslie. If you want this place, it's yours – gratis.'

I was flabbergasted. 'How?'

'Ginny and I had to take two separate apartments so the League of Decency won't realise we're living together. It's bloody ridiculous, but you know what they're like out here and with this new magazine *Confidential* getting inside everyone's underwear...' he shrugged. 'This place is paid for and going spare; we never go near it except to pick up my post, so you might as well move in.'

'That's wonderful!' I was staggered. 'I'll get my stuff from the hotel.'

'It's already here. I got them to put it straight into my car,' Bill laughed.

Bill and Ginny were marvellous to me. He was

making a film called *The Seventh Sin* with George Sanders, who told me that he, like me, had started his career as a struggling young actor in London.

On the whole, the studios were generous to me. They arranged a big convertible Chevy to drive around in – as I soon discovered, nobody walked anywhere in LA, other than from their car at the kerb to the door of whichever shop or restaurant they were going to spend their money in. In some respects, the studio even spoilt me, really, because that was what American movie actors had come to expect, and a great deal more.

Nevertheless, after a few weeks in Los Angeles, I came to the conclusion that I was an inescapably English sort of chap – that was, after all, what got me the part. Luckily, I was saved from feeling a complete alien by Bill and Ginny and a few other English friends who were in LA to work.

My first meeting with my new director was less than auspicious. George Cukor was awesome, as they say in America, no question about it. He carried an incredible reputation before him. By this stage in his career he had some fifty movies under his directorial belt, including the Mason/Garland version of *A Star is Born*, *The Philadelphia Story* starring Katherine Hepburn and James Stewart, and some of the best, earlier scenes in *Gone With The Wind*. He was not, however, at all prepossessing at first sight, nor, indeed, at any subsequent sight. He retained the strong remnants of an accent from one of the less salubrious New York boroughs – and the manners to go with it.

On my second day, I was picked up at the appointed hour in a studio limousine, driven along the great boulevards to MGM's massive studios in Culver City and delivered to Cukor's office (I hadn't the nerve yet to risk the Chevy on LA's roads). I sauntered sunnily through the door, more or less in the character I habitually adopted for this sort of encounter. He looked up at me and scowled.

'Hello, I'm Leslie Phillips.'

'Yah? You any good?'

I chuckled, inclined, like most Englishmen to self-deprecation.

But Cukor had already made up his mind. 'You can't be; you're too fuckin' cheap!'

Inwardly cursing my agent, I countered this with a suggestion that they put my money up. Cukor liked that.

John Redway had got it wrong. 'We mustn't go crazy,' he had said when I asked him to go for more money. 'This is your first chance in Hollywood; we don't want to scare them off by being greedy.'

All wrong, God bless him; he ought to have known that the more you asked, the more they would love, cherish and value you. Money wasn't just the primary measure of talent in Los Angeles, it was the *only* measure. As John was married to an American lady, he should have known this.

I left Cukor's office and went off to wardrobe wondering why on earth he had got me there if he thought I was going to be so useless. I wasn't about to go under, though; after all, I'd survived

221

working for Roy Boulting.

That evening Ginny McKenna told me how Cukor had heard of me. It turned out that it was partly thanks to her and Kay Kendall that I was here in Hollywood.

Cukor had been lunching with Kay Kendall in MGM's cavernous commissary, which is what they call the stars' canteen in Hollywood studios. Ginny and Bill were at a nearby table. They knew that Cukor was at the development stage of a musical comedy set in Europe, with Gene Kelly carrying it, and they couldn't help overhearing George's loud voice as, without bothering to complete the mastication process on whatever was in his mouth, he said to Kay, 'OK, darling, but what's his fuckin' name?'

Looking around, Kay saw Virginia and called over to her: 'Ginny, can you remember the name of that nice blond chap with the moustache, good comedy actor; always playing toffs or silly asses?'

Ginny knew at once. 'Leslie Phillips – he's a friend of ours.'

'That's it!' Kay exclaimed with her usual exuberance. 'That's him; Leslie Phillips, he's exactly what George needs for Sir Gerald Wren!'

She turned to tell Cukor, who rang John Redway straight after lunch. On such serendipity are movie careers built.

When it came to making the movie, Cukor's talents were such that one could forgive him his lack of charm. He had an extraordinary mind, walked a fine, potentially treacherous line between vulgarity and art, was fascinated by the

222

dynamic of parties and drunkenness, and was supreme at extracting truly powerful, risky performances from his women stars. Indeed, it was said that he was fired from *Gone With The Wind* because Clark Gable resented his throwing so much of the movie at Vivien Leigh.

In *Les Girls*, he drew from Kay Kendall an astonishing exuberance which stole the picture and earned her a Golden Globe. This was even more extraordinary when one takes into account that Kay was dying from leukaemia. Of course, none of us knew, but I did notice that during rehearsals for the dance routines with the other two girls, Mitzi Gaynor and Taina Elg, she quite often said she wasn't feeling too well and sat out, only coming in for the take. Then, because she was a very astute, creative performer, she often got the moves better than the others, who were tempted to think she was playing some kind of ego game.

Kay and I became great friends just like that. She was one of the kindest, most thoughtful actresses I've ever met. Many evenings she and I went out together, always fun, always platonic. She would never leave her hotel in the evening until Rex Harrison had rung from his dressing room in New York, having just finished his performance in *My Fair Lady* for the evening. He wanted to know exactly what she had done that day, how she was feeling, how her scenes had gone, what she was going to do that evening and, more important, who she was going out with. He seemed very possessive, although it later occurred to me that perhaps he knew about Kay's illness and was taking extra care, but probably he was just very possessive.

If she told him she was planning to go to a party with me, he always gave his blessing, confident that Leslie wouldn't abuse her trust, or his – flattering, in some ways; less so in others. Whatever, Kay was effective in opening doors for me, and eased me into a lot of parties to which, as an unknown Brit, I wouldn't otherwise have been asked.

One evening, after she and I had downed our customary glass or two of champagne cocktails edged with sugar and laced with brandy, we went to a dinner party given by Minna Wallis, sister of the great producer, Hal Wallis. A powerful agent since the early thirties, Minna was very high up the non-acting pecking order in Hollywood, and she knew it. Kay had been asked to bring a friend and so she brought me. This did not please Minna, a famously committed Beverly Hills socialite who took her position very seriously and relished the power she wielded. When Kay introduced us, I noticed, besides her frigid grasp, her nostrils quivering in disdain at my lack of celebrity. She asked me what I wanted to drink, managing to convey the idea that even a request for tap-water would be pushing it. Kay saw this and immediately waded in.

'Champagne, of course, Minna darling. Leslie never drinks anything else, do you, sweetie?' It would have taken a lot more than Minna Wallis to intimidate Kay. Minna quickly produced champagne and soon began to warm up a little.

Her illustrious brother, Hal, was also at her

party that night, along with James Mason, plus his powerful wife, Pamela. James invited me to play tennis with him a few days later, when, despite the advantage of my comparative youth, he thrashed me. Unfortunately, he didn't play me at my game – poker. He's a good actor, too, and a bloody nice bloke. Also at the party was a young actor on everyone's must-see list – Paul Newman. He was then about thirty and fresh from starring in *Somebody Up There Likes Me*, a biopic on the gangster-turned-boxer, Rocky Graziano. Newman was theatre school-trained, and had made his movie debut only a couple of years before in *The Silver Chalice*, a serious turkey. But the new picture was a hit, so now everyone wanted to meet him. Despite this, he seemed to me then a genuine and likeable guy, and I don't think I was wrong. Who else was there? Gary Cooper, tucked away in a corner – it was quite an initiation to the Hollywood scene.

Although I'd made many pictures in Pinewood, Denham, Elstree and Ealing, the scale of the MGM Studios was so much greater that it was hard not to be overawed at first. I had my own personal trailer which was moved around the lot depending on which sound stage we were using. Kay always organised lunch parties with Mitzi and Taina, and we all brought our own contribution: fun. Sometimes we would eat in the commissary, where I soon got used to being surrounded by the studio's major stars. I was glad there was no booze at lunch, not even one glass of white wine; the work was too tough for that.

On one occasion we came across Peter Finch, an actor who I'd first met on *Train of Events*. He'd had a much publicised dalliance with Kay a few years before, but she was now totally committed to sexy Rexy. Finchie was still married to his first wife, Tamara, but as usual was having affairs between bouts of serious boozing.

Our producer, Sol Siegel, was a marvellous man, far politer to me than the director ever was, and, unlike a lot of producers, he didn't come on to the set, possibly to avoid confrontation with Cukor, who took instructions from nobody.

The plot of *Les Girls* is necessarily convoluted, as the story is told from three points of view – which is just as well as there's not a lot of it. Originally it was to be shot on location around the world, but in the end they decided instead to film it all in Culver City, Hollywood – more's the pity. However, with back projection and film trickery it works OK, and was probably a lot easier to make that way.

Cukor's words during our first meeting came back to me one day when I was doing a scene with Gene that featured just the two of us with a good bit of dialogue for me. The lighting camera-man asked George, 'How are you shooting this scene?'

'On the money,' growled Cukor.

I'd only heard that expression before as a Sam Goldwyn gag, but George meant it. The whole scene was to be shot over my shoulder, putting all the emphasis on Gene. I was now beginning to understand what Hollywood was about.

If ever I thought of an idea and tried to tell

Cukor, he would simply turn his back and ignore me. This was frustrating, not to mention rather humiliating. Like a lot of experienced actors, I often saw ways of doing things which a director might be pleased to accept and try. Certainly with most English directors, I could expect a hearing, but here I was in an alien land.

Seeing what was happening, Gene came to my aid: 'Look, Les, that was a great idea. If you get any more, tell me and I'll get them through to George.'

And that's what I did. On one occasion, there was a fight scene between me and Gene, and I thought it would work better if I hit him in a certain way.

Gene nodded. 'That's good.' He turned to Cukor. 'Say, George I think he ought to hit me like this.'

George beamed at his star. 'That's fine, that's a great idea. We'll do that.'

And that scene does look good – at least, my first punch does.

Throughout the production, Gene was a great performer, a joy to watch in the dance sequences and a delightful man to work with. That's pretty rare among movie stars of his magnitude.

I wasn't the only member of the cast who had to cope with the director's hostility. He was even more vile to the third girl in the trio, Taina Elg. We had no idea why. He bullied her so relentlessly she was always in tears. Neither of the other two female stars could do much for her; to have attempted to defend her would possibly have made it worse. I'd already learned it usually does.

It wasn't uncommon for a director to pick on one or two members of the cast in order to demonstrate his authority to those with whom he couldn't risk out-and-out confrontation. Sometimes a male director will take it out on an actress as a kind of courtship device if he fancies her – obviously not the case here, as Cukor didn't fancy ladies. Yet he was renowned as a woman's director. He treated all extras and bit players as the utter dregs. If he needed them moved off the set, he'd just yell to one of his assistants: 'Will y' get all that shit out of here!' Charming!

Although Kay, like me, was English, her performance mattered to him more than anyone else's and he treated her with the greatest respect; perhaps he knew she wouldn't have let him do otherwise, or maybe her connection with Rex helped just a little.

The other male lead was a flamboyant French Basque called Jacques Bergerac. He was a nervous actor, but that didn't matter; he was outrageously good-looking. I went around with him quite a bit, and the women were always all over him from all angles, which did nothing to sweeten relations with his wife, the amazing Ginger Rogers.

Ginger may have worn the petticoats when she was dancing with Fred Astaire, but in her household, she definitely wore the pantaloons, and poor Jacques spent a lot of time being treated like a miscreant pooch. I often went up to their house in Beverly Hills after filming to play tennis on their floodlit court, and he was a very amiable companion. My first experience of that came when we were having a drink in the Polo Bar of the Beverly Hills Hotel and he asked me if I wanted to come back for dinner. Ginger agreed to it when he phoned her. We went to the house, where I discovered it was going to be just the three of us – him, Ginger and me.

When we arrived she wasn't anywhere to be seen. Jacques made drinks and showed me round. It was a palace, all marble and white and sweeping staircases, like the film sets Ginger used to whirl across with Fred. The place was stuffed full of all the latest household gadgetry. I was particularly struck when Jacques decided to light a log fire laid in what looked like the mouth of a well-appointed cave set in the wall. With the merest flick of a switch, some device exploded a massive tongue of flame through the pile of timber, and in seconds the thing was roaring like a witch's pyre. I thought we might have to call the fire brigade.

Ginger still hadn't appeared after an hour, by which time Jacques and I had downed several cocktails and were hovering around the magnificent dinner table laid for three, ready to eat. Suddenly she staged the most magnificent entrance, appearing, dressed to the nines, at the top of the stairs. Then, as if an orchestra had struck up, on cue she swept down the stairs, just as she might on a Broadway stage, looking a million dollars. No, two million.

When she finally sat down, she was very charming and friendly, and chatted away, but exclusively to me. I was fascinated how these megastars could really turn on the charm when required.

Obviously she and Jacques were in the middle of a row, and I was piggy in the middle. She wouldn't talk to him at all, but she occasionally asked me to pass on a message to him. A few decades later, it would have been emails.

The only way I could deal with this bizarre situation was to make a joke of it. She continued, though, to be very attentive to me, and told me all about her mother, who still seemed to be a controlling influence in her life. After a super dinner and a one-sided chat, she showed me round the house herself, opening a drawer stuffed with what seemed like a thousand lipsticks, all different colours for different moods and outfits. She held my hand and used one of her lipsticks on me, lingering a little over the task. She also showed me some daring shots that had been taken of her that showed off her figure to its best.

I came away with the impression that stars of this calibre, unlike ordinary mortals, were accustomed to behaving as if they were gods. But I won't forget that kiss or the lipstick, or that one nude figure, give or take a loose scarf. Above all, I won't forget dancing with her, even if I was never going to be in Fred Astaire's league.

Looking back, it seems the round of parties was endless and they all rather melded together in one's memory. However, I do recall a party given by Kirk Douglas, whom I found to be a very bright, exuberant man. The place was full of big stars and he sat down to entertain them all, playing the drums and singing. I bumped into Roger Moore, who was living in LA then, with his wife, an efficient fixer who asked me to a couple of parties at their place. There was almost a major drama one night at the Moores' when someone dropped a lighted cigarette on to an immensely deep woolly carpet. It was buried so deep in the shag pile that it burned undetected for a long time, creeping along the underside, until people started sniffing suspiciously, and we realised the whole thing was about to burst into flames. Just in time, the soda siphons were brought into play and a major conflagration was averted.

I often went with poor Jacques to parties, plagued by women, as ever. Obviously he enjoyed their company, but this overwhelming attention could become tiresome, especially when the salacious gossip magazine, *Confidential*, started to report his exploits, usually complete fantasy. Scantily clad girls were often sent to these Hollywood parties where they would entice stars like Jacques into a compromising position; *Confidential* would have a photographer standing by to capture the moment for the next issue, and the more daring the pose the higher the fee. And they would make sure a copy was delivered to the wife.

When Robert Harrison launched *Confidential* in the mid-fifties, he unleashed a reign of terror among public figures across the nation, and especially in Hollywood. For years, the studios had been able to suppress any stories that threatened to expose some of the grosser hypocrisies surrounding the major stars, but *Confidential* changed all that. The publication had no mercy, no qualms about who or how they attacked, and a sort of press paranoia was plaguing the movie industry. Each issue, the stars trembled in anticipation of headlines like *The Joe who said 'No' to Jane Russell* or *Sinatra – the Tarzan of the Boudoir!* Ironically, these would be emblazoned above a strap-line that read: 'Tells the Facts! Names the Names!'

Although I seldom had a night in on my own during my time in LA, I never engaged in dalliance of any kind – it honestly never occurred to me, so I had nothing to fear from *Confidential*. That may seem like a bit of a lost opportunity, being alone in Hollywood for five months, but the truth was, Kay was spoken for and American women didn't appeal to me in the same way. Besides, I truly didn't want to do anything that would put a strain on my own marriage. I really missed my family and Mill Hill, even London itself. It would have been impossible to have them all with me. Hollywood would not have pleased Penny, and our three children would have been taken out of their familiar environment.

Over the course of filming, I was able to renew an old friendship with Patrick Macnee, who was playing a barrister in *Les Girls*. I'd known Pat since he'd turned up to take over Geoffrey Edwards' part in *Doctors' Dilemma*. Like me, he was an Englishman trying to make his way up. He'd arrived in LA thinking he might have a slight advantage, being a cousin of David Niven. However, that quintessential English gent of Hollywood turned out to be, in Patrick's words, 'No fucking help, whatsoever.'

Pat was an easy-going man with a wry sense of humour, which is something you can easily miss in LA. We drove out to Palm Springs together to a wonderful spa hotel in the desert. Palm Springs' sole purpose in life appears to be to provide a haven of sybaritic pleasures for rich people escaping the LA smog. The weather's always wonderful and the food supreme. It was remarkably relaxing – a great place to chill out, as they say these days. They've taken to playing a lot of polo there, to give themselves some kind of *raison d'être*, but nobody actually makes anything, there's no coast, and no skiable mountains, though the San Jacintos do rear up rather beautifully to the west. Somewhat to my surprise, I found that it was possible to have a great time doing absolutely nothing except lying in the sun and looking at the girls around the pool.

I also did a lot of sightseeing with Bill and Ginny. We once drove up to Las Vegas, along with Taina Elg, to see our co-star, Mitzi Gaynor, appearing in cabaret, which was always a strong side of her career. She'd been a star since she was a kid, a fine singer and a great dancer – worth seeing in the Marlon Brando biker sequence with Gene in *Les Girls*.

Although Las Vegas was not as enormous as it is today, it was still a mind-blowing experience with it massive casinos and lavish shows. I found it quite amazing that all this had sprung into existence only ten years earlier (the first big hotels went up in 1945); before that the city had merely been a railhead for the building of the Hoover Dam.

Mitzi Gaynor wasn't just a great talent, she was great fun. Still very young, she had become a star in her teens. The man in her life was her manager, Jack Bean, one of those unfathomable movie industry wheeler-dealers who are into all aspects of the business: PR, developing, producing – it's a big trough. They were a super couple and both became good friends. In fact, Mitzi became godmother to my second son, Roger, born a few years later, and after that they always looked us up when they were in London.

One day, during a gap in shooting, Jack said, 'OK, Les, we're going up to San Francisco. You coming?'

We flew up for a weekend of non-stop partying as Jack and Mitzi kept running into people they knew. One night we ate in a wonderful revolving restaurant at the top of a hotel with a view across the whole bay, the city and the Golden Gate Bridge. I fear it may have closed now, but that night, in this spinning eatery, we bumped into Frank Sinatra and I was introduced. Everyone was so welcoming.

I managed a couple of days' raw tourism, all the usual stuff: scoffing noodles in Chinatown, rattling along in little cable-cars climbing halfway to the stars, listening to jazz in seedy bars, and writing 'Wish you were here' on postcards of Alcatraz to send to my friends.

One of the people I was most pleased to meet in San Francisco was an old hero of mine, Edward Everett Horton, whom I bumped into at every party we went to. He was a great character actor I'd admired on the screen for years. He'd made his first picture in 1922, and by the time he died, in 1970, he had over 140 films to his credit. He was now seventy, tall and camp, he delivered his catchphrase, 'Oh really,' with a distinctive quavering voice. He gave me a tremendous greeting because I was from England and Mitzi had given me a bit of build-up when she'd introduced us. He and I hit it off at once and he was full of outrageous stories about everyone he'd worked with. Years later, now that my job has shifted from comic/romantic lead to character parts, I think of him and his way of handling those roles.

Spending a few days at a time with Mitzi and Jack showed me again how different the Americans are to the British, especially in matters of money. Here in England, unless you happen to be half American, one doesn't really talk about money. But in California, it's all very up front.

'How much are you getting for this movie, Les?' Mitzi asked me.

I demurred with an embarrassed laugh. I was caught off balance, quite shocked to be asked right out like that.

'Well,' Mitzi said, 'I'll tell you what I'm on. I'm getting half a million bucks. So, what are you getting?'

'I couldn't afford your agent's commission,' I said, with a laugh. 'No, I don't think I dare tell you.' And I meant it. Once again, I thought of my friend and agent.

I couldn't help noticing how my American friends could be astonishingly direct at times. When we got to the airport to fly back, Jack wanted to change his flight and went up to one of the check-in desks.

The girl behind it gave him one of those bland, meaningless airport smiles.

'How may I help, sir?'

'I wanna change my flight.'

'All right, sir. You need to go to a desk where they have a telephone. I don't have one right here.'

Jack didn't budge. 'Go find one,' he said, no top dressing. I think most of us Brits find that sort of thing difficult to take. We are so polite about things, and often use too many words (particularly me).

We got back to LA and carried on filming. Having met the great Frank Sinatra, who hadn't really registered my existence, a few days later I met the even greater Bing Crosby. It turned out that Kay was mad about Bing, though she'd never met him; we were working in the studio when he suddenly walked in unannounced, carrying a big package tied with a silk ribbon. He walked straight up to Kay. 'I believe you wanted to tell me you're mad about me?' He gave her the package he was carrying.

She went weak at the knees and opened it with a squeal of delight. Bing had brought her an original 1934 recording of 'Love in Bloom', one of his biggest hits. He was charming and sincere, exactly as he came across on the screen.

After that he introduced himself to the rest of the cast, and for me it was the start of a friendship that lasted throughout his many visits to England over the next twenty years, until he died.

When he came to London we would often meet up. The two of us did several joint charity gigs at the races and golf clubs, which he loved, and he would often come to Brighton, where we'd meet at Wheeler's.

He had, unlike many of his countrymen, impeccable manners. He always remembered names from year to year, which has never been one of my talents: great with faces, but not names.

I last saw him in Brighton in the autumn of 1977.

'How are you, Bing?' I greeted him.

'Hi, Leslie, not bad, for an old 'un.'

The following week, dear Bing died on a golf course in Spain.

I was introduced to the seamier side of LA by Jacques Bergerac's brother, Michel, who was, to put it politely, a less sophisticated version of Jacques and not as handsome (no one could be as good looking as Jacques). He was, however, immensely good-natured. He took me downtown to the Mexican quarter – a very different place to Hollywood and Beverly Hills. It felt dangerous and exciting just being there. The first time he drove us there, we hadn't gone far when he just caught some poor chap crossing the street. But Michel didn't stop. I was rather alarmed; it didn't seem at all right.

'I say...' I started to protest.

Michel laughed. 'Don't worry about it; it's some asshole trying to make a buck.'

Apparently they would step in front of a car and pick up an injury in the hope that the driver was drunk and would pay a hefty bribe to avoid involving the police.

The first bar we went into looked like a saloon in a John Wayne picture. The place was seething with hostesses in outfits that left little to the imagination. I sat on a stool at the bar, and moments later a girl in a frock made of pink satin and a lampshade fringe came and sat down beside me. Her vermilion lips were set in a kind of smile as she showed off her beautiful tits. They were clearly on offer, but it was an offer I could refuse – just. I returned her smile and she reached across and grabbed my complete wedding apparatus, squeezing firmly until I gulped.

This had never happened to me before. It soon became apparent that the price of release would be a tequila sunrise, a pack of cigars, and a sum of money. I paid, and breathed a sigh of relief. Once she had her drink she listed some of the other services she could provide, but I didn't feel inclined to take up her offer.

Michel had by this time gone home, leaving me alone in this hellhole. As I waited for a car to take me back to my apartment, I thought about the extraordinary contradictions of LA: the seediness of the downtown area side by side with hermetically sealed Beverly Hills; everything's either too clean, or too dirty. In the Hollywood food markets, I didn't like the way the vegetables were all scrubbed pristine. In London I was used to buying in Berwick Street Market with a bit of honest earth still clinging to them.

I found that restaurants in Hollywood were

graded according to who used them – directors, producers, hot stars, middling and bit-part actors. But there were some with sufficient self-confidence to straddle these distinctions and happily cater for a broad spectrum of clients.

In one such place on Sunset Strip, divided into two- and four-seat cubicles, I was having dinner with Patrick Macnee when we overheard from the adjoining cubicle a conversation of such startling horniness that one was almost shocked just listening. I was beginning to find it rather embarrassing when suddenly the whole timbre of the conversation changed. The woman (one couldn't call her a lady, on account of her very rich language) was accusing the man of having shown an interest elsewhere. The more he denied it, the angrier she became, her insults became more widely targeted about her partner's anatomy.

Our own conversation had come to a standstill by the time a crescendo was reached, and the two of them burst from the cubicle, revealing the speakers as the late Judy Garland, and another distinguished film actor whose name escapes me.

Encounters like these did much to keep the excitement level high in LA. But while not wishing to malign a whole nation, there were aspects of American life which I found difficult to handle. That's almost certainly why I never wanted to settle there, however much I enjoyed working there.

Dining in a restaurant one night with Bill and Ginny, we noticed that a fellow had passed out under a table. Ginny went to see if he was all right, but whatever was wrong had deprived him of speech. Solicitous as always, she asked the maître d' to call an ambulance.

'Does he want an ambulance?'

'Of course he does – look at him!'

'Did he ask for an ambulance?'

'He's passed out. He can't speak.'

'If I call it and he don't want to pay – who do you think gets the bill? Huh?' He stabbed himself in the chest with a podgy finger and turned on his heel.

The authorities had their engaging little ways too. I had to go and square my temporary tax status with the US Internal Revenue.

'OK,' the gimlet-eyed, dark-jawed official said. 'So you're here and you're single.'

'Oh no, not at all, I've got a family.'

'What you got?'

'A wife and three children,' I answered, not without a hint of pride.

'Have you got 'em here?'

'No. They're in London.'

'If you ain't got 'em here, you ain't got 'em.'

Towards the end of my stay in LA, the crisis in Suez came to a head when Anthony Eden sent in British troops. The American press and most of their readers were in no doubt that the whole destabilising nonsense was our fault. They were right, of course, though I felt it was unreasonable for them to blame me personally. For a while an English accent was a distinct disadvantage. At the Beverly Wiltshire, when I asked the usual doorman to park my car, he snapped, 'You're

British! Park your own car!'

In general, I found that you had to be careful what you said to Americans; they didn't seem to understand criticism. I suppose, too, that the obsessive preoccupation with money and financial success is alienating to most English people. It's not that we don't like success, it's just that we measure it in different ways. For all the spectacular kindness of my American friends, I never did feel entirely settled in California.

In the end, the decision had to be made: did I want as much money as I could put my hands on, which would entail living in LA, or did I want a civilised life in London? Answer: a bit of both! However, I'm a Londoner, through and through; it was no contest for me. Before leaving I'd already made up my mind that a Hollywood career was something I could do without, and even when, a few years later, the success of *Carry on Nurse* and *Doctor in Love* brought many tempting offers my way, I couldn't imagine living in LA full time.

Nevertheless I was sorry to say goodbye, particularly to Kay; it seemed so final, and she and I had become very close. She was so strong, so charming and deliciously honest. She was an incredibly lovely person with a streak of warmth that isn't easy to find in the movie world, especially in Hollywood, and I think she was one of the finest women I've ever met. I'm glad to say that Rex married her the following year, but tragically, two years after that, Kay died. I'm very proud, though, to have been involved in one of her extraordinarily exuberant performances.

On my last day in LA, Patrick Macnee drove me to the airport, and I had my first and only experience of an LA storm. I've never seen so much rain descend so thick and fast, turning all the freeways into rivers. It was only then that I realised why there was a groove down the middle of every road, with both sides cambered towards the centre.

In retrospect, I really enjoyed my time in America, and it helped me learn about them (as many of my American friends find a visit to London helps them understand the British). In the end, however much I enjoy working abroad, I always love coming home. And it was time to do just that.

8 • Pinewood Again and Again

I'd had a wonderful six months in America, and now emerged even more English than I had been before. I needed to get back to London and my wife, children and friends. I had missed them all, as well as the rain and the foggy, snarled-up streets – and, of course, Perk House. It took me a while for it to sink in that, only a month or so before, I had actually been kissing Ginger Rogers, swapping yarns with Paul Newman, and being thrashed at tennis by James Mason.

Even if I'd wanted to, I couldn't have stopped myself being aware of my new status as a 'Hollywood' actor and I decided to confirm this by buying a suitable car – not a flashy convertible, like the Chevy in which I'd cruised Malibu and the boulevards of LA, but a quietly superior R-type Bentley. It didn't cost a great deal; it was second-hand and six years old, but I loved it. You might have thought for a thirty-three-year-old man with a young family, a car like this was a bit much, but it did the trick for me. The gentle purr of the 4½-litre engine, the warm musky odour of the leather upholstery, and the elevated driving position were terribly reassuring to a man who had left his mother's modest little house in Chingford less than ten years before.

The R-type was to be the first of two Bentleys I owned. As the advertisements claimed, 'The loudest sound you'll hear is the ticking of the clock.' They are a pleasure to drive and I grew to enjoy them very much. Somehow the new futuristic barouches being produced by a factory in Germany have none of the subdued, under-stated opulence of the R and S Series.

Penny, to my dismay, was not so delighted with the Bentley. She didn't like being dropped off in one for a morning's shopping as it was too ostentatious. Looking back, I wonder if there was an element of frustration that the Bentley under-lined the progress of my career. Peter Ustinov once said to me that it was risky for an actor to be married to an actress, because both parties would always be competing. This wasn't what I wanted; as far as I was concerned, my success was our success, and vice versa, as in the early days when her career was going better than mine.

Nevertheless, Penny now seemed to have accepted the demise of her own career. She made one last film, *The Big Chance*, with my old friend (and wartime colleague) Peter Graham-Scott. For some reason, neither she nor Peter told me about it until long after the event; being so busy myself or possibly away at the time, I hadn't been aware of her going off to the studios during the day. I don't know why she was so secretive about it, but I knew that she was now totally committed to the children. The girls, seven and five, were developing rapidly, while Andrew was showing signs of great charm in the face of Caroline's childhood bossiness. Penny was anxious that they should have an upper-middle-class background and education to go with it, with nannies, tea parties, parents back for drinks, coats with velvet collars and shiny buckled shoes.

I could see that, if it were to live up to Penny's expectations, the future was abundantly clear. I thought to myself, if that's what she wants, that's what I'll try to provide – one of the best sources of motivation known to man – and threw myself into the task of earning it. At the same time, I was conscious of Penny's mild resentment that I was away from the house too much. No doubt I was becoming a workaholic, but I was bringing home the dosh. Frankly though, I've often thought of myself as a good father, but a doubtful husband.

The process by which it is decided which film will be shown to the Royal family for the Command Performance is a mystery to I. Perhaps the presence of two English actors, Kay Kendall and me, in what was an American movie, set mainly in Paris, was a significant factor. Whatever the reason, it was a great moment when *Les Girls*, my first Hollywood movie, was to be shown to Her Majesty the Queen and Prince Philip at the Odeon, Leicester Square, in the spring of 1957.

It is the custom to have as many of the actors as possible present at this performance in order that Her Majesty might inspect each of them in the flesh, so to speak, much as she might a promising young racehorse, or a Derby winner. As it turned out, I was the only member of the cast able to make it, so I had Her Majesty all to myself. The Queen was lovely, and indeed, has always been on subsequent encounters at the Royal Theatrical Fund events at the Garrick Club, when she generally comes along on her own and lets herself go a little more. I found her a remarkably attractive and amusing woman. I also met the Queen Mother, who was good enough to say that I was among her favourite actors; reciprocally, she was always a lovely Queen Mum.

As a result of the publicity surrounding the Royal Command Performance and the critical and financial success of *Les Girls*, I had moved up the ladder a few rungs. Now I was being offered more starring roles. People were stopping me in the street and waiters in French restaurants were almost polite to me. The phone was ringing non-stop and scripts for plays, TV, radio and movies were plopping through the letterbox frequently. I could hardly believe it, but I was now officially 'hot', it seemed.

The most pleasing news I had on returning to England was that I was to work again with Ginny McKenna and Bill Travers in a film called *The Smallest Show on Earth*, with my old mentor, Basil Dearden, directing. Still, in my view, an enchanting movie with a delightful plot and some wonderful character roles, *The Smallest Show* is about a young couple (Bill and Ginny) who inherit an ancient and commercially defunct cinema, the Bijou, whose equally ancient employees are determined to keep it and their jobs open. It had a marvellous cast, with Peter Sellers in one of his earliest film roles as the drunken film projector operator. He already had an aura about him that smelled of stardom, and agents were hanging around like flies – at least, John Redway was down on the set every day hoping to sign him up.

Margaret Rutherford, already in her mid-sixties, was magnificent as Mrs Fazackalee in the box office. She was one of the outstanding female character actresses to emerge since the war, and her triumphs included Madame Arcati in David Lean's *Blithe Spirit*, and she later became the archetypal Miss Marple. She was married to a gentle character actor called Stringer Davies and, such was her unique appeal to audiences, she was able to make a role for her husband a condition of any movie contract she signed. In *Smallest Show*, Stringer played Emmett, an old retainer of the Bijou cinema, while the makers of the *Miss Marple* films even wrote in an entirely new character called Mr Stringer for him to play. She was a first cousin of Tony Benn's – though I'm sure that had no bearing on her being made a

246

Dame in 1967, it was richly deserved. She was always warm and wonderful to work with; while appearing with her in this film at Pinewood, she and Stringer would turn up, full of vim and enthusiasm, announcing that they had stopped at some wild, fast-flowing river or placid lake for a bracing swim – probably in the buff, knowing her! Stringer would keep his pants on, I'm sure, and always have a towel at the ready to rub down his wife.

Bill Travers' quiet, understated way was just right for the role of Matt in *Smallest Show*. I played the solicitor who dealt with the will, and the eccentric Bernard Miles played the commissionaire. I worked with Bernard in the theatre several times and he was full of surprises. I remember being with him on the roof of the Mermaid Theatre, where he was artistic director, when a barge trundled up the river within hailing distance. He stopped rehearsing, leaving the rest of the cast waiting, and called out through cupped hands: 'Ahoy there, bargee! Where be you going this bright sunny day?'

The bargee yelled back: 'Bollocks!!'

I'm often reminded of the fun we had making the film because the false frontage of the Bijou cinema was set next to Kilburn Station and onto an old bridge, just up the road from where I've lived for the last forty years. Every time a train passed over this railway bridge, the whole cinema shuddered like the bowels of a flatulent whale. In fact now, in 2006, the old bridge has just been declared too tremulous for safety and is being replaced.

One of the more bizarre and, you might think, unseemly aspects of this production was the performance of our producer, Michael Relph. Most of the interior shots were being filmed at Pinewood. The girl who sold the ice-cream in the Bijou was played by a pretty, brassy girl who, not without some justification, liked to flaunt her physique as well as her ice-cream. I soon noticed, along with everyone else, that she'd caught the eye of Michael Relph, but I couldn't help feeling a little taken aback when one of the crew asked me to place a bet on how long it would take our producer to move in on the ice-cream girl.

'What on earth are you talking about?' I asked.

'Michael always finds one he fancies on every picture,' the chap who was making the book replied, 'And this girl's the only candidate, really.'

The last part was true enough. Ginny McKenna was thoroughly entwined with Bill Travers, and Margaret Rutherford was hardly an option with Stringer.

Although I'm not a prude and I certainly don't mind gambling, I felt I didn't like or want to be party to this, so I declined to bet. However, I heard that there was soon a full book, at widely varying odds, on possible times for this meeting to take place. Going, I was told, on past films, the closer to the start of the day, the shorter the price.

From the moment she arrived at the studio, the girl was stalked relentlessly and not very discreetly everywhere she went. At last, thinking the coast was clear, he took her into his room, where the spies checking through the window subsequently confirmed that the encounter had taken place. It happened late in the day, probably as a result of the crew's vigilance, and the winner was paid off. It surely must have been some kind of bad joke.

That apart, it was a happy and successful movie, although it was to be the last I made with Basil Dearden.

Later that year, I got a call from Alastair Scott-Johnson at the BBC, asking me to come in and talk about a new comedy series written by Laurie Wyman with three prospective stars in mind: Dennis Price, Jon Pertwee and me. Although it was a wonderfully conceived idea with well-drawn characters in an unexpected and original setting (in the same genre as *Dad's Army*), no one could ever have predicted just what a phenomenon *The Navy Lark* would become.

This comic saga of naval incompetence was to become a national institution (even an international one, through the BBC World Service), and over the next seventeen years, I recorded some 250 episodes. I didn't miss a single one and, such was my love of the show and my loyalty to it, that I once flew back from Rome, where I was making an Italian movie *Fernando, Re di Napoli*, to record an episode before flying straight back. My rather insubstantial BBC fee didn't cover even half the cost of the trip, but *The Navy Lark* was one of those jobs where the money was irrelevant (and there aren't many of those in the average actor's life).

Money for the Italian film, on the other hand,

was only too relevant. I had been warned to make sure I got anything owing on my fee before they finished shooting my part. Once they'd got what they needed of me in the can, the incentive to part with further wads of *lire* would be greatly diminished. Needless to say, I ended the job still owed money. I left feeling dejected, ready to write it off. Imagine, then, the ecstasy of opening the door of my house in Mill Hill a few weeks later to a shortish, darkish, continental-suited fellow who handed me a suitcase full of pristine Italian currency. He left with barely a word and never even asked for a receipt. Give or take, allowing for the fluctuations in the naturally ludicrous exchange rate, I'd been paid in full. Thus my faith in Italian film-makers has remained intact (although I've not worked for an Italian director since). I even felt a little guilty when the film turned out to be a great big flop.

It shouldn't have been. Gianni Franciolini was a highly respected director with a wonderful cast of great Italian (mostly Neapolitan) actors: the De Filippo brothers, Peppino and Eduardo, and their sister, Titina; Vittorio de Sica, who had won Oscars both as director and actor; Renato Rascel, Jaqueline Sassard (a gorgeous French actress I played opposite), and a young Marcello Mastro-ianni. I had a delightful time filming in Naples and Rome, where I started off living in a hotel at the top of the Spanish Steps, but moved every couple of weeks to a new hotel in order to get a broader view of the city.

We were wonderfully looked after in Naples. On several occasions we were joined for dinner by Toto, the legendary star, who possessed about a dozen dukedoms and marquisates, as well as one of the strangest, most twisted noses I have ever seen. We would eat out on a terrace over the river, and the ragged desperate slum children would shin up the jetty pillars and poke their grubby little faces over the rails, and stay there watching us dine until they were thrown some money, which the Italians did without a thought. It was, they said, expected and the thing to do.

The film was shot in Italian, but as the only Englishman in the cast, I was allowed to deliver my lines in English, to be lip-synched in the vernacular. To assist me, I was assigned a lovely girl who told me what everything meant, so that I could react correctly. It's not the easiest way to do the job, but the Italians have always had a pretty cavalier attitude to the soundtrack. I could barely recognise myself speaking Italian. It reminded me of Peter Finch in *Train of Events* when they dubbed his part with an entirely different voice with a strong German accent. It ruined his performance and he was furious about it. In this case, I couldn't understand enough of what was coming out of my mouth to mind very much.

Back in England, as my workload in films grew, I was having to turn down a lot of theatrical productions. I still managed several stage appearances (*Three Way Switch*, with Brian Forbes; *Double Take; We'll all be Millionaires*, written by Roy Plomley and directed by me), but with appearances in so many films released in this period there was little time for anything else.

One of the films I made at this time, *I was Monty's Double*, took me back to my Durham Light Infantry days at Haverhill when the real Monty came to see us. The film starred Meyrick Clifton-James, the original double playing the role of Montgomery, while I played ADC to the double. I think even Meyrick would have agreed that he wasn't the greatest actor of his period; he got the job through one of the most bizarre pieces of casting in history. During the war, he had been appearing in a play in London when, unable to find his hat for the final bow, he plonked a handy black beret on his head and walked back on stage. The audience assumed, without question, that Field-Marshal Montgomery had just walked on, and they all got to their feet and cheered.

When Military Intelligence got to hear of this extraordinary incident, they immediately booked him to masquerade as Montgomery in several ploys concocted to fool the Germans over Allied plans. They took him to Gibraltar, knowing that southern Spain was teeming with Nazi spies and sympathisers who, seeing 'Monty', would come to the conclusion that the Allies were planning a landing in another location.

Soon after I'd finished *Monty's Double*, I was cast in another film that was to become the most significant (if not the most financially rewarding) of the first half of my career.

Initially, I wasn't very excited when John Redway rang to say that I'd been offered a leading role by Peter Rogers, a producer for whom I'd played a small part in *You Know What Sailors Are* about four years before. On the face if it, the new movie wasn't much of a proposition, with a budget for the whole thing which these days wouldn't keep a Chelsea footballer happy for a week. However, I said I'd have a look at the script, and that evening it dropped through the letterbox with a portentous thud, delivered by John on his way home (he also lived in Mill Hill), along with a covering note: *The money's rubbish but it's only five weeks' work. I think it's very funny. Give it a read and see what you think.*

I picked up the packet and took it through to the drawing-room, where I curled up on the sofa with darling Pippa, my yellow Labrador, and started to read. I was soon chuckling quietly, then laughing out loud. John was right. The script was bloody funny, and I could see it working very well.

Peter was an independent producer who worked alongside the Rank Organisation at Pinewood. He had lined up Gerald Thomas to direct. The script was written by Norman Hudis, who'd been a staff writer at Pinewood, but was now working freelance and clearly knew what he was doing. It was loosely based on an existing property, *Ring for Catty*, written by Jack Searle and a friend of mine, actor Patrick Cargill. It was now to be entitled *Carry On Nurse*. The story featured a pair of lovers caught up in a series of funny and sentimental scenarios, to the backing of a sort of Greek chorus of character comedians.

John was right about the money too: there was a distinct odour of ordure to it – five weeks' work at £100 a week. Even for Peter Rogers, who had

253

a reputation for being as tight as a serpent's arse, it was mean. While I'd been in Hollywood on *Les Girls*, MGM had given me £500 a day expenses. Now here I was, not much later, being offered a measly £100 *in toto* by Peter Rogers for a complete film!

I could always have said no, I suppose, and told the producer to 'Bugger off!' like Richard Burton, who I'd worked with a few years earlier on *The Woman with No Name*, his first film before he went off to become a fully paid-up Hollywood star in *The Robe*.

But I didn't; I complied with advice I'd heard years before, a quote from the great silent movie star, Mary Pickford, who concluded that there were two routes to stardom – either be very picky indeed about which parts you take and be consistent with it, or do anything and everything that swims within range, while you build experience and a name. For better or worse, I'd always taken the latter route. And this script was bloody funny.

I had to make a swift decision; Peter Rogers was anxious to get on with the film. So I said I'd go for it – I was already busy with *The Navy Lark*, and I had just finished playing the lead in *Three-Way Switch*, a promising play that seemed certain to transfer from Windsor to the West End (and did so later). I had a good chance of picking up another TV play and two more movies were lurking on the horizon. There was no shortage of work in my life then; on one occasion, I performed in all four media – theatre, television, radio and film – on the same day. And all the while, the money was going up – except for Peter Rogers' newly born *Carry On Nurse* cast. In spite of the crummy wages, Leslie Phillips – complete with bunion – would be turning up at the studios to appear in *Carry On Nurse*.

After an early call on the first day of shooting, I arrived at Pinewood, by then almost a second home to me, setting a pattern for the next five weeks. I would wake, gently kiss my still-sleeping wife and, leaving her in the warm matrimonial bed, get dressed, climb into my Bentley and drive to Pinewood, where I would get undressed and climb back into bed, usually with June Whitfield standing watch over me.

The cast had been well chosen by Peter and Gerald. They were, for the most part, strongly individual, experienced comic actors – certainly those who were to go on and form the backbone of what Peter wanted to call the *Carry On* team. We were all on the same lousy wages, which Peter Rogers tried to justify by claiming he didn't want a 'star-driven' series. He was taking a punt that, once they were in, like most actors, they'd be reluctant to duck out, whatever the money. He was generally, if not entirely, right. I'd met most of the cast before and worked with some of them – Kenneth Connor, Hattie Jacques, Charles Hawtrey, Joan Sims, and the one and only Kenneth Williams.

On day one, my first full scene on *Nurse* was set up 'on the floor'. My character, Jack Bell, was arriving at Haven Hospital for an operation to

255

remove a bunion – it was that kind of script. Gerry Thomas was a lovely chap, as well as an amiable and easy-going director – in sharp contrast to the overbearing, dictatorial George Cukor. When we were ready to shoot, the first assistant called for quiet. I cast an appraising glance over the actress with whom I was to share the scene – the deliciously sexy Shirley Eaton. She was jaw-droppingly beautiful, and it came as no surprise when, a few years later, Cubby Broccoli asked her to bare all for the cameras in a James Bond movie, albeit thickly coated in gold leaf. Her performance as Nurse Denton was to heat up the cockles of a generation of lusty young men, and not a few older ones. I'd worked with her before and knew her a little. Easy as I found it to share the impure thoughts of the male film-going public, I restrained myself. Nobody seems to believe it, but in contrast to my screen image, I was a loyal and dutiful husband and dad.

As it turned out, though, a few weeks after filming *Nurse*, I was offered a bonus if I decided to do the next film, *Carry On Constable*: a shared scene with Shirley in the shower. She would shiver beside me in elegant nudity, wearing nothing but two small pieces of flesh-coloured sticking-plaster over her nipples, so I decided to do that film, too. *It's going to hurt a lot to pull those off*, I thought with concern, and would have been more than happy to lend a quiet, unhurried hand.

Back on the set of *Nurse*, I overcame any un-gentlemanly urges while an assistant labelled the scene with his clapper-board. Alan Hume, friend and favourite camera operator, confirmed his

The Phillips family on holiday in Ramsgate. (Above left) Me
entered into a beauty contest, with inked-in shorts to cover my
unbuttoned flies; (above right) with elder brother Fred; (below)
the entire family sits down for a cup of tea: Dad Frederick,
Mum Cecelia, sister Dolly, Fred and me.

With Dad and Fred in Folkestone, 1934. The following year, father's always frail health finally gave way, and we were faced with the challenge of making ends meet.

Mum and Dolly work on my first car, many years later.

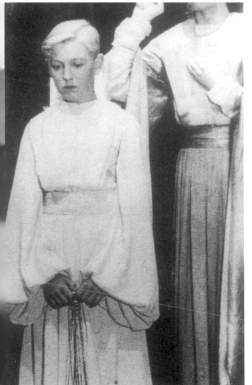

Two shots from my appearance as John Napoleon Darling in the 1938 *Peter Pan*, alongside Jean Forbes-Robertson and Sir Seymour Hicks.

As 'the sweetest little cherub that ever came to life from a stained-glass window' in the Dorothy L. Sayers play, *The Zeal of Thy House*, which earned me the then huge sum of five pounds a week.

Bobby Desmond and I were to be partners in crime as young actors, and remained great friends.

An early publicity shot, though Italia Conti was not happy with the size of my nose.

My Guildenstern in the Dundee Rep's performance of *Hamlet* in the winter of 1944/45 was not a success, and a kindly director found increasingly imaginative reasons to give my lines to Rosencrantz. I had much to learn.

Three uniforms in wartime: (right) in the Home Guard in Stevenage, 1942; (below) in the uniform of the Royal Artillery; (below right) aged nineteen in the Durham Light Infantry, following my request to join either the Middlesex or the Essex regiments.

Joy Herbert, my fiancée, who decided she'd rather marry an officer than an actor.

My wedding to Penny Bartley on 30 May 1948 in St John's
Wood, after which we went to Lake Lugano for our honeymoon.

Our daughter, Caroline, is born on 31 October 1949 to the
huge joy of her doting parents.

My first big film role, in Basil Dearden's *Train of Events* in 1949, where I played a fireman to Jack Warner's engine driver.

With Earl Cameron in the 1951 thriller *Pool of London*, also directed by Basil Dearden; it was the first of eleven movies I made with James Robertson Justice.

My name in lights for the first time, in *For Better, For Worse* with Geraldine McEwan. The play ran for more than 500 performances, and even got me the chance to meet Marlene Dietrich.

Pippa, our Labrador at Perk House, one of very many family pets.

Appearing with Bill Travers and Virginia McKenna in
The Smallest Show on Earth in 1957. They had been so helpful
and supportive during my stay in Hollywood, I was delighted
to be working with them.

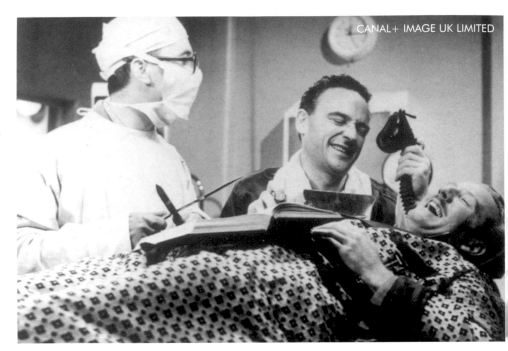

Ding Dong! (Above) Kenneth Connor lets loose the laughing gas in *Carry On Nurse*, and the whole nation laughed. While (below) I work very hard on trying to say Miss Allcock (played by Joan Sims) in a way that didn't risk the censor's wrath in *Carry on Teacher*.

Carry On Constable. (Above) The Shower scene, *Carry On* Style, with Kenneth Connor; (below) with Kenneth Williams, who used the uniform to good effect when filming stopped — along with the traffic.

The Navy Lark ran for seventeen years, and I appeared in more than 250 episodes, never missing one. From left to right: Ronnie Barker, Jon Pertwee, me and Stephen Murray.

One of the most extraordinary characters I ever worked with: James Robertson Justice was my co-star in all three *Doctor* movies I made. Producer Betty Box also ensured that this work was far more lucrative than the *Carry On* movies.

Working with Robert Mitchum in the 1959 film *The Angry Hills*.

All aboard for the holiday to the Côte Sauvage, with Andrew, Caroline, Claudia, Penny and Roger, but it was our au pair Renata who was to save the day when the French coast lived up to its name.

Two movies directed by Ken Annakin. (Left) With Stanley Baxter, an enormously versatile actor, in *Crooks Anonymous*; (below) a scene from *The Fast Lady*. These films also gave a break to Julie Christie, whose unusual beauty wasn't to the immediate taste of all, but whose talent shone through.

'Oh Lesley, why did you do it?' was the agonised cry of one reviewer of *The Man Most Likely To. . .* However, the play, which opened in July 1968, was to run in various incarnations for years to come.

TRINITY MIRROR

Angie Scoular gives me a helping hand, while Freddie Jones tries to pick me up in drag in *Doctor In Trouble*.

GRANADA

During the era of *Casanova '73*, my reputation for playing smooth-talking philanderers took a further turn, as we brought sex to television, much to Mary Whitehouse's concern.

Working with Terry-Thomas on *Spanish Fly*. Unfortunately, by then he was ill and no longer the tremendous raconteur he had once been.

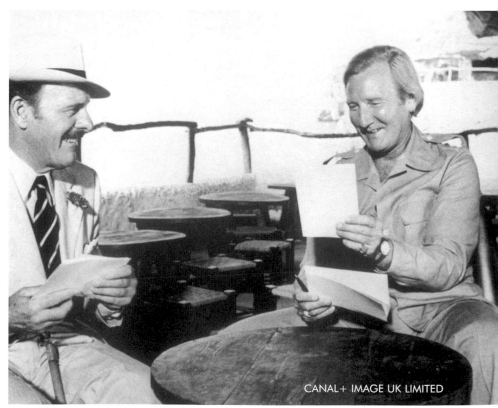

With Carrie Mortimer, who I met while working on the play *The Big Killing*.

The successful TV series in which I played a vicar, *Our Man at St Mark's*, was dropped after my relationship with Carrie became public knowledge — in those days it was deemed inappropriate!

The *finca* we found in Ibiza — forty years on, it is much changed, but it has always been a wonderful place to go to get away from it all.

When the salesman parked this Mercedes 220OSE outside the office I was working in on the Strand, I was immediately hooked. In the background is our house in Maida Vale and the magnolia that Carrie and I planted when we moved in.

An exciting new role for me: as producer of the film *Maroc 7*.

Prawn, whose genes still run through the cats in our house, twenty-five years on.

Angie and me on our wedding day.

With my four children at my seventieth birthday party. Left to right: Andrew, me, Roger, Caroline and Claudia.

The results of my decision to take on more serious work: (top) with the hugely impressive Steven Spielberg and Christian Bale in *The Empire of the Sun*; (centre) playing Lord Astor, with Joanne Whalley as Christine Keeler in *Scandal*; (bottom) as James Blake in the successful TV series *Chancer*, alongside Clive Owen.

PHIL CUTTS

Tony Hopkins' adaptation of *Uncle Vanya*, renamed *August*, was performed by the same cast on both stage and film, and was exactly the sort of role I have enjoyed in my later career.

(Below left) Returning to Shakespeare, this time with the RSC, as Falstaff in *The Merry Wives of Windsor*, which I was thrilled to be asked to do.

(Below right) My co-starring parakeet in the RSC production of the Tennessee Williams play *Camino Real*.

CHARLES GREEN

Angie and me at Buckingham Palace after I got my OBE from the Queen in 1998.

Hard at work finding all the right materials for our *finca* in Ibiza; with the end result looking spectacular.

MAIL ON SUNDAY

One of my more unusual roles, as the Sorting Hat in the first two Harry Potter films — the first time in a long career I'd ever played a hat!

Presenting the 2003 Comedy Awards with Katie Price, aka Jordan.

Alongside Peter O'Toole in Roger Michell's wonderful film *Venus*.

equipment was ready to roll and nodded at Gerry Thomas.

'Action!' Gerry said, and we were off!

I walked in. 'Hello, chaps!' I greeted everyone in the prescribed tone of honey-smooth bonhomie.

'Mr Bell?' asked Nurse Denton, with fluttering eyelids and quivering breast.

I moved closer to her and gazed into her eyes for a brief moment.

'Ding Dong! You're not wrong!' I said, then spun away, without giving the line a second thought.

My character, Jack Bell, had, unsurprisingly, been lumbered by Norman Hudis with a number of catch phrases, including that one – 'Ding Dong'. The first time I'd uttered those two words, I would never have believed that I would become so inescapably linked with them in the minds of the public for the next fifty years, and still counting. Even today I'm regularly Ding-Donged as I walk through the streets of London, and not long ago, having performed a small favour for a Ms Jerry Hall, I received a nice *billet doux* from her informing me that she, too, would 'like to ding my dong' – a heart-warming sentiment for an octogenarian trouper. I haven't seen her since to take up her offer, more's the pity; she's smashing.

That scene from *Nurse* where my nutty fellow patients attempt to remove my bunion in the operating theatre remains with me most vividly. It was a supreme moment of what came to be recognised as the *Carry On* brand of cinematic humour, with the cast losing all dignity as a result

257

of a dose of laughing gas being squirted into the atmosphere. In all my years of film-making it was one the funniest experiences I ever had on camera. Our hysteria was entirely spontaneous and set the tone for the umpteen years of *Carry On* slapstick that followed. And thank God I wasn't going to be there for all that!

But the laughter wasn't only in front of the camera. Alan Hume, an inveterate giggler, was laughing so much that several takes were unusable as a result of camera shake from his quivering hands – and this was the man who went on to shoot a string of James Bond movies for Cubby Broccoli. We had to deal with him by stuffing a large handkerchief into his mouth.

A magic had been born among the team; the interplay and energy was amazing, inspiring the most glorious improvisation. It was, in truth, a tremendously happy film to make, with the strongest sense of camaraderie I've ever come across, partly due, of course, to the effortless direction of Gerry Thomas. It set the seal, I think, for the success of the movie and a lot of its sequels.

The scripts of the *Carry Ons* conveyed the World According to P. Rogers – not a message of great gravitas, it must be said, but nevertheless relevant, and a hint to an orderly nation that our great institutions were not as beyond reproach as was widely perceived, especially, in this case, the NHS.

Towards the end of filming, Peter Rogers sidled up to me in the bar at Pinewood for a quiet chat which carried over into lunch.

'This is going awfully well,' he said, pouring a glass of champagne with a knowing nod. 'I think we might have a bit of a hit.'

I've always been fairly circumspect about this sort of prognostication, but I had to agree – and, with work to do after lunch, I didn't accept the drink.

'I've got two more planned, *Carry On Constable* and *Teacher*. I'll start shooting in a few months,' Peter went on. 'You'd like to do them, wouldn't you?'

'I expect so,' I answered cautiously.

'I hope so, because there are six people I'd really like to be in the sequels – the two Kens, Hattie, Joan, Charles and you. And for those who sign up, I'm going to work out a really good contract.'

By that I assumed he meant a percentage deal – what else?

'I might be on for that,' I answered, though not too enthusiastically, while thinking a slice of the action could be worth having if it was a success.

'Good,' Peter said, with the glowing eyes of a man who thinks he's just saved money. 'I'll be in touch.'

I could only think his motive in offering to part with a share of the profits was to get us cheap while it was still speculative. Or maybe he realised there was a vital dynamic among the cast which it was vital to preserve, and this was a way of ensuring that we all stayed in. I was almost tempted to think it was an act of generosity on his part. It would be the talk of Pinewood if it ever came to pass.

At home in Mill Hill, life had settled into a routine that was comfortable, if a little too pedestrian for Penny who, with her series of boot-faced au pairs, was fully occupied in bringing up the children – a task I joined in with as often as work allowed. I was, however, ridiculously busy. My habit of taking every job that came along was so strong that, now I was being offered far more than I could handle, there wasn't a minute to spare. Penny began to complain at my absence, constantly in studios by day and theatres by night. I admit that I was guilty of neglecting the family a little as a result, but she made no objection to the money coming in and I took the view that an actor's life is so precarious, one doesn't have the luxury of turning stuff down while the going's good.

Even my radio career was buoyant and, by the middle of 1959, *The Navy Lark* had already shown its mettle. After a first series of sixteen shows, we launched into a second, this time of twenty-six episodes, with pretty much the same cast apart from Dennis Price, who'd gone to New York to do a play which died after a single night. He cried when he couldn't get his job back on *The Navy Lark;* Stephen Murray had already been appointed the new No.1. It was a great pity as I liked Dennis very much.

The Navy Lark was a show blessed with a remarkable and astonishingly long-lived bonhomie. I formed some great friendships, most especially with Ronnie Barker, who as A.B. Johnson, along with numerous other parts, appeared continuously from the first episode until the 160th in 1967. I realised from the off that Ronnie was a character actor of mind-boggling versatility, perhaps one of the greatest comic actors of his day, and brilliant on the writing side. I was thrilled when he was rewarded with success after success until the day he decided to hang up his box of Five & Nine and powder puff to become a part-time antique dealer – a decision of almost unprecedented courage among actors who are in such great demand. I could fill a book with Ronnie anecdotes, but let's just say I loved him.

The script by Norman Hudis for *Carry On Constable* was as well-crafted as *Carry On Nurse*, and I'd have taken it on as a stand-alone job if I hadn't already agreed to do it and *Teacher* for the same lousy fee, pending Peter's proposed contract for any future films in the series. Even though I had a marvellous time making it, I was becoming impatient to see Peter's implied slice of the action become a reality.

With Gerry Thomas' inspired, light touch, it is no surprise that *Constable* was good too. We were lucky to have such an engaging crowd to work with; Kenneth Connor was one of my favourites. He was an enchanting man and a fine actor who, in my view, was seriously underrated. He could have made far more, dramatically speaking, of his part in the *Carry Ons*, if only Peter Rogers, through Gerry Thomas, had allowed him to characterise each role he played. Peter, however, just wanted the self-deprecating whimsy of the small, romantic but ineffectual man that was

Ken's persona in all the films. It caused Ken a lot of heartache, being restrained like this, but, like most actors, he did as he was told to make sure he kept the job. Although he got locked into that character as far as the *Carry Ons* went, he had a diverse career outside them. His work was recognised, I'm glad to say, quite early on with an OBE. I often worked with him on radio, where he was always a superb performer. On a personal level, I had a great deal of time for Kenny, got to know his family, and spent many happy hours at parties in his house.

Hattie Jacques, too, was an interesting character with whom I worked on a lot of films besides the *Carry Ons*. She was a splendid comic actress, perhaps because she always played it very straight. Her lifelong friend, Joan Sims, became known as the First Lady of *Carry On*, having appeared in twenty-four of them (although Barbara Windsor was crowned Queen of *Carry On* from just nine appearances, which probably didn't impress Joan much).

Joan was a marvellously versatile actress who, unlike the rest of the team, managed to escape being typecast by Peter Rogers. She'd already had screen hospital experience in *Doctor in the House* as Nurse Rigor Mortis. This hysterically funny, talented lady spent a lot of time kidding, laughing, and cheering us all up, though, sad to say, she had a slight weakness for the booze and never found anyone she wanted to marry. I fear she was sometimes quite unhappy beneath all the jollity. I'd worked with her before on *As Long As They're Happy*, and was to be with her in many other movies and *The Canterville Ghost* on TV, our last job together. I always admired Joan's madness and joy in her work, and we became good friends. I missed her when she died in 2001. I rather feel the alcohol didn't help her very much; it never helps anyone actually.

Charlie Hawtrey was also an important *Carry On* face and another big talent. With his skinny, birdlike frame, National Health specs and prim, posh delivery, he was distinctly a clever oddball, as strange in life as his film persona. I met his brother once, years later; he was utterly different, a butch, warm friendly man. Charlie was gay, of course, and liked his drink, although he generally kept that under control with endless pots of Earl Grey tea. He had a real talent for reproducing that fey, feeble character he'd aired in many previous films. He could also be fastidious and difficult at times, refusing to go naked in the crazy shower scene in *Constable* until, eventually, we persuaded the make-up man to put a bit of powder on his bum to reduce the shine, which worried him enormously. Once he'd warmed up, though, we were all amazed by the size of his willy. We finished the scene and, still fairly hysterical, measured up for a wager, which Charlie won, although Kenneth Williams, of course, accused him of cheating by giving himself a helping hand, so to speak.

I suspect the most memorable member of the *Carry On* team must have been the ubiquitous and permanently attention-seeking Kenneth Williams. Kenny was, by any standards, an extraordinary man. He'd been a friend since I first met him in the Salisbury Arts Theatre, but working with him now on these three movies, more or less back to back, I came to know and like him even more. He could be tremendously stimulating to work with, though it was often difficult to cope with his unpredictable adlibbing and spontaneous business, not to mention his habit of goosing us all when we were trying to work. He was always putting his finger up people's arses – please don't misunderstand me!

Since our first meeting, back in the days when his ambition was to be a serious dramatic actor, his taste and innate talent for comic performance had developed considerably. He had a vast knowledge of history, literature and art, and a perceptive, very acerbic, wit. He could also be colossally irritating if he felt he was being ignored for more than a minute or two. He craved the response he got from performing, as if it was a drug he couldn't do without.

Making *Constable* on location around the streets of Ealing, we had permission to stay in somebody's house while we filmed in the road outside. Between shots, Kenny went out on to the street in his full policeman's uniform – helmet, whistle and all. The rest of us watched from a window, wondering what on earth he was going to do. Placing himself squarely in the middle of the road, he raised his hand and blew his whistle. The first car to come along assumed he was a genuine copper and stopped, then another coming the other way also stopped, then a few more, until he'd built up two massive queues down the road in both directions – for no reason at all. The drivers all waited patiently (this was the fifties, remember), while Kenny kept a straight face, glaring haughtily at them over his large proboscis, then turned to us and delivered one of his now famous grimaces.

He kept the drivers there for several minutes while we fell about laughing inside the house, until, having had enough of that joke, he blew his whistle and waved them all on, with the drivers left scratching their heads wondering what had happened. As he walked back towards the house for his applause, we all came out. Giving us his haughtiest look, he announced, 'I want a piss.'

Without a moment's hesitation, he walked to the kerb, unbuttoned his flies and pulled out his cock. An old lady tottering down the street towards him couldn't believe her eyes at the sight of a well-turned-out copper urinating into a drain in the gutter. As he shook his willy and put it away, the old lady hurried off as fast as her arthritic knees could carry her, utterly horrified. None of us could have stopped Kenny – we were all laughing too much, Gerry Thomas more than anyone.

Kenny adored the wild hysteria which his impromptu sessions on the set could provoke, and our appreciation was oxygen to him. He had the capacity to be side-achingly funny on several different levels – his faces, the flaring nostrils, the long nasal howls, the cutting jibes, the inspired puns, all flowing out of him in a spontaneous stream of consciousness, while all the time he was camping it up like a mercurial, gay Peter Pan. He was a true one-off.

Possibly, in the solemn seclusion of his flat, where even his closest friends were seldom admitted, he allowed his permanent mask of outrageous camp to drop and lived an ascetic, almost monkish existence. The diaries he left behind – articulate, dispassionate and dolorous about his own circumstances as they were – would suggest that this was the case.

The Emperor of Camp, he may have been, but I don't believe he was a practising homosexual. Certainly, when he went off on holiday with Joe Orton and Kenneth Halliwell, they subsequently observed that he didn't readily take advantage of what was on offer in Tangier. I never knew him to have any significant relationship, let alone a consistent partner. When it came to sex, he enjoyed a wank and that was it.

I worked with him again over the years that followed, doing voice-overs and various shows, and I feel I became a good, even helpful friend – in so far as he allowed anyone close enough. Naturally, when he was being irritating, which could be quite often, I would tell him so.

During filming, while I was trying to get myself straight and ready to shoot a scene, he would fool around sometimes until the last moment, telling interminable stories, joking and goosing any of the cast who passed within range. I would ask him, quite sharply sometimes, to stop it and into his eyes would spring a startled look. He would be abject in his remorse, needing me to reassure him that I was still his friend. Of course, I always was.

It's true that, when the mood took him, he

could be quite cruel, especially to those weaker than him. Nevertheless I was very fond of him, as were all his friends. He had a host of genuine admirers of whom perhaps the greatest was Maggie Smith. The two of them had a wonderful friendship for many years. Bizarrely, despite the obvious obstacles, I believe he once proposed marriage to the loveable and lovely Joan Sims, who was said to have turned him down on the grounds that he was too selfish and homosexual, and the marriage would never be consummated. No doubt the whole conversation was an example of the wild humour they shared and ended in a burst of raucous laughter.

In that same busy year, I found myself working with Muriel Box, wife of former Gainsborough Studio boss, Sydney Box – a big presence in the British film industry throughout the forties, fifties and sixties. Muriel was a writer who had been working on the fringes of the movie industry when she married Sydney in 1935, after which they co-wrote *The Seventh Veil*, the highest grossing British picture in 1947, which won them an Oscar for Best Original Screenplay.

They carried on working together when Rank asked Sydney to take over Gainsborough Pictures, where they were expected to churn out movies as cost-effectively – that meant cheaply – as possible. In the early fifties, Muriel started to direct in her own right. At that time, she was one of very few women film directors and encountered a great deal of prejudice, which became the subject of several of her films. Regrettably, despite being responsible for fifteen good movies, and earning a reputation in the process for dealing well with topical and controversial themes, she never completely overcame the prejudice against women directors, which only partially persists to this day. Long before she'd exhausted her potential, she retired to write novels and set up a successful publishing house, Femina.

The movie she'd asked me to make was named, perhaps ironically, from *Richard II*'s 'Sceptr'd Isle' speech, *This Other Eden*. Based on an intelligent and well-written play by Louis d'Alton, it raised complex issues about Irish politics, hypocrisy and illegitimacy. It offered me my first chance to make a film in Ireland, leaving behind the crazy comedies for a while to play a serious role. We were to shoot a lot on location, which I looked forward to as I love the country, and at Ardmore Studios in Bray, in the lee of the Wicklows, south of Dublin.

Working with the talented Abbey Theatre players, including the mesmerising Milo O'Shea, Niall MacGinnis and Hilton Edwards, I was the only Englishman in the film. I played Crispin Brown, a wealthy outsider who, as a result of falling in love with a native girl, decides to buy a local mansion and develops a romantic vision of Ireland and all things Irish, becoming more Irish than the natives.

Opposite me, playing the girl, was Audrey Dalton, a beautiful Irish actress who'd moved to Hollywood after Paramount had scouted her at RADA in 1952. At twenty-five, she was already the mother of three children and married to an assistant film director in Los Angeles. She'd come back to Ireland to do this picture, partly, I think because the Ardmore Studios were run by her father, Major General Emmett Dalton, who had been a key figure in the Free State Army, and a right-hand man of Republican leader, Michael Collins. He was a powerful individual with a formidable reputation, who had founded the studios in a bid to bring serious international film-making – with all the employment and investment that entailed – to the Republic. Several members of this big Catholic family were involved in the theatrical business in some way. They lived in Kilgarrig House, a handsome mansion standing in the grounds of the studios and used as a setting for some of our movie.

Audrey was a very striking and likeable woman. She had eyes and colouring that reflected the influence of the Armada sailors who had run adrift on the Irish west coast in the late seventeenth century and subsequently infused the Celtic population with strong Hispanic genes. She could have been a tempting proposition, although it didn't occur to me to see her in those terms. Besides, the father was not, on the face of it, a man who would look kindly on a Protestant English actor paying attention to his daughter. So I concentrated on the job, which was not the easiest I'd ever had.

The screenplay was good but erratic, in so far as the scriptwriter, would enjoy a drop or two in the bar, and then wend his way upstairs each evening in the hotel, and lock himself in his bedroom to work. My room was on the same floor as his and

269

I often witnessed pages of fresh script slipping under the door into the corridor, where the second assistant would gather them up and rush down to the office to print for the next day's shooting, and distribute them.

We'd been filming for a week or so when our cameraman, my old friend Alan Hume, whispered in my ear. 'That woman's potty about you.'

'Which woman?' I asked, genuinely puzzled.

'Audrey,' he said. 'She can't take her eyes off you.'

'Get away,' I said, not surprisingly, quite flattered. Now that he'd mentioned it, I did detect a smouldering heat in her eye. She was very good-looking indeed, and despite everything that told me I shouldn't take any notice, a colossal chemistry began to build between us. At first nothing happened, although we were both totally aware of what could happen, but a few days later, on the set, she asked me to come round and see her in the house where she was staying and meet her children.

Rehearsing every possible excuse to placate her Irish tribe if they should ask what I was doing there, I went round that evening. She was apparently the only member of the family at home; the children were out of sight. We did some work on the scripts, ate some food and all the while I tried to ignore her physical beauty and very appealing vulnerability. Before the rest of the family were due back, I returned to my hotel, rather confused, but I had no idea where this was all going to lead.

The following evening, her father had invited

270

me along to a big dinner at the Shelbourne in Dublin with all his family. During dinner, Audrey kept herself to herself and left early. I assumed she went off to look after her children. We had some good scenes to play the next day and I was looking forward to them. Next day she was very friendly again.

A couple of days later, I was sitting with my feet up in the little suite that the studio had allocated to me, trying to learn my lines but thinking of her, when I heard the rattle of a window being opened in the bathroom. Curious, I stuck my head round the bathroom door in time to see a slender female hand slip in and lift the catch. Audrey must have shinned up a ladder to my suite, one storey up. A moment later, her head and neck appeared and she scrambled through the window. Her dark brown eyes gleamed with the pleasure of conspiracy. 'Nobody saw me get in this way,' she whispered huskily.

My response? I opened my script and said, 'Come on, let's run our lines for tomorrow.'

And that's what we did. With great difficulty, as my heart was beating wildly. And nobody would believe me! It seemed we were both feeling the same about each other, but nothing untoward happened. However, a month or so after my return from Ireland, my old friend and former army medic, Dr Nigel Thornton, rang.

He and I had stayed in regular touch since the war. Though he still had a piece of shrapnel lodged near his heart, he had recovered sufficiently to become a successful doctor again. When I'd said goodbye to Audrey I had told her that if she found herself in London and wanted to see me, she should get in touch through Nigel. He was ringing to say that she wanted to meet me somewhere in Hampstead. We met for lunch, but both of us had confused feelings, especially after her strange behaviour in Ireland, when she had been so daring. In any case, I'd since had time to reflect on my own situation, so our meeting went nowhere, and things sensibly calmed down – a disappointment in some ways; a great relief in others. Audrey had to get back to LA very soon after that, and I didn't see her again for fifteen years, and then only fleetingly. It was a strange, almost unbelievable episode.

When *Carry On Nurse* hit the streets of Britain it was obvious from day one that it was going to do well. I persuaded Nigel Thornton to come and see *Nurse* when it first opened. Though generally hard to please, and a cynical doctor to boot, Nigel left the cinema with tears of laughter in his eyes and said it was the funniest thing he'd ever seen. That, I thought, augured very well indeed.

Ticket sales soon confirmed it as a massive hit, providing Peter Rogers with a strong launch pad for the franchise he was conceiving. I heard nothing more from him about the promised 'slice of the action'. It seemed to me that now the cash had started to pour into the cinema tills for *Nurse*, it had become cheap and easy for him to raise the money for sequels, so he didn't need to involve the actors in getting percentages. I never imagined he'd suggested the deal out of generosity, but I was quite peeved that I ended up doing *Con-*

stable and *Teacher* for the same miserable money.

Call me mercenary if you like, but I still feel thoroughly frustrated that these movies have been shown time and again around the world for almost half a century, earning huge sums for Peter Rogers, while the cast get nothing from the residuals for our part in their tremendous success.

In contrast to Peter's commercial parsimony, though, must be set some considerable acts of personal generosity over the years. For instance, like me he is a great lover of dogs (although his speciality was Alsatians), and when my much-loved Labrador Pippa had her only litter, a van from Moyses Stephens rolled up at the house and the driver offloaded the biggest bouquet I've ever seen in my life – hundreds of pounds' worth. They were from Peter, but they weren't for me or my wife; they were for the proud new canine mum, Pippa.

Quite astounded by this gesture, I presented the flowers to my lovely dog; she staggered to her feet, sniffed them, and promptly peed over them. I don't know what was going through her doggy mind, but maybe, like a number of cynics I know, she thought such an extravagant bunch of flowers was rather over the top.

I've always thought that *Teacher* was the best of the three *Carry Ons* I made. The cast and director were very confident by then, and the franchise was still fresh. Norman Hudis had drawn on his experience in the earlier titles to good effect, though it seems extraordinary now that in 1958 the film censors were so preoccupied by the way I should address the character played by Joan Sims. She was called Miss Allcock, and I was firmly instructed that I should lay absolutely no emphasis on either syllable of her name. The censor had not stipulated what should be going on with my eyebrows and eyes when I uttered the potentially offensive name. However flatly I said it, it was still very suggestive.

A welcome new addition to the cast was the comedian Ted Ray. Ted was immensely popular on the radio, a very experienced stand-up with an inexhaustible supply of material. Many comedians turning to acting find it tricky to adapt to the joint effort involved in film-making. Ted, however, was thoroughly disciplined and turned out to be a convincing actor. At the same time, between takes he kept us all entertained with a constant flow of jokes and observations. On one occasion, when the film was finished, he and I were driven off to do some more publicity for the film in Bury St Edmunds. It was a three-hour drive, and Ted told jokes and stories without repetition, hesitation or deviation the whole way there and the whole way back. He was a delightful man whom I got to know well, and stayed good friends with him and his two sons.

One evening towards the end of *Carry On Teacher* I wandered into the bar at Pinewood. There I found Betty Box who, after a quick kiss and a squeeze, asked me to have a drink with her. I quivered a little. Betty, Peter Rogers' wife, was lovely and, what was more, a successful independent film producer in her own right. By this time, she had produced a number of successful films, including *Doctor in the House* and its sequels, directed by Gerry Thomas' brother, Ralph. She and her husband between them had built up an extraordinary, almost incestuous presence in Pinewood comedy – the dominating genre of British film at the time.

We had our drink and, before she left, she asked if I would meet her for dinner in a couple of days' time. I agreed without hesitation – gentleman actors don't turn down dates with beautiful film producers – but she didn't give me any hint as to why she wanted to see me. When I arrived as arranged at the Dorchester Grill Room – a favoured haunt of mine – I was bounced into considering all sorts of possibilities. She was dressed to maximum effect with an eyeful of cleavage. A bottle of Dom Perignon was peeping over the rim of an ice bucket – very promising!

The mind plays wicked tricks sometimes, and the very idea of naughtiness with Betty was distinctly arousing. Then a vision of Peter Rogers flashed through my mind and, as dinner progressed, it became clear that I'd been suffering from delusions of vanity; it wasn't my body she was after, it was my talent – or, at least, my presence on the screen.

Her first three *Doctor* movies, starring brilliant Dirk Bogarde and the popular Kenneth More, had been solid hits; a franchise, it seemed, had been established and sequels were being planned. For some reason, however, Dirk didn't want to continue and Kenny More was engaged elsewhere, having become a huge star by virtue of the success of *Genevieve* and *Doctor in the House*. Betty was planning to shoot *Doctor in Love* early in 1960. Would I like to take over Kenny's original role? Michael Craig, a close mate, was getting Dirk's part.

Betty may have shared many things with her husband, but not his attitude to rewarding actors. She offered me a very respectable deal and I didn't take long to agree. I saw this as the entrée to a series of movies and, in the next ten years, there were three of them: *Doctor in Love, in Clover* and *in Trouble*. In spite of the gentle ageing which comes to us all, I've yet to be asked to star in *Doctor in Dotage*.

By the time we'd finished *Carry On Teacher, Nurse* was breaking records all over the country. Peter Rogers still hadn't muttered another word about his idea that six of us should have a slice of the cake, and by now it was obvious he was never going to raise it again. We should have known he wouldn't share with anyone except, possibly, Gerry Thomas. Now he wanted to talk to me about the next titles in the series – *Carry on Regardless* and *Cruising*. There would, he said, be nice roles for me, and he assumed I'd be staying on board.

He assumed wrongly.

I could see what was coming and had no intention of getting locked into an interminable series with the risk of getting totally typecast across the world. Even if there'd been a respectable deal in it, I still didn't want to know. But I doubt that would have been on offer, after all I believe he had once said to someone: 'I'll do anything for my actors, except pay them.'

When I told him I wasn't going to carry on (so to speak), he greeted the news with an evil glitter in his eye and uttered what he mistakenly thought would be the ultimate threat.

'I'll get Ian Carmichael!'

'Dear old Ian,' I chortled. 'Do give him my love.'

And that was the end of *Carry On* for me.

Charlie Hawtrey – undoubtedly an asset to the series – also felt that his contribution and experience merited greater recognition and more money. He tried to face Peter down, but was summarily left out of the cast of *Carry On Cruising*, presumably to see the error of his ways. The hard truth was, though, that the *Carry Ons* had brought Charlie far more recognition than anything else he'd done – or ever would do. He bit the bullet, accepted Peter Rogers' measly shilling, and was reinstated for *Regardless*. He remained for a total of twenty-four, until *Carry on Abroad*, in 1972, after which he once again stuck out for more money, this time to be pushed out for good – effectively signalling the end of his career.

By that autumn, perhaps as a result of my attentiveness after I'd returned from Ireland, Penny was heavily pregnant with our fourth child. On 16 November 1959, Roger Quentin Phillips was born not at Casterbridge but at a nursing home in Avenue Road, St John's Wood.

I was delighted with my second son. I had wanted to name him Quentin, after the American war correspondent, Quentin Reynolds, whom I greatly admired. However, Penny, with her friend and new influence in her life, Christine Staley, talked me out of it. They were right, in the way women often are about that sort of thing. Sure enough, poor Roger was deeply embarrassed with Quentin as a second name for most of his childhood, rather in the way I'd been embarrassed about Leslie.

In the meantime, *Carry On Nurse* had opened in New York. The film ends with a wonderful scene in which the irascible Wilfrid Hyde-White – another patient at Haven Hospital – is lying face down on his bed with a daffodil sticking out of his bum. He'd been fooled by nurses that it was an anal thermometer.

Hattie Jacques as Matron comes in and surveys him with lifted brow. 'What on earth *are* you doing?'

Wilfrid turns his head and growls, 'Haven't you ever seen a man having his temperature taken, Matron?'

'Yes,' she gasped. 'But never with a daffodil.'

The audience were still laughing their heads off as they left the cinema and the distributors made sure they were all given a daffodil as a memento. It was inspired. As they poured out into Times Square, clutching their daffodils, passers-by wanted to know what it was all about. Word spread like wildfire, and *Carry On Nurse* went on to become the biggest grossing British film ever in the US.

9 • The Doctor Years

As far as I can remember, by the end of the fifties, youth culture in England consisted of Soho bars selling frothy coffee, Teddy boys, hula hoops, Cliff Richard with a cowlick and the Shadows, while in America, Elvis reigned supreme. The decade that followed seemed to turn everything on its head and, in a way, the not very subtle innuendoes of the *Carry On* films I'd made were forerunners of the massive loosening up of public attitudes to life and sex that began to take place all over the world – although I can't claim to have seen it at the time.

While I carried on making movies back to back, the next two *Carry Ons* had come out to wild success (although none would ever have quite the spectacular reception of *Nurse*), I was tasting for the first time the real impact of being a household name and, for that matter, a household face. The moustache (my own; no glue) had featured in so many of the parts I'd played and had become a permanent fixture, barely having left my visage since. I found I was now being recognised everywhere. This kind of recognition, it would be churlish to deny, can be gratifying, but it's a two-edged sword.

There are times when a little privacy can be welcome. Nevertheless, I've always accepted the public's right to think they own a bit of me.

Kenny Williams, on the other hand, although he loved an audience of any sort when he was performing, loathed being approached in the street or in restaurants by total strangers who seemed to assume he would know them as well as they knew him. He would tilt back his head, gaze down his hooter at the intruder with deep opprobrium and tell them to get lost – and that's putting it politely.

In 1960, I made the film *Weekend with Lulu* with Bob Monkhouse and directed by John Paddy Carstairs, found time to do a new series of the *Navy Lark* on the radio, and several TV shows, as well as directing a play, *Roger VI*, at the Westminster Theatre. Amid all this activity, by far the most significant project for me that year was the making of Betty Box's *Doctor in Love*.

The director, Ralph Thomas, had the same light touch as his brother Gerry, who directed all the *Carry Ons*. They worked in similar ways and indeed sometimes worked together. They were a lovely pair to work for – great fun, and one felt appreciated and cocooned in an atmosphere that created the right mood of humour and lightness so evident in their movies.

The *Doctor* films were already an established franchise, but taking over the role of Dr Tony Burke (colleague of Dr Richard Hare – geddit?) from the immensely popular Kenneth More, I had to be sure to put my own stamp on the character. It was in this role that I uttered on screen the simple word 'Hello' for the first time, in such a way as to imbue it with a plethora of meaning and overtone that immediately caught the public imagination.

It's hard to see how a short, everyday word like 'Hello' could have become a catch phrase, but it did, and shows no signs of going away – hence the title of this little compilation of memoirs. Even now in the streets, when people aren't chorusing 'Ding Dong' at me, they're attempting to reproduce my particular delivery of two simple syllables of greeting – Hell-*oh*. I'm told the word has now been used this way all over the English-speaking world as an instant chat-up line (though no one can ever seem to get it quite right). I've never really escaped it; I even wake up from dreams in which the epitaph on my grave reads, 'Hell*o* … and good*bye*' with 'Ding Dong!' underneath. Heaven forbid.

The making of the *Doctors* was an altogether classier and better-budgeted operation than the *Carry Ons*. Ralph Thomas usually had a stronger script, with more storyline than his brother Gerry had to work with on the *Carry Ons*. Many years later, when I was being interviewed on the BBC's *Pebble Mill* programme, the producer asked if I would mind their house doctor sitting in; of course, I agreed. He told me that my portrayal of Tony Burke in *Doctor in Love* was what had first awakened him, as a youth, to the possibilities, the fun and fulfilment to be had in being a real doctor and, what's more, once he'd qualified, he hadn't felt deluded. Very flattering, though I'm not sure what it says about the NHS!

The film had a cast of good comedy actors.

Michael Craig had the unenviable task of taking over his role from Dirk Bogarde, who at that stage was one of the biggest heart-throbs in the country (and incidentally a great friend of Kay Kendall's). I liked Michael, he was a mate and I missed him when eventually he went to work on Australian TV, got married and stayed there.

We were both enthusiastic members of an eclectic poker school run by our friend Bobby Desmond in his flat in Notting Hill. This was a time when I loved playing poker – not because I thought I was going to get rich from it, more for the total absorption it provided and the friendships we developed away from the tensions of filming and theatre, which is perhaps why it's so popular among actors. Stanley Baker, Michael Craig's brother Richard, comedy writer Jimmy Croft and racing driver Les Leston were all regulars in our school, which included visits from Carmen Silvera. We played every week, often after the curtain came down in the theatre on a Saturday night. Drinking was strictly forbidden; we only had coffee and sandwiches. We set a time limit, usually the next (Sunday) morning, though for one monster session that got extended to Monday morning, which as you can imagine caused a bit of friction with Penny.

Doctor in Love was the first time I'd worked with Virginia Maskell, who played one of the lady doctors. She was a lovely girl, beautiful, intelligent and a super actress. I once went to her house off the Kings Road in Chelsea where, enchantingly, she had an indoor dovecote, which was constantly visited by birds from the garden.

One morning, she didn't show up at the studios. This wasn't like her, so we were all instinctively worried. Our fears were confirmed when we heard that she'd overturned her car on the road leading up to the main gate at Pinewood. Thank God, she was soon all right and back at work, but I always felt there was something delicate about her, and I wondered how she would survive in the hard world of films. I learned later that she'd got herself into a complicated ménage-à-trois with a writer and another mystery person which led, not long after she'd had another big success with *Interlude* in 1968, to a drive to a beautiful spot in the country where, unbelievably, she took her own life. A tragic loss! How can these things happen?

Many years later her son contacted me. He'd been a very small boy when she died and he wanted to know what I remembered about her. I was able to tell him quite truthfully what a really delightful, clever person she was, and that, personally, I loved her dearly. But I couldn't offer any explanation for her sad death – suicide is always so ghastly for the loved ones left behind.

It was a very sad coincidence that another lovely woman from the cast of *Doctor in Love*, Carole Lesley, also took her own life a few years after Virginia. I've never heard the details of that tragedy, but I have found, writing this book, that reviewing one's life can sometimes be extremely painful.

Joan Sims and Fenella Fielding were also in my first *Doctor* cast, along with Irene Handl who was in her usual scene-stealing form, although this is harder to achieve on a film set than on stage, where she was a past mistress at it. One of her ploys was to bring her naughty terrier, Foxy, on to the set, and keep him with her, yapping, generally distracting everyone and drawing attention to Irene. Of course, if you went near her, Foxy would try and have your hand off, or at least a finger or two, providing a few more amazing ad-libs for Irene. For example, there was the scene in *Doctor in Love* when her character had to come to Dr Burke to ask for some contraceptive advice for her daughter. She said, with her trademark simpleness, 'Another doctor told her to take some of them funny little pills, but they was useless; she did put them up, but they kept falling out.' And I had to keep a straight face.

The most striking character in *Doctor in Love* had to be James Robertson Justice, who had already established himself as the irascible though soft-centred and very popular Sir Lancelot Spratt. I hadn't worked with him since we'd both been in Basil Dearden's *Pool of London*, but I'd seen him around Pinewood from time to time. In the end, my final count of films made with him was, amazingly, eleven, and he became a great friend.

James was in his mid-fifties by then, a great bear with a bushy beard and beetle brows who seemed to scare the pants off most people. He was a huge personality, a risk-taker and a raconteur who filled the lens of a camera and brought amazing life to the film when playing opposite him. I had to inject him once and, with no help or make-up, his face went bright scarlet – a great piece of acting.

He always hated learning lines – don't we all – but made no excuses. He simply pasted chunks of script wherever he could read them – on his arm or, in one case, the underside of the bunk he was lying beneath – in fact, anywhere convenient.

Ralph Thomas handled him beautifully. If James didn't feel like doing what he'd been asked, he would roar, 'Bloody hell, man! I'm not doing that!' But somehow Ralph always quietly got what he wanted.

As Sir Lancelot, he oozed power and struck fear into all those around him – on and off set. His mere presence was intimidating and a lot of people in the business took him for a loud, bullying bastard, and a nuisance to deal with. I didn't. I found James fascinating and got to know him extremely well. Once, over lunch, I chatted to him about his childhood.

'My father was a Scottish lawyer,' he told me. 'He made quite a bit of money and sent me to Marlborough. He wanted me to go to Varsity, but I wasn't having any of that. I wanted my freedom and tried my hand at dozens of things – worked on a barge, sold insurance, and started to do a bit of freelance journalism. I thought I'd found my métier, so when I was twenty-four I went over to Canada to try my luck as a journalist there – just before the crash of '29!' He chuckled. 'Timing was never one of my strengths – not like you, Leslie. But when I got back to England, I got a job at Reuters in Blackfriars. Stuffy lot – objected to my coming in for the night shift in my dressing gown and pyjamas. Can't think why. While I was doing that I got interested in politics; life was pretty dull here so I went off to fight with the Spanish commies against the Falangists. That gave me a bit of a taste for war, so as soon as we declared against the Krauts I came back, signed up, and wangled myself a job as an engineer in the navy.'

'I'd no idea you were an engineer,' I laughed with disbelief, thinking of my own massive effort to become a gunnery officer.

'I didn't know the first thing about it, but I fooled them. Got damaged, though, and was invalided out in '44. That's when I tried this game.' He waved vaguely in the direction of the studio where we'd been working. 'I got a few funny little parts and quite enjoyed it. I knew I wasn't an actor, for God's sake, but I needed money to pay for my falconry, wildfowling and plenty of good champagne. And these days I have to subsidise my politics, too.'

'Politics?' I questioned.

'Yes, certainly. I stood as a Labour candidate in Angus and Kincardine in the 1950 election. I had to be a bit careful, actually. I was in a film that had just come out, but had myself billed as Seamus Mor na Feasag. I don't think too many people made the connection – but they didn't elect me either! Anyway, I got lucky after that and went to Hollywood and played Henry VIII for Walt Disney in *The Sword and the Rose*.'

James always downplayed his success as an actor, but I knew that Peter Ustinov, as a director, took him seriously enough, and I thought Betty

Box had been inspired to cast him as Sir Lancelot. They both knew what they were doing.

Working with James, I discovered he had a taste for caviar and champagne, which seemed somewhat at odds with his earlier political tendencies. At some point in his eclectic career, he'd been a racing driver and he still liked fast cars. On one occasion he turned up at the studios in a beautiful gull-winged Mercedes 300SL, with Molly Parkin, the well-known writer, in the passenger seat. We concluded from this that all was not well with his wife, Dilys. I knew there had been some unhappiness in the marriage, not least because their only child had drowned at home in a terrible accident.

However, Molly Parkin apparently took flight when James got a bit too serious and, not long after that, he started an affair with an Estonian aristocrat, Irina von Meyerndorff, with whom he was to live for the rest of his life.

Now that I was seeing a lot of James, I found him delightful – quite unique, well read and extraordinarily erudite. He spoke ten languages, including Gaelic, and if he told a story he always backed it up with a damned good ending.

I was developing an interest in natural gemstones, which was becoming something of a passion, and talking to him about it one day he asked: 'Do you know anything about jade?'

'Actually,' I said, 'it's my favourite stone.'

'Right!' he declared. 'I'll show you a piece of jade the like of which you've never seen. I got it when I was in China just after the war.'

The next day, quite casually, he came into the

bar with a stout leather bag over his shoulder. He put it on the table and pulled out an object wrapped in a square of black velvet. It was a thick chunk of perfect green jade, about 12 x 18 inches, that must have been worth tens of thousands of pounds. I drooled and stroked it before he popped it back into the bag. He never mentioned it again.

Indulging another of his passions, he once brought his favourite falcon, a magnificent peregrine, to the studios and left it on a large wooden perch in his room. The great actor Trevor Howard was working on another picture at Pinewood at the time and came prowling around looking for someone with whom to carouse. Finding the door of James' room unlocked, he let himself in and was instantly attacked by the bored falcon. Trevor, who'd already had a few drinks, went berserk, and rushed out of the room to escape the falcon. He stormed into the bar, where he found James holding court.

'You fucking idiot! What the hell are you doing leaving a lethal bird like that in your room?'

James' pudgy eyelid didn't even twitch. 'What the bloody hell do you mean by going into my room without asking me, you piss-artist?'

James would let slip when talking about women that he was something of a sexual daredevil. That was his business, but I was surprised by an event a couple of years later, when we were making *Crooks Anonymous* with Ken Annakin at Beaconsfield. I wanted to see James, knocked on his dressing room door and, out of habit, went straight in. There was a young girl with him who jumped up, scarlet-faced. I apologised and went straight out, though James didn't seem particularly embarrassed.

Another time, some girls had come to visit Pinewood studios and were in his room. James opened the door and the girls rushed out, obviously upset about something. James laughed as they went. Both these events puzzled me a bit, but the image of the first girl stayed in my memory.

Many years later, I was visiting my stepson, Daniel, at his prep school, Swanbourne House. It was one of those parents' gatherings they put on to show you where your money's going. A young mum came over to me.

'Hello, Mr Phillips. Do you recognise me?'

'I'm afraid not,' I admitted, hoping it wasn't someone I should have known. 'I don't think we've met.'

'We have actually,' she said. 'I was the little girl in James Robertson Justice's room at Beaconsfield years ago when you came in.'

I was absolutely staggered. 'Oh yes, I remember. How nice to meet you again. What are you doing here?'

'I have a son here, in the same year as yours,' she said.

'He's my stepson, actually,' I muttered.

'I thought he might be. That's my lad over there—' She pointed to a happy-looking child about the same age as Daniel.

'How extraordinary that I should meet you here,' I said.

'I expect you're amazed, considering how we first met.'

'Well, yes. I was a bit worried about you.'

'I realised that at the time,' she nodded. 'James was like an uncle to me. You may find this extraordinary, but he was always incredibly kind. My mother and father were very upset when he died – and so was I.'

I never saw her again, or discovered her name.

Doctor in Love came out in 1960 to a great reception in Britain and in the States. Like *Carry On Nurse*, it became one of the biggest grossing British films to date. It is a distressing irony that these two films, which were undoubtedly two of the most significant of my career, should both have earned so much for their producers (Peter and Betty Rogers), and so little for me. Still, we all managed to stay friends and work together again, several times. I was very fond of both of them, though Betty's not with us any more, and Peter's in his nineties. Indeed, Peter still goes into his office every day, with his dog, of course.

In the years following the release and huge success of *Doctor in Love* all over the world, I had film and television jobs running pretty much back to back, and I only ventured on to the live stage when I smelled the prospect of a sure-fire winner – although it's about as easy as picking the winner of the Grand National. That said, I've often managed to be lucky – on both counts.

Curiously, the next Peter Rogers picture I did at Pinewood, *Raising the Wind*, was distributed by Anglo-Amalgamated, whose boss, Nat Cohen, was a keen racehorse owner. When his horse Kilmore was declared to run in the 1962 Grand

National with Fred Winter on board, he told all of us on the picture to back it. I'd known for years, of course, that the worst possible tipsters in the world were owners tipping their own horses. Feeling a bit of a fool, I piled in along with everyone else – plenty of ante-post and a load more on the day. He told us the race plan for the horse was to hug the rails the whole way round, taking the inside track and shortening the journey by a significant amount over two complete circuits of the famous course. Imagine how clever we all thought we were when Kilmore did just that and came in first at 28–1.

Raising the Wind had a similar quality to a *Doctor* film, only not medical but musical. It centred around a group of (it must be admitted, rather mature) music students: me (aged thirty-five), Kenneth Williams and Paul Massie, all aiming for their final exams. My friend, Nigel Arkwright – who, along with his wife, regularly came on holiday with Penny and me – was playing a musician; it was one of the few occasions we'd actually appeared together on film.

The story and the screenplay were by Bruce Montgomery, who was also the musical director and composer of the original music – so it was very much his baby, although Gerry Thomas was directing once again. Bruce was a wonderful musician who'd written or produced the music for many Peter Rogers pictures at Pinewood, where he had his own little musical kingdom. But when it came to the crunch, he was not a great comedy script writer – this was the first and last film he ever wrote. However, I enjoyed working with Bruce and the musical element of the film enormously.

One of the hoops through which the students had to leap in their final exams was to conduct a full orchestra. Each of us in turn would have to conduct part of Rimsky-Korsakov's *Scheherazade*. Bruce went through the rudiments of the process with us and gave us some coaching in how to conduct a full orchestra. I'd had a love of orchestral music since my childhood appearance at Covent Garden, and this had been strengthened by my visits to the Proms with my girlfriend Jane Greelish just before the war. I wanted to do more than just pretend to conduct, and I told Bruce how much I was enjoying it.

'You do it very well,' he said, 'quite naturally, as if you know what's going on in the music.'

'Can I do more?' I asked. 'Try and conduct for real, so the musicians will actually be following me?'

Bruce thought it was a great idea. As a musician first and foremost, he liked the idea of actors doing the job in a way which would convince any music buffs who might come to see the movie.

Over the next four weeks, when I wasn't needed on set, I was working with Bruce on the actual conducting. I learned the piece carefully, got to know my way around the score and identified when each section of the orchestra came in, and how. I became fascinated by this.

A full-scale concert orchestra, the Sinfonia of London, came down to Pinewood to play live for the final conducting scenes. The students were to be filmed for a few minutes each, doing their conducting. They had only to walk in and stand on the dais while the players took their time from the first violinist.

Kenneth Williams was before me and, predictably, over-egged his performance with much contorted arm-waving and extravagant nostril flaring. When he finished, the crew laughed, and so did the orchestra.

I got up for my turn, walked on to the dais, stood for a moment to make eye contact with every member of the ensemble, then lifted my baton and tapped the music stand. I raised it again, confident that I knew every note of the piece I was about to conduct, paused for a moment, and lowered it. To my supreme relief, less than halfway down the stroke, the orchestra came in and were playing. After a minute or two, I felt that they were really following my direction – amazed, but they were apparently prepared to take their lead from what I imagine they had first assumed to be nothing more than a half-witted actor. But I had genuinely taken control of the orchestra. It was the most wonderful feeling – an extraordinary sense of satisfaction to have such complete influence over the music they were making. Bruce, of course, was thrilled.

Gerry Thomas only needed a few minutes' footage of my conducting but, to my great surprise, he let me carry on right to the end of the passage, which he hadn't done with any of the others. It only occurred to me later that perhaps Bruce, proud of his pupil, had persuaded him not to stop me. When I finished the section I'd learned and brought it to a close there was a great, unexpected burst of applause from the film crew; unknown to me various producers and their families had come in to the studio to watch. To my even greater astonishment, there was also a very gratifying rattle as the string players showed their appreciation in the traditional manner by tapping their instruments with their bows. It was a super bit of fun for me. For that reason alone, I will never forget *Raising the Wind*.

During a long run of making films at Pinewood, I witnessed many bouts of excessive behaviour – the results, usually, of too much drink or too much ego – or, in some cases, like Peter Finch, too much of both. I'd often seen him around, having a good time, and remembered with some awe how angry he had become about the German voice they'd dubbed him with when we were making *Train of Events* in 1949.

One winter's day in Pinewood, while Finchie was making *No Love for Johnny* for Betty Box and Ralph Thomas, he went on the rampage with Earl St John, a flamboyant Texan whom Rank had appointed executive producer of the studios a few years earlier. They staggered into the sound stage where I was working and wandered around, very pissed, roaring and joking and generally enjoying themselves. Peter was a big star by now and he was with the boss; everyone was happy to laugh with them until they moved on to cause havoc in the next studio.

An hour or so later, after lunch, I was in the bar having a quick ginger beer with some of the cast before getting back to the studio. The bar and dining-room in Heatherden Hall are an elegant suite of oak-panelled rooms, complete with chandeliers and baronial stone fireplaces. It was a cold winter's day and a brace of spruce logs were blazing impressively on the fire in the bar as we all stood around finishing our drinks. Derek, the longstanding barman and a man of legendary good manners, was starting to close up, complying with the archaic licensing laws of the day. He was just putting everything away when Peter Finch and Earl St John burst in, Earl demanding two large scotches. Derek said he couldn't serve them as it was now after time, and apologised politely.

Finchie wasn't happy about this.

'What?!' he roared. 'If you don't give my friend a drink, I'll put out your fucking fire!'

We stood by, wondering what would happen now.

'I'm sorry, sir,' Derek said again, standing his ground. 'But the bar is closed.' He turned away to finish the process.

Peter Finch fumed for a moment, as if he were about to leap over the counter. Deciding against it, he strode over to the blazing fire, unbuttoning his flies on the way, and without an iota of modesty, he pulled out his willy, pointed it at the leaping flames and peed straight into them with a mighty hiss.

Unfortunately for him, even the quantity of booze he'd drunk couldn't generate enough liquid to douse the fire completely, and it occurred to me that perhaps his pee was so full of alcohol, it actually helped to keep the fire going.

They didn't get the drink they wanted, but they got a lot of laughs.

Amid all my frenetic activity in the film studios, on which I admit, I thrived, I hadn't quite lost sight of the fact that I had a family and a home life to keep going – which was the point of it all. In truth, every spare moment I could, I tried to spend with Penny, the children and whatever hatchet-faced foreign girl we were housing at the time. I realised I was over-working and wasn't seeing as much of them as I should, but I didn't just take off for the golf course at every opportunity, like others in my profession.

When I could get away, I took the whole family off on holiday and, in the summer of '61, with my youngest, Roger, now walking independently, we set off for a couple of weeks in Brittany – near enough to reach without too much trouble; far enough to feel we were abroad. The Swiss au pair, Renata, came with us, somewhat to my discomfort; besides being on the bulky side, I couldn't get on with her at all. There was something altogether too Wagnerian about her for my taste. But Penny needed the help, and was adamant that she was a very able girl; I bowed to her superior knowledge.

The beaches on the Côte Sauvage, between Le Croisic and La Boule were wonderful in those days, and not over-populated. We rented a cottage and we'd spend hours of relaxing fun among the rock pools and the sandcastles, interrupted only by long, lavish picnics.

One day, having found a sheltered, sunny spot

backed by a low cliff, we spread a blanket on the warm sand and laid out a mouth-watering feast of chicken and crusty *fromage*-filled baguettes for the children, and a basket of *fine clairs* for Penny and me. When Penny, Renata and I had finished unpacking the picnic, I looked down the beach to see what had happened to the children.

The Breton coast at this point faces the Atlantic head on and is exposed to the full force of a sea that builds over thousands of miles. A brisk westerly blew up – nothing unusual about that in Brittany or Cornwall, where the trees all bend eastwards like lopsided wigs on their stands. But we didn't heed the warning, and got a terrible shock when suddenly we saw a massive wave racing towards the beach, building up in height and power as it came.

There were a lot of people on the beach by now and we could only gape in horror as the wave swept up and over us all. There was no time to escape; we were caught behind a mini-headland of rocks and enveloped by the charging wall of water. We could see Andrew and the girls struggling towards us as fast as their little limbs would drive them. But we were all caught up and the wave lifted us into the air, sweeping with it our picnic basket, the blankets, my camera, passport, wallet, travellers' cheques – everything a traveller must have – and dashed them against the rocks.

'Where's Roger?' Penny gave a yell that turned into a scream as the wave started to withdraw and she saw the tiny boy being carried out to sea.

The cry had hardly died on her lips when Renata, who only a moment before had been licking her fulsome lips over the picnic, was racing through the water like a galleon in full sail. While we ran after Renata, already knowing we wouldn't get to Roger in time, she charged on like a Valkyrie. We watched, mesmerised, as in the foaming aftermath we saw her catch hold of Roger and start to swim through the powerful backwash towards us. We were almost dragged off our feet by the undertow, but once the giant wave had done its worst, it subsided and the surface of the sea settled down.

The girl emerged triumphantly clutching our youngest child; Penny wept with relief and hugged them both. I think I even managed to give Renata a kiss; the girl had certainly saved Roger's life.

We walked back up to find everything swept away, washed God knows where among the rocks and shingle beyond the high-water mark, or dragged back into the Atlantic to emerge as flotsam on some shore miles away. Thankfully, all the family were safe.

We made our way around the headland and, closing the door after the horse had bolted, perched high up on the dunes behind the small cliffs while we tried to sort out what to do next, although we realised how lucky we were to have everyone safely with us.

The next task was to try to get some money. We contacted Penny's always reliable father who arranged to have money and passports sent over so that we could get back to England. In the meantime, we had to blag our way into dinner in a restaurant who, having heard about the tsunami, believed our story and trustingly gave us credit.

The French were fantastic, and within a few days help had arrived; we were solvent again and ended our holiday on a bright note. I also viewed Renata in an entirely new light – and vowed, in future, never to make judgements solely on appearances. I even, briefly, blessed my mother-in-law's au pair rules. However, none of us have ever forgotten that holiday on the appropriately named Côte Sauvage.

10 • A Man of Many Parts

Once we'd returned to Mill Hill after our misadventure, we forged links with two schools that were to last the next fifteen years. Caroline, my eldest daughter, went off for her first day at a small independent school for girls, The Mount (what a name for a girls' school!), where my second child, Claudia followed her a couple of years later and eventually became head girl.

My eldest son, Andrew, began at Belmont, the prep school to Mill Hill, where he and Roger would continue their schooling. Mill Hill is a fine school, housed in a beautiful, late Georgian mansion amid stunning grounds, which were full of exotic plants discovered by the first owner. Although, like The Mount, it was very close to our house, Andrew boarded for a while, and so did Roger when he went there, but he wasn't too happy being away and was always stealing back home. Despite this early lack of security, Roger became a top student in every subject and eventually went on to Cambridge.

Andrew's connection with Mill Hill was to extend well beyond his own school days. After a getting a degree at Kent University and teaching at Christ's Hospital, he came back to teach at Mill Hill and run Collinson House, where he'd been as a student. His eldest son, Matthew, carried on the chain at Belmont and made a promising start there.

I always took a great deal of interest in the children's schooling and inevitably was in demand to attend all the shows and assorted thespian experiments they put on. I didn't mind; I enjoyed watching the children 'act'. In retrospect, I'm glad that none of them decided on it as a potential career; Andrew had a sniff at it, but in the end used his obvious linguistic skills to teach. In fact, both my sons were much more interested in sport.

I was always aware that educating four children privately was going to be expensive, and, along with all the cost of running a fairly big house to our demanding standards, there was no let up in the need for a regular income, and as large as possible. It was lucky, then, that the work continued to pour in and my children were able to have a first-class education – unlike me. This was without doubt due to Penny's strong endeavour to bring this about. She was single-minded about the importance of a good education for all the children.

I still hadn't broken the habit of accepting any

job offer that was halfway decent. A couple of good movies came my way in the early sixties from Ken Annakin, a director who'd previously given me small parts in *You Know What Sailors Are*, *Value for Money* and, more recently, a lead role in *Very Important Person*, with James Robertson Justice. James also appeared with me in Ken's next two films.

In the neatly turned comedy, *Crooks Anonymous*, I was to take the lead role. Made in black and white, it was the story of a thieves' and safe-crackers' version of Alcoholics Anonymous, a good idea with a strong comedy cast – as well as James, there was also Stanley Baxter, Dick Emery, Wilfred Hyde-White, Arthur Mullard and John Bennett. However, by far the most interesting piece of casting was the female lead.

Apart from one very small part in an episode of *A for Andromeda* for BBC TV, the actress Annakin and his producer, Leslie Parkyn, were considering hadn't done anything, so they arranged a screen test. As I was due to play opposite her, I was invited in for the viewing. I couldn't believe the others' crass reactions, tearing her apart as they looked at her test, although this is quite normal on these occasions.

'Just look at her mouth! It's no good.'

'Yeah, what about that upper lip, for Christ's sake!?'

The poor unfortunate girl was Julie Christie.

Personally, I thought she looked bloody lovely, with the sort of unusual beauty that had every chance of leading to stardom, and we'd be lucky to get her. In the end, after a lot of humming and hawing, they decided to use her in *Crooks Anonymous* opposite me, and Ken went on to put her in his next picture, *The Fast Lady*, in which I also starred with Stanley Baxter, James and a beautiful 1924 Racing Bentley.

These films led quickly to her real break – working with Tom Courtenay in *Billy Liar*. After that, she did *Darling*, with Laurence Harvey and Dirk Bogarde, and never looked back. Nor, as it happened, did she ever mention again the first two pictures she'd done for Ken. I can't say I blamed her. Her new films were at the top of the ladder, and our two weren't quite in that class. But Ken had provided her first break, tough as he was on her. On one occasion he sent her home, complaining that she'd turned up looking too tired and washed out for him to film her. I bet she didn't like it, but no doubt she learned from it. Filming is a tough world and she went on to make it to the top very quickly. I'd love to read what she has to say now about those first movies.

I'd worked with Stanley Baxter before and we were good mates. On *Crooks Anonymous* he produced a great performance. Like Alec Guinness, he had the ability and desire to play men or women, thanks to his extraordinary rubbery face and his versatility.

The next picture I did with Ken Annakin, *The Fast Lady*, was the first of three I was contracted, through Leslie Parkyn, to make for Rank at ten grand a pop. While this deal paled into insignificance when compared with what the Hollywood stars were getting, it was a hell of a good deal by British standards at the time, and I realised that I was now one of the top earners among domestic film stars. All those years of slogging on the stage from Plymouth to Dundee, the endless months in hit West End plays, and the trip to Hollywood, had paid off.

The Fast Lady was right up my street, featuring a 1924 Racing Bentley. As I'd recently upgraded from my Bentley R-type to an S1 (the first of that very elegant series, and still, in my view, the archetypal Bentley), I was delighted to be paired with such a lovely old model.

Lucky Stanley Baxter was playing opposite Julie Christie, not me, and there's no question that she looked absolutely gorgeous in this movie, a Technicolor production with a bigger budget than *Crooks Anonymous*.

The casting worked very well. Julie's character was the daughter of a car manufacturer, played by James Robertson Justice, who hated cyclists. She falls in love with Murdoch Troon (Stanley), a puritanical Scots cyclist. J R-J won't allow Stanley to marry his daughter until he passes his driving test. Enter yours truly, the silver-tongued car salesman with an old car to shift, who says he'll give Stanley lessons if he buys the old banger (the Fast Lady).

It's well set up, well written and directed, and I've always looked back with pleasure on the movie. It also yielded a bonus in the car itself. I borrowed it a few times, and Leslie Parkyn even offered it to me for the friendly price of £100 at the end of the movie. I wish I'd taken him up on it – the car would be worth many thousands now.

I did, however, use it to take my advance driver's test, which came as a serious shock to the poor examiner who met me on Hampstead Heath. It was tremendous fun to drive, and I took the view that if I could pass the test double de-clutching in a 1924 Racing Bentley, I'd passed well and truly. I'm glad to say, I did.

While I was at Beaconsfield making *The Fast Lady*, I had a few drinks with Richard Harris, who was making *This Sporting Life* at the studios. With his customary forthrightness, he put his arm around my shoulder one day.

'I'll tell you something, Leslie,' he said in a primeval Celtic growl. 'You're probably shooting a load of crap – I don't know – but I'm shooting a wonderful, brilliant fillum. Yours is going to make a load of money; ours'll be a financial fockin' disaster.'

He was more or less right: *This Sporting Life* was a great critical success and, of course, became a classic, while *Fast Lady* was a popular and box office success. I had the opportunity to work with Richard many years later in the first two Harry Potter movies.

Soon after we finished filming, Ken Annakin went over to Hollywood where he made several big American comedies including *Those Magnificent Men in Their Flying Machines*. He never asked me to join him in LA, although he got Terry-Thomas over once or twice. Maybe he'd heard me expressing my strong views on life in Hollywood and thought I wouldn't miss it. He would have been wrong, in fact, as I loved working in

LA, but just didn't want to live there.

The second in my Rank three-picture deal was *Father Came Too!*, directed by my old childhood theatre chum and army colleague, Peter Graham-Scott. James Robertson Justice was in it too, and my treasured friend from *The Navy Lark*, Ronnie Barker, who was already showing the genius that was to make him one of the great comedy character actors of all time, and one of my dearest friends in the business.

It was to be the last film I made at Beaconsfield for some years, as the third in my deal with Leslie Parkyn was a long time maturing. When it was finally proposed, the script was so bad that my co-star, the iconic French beauty Brigitte Bardot, took one look and turned it down. Much as I would have enjoyed working opposite this famous animal lover – not to mention her looks – I could only agree with her judgement. Her decision left me with a third of my contract to fulfil.

Having loved Italy on the couple of occasions I'd filmed there, I decided to take a summer holiday there with the whole family – plus the latest au pair, a German girl with unshaven armpits. I vividly remember Marie Anna for, despite skimping on the lady-shavers, she was exceptionally good looking for a Phillips family au pair. Somehow this lovely girl had slipped through the net and she arrived very shortly before we were due to set off, otherwise Penny might have had time to consult with her mother and trade the girl in for something less glamorous.

We all piled into the Bentley and glided over the Alps, via the Simplon Pass, down the spine of Italy to an old fishing port on the coast between Rome and Naples. Sperlonga Mare was at that time a very low-key resort, and I had rented a lovely house a short stroll from the azure Med, surrounded by orange groves filled with wild-flowers and cicadas putting up a racket of trilling and whistling like a crowd of Millwall supporters.

It was as idyllic as anyone could have wished. I've always adored the warm corners of the Med and the family loved the place. Nor did I object to having the view enhanced by Marie Anna. I soon realised that she was massively flirtatious and, frankly, not a little tempting. But, as usual, I made no response, not least because another distraction had recently entered my life back in London, more potent than anything before, and I wasn't at all sure how I was going to deal with it.

After my failure to respond to her advances, it came as no surprise when Marie Anna turned up one evening with a young Italian man. She told me she'd been invited on an all-night trip on his fishing boat.

'What on earth for?' I asked fatuously.

'To catch crabs.'

Looking at the smouldering young man, I thought it very likely she would catch more than that. After that she spent all her free time fishing, and I have an idea that she went back there, and never returned home to Germany – but that was after her brief sojourn with us.

Although I made several films in the early sixties, I was still keen to keep my hand in at live theatre, and a few opportunities always cropped up. The year before, I'd been approached to play the leading role in *The Thurber Carnival*, which was a big hit in New York. I read the script and loved it. Thurber's idiosyncratic wit was marvellous. The Alberys, who were producing, asked me to come down to what was then the New Theatre (now the Albery) in St Martin's Lane.

When I arrived for the meeting, they said Mr Thurber was sitting down in the stalls and would I go on stage and read some of the part. At that point in my career, I didn't generally expect to do auditions. I'd done enough plays for producers to know what I could do, and either they wanted me or they didn't. That's how it was then; nowadays it seems everyone's expected to read or be photographed in some way, whoever they are.

The director was apologetic. 'I do understand, of course,' he said. 'But the problem is that, although Mr Thurber is in the auditorium, he's almost totally blind now. It's no use you going down to the stalls and saying "hello". He wants you to read so he can hear your voice.'

I was amazed. I'd had no idea Thurber was blind. After all, he was as famous for his cartoons as his wonderful humorous writing. I learned afterwards that he had been blinded in one eye as a result of a childhood accident and the other eye had become progressively impaired, until in later years he could only do his cartoons on huge sheets of paper with a thick black crayon.

'I'm sorry,' I said, 'I won't read. But I'll tell you

what I'll do, if it's OK by you. Give me three days, and I'll learn a passage.'

'What do you mean?'

'I've read *The Night The Bed Fell In*, and I thought it was brilliant. But it's quite long; if you give me a date to come back, I'll do it on stage, without the book.'

'Gosh! That'd be great.' He looked delighted and went down to ask Thurber, who said he thought it was a fabulous idea.

Three days later, I returned as promised and delivered the whole piece without drying. Thurber asked me to come down to the stalls afterwards.

'You've just done me a great service,' taking my hand, he said, with genuine warmth, obviously thrilled, 'because I've always written in what I call English, but there are those who think, because I'm American, I can't do that. Now I've just heard you deliver my lines, in perfect English. I want you to do my production.'

The producers asked me to join them for dinner at the Connaught Hotel where they told me they definitely wanted me for the lead. 'But we also need someone really good for a big character part. Have you any ideas?'

'Ronnie Barker,' I suggested, knowing he'd be just right for it.

'Who?' one of the Alberys asked. 'What does he do?'

'He's a fantastic character actor,' I told them. 'You may not have heard of him yet, but he's in *The Navy Lark* with me, and he's one of the most versatile actors I've ever worked with.'

They said they'd think about it, but looked

doubtful. I subsequently learned that they'd ignored my recommendation, because, I gathered, they wanted 'a name'. Ironically, when I next saw Ronnie he was working in a show for the Alberys, and they hadn't even realised!

The production wasn't due to start for a while, but I kept myself open because I liked the part. However, before production plans for *The Thurber Carnival* had been finalised, I was offered the lead in a new play which was all set to go on tour. When eventually the Thurber play did open, a long time later, somewhat to my regret, it did so without me or Ronnie Barker. Sadly, by then James Thurber had died and the play, despite its success in New York, flopped disastrously in London.

Towards the end of 1962, I was devastated by the death of my friend, Nigel Arkwright. He'd been very close for a long time and, although I'd lost an awful lot of good friends during the war, comrades from the Durham Light Infantry and men I'd got to know from the Scottish units on the way through Chadacre, Nigel was the first who'd died since then – and this was made worse by the tragic manner of his going.

Poor Nigel had just started work on a new picture. He'd gone out with some of the other actors for a quick lunch but, complaining of a dodgy stomach, he'd opted for a pint of bitter and nothing to eat. Afterwards he went back to the studio and collapsed in the studio restaurant. His colleagues laid him down and called a doctor. Less than half an hour later, he was to die on that floor. A post mortem discovered he'd died as a direct result of being laid down and choking on his own vomit. It was an awful way to go. He was still young; he loved life and his lovely wife – the 'Other Penny' Williams. He got a great deal of pleasure from his work and was one of those friends I always enjoyed seeing. Inevitably, his funeral was a gloomy day for us. It was like the closing of a much-loved chapter in the story of our life. He had been my best man back in 1948 and, with his Penny, had shared the early years of married life with us. We'd all been on holiday together several times in Jersey, which our kids had loved as much as we did.

My next play was *The Big Killing*, a clever thriller written by TV dramatist Philip Mackie. I played a racing driver, a smooth, evil shit who's been offered a bet by a rich landowner that he can't kill the man's wife and get away with it – at odds of £25,000/£1. It was a tricky part to play effectively, but I was reasonably confident I could pull it off. After touring, the play came in to open at the Prince's Theatre (now the Shaftesbury), where it did well, even attracting a visit from Her Majesty with Lord Mountbatten in tow. It was also to produce other, more profound, repercussions for me.

The ASM and understudy to the leading lady was a thoroughly alluring choc-eyed beauty with lustrous dark hair by the name of Caroline. Though she was only nineteen, she already had some dramatic experience; at fifteen she'd been ASM at the Royal Court, before going on to

RADA. She had a bizarre family background which must have been a major influence on her, making her sophisticated beyond her years. Her mother was the well-known writer and demi-bohemian, Penelope Mortimer, an extraordinary, vivid person, with four acclaimed novels to her name and one just completed, about to be published, called *The Pumpkin Eater*.

In 1947 Penelope had married the barrister/playwright John Mortimer, but before that she'd had what could be described as a self-indulgent love life, resulting in four daughters. Madelon and Caroline were by her first husband, Charles Dimont; Julie was by Ken Harrison, and Deborah by Randall Swingler. With John Mortimer she went on to have a lovely fifth daughter, Sally, and a son, Jeremy (now a top BBC radio director, who I worked with on *Les Misérables* on Radio 4).

When I met Carrie (as I knew her), I was thirty-seven, but the eighteen-year gap between us was irrelevant; Carrie was passionate, strong, opinionated and far too confident to settle for a relationship with a man her own age. The mutual attraction was palpable and profound. Meeting her presented me with a dilemma. I had been by most standards – and especially by those of my profession – a loyal and faithful husband. I wasn't the straying type. It was in my character to be loyal, but in this case such was the attraction that Carrie did not have to pursue me to catch my interest. Nevertheless I had to battle with my conscience before I allowed anything to happen, and I held back for some time, reluctant to get involved in anything that might adversely affect my family.

Even then, in the early days of our relationship, I didn't think it would, or could, last. Despite my wife's growing tendency to distance herself from my career and her objections to the ridiculous amount of work I was doing, I still loved her and respected her as the mother of my children.

Inevitably, as the play's run continued, Carrie and I came together more, and began seeing each other alone. I met her mother and some of her siblings. I was certain at first that they didn't consider me very suitable, and not just because I was older. Penelope Mortimer took a long-nosed view of the kind of light comedy in which I'd had so much success. Perhaps, like many people, she didn't appreciate that, from a technical point of view, it was often a great deal harder to bring off than straight drama.

I soon found I didn't like too much direct confrontation with Carrie's mother and generally avoided it when I could. Our affair began to gather momentum, although it's quite possible that it would have run its course and petered out – as thespian liaisons so often do when their lives move on – had it not been for the interference of one of my wife's closest friends. She was an actress with a women's theatre group and had formed a very close bond with Penny. She was always hanging around the house and I must confess I didn't like her.

She had a friend in the cast of *The Big Killing* and her antennae had picked up the rumour that Carrie and I were having an affair even before it had started. She conveyed the gossip posthaste to

312

Penny, who was inconsolably bitter. Of course, I'd noticed rumblings of dissatisfaction in her, but on the whole we got along well and made a good team when it came to running the family. She knew that I would be tempted from time to time. She also knew I worked bloody hard, making hay for the possibly brief season that the sun might shine on my career, in order to maintain the high standards we had both set. We were six interdependent people, or so it seemed to me, who would all suffer if we split up. But Penelope was adamant; she wanted a divorce. Until that point I'd been uncertain how far my relationship with Carrie would go.

In the end I was left with no choice but to move from Perk House, the home on which I had lavished so much time and work, and which I loved just as much as Penny did. There was inevitably an ambivalence about my situation now. On the one hand, I knew I'd have given anything to keep my family together, but there was no compromise, it seemed. When I realised this situation had become impossible and that Penny was determined to divorce me, I wanted it done as calmly as possible. I loved my children and would always go on looking after them, sparing them any unnecessary anguish. Unfortunately, divorce is always hell but worse when children are involved. Whatever it took, I was going to make it a hundred per cent certainty that I never lost them for a moment.

At that time, I was appearing in *Our Man at St Mark's*, a popular BBC TV comedy series about an unusual vicar. I was being very well paid for it, too, and for a while was the highest paid TV actor in Britain. Sadly, this was brought to an end by the publicity surrounding the rumours of our marriage break-up. Stories of vicars (even those who merely portrayed them on the small screen) having affairs were meat and drink to the low-brow press. So I had to give up the vicarage of *St Mark's*, to be replaced by a friend of mine, Donald Sinden.

However, the drama progressed in more ways than one. As eccentric as they were, Carrie was close to her mother and sisters. Penelope was a highly strung, complex character, about whom there was something vaguely self-destructive. She was a woman of sharp, wicked wit and cynical perceptiveness. Carrie and I used to refer to her as the TCM: Tiny Complicated Mother.

In the beginning, I saw quite a lot of Penelope. The autumn after we'd met, Carrie and I were invited on a publicity voyage to Istanbul aboard a new Turkish cruise ship, the SS *Ackdeniz*. Penelope had been unwell and Carrie asked her if she'd like to join us. She agreed, and we flew down together to board the ship at Marseilles.

Penelope had been going through one of her great glooms, triggered by a family crisis. She was also on edge because her new novel, *The Pumpkin Eater*, had just been published and the reviews hadn't yet appeared. The ship contained a motley selection of what would now be called celebrities, and journalists. Penelope was involved with a German journalist, a handsome, self-assured man who may or may not have been an officer during the war.

When we reached Naples, Penny bought a copy of the *Daily Express* and found a review of her book and a story about her 'nervous breakdown'. She rushed off and was violently sick in the loo. By the time we reached Istanbul, more favourable reviews had appeared, prompting Penelope, in a complete reversal of her earlier gloom, to sit in the back of a horse-drawn *carozza* singing, 'I'm a genius; I'm a genius!'

I enjoyed the time I spent with the Mortimer family. Sunday lunches when they were all around the table were very memorable. John would carve the joint, helping himself to slithers of beef as he did it, always keeping up a barrage of witty conversation and banter with his wife and all her children. Penelope's mother would sometimes be there – the splendid widow of a distinguished country clergyman. She loved word play and suggestive puns. When playing Scrabble, she would go to great lengths to shock us by placing four-letter words. Once, on spotting a colossal flower arrangement in the middle of the dinner table, she cried, 'Oh, what a lovely erection!'

She must have liked me, at least a little, because she gave me the most lovely red rose to put into my garden when finally I found myself a new house. It blossoms there still.

Curiously, I didn't get to know John really well until several years later, when he and Penelope were no longer together and he came to see me in a Chekhov play, subsequently asking if I would play a judge in two of his television dramas.

After *The Big Killing*, I took over a lead role in *Boeing Boeing* at the Apollo. I'd once seen an unimpressive production of the original French play in Paris, but the English translation worked a lot better and the quality of the London production was much higher, making it an unexpected hit. It was a complicated comedy about two men who play the airline schedules to run busy sex lives with a string of air hostesses. My part had originally been played by my old chum David Tomlinson, who told me he'd had a riot in the part. David was a delightful, funny man, who loved to play games on stage and off. Patrick Cargill, another great friend, was my co-star. Business at the box office was already brisk, and it went from strength to strength, so that it took over my evenings for the next two years or so and was one of the most enjoyable stage comedies I ever played in.

One evening in late November, I came into the theatre ahead of the performance to do an interview with a journalist from one of the Sunday papers. We were just settling down in my room when the stage doorkeeper hurried in to ask if he could put through a phone call for the journalist. Looking suitably embarrassed and apologetic, the journalist picked up the phone. A few moments later he let out a great shout of despair and collapsed as if he'd been sandbagged.

'What on earth's happened?' I asked, thinking it must have been some personal tragedy.

'That was my wife – she's American. Her sister just called from the States. Kennedy's been assassinated!'

'What!' I gasped.

He nodded dumbly, in a state of shock, which to some extent I shared. I was certainly conscious that this was an absolutely momentous event.

'Look,' he said, 'I'm sorry, I can't do this now. My wife's hysterical.'

I quite understood. I didn't much feel like it myself.

By now the management had heard the news, and we gathered to discuss what changes we needed to make to the script to avoid causing any offence. We didn't think, in any case, that many people would turn up.

However, either because they hadn't heard, or didn't want to sacrifice the price of their tickets, we had a nearly full house who laughed as loudly as any audience. We did make the few cuts we thought judicious, but I don't know that anyone would have minded if we hadn't.

During the run, I had one or two surprising visitors back stage. One of these was Minna Wallis, the powerful Hollywood agent who had been so snooty when I'd turned up at her party in LA with Kay Kendall. For some reason she was accompanied by Hugh Hefner, proprietor of the massively successful Playboy empire (where did all those Bunnies go, I wonder?). In contrast to our first encounter, she was very gracious this time around and treated me as a star.

More flattering, perhaps, was a visit from Van Johnson, the veteran American star, who came in wearing his trade-mark red socks. When I say veteran, I mean he was eight or nine years older than me, and was thinking of doing my part in a movie version of the play. He was very charming, and generous.

'Listen, Leslie, you're so good in this, you should be doing the movie. I couldn't do it better than you.' What a nice chap!

As it turned out, Minna's brother, Hal Wallis, produced that movie, with Tony Curtis and Jerry Lewis in the starring roles. Perhaps they were both clients of Minna's.

I was also visited one evening by a gruffly affable James Robertson Justice, who seemed to be in every film I had made of late. He was all on his own.

'Hello, Leslie. Just thought I'd come round and see you. What about a drink?'

It was unexpected, but I was delighted to see him. We had most recently worked together a few months before in *Father Came Too!* I offered him a glass of champagne and we settled down for more anecdotes from his extraordinary past.

When he left, we promised to keep in touch. 'See you for the next *Doctor* otherwise,' I joked. As it happened, I missed appearing in *Doctor in Distress* due to an irreversible conflict, but Betty Box had promised I'd be in the next.

There was more reminiscing when Fay Davies, now head of the box office at the Apollo, would drop by my room. Eighteen years earlier, I had been No. 3 to Fay's No. 2 just down the road in the Lyric box office. We had a great time recalling all the pranks our No. 1, Bobby Roberts, used to get up to.

It was Fay who relayed to me the details of a drama in the Apollo box office. The manager,

Grimond Henderson, had been coming down the stairs from the stage door when he spotted someone he didn't recognise going up. A short while later there was uproar from the cast when they discovered a thief had been through their dressing rooms. Grimond rushed out and caught sight of the man running off down Shaftesbury Avenue with a cloth bag in his hand. He sprinted after the thief and saw him leap into a taxi, which promptly got stuck in a jam. Thinking quickly – or not at all – he caught up, leapt into the cab and struggled with the robber for a few moments, trying to wrestle the bag from his hand, while the cabby navigated Piccadilly Circus in some consternation. The thief broke free and managed to get out of the taxi on the other side, still clutching the spoils, dodging the traffic streaming up and down the Haymarket. Grimond, determined not to be beaten, shot out of the cab to give chase, only to be brought up sharply by a bellow from the cabby. 'Oi!! 'Oo's going to pay my bloody fare, then?'

But Grimond was already in full flight, screaming, 'Stop thief!' with no one taking any notice, until the robber found another cab, jumped in and got away with all the loot.

11 • The Producer

In 1965 I returned to Pinewood for the first time in nearly four years to play Dr Gaston Grimsdyke in *Doctor in Clover,* my second of the series, with Betty Box producing and Ralph Thomas directing. With hindsight, it was the best of the *Doctors* for me and it was no coincidence that we were howling with laughter through the rushes most days.

My character, in order to attract a bride, a condition of his taking up a high-powered job in America, tries to make himself look younger, starting in Carnaby Street and getting worse. Jack Davies had written a string of comic scenes that work wonderfully, while Ralph was on top form and brought more sophistication to the picture than would have been possible in the '50s.

John Fraser, who played my brother, Dr Miles Grimsdyke, was a good-looking, affable chap. We sometimes lunched together and one day when we were making our way to the restaurant, he told me about his small Georgian cottage in the Chilterns, which he wanted to sell. I love Georgian architecture and Carrie had grown up in the Chilterns, where Penny and John Mortimer had lived. 'Where, exactly?' I asked.

'Bledlow Ridge, just west of High Wycombe.'

'I'd love to see it some time,' I said.

John looked at his watch. 'If we skip lunch, we

could get there, have a look at it and be back in time for the afternoon session.'

My motto has always been, *If t'were done, t'were well t'were done quickly,* (though I didn't write it myself). 'Good. Let's go, then.'

The house was perfect for our purposes – pretty, warm, with wonderful views of the Wycombe Valley and a sweet nineteenth-century garden. By that evening, the deal was done, we shook hands and I was the new owner of Retreat Cottage, Bledlow Ridge.

It was an enchanting cottage and during the long period when all was not well at Mill Hill, it made a perfect hideaway where I could escape with the children, and Pippa the yellow Labrador could join us on long country walks. We cooked and entertained there, and lavished our enthusiasm on the garden. I even lived there for short periods when I was filming at Pinewood. It was with considerable sadness that I parted with the place forty years later.

Clover had a marvellous cast: James RJ, of course; Joan Sims again – as heavenly as ever to work with; the lovely Shirley Anne Field – so sexy she could raise the temperature of a corpse by just lifting an eyebrow; clever beanpole Jeremy Lloyd, a great friend who had been in *Crooks* and *VIP* with me; and a gang of comedians who had cleverly turned themselves into actors – Arthur Haynes, Eric Barker, Norman Vaughan among them, and two super comic actors, Terry Scott and Alfie Bass.

I was fond of Eric Barker, but he was a dreadful

worrier, and I felt it my duty to tease him a little, perhaps to help cure him of it. When the camera was on him for quite a long speech, I placed myself right behind him, where he couldn't see me, even from the corner of his eye, but I was visible to everyone else over his shoulder when the camera rolled (Alan Hume behind the lens, of course). After he'd delivered about three lines, I started very deliberately and extravagantly to pick my nose. Alan managed to hold it together, and Gerry Thomas let it roll, but everyone else on the set began to crack up and Eric sensed that he was being sent up.

Determined not to abandon his lines or be seen to give in, Eric ploughed on to the end of his speech before he finally capitulated and spun round to vent his frustration on me. He forgave me later, and the rushes next day were hilarious.

Wrapping *Clover* was rather as I imagine the last day of term at boarding school must be, when you know you'll all be getting back together and picking up your friendships again as soon as the holidays are over. As it turned out, though, we didn't start making *Doctor in Trouble* until 1970.

Two years had passed since Penny had started divorce proceedings against me. It had been a long, harrowing process; more than anything in the world, I'd wanted to keep our family together and would have been willing to make any sacrifice in order to achieve that. But it seemed divorce was inevitable, and in 1965 the legalities culminated in a decree absolute.

Despite Penny's antagonism, I refused to be

deterred from seeing the children, whom I adored. I had no intention of shirking my paternal responsibilities either: I paid off the mortgage on Perk House and whenever the family went off on holiday I'd wait till they'd gone before entering the house to empty the fridge, check that all the windows and doors were locked, and deal with any repairs that needed doing, so that everything would be in order when they came back. Keeping all this going, and making certain that I saw as much as I could of my children while under a lot of pressure from work, was not easy.

Penny's friend was still lurking around Perk House, and upset me one last time when Penny took the children to Corsica and left my dog with her. Pippa became seriously ill and she had my beautiful golden Lab put down without even consulting me. It was a black day when I found out. Pippa had been my friend since the morning I'd driven her home as a puppy and she'd rested her head on my knee the whole way, and I loved her almost as much as my children.

I'd been in *Boeing Boeing* at the Apollo for over two years by this time; *The Navy Lark* was still going strong, and I was getting so tired shuttling between jobs that I succumbed to Nigel Thornton's suggestion that I should get myself a driver for the Bentley.

A friend recommended one of the doormen from Annabel's, Mark Birley's new Berkeley Square nightclub, which had been an instant, if exclusive, hit. This burly individual (the doorman, not Mr Birley) was looking for a job as a chauffeur, and he seemed like a handy sort of chap to have around. It went well enough for the first week or two, but one night as we pulled up at a red light on the way home from the Apollo, the driver of the car alongside said something aggressive to him and accompanied it with what the police call an 'offensive gesture'.

I watched appalled as my driver stiffened and the hairs on his neck prickled like a hedgehog. Suddenly he bounded from the car, opened the door of the adjacent vehicle, pulled out the driver and pummelled him like a loosely packed bag of porridge, until the poor man lay limp and senseless across the bonnet of his car. Dusting off his hands and giving his knuckles a quick flex, he came back, climbed into his seat and drove us away, leaving the other vehicle sitting at a green light with his victim still slumped across the bonnet.

I protested with an, admittedly, fairly hopeless demand that he should go back and help the man, but he ignored me. I was worried that, as the employer of this wild beast, I might be held responsible for any damage or, in this case, GBH he had caused while in my employ. When I consulted my lawyers, they told me there wasn't a problem, but I certainly wasn't going to take the risk and decided my chauffeured days were over.

An old acquaintance of mine who did like to be driven was the up-and-coming film director Michael Winner. He was more or less established by then, having made a string of low-budget pictures that had done well in the burgeoning 'youth' market, as he was to do again with the big-budget Hollywood *Death Wish* films.

Back in 1950, he'd turned up on the set of *Pool of London* as a cub reporter trying to chivvy the cast for interviews. I was the only member of the cast prepared to talk to him. Years later he asked me to lunch in the Lyons Corner House in Coventry Street as a retrospective thank you for being so kind to him in his struggling youth.

'Do you remember me?' he asked.

'Yes, of course I do. You interviewed me for the *Hackney Times* or some such organ – about fifteen years ago.'

He was delighted and asked me if I wanted a part in his new movie, *You Must Be Joking!* – a phrase he frequently used himself. It turned out that the picture was stuffed with old friends of mine – James Robertson Justice (again), Terry-Thomas, Wilfrid Hyde-White, and Denholm Elliott, with whom I hadn't worked since David Lean's *Sound Barrier*. It was a piece of swinging slapstick, based on the story of a group of soldiers going about an initiative test, culminating in their pinching the Lutine Bell from Lloyds of London (something I was quite tempted to do myself years later after suffering substantial losses there).

Michael had got himself a reputation for being a very daring director who didn't care what he did or who he upset. He had borrowed an apartment above Harvey Nichols, which was meant to be my character's flat, and smashed the whole place up, seemingly oblivious to the consequences, so long as he got the shots he wanted. The owner of the property was expecting to have it back in pristine condition at 8 p.m. God knows how he wriggled out of that one.

On another occasion he was exasperated with an actress who couldn't deliver what he wanted, and chivvied her in front of the whole cast and crew.

'Come on, for Christ's sake, darling!' he spluttered. 'Put some life into it. You did promise me you'd do anything I wanted if I gave you the part!' This sort of joke was not necessarily designed to win friends and influence people.

It was great to see more of Denholm Elliott, whom I'd always liked. He and my *Navy Lark* colleague, Jon Pertwee, who was also in the film, suggested that I should come out and spend some time in Ibiza where they'd both bought houses and were having a wonderful time. I'd never been there, and the idea appealed very much to Carrie.

The following spring, we made time for a short holiday between jobs and set off for our first visit to this Balearic island. In those days, one flew to Valencia, unloaded one's baggage, cleared Spanish customs and passport control, lugged the bags back on the plane and flew the last hundred miles over the Mediterranean to Ibiza.

The island lay like a dun-green stone on a cloth of aquamarine silk, and as we crossed the southern sierra to touch down, we were surprised to see that most of the higher ground was covered in thick pine forest. The whole island at that time of year was much greener than I'd expected, although it was already bathed in sunshine. The airport then was a primitive affair, though charming: a few shanty sheds with straw roofs and a fly-blown bar where people hung about waiting for friends to arrive. We felt transported back thirty years and were immediately enchanted.

There were no buses and only a couple of ageing taxis to take us into town. Carrie's eyes lit up when she saw the place. If you didn't mind the clusters of sun-bleached proto-hippies spilling from the bars (which we didn't), Ibiza was completely unspoilt, and still with its integrity intact.

From the start we were hooked by the wonderfully laid-back air and the easy-going attitude of everyone on the island. It was less than a decade since artists and beatniks from Northern Europe and America had started colonising the place. There was little history of tourism and, at that time, no signs of the depredation it tends to bring. It was still a glorious and peaceful haven for artistic people.

We stayed at a delightful small hotel, white adobe outside, thick-walled and cool inside, with a terrace overlooking the sea on the southern outskirts of Ibiza town. The next day we drove our hire car up the east coast to the small town of Santa Eulalia del Rio. As instructed, we made our way first to a bar, *El Caballo Negro*, owned by an Englishman named Sandy Pratt.

While we relaxed and downed a few lunchtime cocktails, it became clear that Sandy's Bar, as it was always called, was the hub of the local ex-pat community. Sandy himself was a one-off – known, with great respect, as 'Lord of the Island'; I prefer to call him 'Peter Pan'. He never seemed to age – or charge his regulars for drinks. He

327

chalked them up somewhere and relied on one's honesty and memory to pay. He was loved by everyone, and still is forty years on.

Diana Rigg, Terry-Thomas, Nigel Davenport, Laurence Olivier and Robin Maugham were all regulars, as well as Denholm Elliott and Jon Pertwee, who soon joined us there. What a welcome!

That evening we went back to Jon's house – a squat, somewhat enlarged, white Eivissenc farmhouse, like a misshapen sugar lump – which stood between clusters of Aleppo pines on the side of a hill in the village of Jesus, with a staggering view over Ibiza town. Gregarious as always, Jon had built up a big group of chums, imports and locals, to keep him entertained; he immediately organised a tremendous party for us, with invitation by a single card put up in Sandy's Bar and bush telegraph – no mobiles then.

I played the bongos; Jon told stories and sang. He was a brilliant entertainer and I always felt he had more talent than ambition and never really made use of all that he had to offer. Although he and Denholm were friends, they were very different sorts of people; Denholm was more inward looking and an instinctive actor whose career just got bigger and bigger in a way that allowed him to hang on to his distinctive identity.

Despite the contrast between the kind of work Denholm and I did, he'd often said he admired my comedic skills and the way I handled an audience; he claimed he was too scared to do it himself. In return, I loved the slightly sleazy and eccentric characters he played so well. I also admired him for his wartime bravery, when he'd flown for the RAF, been shot down in 1942, and festered for the next three years in a Stalag PoW camp in Silesia. We became a mutual admiration society, although, as time went on, our roles were somewhat reversed as I became more involved in serious acting and the kind of parts he'd been good at, while he played more comedy.

He'd been married to Virginia McKenna in 1954, but only for a few months; later he'd married an American girl called Susan Robinson. They'd come to Ibiza a few years before and had a house built on the northern slope of the Eulalia valley. Susan had recently given birth to their first child, Jennifer. I enjoyed seeing Denholm very much, and Carrie and I spent a lot of time with them as we joined in the Ibicenco life. We'd only come over to see a couple of mates, but quickly found ourselves swept away by the place. When I told Denholm I was thinking of buying a house on the island he was delighted and keen to look after my interests.

'It's very easy to get stitched up,' he warned. 'One has to be very careful about the legal and money side of buying property here. It's full of pitfalls.'

When he'd first come, he'd trusted a chap who filleted him like a kipper and very nearly ruined him, he told me. 'It happened to some friends of mine, too. But I can put you on to someone who'll help you find a place and deal with anyone you have to buy from, which can be tricky if you don't speak Eivissenc.'

Thus I met Chiqui, a lovely Spanish/Ibizan lady, and her German husband Messcher-

329

schmidt, an artist. I liked them both on sight. She was well connected, Catholic, of course, and had set herself up as a go-between for tourists like me who wanted to live there, and the locals – or, as we called them in those days, the 'peasants' (whose offspring now all speak fluent English and drive BMWs). She knew a lot of the indigenous families; they trusted her, and so did I.

We'd already decided that Santa Eulalia was the place for us – small and not too over the top, with the benefit of Sandy's Bar and Denholm close by, so we decided to look in that part of the island. A few days later, Chiqui announced that she had three places for us to see, all old *fincas* in varying states of decrepitude.

The first we saw was in the hills on the western edge of the village, approached by a long, dusty track snaking between gnarled old trees. Perched on the side of a small mountain and bounded by drystone walls, it was a very charming little *finca*, some two or three hundred years old, with no sanitation or electricity.

Absolutely beautiful and very basic, it hadn't been lived in for years. Although devoid of modern conveniences, its water supply came from an ancient brick *cisterna* sporadically fed by a small spring. Animals belonging to the family who owned the place were wandering about, tugging away at the untamed vegetation surrounding it. It had a wonderful outlook, straight across the river valley to Denholm's house on the far side and the sea in the distance to the right. The only drawback was the sunset. The *finca* was perched on the north-eastern slope of the mountain behind which the sun dropped long before it set, though later we found we could enjoy a beautiful reflected sunset on the other side of the valley, and naturally we had wonderful dawns that encouraged one to be up and about early, bursting with energy to get down to the local market and buy up the best vegetables.

As we walked around it that first time, the look on Carrie's face told me she already loved it as much as I did, but Chiqui whisked us off to look at two more houses nearer the coast. Both were charming in their way, but afterwards we asked her to take us back to the first. We looked all over it again, established what land was on offer with it, and discussed the possibility of installing some kind of electricity. After half an hour, my mind was made up. I said I'd have it. The process of transferring ownership was extraordinary and very convoluted. The head of the family, Señor Plannel, couldn't write and signed all documents with his own distinctive 'X'. He was a lovely man, though, and as the years went by, he became a close *amigo*.

I returned to London in a state of great excitement; after all, I'd only popped over to spend a few days in the sun with friends and now I was leaving as a resident myself. I was so thrilled I could hardly think of anything else, although, of course, as soon as I was back in London, reality and the need to pay for the place soon brought me down to earth.

Acting in films had kept me very busy for the past ten years, but of late I'd become more interested in the business side of the industry and had started working on a big new project. The time had come to invest some of my own money as well as my acting talent: I was going to produce a film. I was more excited about this than I let on. John Gale, the energetic producer of *Boeing Boeing*, had agreed to join me. Along with a third director, Susanne Skyrme, heir to a sugar fortune, we formed Cyclone Films. John then brought in an assistant, Martin Schute, for the first project.

We found a script we liked and I persuaded the Rank Organisation to make it the last leg of the three-picture deal I'd done with them through Leslie Parkyn. I had completed only two films (*Fast Lady* and *Father Came Too!*). The third, in which I was supposed to have played opposite Brigitte Bardot, had fallen out of bed. Obviously I felt cheated I hadn't fallen into bed with Brigitte B; instead I was left with an outstanding commitment to make one more film for them. Rank told me I could either wait until a better script came along, or I could give them their money back – which didn't sound like a good idea; I had a better one.

I would produce a film in which I would also act, thereby fulfilling my contract, only they'd be putting up the bulk of the production cost. I showed them the script by David Osborn; set somewhere in the Middle East – Egypt or Israel – it revolved round the glamorous editor of a woman's fashion magazine who turns jewel thief. They liked it and told me to get on with it, thus guaranteeing funding and distribution for our first production.

We set up a base in John Gale's office above the Strand Theatre, and started planning and casting.

While all this was going on, I found time to film six episodes of a BBC comedy called *Foreign Affairs*, in which I had the lead as a British diplomat, with the brilliant Ronnie Barker playing my Russian counterpart. It's a mystery the series has never been revived. It showed Ronnie at his character-playing best. Not long afterwards, the first series of *The Two Ronnies* took off, and Ron's career with it. We were already good friends through half a dozen years of *The Navy Lark*, which made *Foreign Affairs* especially enjoyable to do. I'm delighted to say that he and I stayed very firm friends right up until his sad death in 2005.

He was a lovely, strong, eccentric man, meticulously tidy and organised. We were both great collectors, not to say hoarders, but where I just put things in rooms to gather dust and then forgot about them, he would go to great pains to show his appreciation by arranging them in elaborate display cabinets. His wife, Joy, was enchanting, too. They lived in the depths of rural Oxfordshire and for years they gave a party every August for all their close friends, which everyone came to if they could. I can't recall any actor more talented and popular than dear Ronnie B.

Talking of treasures, I still have a car I bought at the time John Gale and I were preparing our movie. Nigel Thornton, my old army doctor, had a friend who sold cars from a Park Lane showroom and he told me about a brand-new

Mercedes convertible he had for sale.

'Would you like to see it?' he asked.

'I'll have a look,' I said, but I didn't give it a lot of thought.

A few days later, John and I were in the office above the Strand, poring over budgets for the new film, when the stage doorkeeper came up, wheezing a little.

'There's someone in the road outside who wants you to put your head out the window and have a butcher's.'

Puzzled, and expecting to see an aspirant actress, I leaned out and looked along the Strand. In the road, parked with the hood down, was a beautiful, dark metallic green Mercedes drophead 220SE. I told John I was going down to look at it.

'Here it is,' the salesman said smugly. 'The last off the line.' He handed me the key and opened the driver's door for me.

What could I do?

I let myself in and drove it away. I eased into the traffic on the Strand, and made a long block via Northumberland Avenue and the Embankment. When I got back, the chap was still smiling smugly, as well he might. The Merc was magnificent, quite the most impressive motor I'd ever driven, and aesthetically superb.

'Well?' he asked.

'It's lovely,' I said. 'I'll have it.' And carried on casting my picture – a job I enjoyed very much.

To give the film the best possible chance of worldwide distribution, we aimed to have an international cast. Gene Barry (an American)

334

took the lead role, Cyd Charisse (American) and Elsa Martinelli (Italian) played the leading women, along with the lovely Alexandra Stewart (Canadian) and Angela Douglas, who had brought a bit of class to the recent *Carry Ons*. I had a nice role for Denholm Elliott, as a French detective. We also had the pleasure of selecting several more assorted lovelies to play the models in the film, and I was able to give myself a good, tricky role as an evil smoothie – the kind of part no other producer would have considered for me, blinded as they were by my seemingly inescapable *Doctor/Carry On* image.

As we were finalising arrangements, Eric Barker suffered a stroke. He was an old friend, still married to Pearl Hackney (their daughter, Petronella, went on to marry Anthony Hopkins). It so happened one of the characters in my film, Professor Bannen, was confined to a wheelchair after a stroke. Eric was paralysed down one side, and I immediately wondered if I dare offer him the part. I asked mutual friends, who couldn't agree whether or not they thought he'd be offended to be asked – or if, indeed, he was able. I took a chance, and rang Eric's agent to ask him. He thought it a daring and amazing idea. I said I would personally take care of him and arranged to pick him up and take him out to the shoot in North Africa myself. When it came to filming, though, the heat and the strain were pretty tough. Because Eric was genuinely paralysed, it was very emotional as well. He was terrified that he might pop off in Morocco, but I got him back safely to England. Of course, Eric was very grateful for the part, but it was to be his last.

We had considered various locations in Egypt and Israel, but finally chose Morocco, which fulfilled several needs. It was an unusual location that was becoming more fashionable now that *Lawrence of Arabia* had given the Moroccan royal family a taste for movie-making. King Hassan's sister, Princess Lalla Aisha, was the Moroccan Ambassador in London and she promised all the help we needed, which, coming from the sister of an absolute monarch, meant something. In addition to these advantages, and its beautiful locations, Morocco was very cheap. That clinched it, and our film was now entitled *Maroc 7*.

By the end of May, everything was in place and we were ready to go. The royal family had given us carte blanche to go wherever we wanted, and we made our production plans in conjunction with them. We based ourselves in a splendid hotel in the ancient city of Meknes, by the foothills of the Middle Atlas mountains. It was a big undertaking and strange to see it all happening from a producer's perspective. The cast and crew comprised around fifty people, some with their own hangers-on.

The royal family loved the movie business and the princesses or their husbands often turned up to watch, especially one of the princes, an affable chap who became a friend of mine. He took a healthy interest in the film – particularly the female members of the cast.

Carrie, of course, had come along with me, although she had to fly back to London from time to time to work. A steady stream of friends turned up to watch the fun, including Sandy Pratt from Santa Eulalia; Lionel Bair, who appeared from nowhere and practically insisted on being found a part – I cast him as a receptionist.

We were allowed to shoot more or less anywhere; even if we needed a palace, we would be offered a choice. Under the old city of Meknes, beneath grilles set in the stone foundations, was an enormous prison that could contain hundreds of prisoners. Laced with waterways and sewers, it was a marvellous location. We went out to the desert to shoot a big scene involving a large tribe of Berbers – dark, aloof and draped in blue. For them I had to provide fifty expensive Arab horses which had to be moved around from place to place. They cost more than the Berbers, and disaster struck when they caught a virus diagnosed as swamp fever and started dying. Up until then, I'd always assumed that Equine Flu was just an excuse English racehorse trainers used to justify the poor running of their clients' expensively maintained animals. But now I saw the real evidence of it and nearly wept with frustration (and compassion, of course). I was beginning to discover that being a producer was ten times more stressful than just acting in a picture, which I was also doing.

On a social level, we were regularly invited up to extraordinarily lavish parties at the Royal Palace in Rabat. I half expected Scheherazade to prance on to the floor in front of us, flourishing a few of her seven veils, or fifty vestal virgins all clad in white. There was always a ready supply of girls, whose charms I did not sample, openly offered by one's hosts much as they might have offered one a brandy after dinner.

I noticed that the prince had his eye on one of the girls in the cast, Maggie London, a gorgeous model married to the Manfred Mann singer Mike d'Abo. She had also caught the eye of his brother-in-law, and a little rivalry was brewing. If he realised he couldn't expect me simply to deliver this girl to him, it didn't stop him trying.

While we were filming, the early rounds of the 1966 World Cup had been going on and, of course, we were all following it with mounting excitement. When England made it to the final against West Germany, the prince asked me what we were going to do about watching it. I told him we would stop shooting for the day and watch it in the hotel. I invited him and other members of the Royal family to join us.

We were standing around after a long lunch, waiting for the game to start, when he turned to me.

'Who do you think will win?'

'England, of course,' I answered.

'I think Germany.'

'Well, they're a good team,' I conceded politely. 'It's possible.'

'We will have a wager,' he said, thumping me on the back.

I felt it would be unsporting, and a little tactless to refuse. In any case, I always rose to a gamble. 'Why not.'

'I give you three to one.'

'What stake?' I asked nervously.

'Women!' he said. 'I bet you three Moroccan women...' he paused and pointed at Maggie London, innocently laughing with a couple of friends and, it must be said, looking absolutely enchanting, '...to *that* one, Germany wins. Very good odds!' he grinned.

That was true: 5–4 on would have been a fairer price, though hard to divvy up in women.

'I don't have the power to deliver her,' I said, hoping he was joking.

'But you are the producer!' he laughed in a way that made me think he was serious.

I had to take the bet, hanging on to the hope that he didn't really think I had control over the girls' sex lives. Otherwise, I would just have to put all my trust in the England team.

This certainly gave the game an extra edge for me, especially when Germany scored after twelve minutes. I felt the blood drain out of me and nearly fainted. When Geoff Hurst equalised and Martin Peters scored another, putting us 2–1 ahead, I relaxed a little. Then, a minute before full time, Wolfgang Weber took a free-kick and managed to poke the ball in for a second German goal.

Two-all at full time! I was dripping sweat. The prince was almost foaming at the mouth and I was sure now he would expect me to deliver Maggie if he won the bet – no excuses!

As they went into extra-time, I think I must have held my breath until Geoff Hurst scored again with a dodgy shot that ricocheted off the bar and only just crossed the line. In the last minute of extra-time, I threw myself on my knees as Hurst raced through and scored his third – 4–2 to England – and Kenneth Wolstenholme uttered his legendary line, 'They think it's all over! It is now!'

Still on my knees, weak with relief, I'd completely forgotten I'd just won three women. The prince hadn't and was very sporting about it. He took his loss with good grace and a rueful look at Maggie, aware, perhaps that gaining her any other way was unlikely. 'Do stand up, dear boy,' he said as he helped me to my feet. 'Where would you like me to deliver your winnings, my friend?' he asked. 'One of the palaces – Marrakech, Rabat, Fez?'

Maggie had no idea what had gone on, nor what a narrow escape she'd had; and I didn't want to upset her by telling her.

By the time we'd finished filming a month or two later, I still hadn't taken delivery. When I saw the prince I joked that I was now owed a little interest on my winnings – an extra couple of women to take account of inflation. I continued to make excuses about not being able to take delivery just yet, and in the end, I never did. I'm not sure what I would do with them if they turned up now, especially with forty years' worth of inflation added.

When we wrapped in Morocco, I badly needed a rest. It hadn't been easy; the director had been struggling and John Gale had tried to persuade me to take over. I didn't because I knew it would double the cost, and we ploughed on, bringing the picture in dead on target at £100,000 – some achievement for a big-scale production like this. I'd found the whole business of producing too nerve-wracking to be enjoyable and had decided that it wasn't something I wanted to do again. I couldn't wait to go back to Ibiza and continue negotiations over the *finca*.

We weren't disappointed by our second visit – far from it. We were welcomed back to Sandy's bar and renewed the many friendships we'd already launched. There was a wonderful, care-free, joyful ambience among the artistic community of writers, painters, actors, sculptors, and now a producer who thrived there. There never seemed to be a dull moment, though if you wanted peace, you could easily find that, too.

Sitting in Denholm's house in the heat of high summer while the cicadas rattled their backsides off, looking across the unchanged landscape at what would soon be ours, was the best possible antidote to the stress of producing. Chiqui was making progress with our purchase, but it was a tortuous affair. There were a lot of points where we could have tripped up and lost out if we'd had a dodgy lawyer, but Chiqui was very helpful in recommending banks and *avocados* who wouldn't fleece us. The family from whom we were buying the house were like figures from another century, ultimately honourable and full of good will.

I soon had to accept that the problems of getting money out of Britain were substantial and, in desperation, I asked Laurie Main if he would like to take a share in the place with me. Since he'd gone off to LA, leaving me his mews house in South Hampstead, he'd done very well in

American television. Funds were more easily movable for him, and he agreed at once. In fact, it turned out that he never came and saw the place. A few years later I was able to buy him out, giving him a decent profit on the deal.

It didn't take me long to find a thriving poker school in Santa Eulalia with an interesting bunch of artists, layabouts and hard-nosed gamblers. One of the older members was an extraordinary and infamous Hungarian art forger, Elmyr Dory-Boutin, better known as Elmyr de Hory. Elmyr had sold thousands of high-quality fakes all over the world – starting with Picassos, but including Matisses, Modiglianis and Renoirs. He was manipulated by a pair of dodgy dealers who had built his house in Ibiza and drip-fed him just enough money to keep the fakes coming. Also playing was little-known American writer Clifford Irving, who had settled on the island a few years before with his wife, an English model whom he'd recently divorced as a result of an affair he was still carrying on with Baroness Nina van Pallandt, a Danish singer who was half of the duo Nina and Frederick.

I made no claims to be much of a player, and as the five of us settled down I noticed a predatory gleam in their eyes. It was a long session. Carrie came, but not to play; she sat at the side of the room reading, getting through a couple of novels as we played until the sun was well up. I won almost every game that night, and had a hell of a shock at the end when I discovered that we'd been playing for ten times more than I'd realised; when I bought my chips, I'd muddled the value of the currency, jumping as I had been between the franc-related Moroccan *dirham*, and the more highly inflated *peseta*. I was rich!

Naturally, they asked me to come back the next day, which I couldn't fairly refuse since I was leaving with my pockets stuffed full of their money. The following night, after three hours, I'd lost every *peseta* back, before slowly regaining it all by the time the morning sun began to glimmer on the Mediterranean to the east.

On the third session, I was the only winner yet again. I have never – before or since – had such a consistent run. But out of the proceeds of this three-day session, I bought all the furniture I needed to furnish my newly acquired house from top to bottom. I also installed a small oil-fuelled generator to provide basic electricity and had the house decorated enough to make it comfortably liveable. There was even a little left over to get the gardens tidied up. Fortunately, the people from whom I'd won became good friends, as I returned to Ibiza countless times from then on, and for the next forty years. I was especially delighted when, to celebrate my buying the *finca*, Elmyr gave me a lovely painting he'd done in the manner of Dufy, which still hangs in my London house.

But I never played poker with them again – perhaps they had no intention of inviting me back after that experience.

12 • The Man Most Likely To...

Over the winter of '66/'67, I was beginning to wonder if I had developed a new kind of mental disorder – Repetitive House Purchase Syndrome, perhaps – when I found myself buying a third house in under a year. Retreat Cottage was already a great success, although inevitably not used as much as planned since Ibiza had swum into my vision and I'd finally tied up the purchase of my new Eivissenc *finca*. Having accepted that I was never going to move back into Perk House and, perhaps, to put my relationship with Carrie on to a firmer footing (I wasn't ready to remarry), I had been looking for a decent London residence of a type I'd always wanted. When I found it, I already knew the house from the outside. It wasn't far from Westbourne Terrace Road, and even closer to Belsize Lane – an elegant, early Victorian town house standing right on the old North Road out of London – Watling Street to the Romans, now known as Maida Vale.

It was early Victorian, rather than my preferred Georgian, but it had lovely tall Georgian windows and large, light rooms, with a big garden secluded by a high brick wall. There were already some good small trees and shrubs amid the untamed jungle, but one of the first things I did after Carrie and I had moved in was to plant a small magnolia tree right in front of the house.

That same year I planted a baby date palm at the *finca*. In the forty years that have since elapsed, both trees have flourished and are now enormous and vivid reminders of the length of time I've spent in Maida Vale and Santa Eulalia.

I hadn't been in my new house very long and was pottering around in the garden, wondering how to deal with the dense growth of weeds it contained, when I was greeted by a faintly familiar, warm contralto voice.

'Hello, Leslie!'

I looked up to find a head had popped up over the back wall. I was amazed and enchanted to recognise Anna Neagle, my very first *Peter Pan* leading lady. Of course, I'd met her quite often over the intervening years, in the inevitable shuffle to the Music of Time, but it was wonderful to find she was now my neighbour. A fine actress and more distinguished than ever, a few years later, in 1969, she was to receive a much deserved damehood from the Queen. I felt it a marvellous good omen that I should have moved in without realising I would be living beside one of the great theatrical personalities of my youth.

At the end of March, *Maroc 7* opened to a curate's egg of reviews. As producer and one of the stars, I was aware of some of its shortcomings, but on the whole, I was pleased with it. The critics were generally warmish rather than ecstatic, and in a couple of cases, downright hostile. It was never a big hit, but, over the years since, when it's been given an airing, retrospective appreciation has been greater. I hope one of these days it will get a release on DVD and be seen by a new audience as a well-made period piece.

As a result of my experiences, one thing was sure – I wouldn't be producing movies again. Nerve of steel, hide of rhino, patience of Job and very deep pockets all seem to be essential in that role, and I wasn't sure I could provide all, or, indeed, any of them again.

I was, however, still very interested in directing, perhaps films, but more immediately, theatre. With that in mind, I teamed up with Henry Sherwood to produce a play called *The Deadly Game*, adapted by James Yaffe from Friedrich Dürrenmatt's novel. I'd played the lead in the only production of the play so far, at the Ashcroft Theatre in Croydon, directed by Hugh Goldie in 1963. I thought then what a clever, intriguing play it was, and I was surprised that it had never been taken to London. Now that I had the chance to play the same part and direct it myself, we started casting and booked the Savoy Theatre. It was a far cry from the usual light comedy I was known for and it represented quite a challenge for me.

It's a brilliantly conceived story, set in the Swiss Alps. A travelling salesman is driving through a night-time blizzard in the mountains when his car breaks down. The only lights are those of a large, solitary house. He staggers through the wind and snow and knocks on the door to find it occupied by a group of old, retired legal men having dinner and entertaining themselves. They invite the salesman to come in and dine with them, then propose that he should participate in the entertainment by subjecting himself to the legal process of prosecuting him for an imaginary crime. The game sounds fairly pointless, but since they're all in their dotage and they've given him a marvellous dinner with superb wines, he agrees to join in to humour them. As he's never been guilty of a crime in his life, he can't suggest anything they can try him for, so they move on to Stage Two – questions on past life. After a while, one of the men, a retired public prosecutor, accuses him of having caused the death of his boss.

At first it's all wild improvisation, but little by little, the prosecutor, using the answers he's given, creates from the fantasy a plausible case for accusing him of murder. The trial becomes so real that under cross-questioning the defendant keeps tripping himself up and begins to think that he has actually committed this murder. When the hangman appears at the end in the shape of an old butler, he's sure he has; the story ends with him hanging by the neck before he has been proved guilty, depicted on stage by a shadow swinging against the backdrop.

It was a dark, fascinating play, so well written that it convinces utterly and shows how blurred the line between fact and fantasy can become under powerful persuasion.

Kurt Jurgens was a client of my agent, John Redway, and he agreed to come to London to do it. I was thrilled – he was a super actor, strong, Germanic, and a name, ideal for the part of a heavyweight prosecuting lawyer. I also gave a good part – the defence lawyer – to Wilfrid

Brambell, always remembered as Pa Steptoe and a very good actor in spite of his devotion to gin. We gathered for the first read-through, all old men except me, but Kurt Jurgens didn't appear. I knew he was already staying next door at the Savoy Hotel and I rang up. I was told he had some problem and couldn't come today. We were all waiting for him; I was rather put out and rang John Redway to find out what was going on.

John was very apologetic: 'I'm sorry, Leslie, but Kurt didn't realise you were having only three weeks' rehearsal. He says he needs three months.'

'For heaven's sake!' I said. 'We only ever have three or four weeks, but I could scrape four, I suppose, as we're in good time.'

'He says he's never learned a play so quickly; he's used to having at least eight or ten weeks.'

'But that's ridiculous!'

I went up to talk to Kurt myself. I'd met him and seen something of him a few years before when I'd been filming with Eva Bartok and he'd been wooing her successfully. He was in a dressing gown now, relaxing in his room with a beautiful woman while I did my best to persuade him that it was perfectly possible, indeed normal, to achieve top-quality performances within the kind of schedule we were proposing. But he was firm; he couldn't do it without the rehearsals he thought he needed, and he just wasn't going to come other-wise. I gave him time to reconsider and left him with his companion, who looked a relaxing sort. But this game went on for days, to no avail, until I had no choice but to tell him in that case, we couldn't use him. I managed to recast, replacing him with my *Navy Lark* colleague, Stephen Murray.

We went on tour and the play came along well; I was quietly confident as we headed back to London to open at the Savoy in late June. A few weeks after we opened, the Six Days' War in Israel erupted. The world watched and held its breath and the London theatres emptied as if someone had pulled the plug. For one thing, the Jewish community were the strongest supporters of the London theatre and the arts generally. Nobody else felt like coming out either in that alarming climate, and the West End went dead.

Sickeningly, we'd had good notices without a proper chance to capitalise on them and recover. The play had to come off and Henry Sherwood lost all the money he'd put up. I told him not to worry; we'd get it back. I'd find something else, something lighter and easier – a comedy – and perhaps we'd recoup his money.

One of the scripts I looked at was potentially a good comedy about an income tax collector. It had a wonderful leading role, which wasn't for me, and in any case, I wanted to direct. I was happy to direct when also acting in a play, but it could be a lonely business, since grumbling about the director is an important outlet for an actor during tricky stages of a production. I thought the role might suit Ronnie Barker, who wasn't a star then (though I already knew how special he was), or Tony Hancock.

I didn't know Hancock well, only as someone I met through Galton and Simpson from time to time, but, of course, I knew his work. A few years before, in the summer of '62, on holiday in Antibes with the family and Penny, I'd found him on the beach with Peter Sellers and Brian Forbes. It was the day Marilyn Monroe died and we were all feeling rather morose. Hancock, truculent and very drunk, adored Marilyn and abruptly announced in a loud voice that he was going to take his wife out on a pedalo. I wasn't going to miss this and picked up my newest toy, a 16mm movie camera. In a minute he was staggering down to the sea and trying to clamber aboard the rocking craft, falling off either side a few times. I still have the film somewhere, buried under a deep pile of old scripts and collectibles. It could be valuable, but it wasn't an edifying sight. He was nevertheless an actor I admired very much. He had a wonderfully comic way of reacting – a plastic face with an alarming ability to convey gloom and inner despair, which he had in great measure.

I sent the script to him and asked if we could talk about it. We arranged to meet at his flat just around the corner from Olympia. I knocked and he opened the door, inebriated but disguising it in the way of the well-practised drinker. Music from *High Society* was blaring from his drawing room, and on a chair beside the gramophone was an enormous, human-sized teddy bear. There was no sign of a woman. I wasn't surprised. Hancock's personal life was always complicated, not to say downright messy. He had until recently been married to his publicity agent, Freddie Ross, who'd been his mistress and mentor for years until he'd finally divorced his first wife, Cicely. By this stage he was a very unhappy man in the last stages of his divorce from Freddie, although he had been comforted, and to some extent looked after, by Joan, the wife of his great friend John Le Mesurier, in a strange sort of compact. His career was in decline, probably more than anything as a result of his decision a few years before to dump Ray Galton and Alan Simpson, the script writers of the best thing in his life – the massively successful *Hancock's Half-Hour* – perhaps because he feared he was becoming too dependent on them. He'd also seen off another reliable asset in Sid James, and nothing had really fired for him since – television or movies. A far as I could see, all he needed was the right script.

Hancock made a pot of tea and we settled down – to talk about music from the shows. He loved musicals and hummed the tunes cease-lessly. He kept getting up to change records and discuss them. The script lay tantalisingly on a coffee table and I could see that it had been thoroughly read, but every time I tried to pitch the conversation around to it, he batted it away. In two hours, we didn't broach it.

In the end, he told me rather shamefacedly that he was booked to go to Australia to do a series of shows there, and presumably couldn't have done my play anyway. I suppose he could have told me on the phone, but perhaps he felt like a chat. In any event, within a month he'd gone. Twelve weeks and a few disastrous shows later, he was found dead of an overdose in a borrowed flat in Sydney – a foreseeable, but very tragic, end to a great talent.

A month or so after *The Deadly Game* had come off, I was sent a play with the somewhat ungainly title, *The Man Most Likely To...* by a novice playwright, Joyce Rayburn, who looked like a Worcester apple, perhaps out of excitement at having her play put on in a smart out-of-town theatre. This one was being done at Windsor. I read it and thought it had a bit of a spark about it and the principal plot idea was original, although not very complex.

The twenty-two-year-old son of the family in whose house the play is set has brought his delicious and overtly sexy girlfriend home, expecting to quite openly share his bedroom with her – with his parents' full knowledge. Also staying the weekend, and causing diversion and sub-plot, is a former boyfriend of his mother, flirting madly, while the father just wants a quiet life. The girl herself is delighted to be there and the mother, expecting a fun weekend, is very relaxed about it.

It doesn't sound particularly shocking now, but the permissive sixties had not yet really taken hold, especially in the cosy commuter belt of the Thames Valley, where it's set. It had some good lines, but there were substantial flaws in construction and initially I said 'No'. However, with a spare evening, when it opened I thought I might as well go down to Windsor with Henry Sherwood, the wounded producer, to see if it worked on stage.

It didn't, but I was very impressed by Angela Scoular, a young actress not long out of drama school, who was playing Shirley, the girl. She seemed to have a real feel for the comedy, such as it was, and she looked stunning. However, Henry and I didn't go backstage afterwards and ungraciously slid out to have dinner in a little Italian restaurant next to the theatre.

'Why did you bring me to see this?' Henry asked. 'It's terrible.'

'Yes, I know, but it's got the germ of an idea that could be very commercial, and we're looking for a commercial play, remember.'

The next day I rang the author's agent and said I'd like to option the play, provided I could do whatever rewriting I thought necessary to make it work. Joyce Rayburn rang back, reluctant to have anything changed.

I shrugged down the phone. 'If that's what you feel, forget it. We'll keep looking.'

However, she must have thought about it when she saw the chance of a West End debut slipping away; within a week she'd changed her mind.

I rolled up my sleeves and, with a lot of help from Carrie, sweated into the night in Maida Vale rewriting the script, sometimes wondering why on earth I was bothering. But it was slowly coming together, and one big bonus would be having Angie Scoular to play the girl. I went to see her again at Windsor to ask her if she would like to do it in London. Unfortunately for me, she'd just been cast in Peter Shaffer's new hit, *Black Comedy* in London, which she had no intention of turning down. I couldn't say I blamed her.

By the time we were rehearsing *The Man Most Likely To...* Carrie and I had ironed out most of the problems, and for the part of Shirley, after auditioning twelve excellent young actresses, I'd found Ciaran Madden, a stunning girl straight out of drama school, who played it with great energy and fizz. It was one of those roles that needed a strong presence and a lot of sex appeal; Ciaran had plenty of both.

Since first seeing the play at Windsor, my complete overhaul of the script had resulted in several tough sessions with Joyce Rayburn, the author. Now, she insisted that Ciaran was wrong for the role.

'Listen, my dear,' I said. 'You don't have to worry about the girl; she'll do very well and be a great success. It's what the critics say about the play that should worry you. I'm afraid it will not be their idea of a night out.'

There was a rumpus; but Ciaran stayed in the show.

In spring '68, we set off on tour, knowing there was still a lot to be done to the play, with Dermot Walsh, Diane Hart, Ciaran, and me, playing Victor Cadwallader, the father. The play went down well enough with the provincial audiences, as I knew it would. There was, luckily, a loyal crowd of fans who would still come out to see me, and I didn't feel I was letting them down.

In York, at my old home from home and early training ground, the Theatre Royal, every performance was sold out three weeks before we arrived – a gratifying testament to the loyalty of the audiences there. Sadly, my great friend the former mayor had died, but twenty years on there were still quite a few of my old friends from rep days around.

While we were all staying at the Knavesmire Manor Hotel, opposite York race course, I got to know Ciaran a little better. She was a very attractive girl, with fantastic spirit, but extra-ordinarily unprofessional.

'I suppose,' she said one night after dinner, 'to get on really well with you I ought to get drunk and take all my clothes off.'

'Do you seriously think the only way to get on in this business is to drop your knickers?'

'Why – isn't it?'

'Not every producer or director feels he has *droit du seigneur* over the female members of the cast; I certainly don't,' I added primly, and with partial truth.

And, hard though it proved to be, I never touched her. There were other things she still needed to learn. Once or twice, when the matinee was due to start in a few minutes, she hadn't turned up. On one of these occasions I rang the hotel.

'Ciaran, darling,' I said icily, trying to keep calm, 'you do realise you're on stage in ten minutes, don't you?'

'Oh ... am I?' she said sleepily. 'Is it that late? Oh well, I'll jump in a taxi and see you in a mo!' she fluted.

I was beside myself with frustration when she arrived, and the punters were rustling restively in their seats. She wasn't impressed. 'What's all the fuss about?' she asked. She would go on and give her usual zingy performance and it worked. She had the power and the charisma, and the audiences loved her, which was the most important thing.

On 4 July 1968, *The Man Most Likely To...* opened in London at the Vaudeville Theatre. The critics, predictably, savaged it like a pack of lions on a freshly downed gnu.

Barry Norman wrote scathingly: 'The jokes come whooping out to greet you with the egregious familiarity of old friends.' One female critic headed her slating, 'Oh, Leslie, why did you do it?', which I never forgot. Another complained about the clumsy name – a name which, I might say, stuck in the public's mind from the first time they heard it.

The *Daily Mail*, uniquely, raved about it. And the public *loved* it.

However, it wasn't easy to turn it into an absolute success. I carried on working on it, managed to get an excerpt on television and, by good chance, stumbled on a marvellously effective piece of business.

In one of the earlier performances at the Vaudeville, towards the end of the play, I'm standing at a door, waving 'Goodbye' to the girl, wearing a short dressing gown. I was casually scratching my behind when inadvertently I lifted the garment, thus revealing a patch of bare arse. The audience howled with laughter.

Like Yvonne Arnaud years before in *The Nutmeg Tree*, when her knickers fell down, I turned it to my advantage, behaved as if it were scripted business, and left it in from then on. Peter Saunders, who owned the theatre, was furious when he heard about this unseemly, gratuitous flash of nudity and threatened to take the play off.

I asked him if he'd seen it. He said he hadn't, but found the idea disgusting. I suggested he came and saw it, which he did, and thought it the funniest thing he'd seen in years. It may have been an utterly frivolous, irrelevant piece of business, but such is the anatomy of humour, the complete unexpectedness of it was enough to send the audiences out on to the street and down to the tube stations with big grins on their faces.

To help the production along, I took no salary for the first four months. This constant nursing of the play and keeping costs in hand during the lean patches allowed it to become one of the biggest hits in the West End, and kept it going, and going, and going. That first production ran in London for the next two years.

Although Henry Sherwood had come in as producer of the play, I'd put up quite a lot of the money myself. It had cost us £10,000 to launch, but it took enough money on tour to open in London more or less in credit, which gave us time to build our audience. That, sadly, would not be possible today with start-up costs closer to £100,000, which would have meant sharing it around more. However, this production, I was co-producer, director, leading actor and part writer, so it was very much my baby; mine to nurse and cajole until it became the great success it was and, once the entire production costs had been repaid, I earned nearly a quarter of everything that came in through the box office.

Of course, my involvement in *The MMLT...* didn't stop me taking other work. During the day I was kept busy with radio *(The Navy Lark,* still going), television *(The Culture Vultures),* and the odd film *(Some Will, Some Won't,* a remake of the fifties classic, *Laughter in Paradise).* Caroline, meanwhile, having helped me so much on my play, was occupied with more rarefied material on television, and was whisked off to Italy to make *Amanti* for Vittorio de Sica, with Italian heart-throb Marcello Mastroianni. I hoped his fire would be drawn by Faye Dunaway, also starring, and hot from *Bonnie and Clyde.* I wasn't entirely confident that I would win a no-holds-barred contest with the Italian Stallion. However, she returned, unscathed, to find my play going from strength to strength.

The Man Most Likely To... had been playing for nine months when I decided I needed a holiday, but I didn't want to upset the rhythm of our success by putting up a temporary replacement for the short time I was away, especially as Ciaran had recently been replaced by Mary Land. I concluded it made far more sense to give the whole cast a holiday and close the theatre for a fortnight. At least that way the public only got to see the show they wanted to see. I was the first producer/director to do this for a London play, but it's become quite common practice since.

Carrie and I took the opportunity to get back to Ibiza and wallow in the sublime, positively flaccid atmosphere that prevails there. It felt like another planet, a million miles from London and the perfect antidote to overwork. The island air was dozy-making hot and, as always, Carrie took to the hippy life absolutely naturally – no doubt a result of her mother's bohemian genes. She drifted around in kaftans and kangas (or, better still, nothing at all), barefoot and bandana'd from the moment we arrived. Our garden was beginning to be interesting and we'd built up a good bunch of friends there, besides our long-standing thespian chums.

Clifford Irving had left Nina and was now with a lovely Swiss artist, Edith Sommer. He had been doing rather well out of his friendship with Elmyr Dory-Bouton, who had become even more notorious recently and had sold Clifford the rights to his life story. Elmyr had been sailing tight to the wind with his extraordinary fakes and there was a permanent buzz of scandal around his gay goings-on with Robin Maugham; the previous year Elmyr had been charged in Spain with homosexuality. This had resulted in a couple of months in a Spanish jail, which must have been nice for him, while Clifford's book, *Fake!* was a big hit and the talk of the island.

Within a week of returning to England and the Vaudeville, I was so darned busy I'd practically forgotten I'd been away. Such, I suppose, is the price of theatrical success, but I was delighted that I had unquestionably laid the foundations of a production which, with careful handling, could run for a very long time to come.

I revived it two years later at the Duke of York's, and – quite unprecedentedly – it was a hit all over again and ran for another 700 performances. Over the next twenty years, I toured the play to South Africa, Australia, the Middle East and the Far East, personally playing it over two thousand times. I never did write back to the critic who had asked, *Oh, Leslie, why did you do it?* though I expect she saw the answer for herself.

13 • Theatrical Passports

In a welcome diversion from the now relentless run of *The Man Most Likely To...*, I did a Galton and Simpson comedy for ITV called *The Suit*, with Jennie Linden and a young, pre-*Goodies* Bill Oddie. Sophisticated, undated and well crafted, like almost everything written by this duo, it turned out to be the precursor of a later fruitful relationship with them. I saw a lot of them both, enjoyed their company and loved their work. *The Suit* had a super script and was a great success. Alan and Ray were, I think, keen to do other projects with me.

At the same time, I was becoming more than aware of something which was to niggle me for the next ten years or so. I was concerned that there would come a time when my standard film role of the affable, naughty, persistently woman-ising smoothie would become obsolete. In any case, I had deeper ambitions. I was sure I had a lot more to offer, especially as I approached my half-century.

However, I'm a professional actor and I loved to work; for me to stop performing popular comedies would be like an accountant saying he didn't want to do sums any more. Besides, my agent and my bank manager were content and I still had a large family and house to look after. So when Betty Box rang to tell me she was planning yet another *Doctor* film – *In Trouble*, her seventh, my third – and asked if I would be Dr Tony Burke again, I didn't flinch. 'Give me a pen and lead me to the dotted line,' was my Pavlovian response.

This time, though, Betty was either reluctant to put up all the dough herself or was finding it difficult to raise it on terms she liked, so she asked me if I'd like to invest in the picture by taking a small percentage and less money upfront – to which I happily replied 'yes'. It was the first time I'd taken a cut of the gross of a major film. Thirty-five years on, I still earn sporadic handfuls of peanuts from *Doctor In Trouble* as it continues to ricochet around the world's television stations, though now I find, by a series of arcane deals, the title has changed ownership again, to a French company, *Canal +*, which seems a little *triste* for such a very British movie.

Many of the old *Doctor* team were involved, including Ralph Thomas, who was directing again. Sadly, James Robertson Justice was by now too ill to give his usual amazing power. To carry the bulk of James's part they wrote in a twin brother, Captain George Spratt, played by Robert Morley – who, ironically, had been Betty's first choice for Sir Lancelot when she'd made *Doctor in the House* in 1954. Morley had then turned it down, I believe, because the money wasn't right.

James had been kept in the film so his name would still be on the credits, but he was in a terrible state. His mind had very little control over his body and he was in a very serious condition. Now it seemed it wasn't just his days that were numbered, but his hours. Poor James suffered increasing fits and bouts of depression and loneliness, in spite of all the support Irina gave him, and he died in unhappy circumstances aged just seventy. It was a shock to see him suffer so much, for he was without doubt one of the most singular men I'd ever met and my memories of him have always remained strong, lasting and affectionate.

My fellow medic in the film was played by Simon Dee, already in rapid descent from the giddy heights of his amazing TV chat show, who was now a bit out of his depth. Thank God for Harry Secombe, Joan Sims, my friend John Le Mesurier and a young, pre-*Python* Graham Chapman as a camp photographer, and welcome to some lovely dishy new ladies, especially for me, according to Ralph, and hand chosen by him.

Angela Scoular was playing my love interest, fashion model Ophelia O'Brien. Having tried to persuade her to play Shirley in *The Man Most Likely To...*, I was delighted that this time she was free. She was also in the early stages of pregnancy during filming, though this was largely kept under wraps.

Once, in a proud moment of gallantry, I stopped a nude photograph of Angie being taken and used for posterity or dodgy magazines. In a scene on what was meant to be a 'closed' set, I spotted a nasty little photographer poking his long lens around the side of a flat, ready to click away at poor Angie in the semi buff. I immediately wrapped my own coat around her naked form, and called over to Ralph Thomas, 'Can you please get that bloody photographer off the set.'

'What bloody photographer?'

'There's one hiding behind that flat taking pictures of Angie.'

The chap was removed and Angie did not subsequently appear on Page Three of the *Sun* newspaper. She was very grateful; contrary to popular belief, there are not many actresses who actually enjoy taking their kit off in public.

There were some wonderful unscripted comedic moments in the film, such as the one where I emerge from a ship's funnel (we are on a cruise ship, again!), covered in soot, and Angie is helping to pull me out when, rather cheekily, my willy partially pops out of my scanty shorts. Ralph left it in the final cut – perhaps he didn't notice it. Angie always thought the film was worth seeing just for that moment.

In February 1970, after 655 performances, I handed over the part of Victor Cadwallader in *The Man Most Likely To...* at the Vaudeville to my old schoolfriend and H.M. Tennent's colleague, Jack Watling. Neither of us missed the irony that twenty years before, I'd been *his* understudy.

I was also dreaming of making a dramatic new leap in my career. Thanks to a combination of the tremendous receipts from *The MMLT* and six years of punitive tax laws imposed by Harold Wilson's government, I was finding myself handing over distressingly large sums to Her Majesty's Collector of Taxes. Don't misunderstand me, I accept that the government has a lot of bills to pay and I've always been ready to chip in with a reasonable contribution. However, when the Chancellor warned us he would squeeze us until our pips squeaked, it reached a point where for every net pound I earned I had to give them 15/- (or was it 17/2d?), and I thought enough was enough.

My accountant advised me it would be sensible to work abroad, preferably before the current tax year ended on 4 April. Provided I was away for a year and a day, legitimately working, I would be excused taxes due on the previous year's earnings. It made sense as I'd had many good offers, so at the beginning of April 1970, I set off to tour a new production of *The Man Most Likely To...* in South Africa.

I was heavily criticised for actually going to South Africa during the height of the apartheid era, but while I deplored the regime as much as anyone, I felt one could do some good for the majority black community by *not* ignoring them, and in our case, as far as possible, taking some external culture to them. We opened in the Academy Theatre, Johannesburg, before touring every single habitable white theatre in South Africa. I badgered the authorities to let me bring in audiences from the townships. They said the black population weren't interested in theatre, and refused permission. However, after persistent and high-profile representation, including appeals to my new-found friend, the mayor of Johannesburg, they let me take my company into Soweto and help a small drama group with a Shakespeare play they were putting on. Far from not being interested, the Sowetans had a marvellous grasp of the text and a real taste for the raw drama of it. The commitment and skill of some of the actors, especially in the unfamiliar medium of sixteenth-century English, was quite amazing.

Unfortunately, just before we were due to put on our production there, one of the notoriously unsound trains that brought African workers into Johannesburg from the townships crashed, I gathered through lack of maintenance. The Soweto community were up in arms over it, there were some ugly demonstrations, and we were warned not to go.

I insisted we already had some friends there and wouldn't be affected, so we went anyway. I was very glad we did. We gave several performances of the play with an all-white cast, which had never been done there before. We were 'protected' by black police officers armed with guns, chains and whips, which must have deterred some people from coming, but they got in through the back entrance. The black audiences took our light-hearted comedy quite seriously and when the leading girl (played by the delectable Gail Grainger), and the father (me) looked as if we were going to sleep together, the audience were expecting at least murder in the family – not

365

humour. They loved it and told us the same situation sometimes arose in their own families.

I was shown more of the township while I was there and witnessed many of the difficulties for the black South Africans. I visited an accident clinic where they were treating the horrendous injuries caused by stiletto knives made from sharpened bicycle spokes, inserted into a precise spot in the victim's spinal cord to paralyse them. I'd never before seen the effects of such wanton and expertly applied violence.

Back in the comfort of Johannesburg, I asked the mayor when he thought the unjust and inherently unstable apartheid regime would come to an end. To my astonishment, he said he thought it would happen in about twenty years. At the time, it didn't seem remotely possible, and yet, in February 1990, his prophecy came true and Nelson Mandela was released.

As I knew I was going to be in Africa for the better part of a year, I wanted to use my spare time to broaden my horizons, so I had my convertible Mercedes shipped out. The South African climate was ideal for driving a big, comfortable drop-head and, fortunately, they drive on the left. I loved having it there, although, one day in Johannesburg, I was giving my lovely black cleaning girl a lift when I was stopped by the police.

'Not allowed, sir!' Somehow I avoided getting into further trouble.

During my year in South Africa I formed a group of black girls and boys for drama, general interest and shared understanding. It was marvellous to see how they responded and what they offered us. When I was leaving to go back to England, they presented me with a scroll of appreciation with all their signatures. Thirty-six years later, it's still a treasured possession.

My car also gave me an opportunity to see a great deal of South Africa which, despite its political shortcomings then, was one of the most beautiful countries I'd ever seen, especially the game reserves and the astonishing wildlife. I went into Lesotho and Swaziland, where I was strongly drawn to African art and traditional culture. While I was in Rhodesia, I found a black sculptor who worked in wood. One of my most loved pieces of art is a wonderful head and shoulders of a mother and child which he carved exquisitely in very dark mahogany tree trunk. I visited him several times and watched fascinated while he was carving it. When it was nearly finished, he priced it and I bought it. It stands in my hallway still. In the same way, I found some beautiful pieces of carved soapstone and I was also able to indulge my love of gemstones and crystals. Most of the artists I found were supplied with their materials – hard wood, soapstone and so on – by the white farmers, in return for a small percentage of the finished price.

I didn't miss the chance to get up to the Victoria Falls, where the Zambezi crashes thunderously out of Zambia into what was then Rhodesia. The Falls were as awe-inspiring as everyone says, although, unexpectedly, I heard them long before I was in sight of them. Driving back alongside the yawning gorges gouged by the river in the earth's crust, I went to see the elephants, lions and buffalo herds that roam through the curiously named Wankie game reserve. It was a park so huge it's hard for someone from our tiny island to take in: 14,500 sq kilometres, with over one hundred different species of animals, and four hundred types of birds.

I went on to do the play in Salisbury, where I met that mildest of rebel leaders, Mr Ian Smith. He'd declared UDI in 1965, and proclaimed Rhodesia an independent republic in 1970. Britain had imposed sanctions that were beginning to bite into the economy there, and he asked me if I could put in a good word for him with our government. I was rather surprised. I thought it unlikely Mr Heath would listen to what I had to say on the subject, but said I'd do my best. That seemed to please him and he was very charming about it.

When we left Salisbury, I embarked on an epic drive the length of South Africa to Cape Town – a wonderful journey despite my discovery that someone had forgotten to put back the oil cap of my motor and most of the oil had drained from the sump; even a Mercedes doesn't take kindly to that. Fortunately, I noticed before any serious damage was done, and after a break of two days while it was put right, and a quick view of provincial Afrikaner life, I was on my way.

I'd been in Africa many months by now. It was the first time since Hollywood that I'd been away for a long period and I was missing my family very much. It was the summer holidays back in England and I persuaded Penny to let the boys fly out to spend some time with me.

I was thrilled to see two bemused, excited faces emerging from a plane at Jan Smuts airport. Roger was eleven, Andrew sixteen and they chattered away excitedly as we drove back into Johannesburg with the roof down, loving the heat, sights, smells and sounds that were so unfamiliar to them, especially the ceaseless chorus of the cicadas. It was great to have them to myself. Because I was working, they came into the theatre each evening, and we spent the days together. They both loved golf – in fact, Andrew had such style I thought he might even have a future career in it – and we played on some of the most beautiful courses on the continent.

The boys were also very eager to see some wild-life, and when I had a couple of clear days, I drove them to the Kruger National Park on the Mozambique border. To make the most of our time, we did the 250-mile journey at night. On the way we passed a massive bushfire and the craggy soaring silhouette of the Steenkampsberg Mountains. In one of the villages the locals were selling vast quantities of soft, ripe avocado pears. Roger adored them, so I bought him a crateful – bliss!

In the Kruger I was as excited as the boys. We stayed in a *rondeval*, a traditional circular thatched house, much the same as our own Iron Age ancestors would have occupied. We were lucky – from the moment we entered the park we saw huge numbers of animals, and we would get up at dawn to go and watch the activity at the busier waterholes.

We were told where we would find elephants, but as we got close to where they should have been we couldn't see any, surrounded as we were by thick bush. I stopped the car to look more closely and turned the engine off. Immediately, we heard the most tremendous crunching, munching sound of a whole herd having their breakfast. Eventually, following this noisy mastication, we found them hoovering up the vegetation at an astonishing rate that made it clear why they needed such a vast territorial range. That same day, we also had a wonderful view of a family of giraffes, two adults with a young one which they were teaching how to move, eat and drink, always a little awkward for a beast shaped the way they are. It was a very touching sight. I pulled out my movie camera and faithful Rolleiflex to get some wonderful footage. On another occasion, just as I stepped outside the car to take shots of some lions, a ranger rolled in from nowhere and gave me a severe bollocking for frightening the animals! Roger was highly amused to see his dad being chastised and he and Andrew haven't forgotten the incident to this day.

The most beautiful aspect of the park for me was the bird life, which was almost unbelievable in variety and colour. A wonderful picture of a pink cloud of flamingos lifting off a small lake in the dawn light has stayed with me ever since.

After two lovely days I had to get back to Johannesburg to do the play, so we set off on the return journey. Halfway back, Roger suddenly burst into tears and told me he'd forgotten his mac.

'It doesn't matter,' I said gently. 'I'll get you another; I can't go back now.'

'But my teddy bear was in the pocket!' Roger wailed.

This was serious. He had adored this small lump of stuffed plush as long as he could remember.

'Well, don't worry,' I said, groping for a silver lining. 'If you love Teddy, think of him, back in the world where he came from; he'll meet up with all his friends and have a wonderful new life!'

Despite its zoological inaccuracy, the thought cheered Roger immediately and we carried on while he solemnly munched his way through another avocado, which kept him quiet.

Back in Johannesburg, I took them to Soweto so they could see the realities of the place for themselves. I told them how poor the people were, and yet they were still interested in drama. It must have been a startling eye-opener for two boys brought up in the verdant heights of Mill Hill. They never forgot the trip, and they never will. Roger's forty-five now, but he still remembers Teddy and the *avos*.

When my year away was almost completed in the spring of '71, I headed back towards London, taking the opportunity to meet up with Carrie in Ibiza on the way, because I couldn't arrive back until 6 April, or HM Collector of Taxes would have had a field day.

By now Ibiza had become an integral part of my life and my little *finca* was as important as my London house. It served the vital function of allowing me to relax totally, as I never can in

371

London where work always comes first. Finally I arrived back after my longest absence from the town I loved. The South African tour of *The Man Most Likely To...* had been an unqualified success; the audiences loved it, I'd made excellent contact with the black community, we had tremendous houses and had taken a lot of money.

In London, production hadn't gone so well with Jack Watling at the Vaudeville. They weren't pulling in the punters and, a matter of weeks after I left, Henry Sherwood decided that the show would have to come off. This was a shame, but we'd had a tremendously good run and been amply rewarded for recognising its potential, even if the critics hadn't.

While in South Africa, I'd been beavering away at a movie version of the play, which was now complete. On my return to London, I began rounding up some potential backers for it. Astonishingly, they hadn't seen the play during its two-year run at the Vaudeville, and they asked me if I could put it on again somewhere so they could see it for themselves. As it had already done a long West End run and a previous tour, I wasn't sure whether it was worth it, but I was so keen to see it turned into a movie, I arranged a short tour, this time using some of my own money.

This time around, I'd ironed out all the wrinkles in the script and had the production honed to perfection. Everyone in the sticks who'd missed the first tour came to see it. It went down astonishingly well. Even I, ever the optimist, was a little surprised the jokes still sounded all right –

the dependability of old friends, I guess. By the end of the tour, people were suggesting I take it back to London's West End again. It hadn't crossed my mind to do that, but I rather liked the idea – it would be so amazing if it succeeded yet again.

On the face of it, this was a fairly preposterous suggestion. It had, after all, only come off less than eighteen months before. But I was persuaded by the success of the tour and managed to secure the Duke of York's Theatre for early 1972. We reopened, and it was a hit all over again. This was unprecedented in the London theatre scene, and one in the other eye for those critics who'd rubbished it. At least, now, we were graciously welcomed back, and the advance bookings were staggeringly good.

I'd no sooner settled back into the weekly routine of *The Man Most Likely To...* – six nights a week, plus two matinees – when Ray Cooney asked me if I would take the lead in a movie called *Not Now, Darling*. It was the usual sort of role for me, and an excellent part for Dudley Moore as the other male lead, so I agreed to do it while still in the play.

When it came to rehearsals, Dudley had a problem so Ray stepped in and read the part. Then we learned that Dudley had landed a bigger film in the States and wasn't available for ours. Ray quickly announced that he'd got Terry Scott instead, but, as Terry was ill, Ray carried on reading the part. The following week, Terry's illness turned into an aneurysm. Ray said it was too late to cast anyone else, so he would play it himself, which, I suspect, is what he'd fancied doing all along. Oh well, I thought, I always enjoyed working with Ray and he was a great friend.

The film of *Not Now, Darling* was very funny indeed and the first of what Ray hoped might become a franchise of *Not Now* films, like the *Carry Ons*. But after we made *Not Now, Comrade* in 1976, the series idea fizzled out, as they so often do.

When Carrie and I escaped to Ibiza for a quick holiday in the early summer, the island was yet again humming with scandal. My poker friend Clifford Irving and his lovely wife Edith had had their collars felt by the Swiss police for a major fraud.

It had all started as a daring idea for a clever hoax. A couple of years earlier Clifford had bumped into Dick Suskind, another writer, in Majorca. Clifford's book on Elmyr de Hory had done very well and they discussed other projects that might have the same impact. One of them hit on the idea of writing an 'authorised' ghosted autobiography of Howard Hughes, the reclusive tycoon. They thought the fact that no one had seen Hughes since 1958 would work in their favour. Clifford would do the writing, with Suskind doing the research. By forging Hughes' signature and handwritten notes, Clifford, who already had a good track record, convinced New York publishers McGraw Hill that he had a deal with Hughes to act on his behalf in selling the rights to the book. He managed to extract a cheque from them for $765,000 made out to H.R. Hughes, which Edith paid into a Swiss bank account in the name of Helga R. Hughes.

When it was made public that the book would be published in early '72, Hughes broke cover and appeared in public for the first time in almost fifteen years to denounce the whole thing as a hoax.

After a short while, Clifford and his co-conspirators had to own up and pay back the whole $765,000. He spent seventeen months in prison, while Suskind did five, and Edith got a spell for banking the cheque. It was a shame, really. I'm sure Clifford's version of Howard Hughes' autobiography would have been very entertaining and probably a lot more accurate than the real thing – if that isn't an oxymoron. So Clifford was missing from the island for a while, but we all did our best to keep Edith's spirits up when she came out of jail. I was very impressed when she showed me some of the paintings she'd done while serving her stretch.

Returning to London and my alter ego of Victor Cadwallader, the play resumed its momentum with no obvious signs of letting up. We were doing so consistently well that John Gale and I were on the look out for any interesting film possibilities to invest in.

At the same time I was involved with another group who were trying to buy a theatre. We started negotiations to buy the Duke of York's, where I was appearing at the time, but the place needed a great deal of work. Many of the seats had a restricted view because the circle was held up by columns; to make it viable, these would have to be altered – a massive and very expensive reconstruction. Sadly, although we came close, it never reached a settlement. This came as a big disappointment to me, and not simply for commercial reasons. Since the demise of the St James', I'd been very active in the Save London's Theatres Campaign, fighting to protect and preserve our theatres from developers who cared nothing for history, only the profit to be made from building on these prime locations.

In fact, while I was playing at the Duke of York's, I had an urgent visit from the fireman at the Prince's Theatre, which stood at the top of Shaftesbury Avenue. I'd known him since my early days in the West End and he was aware of my involvement with the Save London's Theatres Campaign. The week before, during a performance of *Hair*, part of the ceiling at the Prince's had collapsed, providing the freeholders with a marvellous excuse to close the place and knock it down. To make certain of it, the fireman had been ordered to turn off the pumps in the basement. Like a lot of buildings in London with deep basements, the Prince's was prone to flood with water from one of many subterranean streams that flow down to the Thames. If the pumps were turned off, the resulting damage to the substructure, together with the collapsed roof, would justify having the theatre declared a hazard. It would then be eligible for demolition. In the time it took to say 'Centre Point', a new, high-rise office building – worth a great deal more than the theatre could ever be – would shoot up in its place.

With the help of Sir Michael Havers, a sympathetic member of the Garrick and Solicitor General under Edward Heath, we managed to get an immediate injunction to keep the pumps going at the Prince's. The building was listed, restored, and renamed the Shaftesbury. It survives in good health to this day. This excellent result also served as a warning to any other avaricious owners intent on making a killing by killing a theatre.

At a later date, Ray Cooney drummed up a group, including a number of West End stars, to form a company which bought the Shaftesbury and founded the Theatre of Comedy. I was proud to be part of that group, which continues to run this beautiful theatre even now, only under a totally different management, with the original group remaining in the sidelines, though Ray is, of course, still involved.

In the spring of '73 I was delighted when the BBC proposed a brand-new series, *Casanova '73*, specially written for me by Ray Galton and Alan Simpson. It didn't represent a great departure from what I'd come to regard as my standard role of smooth-talking philanderer, but I thought that the quality of the writing lifted it into a higher bracket. In fact, it was a spin-off from *The Suit*, a one-off play we'd done for ITV which had gone down so well four years earlier. I had to flash about in an open-top sports car eyeing up birds in minimal frocks. The car, by the way, was my own racing green Mercedes 220SE, now home from Africa and working for the BBC. My character was called Henry Newhouse – hence the title: *CasaNova*. Conceived as a series for all the family, it was very funny and had a unique new ingredient for the sophisticated '70S – SEX!

As a bonus, my secretary was Gail Grainger, the stunner who'd played Shirley for me in South Africa. I had a string of lovely women to dally with, Cyd Hayman one week, Maureen Lipman the next, and in one episode I had to bed Peter Finch's ex-wife Yolande Turner, when I took off some of my clothes, except – with a nod to old-fashioned family values and Mary Whitehouse – my socks. This turned out to be insufficient modesty for Mrs W and her band of tight-lipped observers, who campaigned vigorously against the show. The BBC quickly caved in and pushed us somewhere indecently close to the epilogue, while giving the empty prime-time slot to *Mastermind*, where the now legendary quiz became a great hit. *Casanova '73*, lurking in its late-night billet, was quietly forgotten – all thanks to the super unique new ingredient. The next time I saw Magnus Magnusson at a party, he expressed his great gratitude for our unseemly behaviour on *Casanova*. Two or three years later, no one would have batted an eyelid if the leading actor of a comedy series successfully bedded a lady every week.

However, the following year, I was beginning to think it was time I released myself for something else. I'd been considering touring the play abroad yet again, which had certain attractions, and when I was approached by the biggest theatrical production company in Australia (and one of the biggest in the world) to take the dear old *Man Most Likely To...* on tour Down Under, I was very tempted. However, nearly two years into its second West End run, the play was still doing business at the Duke of York's, and Henry Sherwood was keen to put in a substitute Victor rather than take it off. After what had happened last time with Jack Watling, and acknowledging the reality that the public associated the play so closely with me, I thought it wouldn't be a good idea. However, he cast the delightful Henry Magee, a very reliable and funny actor, to take over this time. Henry was a lovely chap, and a valuable fellow director of the Royal Theatrical Fund, who sadly died recently after a long, ghastly illness.

In the meantime, I hoped to improve my chances of landing a good television series in the UK by signing a contract with Stella Richman's production company. I'd known Stella for years in her guise as owner of the White Elephant Club in Mayfair, which she'd taken over from her husband Victor Brusa after he'd died. Wearing her TV producer's hat, Stella had had a string of hit television series to her credit – most recently with Lee Remick in *Lady Randolph Churchill* for Thames Television.

Her new production company's co-owner was David Frost, who, having arrived on the scene as a satirical predator of the Establishment in the sixties, had made the transition to an Establishment figure himself by the seventies. He had the muscle to get the right slots for the company's productions.

There wasn't a specific project on the table when we signed, but we agreed to wait until the right one came along. This hadn't yet happened when I was offered some dates for Australia, so, leaving Henry Magee in the Duke of York's, I set off on my first trip to the Antipodes.

It wasn't only London that I would be leaving behind. After many happy years solidly together with the ever-exciting, always-challenging Caroline Mortimer, we had with some sadness, agreed to split. The principal bone of contention was children. For most of the time I was with her, Carrie had been quite clear that she didn't want children, but she'd now reached a point in her life where the urge to procreate manifests itself overwhelmingly. On the whole, men don't fully understand the power of it and, in my case, I already had all the children I thought I could reasonably handle. In the end it was this and, perhaps, my reluctance to marry again that caused the demise of our relationship. I wished there could have been a workable compromise and I knew I was going to miss her a great deal; she was a strong and very special person.

We said goodbye and I left England feeling alone and uncertain, thinking it was an extra shame not to have Carrie to share the new experience of Australia with me. My sense of loss and loneliness was exacerbated when the movie they showed on the first leg of the long flight starred – surprise, surprise – Caroline Mortimer. Just what I didn't need.

I had no idea what to expect when I arrived on the other side of the world. Shortly before leaving London, I'd bumped into Tommy Steele. I'd known him since he was a kid – he'd had a bit part in *Pool of London*, kicking an empty baked bean tin around the wharf to add atmosphere. When I told him I was heading off to Australia, he grimaced.

'Arsehole of the world!' he declared.

Not encouraging; not accurate either, as eventually I discovered, though when I first arrived twelve thousand miles from home, I'd never felt so disoriented. It was as if I'd become detached from the world I'd always occupied; as if I were no longer a part of it, but on another, parallel universe – even the water went down the plug hole the opposite way round.

This sense of alienation affected me profoundly for the first few days, and I had my first experience of a real panic attack in the middle of the night. It took me back to the last conversation I'd had with Tony Hancock, just before his flight to Australia and his abrupt demise in Sydney. He was already in a state of what I guess was deep manic depression; feeling alone and so far from home must have been hell for him. No wonder the poor man had decided to end it all. Perhaps, if I'd persuaded him to stay in London and do my play, it might have saved his life, but he hadn't been remotely interested.

Once I'd become used to this big, brash, colourful country, I was sure I'd love it. Of course, I couldn't be sure how the play would go here, tried and tested though it was in London, England and South Africa. Audiences aren't predictable, and this was an audience I didn't know at all. Yet, because they already knew me from my films and TV work, advance bookings in Melbourne were very good.

I had the advantage of working with a very powerful production company which dominated Australian theatre. It had the most amazing resources in wardrobe, scenery and all the backup of top theatrical production, and we were wonderfully looked after. Once I'd got over my jetlag, I could cope with casting and the enormous theatres I'd have to face, not least thanks to my childhood experiences in the London Palladium and Covent Garden, which were invaluable.

As there were restrictions on the number of British actors who could work in Australia, I'd had to get a permit to direct and play my own part; but the rest of the cast would have to be Australian. For the girl who played the crucial part of Shirley, I applied the same basic instincts that had enabled me to find Ciaran Madden and Gail Grainger. The moment I cast eyes on Vicki Luke, I knew she had the right combination of sexual energy, striking good looks, wackiness and strength that the part needed.

The cast had all adopted something approximating an English accent for their auditions, but, once the play was on the road, the Australian stubborn sense of independence came to the fore and they all started to revert back to their Aussie sound. It left me sounding a trifle alien, but I don't think the audiences minded too much; they certainly loved the play. Not only did its daring comedy appeal to them but, even more than English audiences, they totally appreciated the element of valid social commentary to it, and recognised that the way families interacted around sexual behaviour was being challenged. We had some fantastic reviews and wonderful receptions, which made even 'the arsehole of the world' a nice place to be. We were also a great financial hit everywhere.

I really loved the country and, as usual, made it my business to have a good look around, helped by a few friends already living and working there – Michael Craig, for instance, who had been my co-star in *Doctor in Love* and an indefatigable member of the old poker school, was now married out there and doing very well on Australian television. But there was one blast from my very distant past that took me totally by surprise.

A woman with a standard Australian accent rang the theatre in Melbourne and said she'd love to see me again. Mystified, I asked who she was.

'Joy,' she said, sounding a little peeved I hadn't got her in one. 'Joy Herbert, from Chingford. Have you forgotten me?'

Joy!?

What memories that stirred! She was my first real love. She'd dumped me, you may recall, for throwing up on the number 38 bus after seeing my best friend Bobby Desmond in the West End. She left me at a time when I felt at my lowest ebb, and flew off with a dashing major.

It was ironic – and I say this without a smidgen of Schadenfreude – that she, having once made me promise not to pursue a career on the stage, was now looking me up because she'd seen a lot of my films and read about me and this play in the papers.

I arranged to meet her for a drink, and waited beside a bottle of excellent Aussie champagne in an ice bucket, wondering what on earth she would be like now – after all, she'd been a real stunner and the love of my life thirty years before. When she arrived, I barely recognised her. Time, it must be said, had not been kind, or even mildly understanding. As I poured a drink for her, I couldn't detect a hint of what had excited me so much in those last days of the war. Now with her not especially desirable Aussie twang, she told me how the dashing major had left her and their two children. As we sat together over the champagne, I looked at this poor creature who had almost broken my youthful heart until, somewhat abruptly, she stood up, scribbled her number on a piece of paper, and left to get back to her children. I thanked God for watching over me and finished the bottle on my own.

I had developed an extraordinary feeling since my arrival in Australia, mainly because I was absolutely on my own for the first time in my life – just the play and the people in the cast. However, I quickly made many friends from the audiences and connections in Australia itself, so I wasn't lonely.

An unexpected call from the UK brought me back to reality. Director Bob Kellett, with whom I'd made a movie a year or two before, approached me to play the lead in another film comedy, which would be shot on location in Menorca; my co-star would be Terry-Thomas. The script, which I had yet to read, was called *Spanish Fly* – not exactly inspiring.

Terry, however, was a good friend and Ibizan neighbour with whom I enjoyed working and I took the view that, provided flights, money and billing were OK, it would give me an easy chance to take a short break in Ibiza before returning at my leisure to London. They agreed to allow me time to wrap up my Australian tour first. Once again, I had plenty of leeway to complete the deal as I hadn't yet used up my period of exile.

I was having a fabulous time in Australia, mostly thanks to Vicki Luke, who was super as Shirley. She was very bright and extremely attractive, but I suspected would become a bit of a handful. Apparently she'd had an accident as a child, sustaining an injury to her head which still manifested itself in extraordinary bursts of irrational behaviour. She'd been thrown out of school at the age of sixteen for having an affair with one of her male teachers. This risk-taking, I discovered, was typical of her. She liked to push everything to the limit, and beyond. She had a great sense of humour, was bags of fun and typically Australian. She loved to show me her country, which I soon discovered was home to more deadly snakes, bugs and beasts on land and sea than any other place on earth. I never ceased to be surprised by it or by Vicki Luke.

Her growing friendship, and her ability and desire to please me, meant we spent a lot of time

385

together, and I even got to meet her parents, who were welcoming and friendly. At that time she was in her twenties, and she made it easy for us to get together, and our relationship progressed. She couldn't wait and neither could I – we became inseparable in every way. I had no idea where it would lead to, all I knew was that she needed me. Happily, everyone in the company accepted the situation, except for one woman. We couldn't work out if perhaps she was jealous of me or of Vicki, or if she just wanted to join in with us both!

The rest of the cast were excellent, even if the Australian twang dominated too much, but we worked on that. Any problems were quickly resolved by the Australian Equity, for whom I had the utmost respect.

There was an education for me, too – something I had never come across anywhere else in the entertainment world. 'Giggling', or what we call corpsing on stage, is punishable in Australia by the company manager – by fining the parties concerned – a funny but terribly good idea, and sometimes very expensive.

Audience reactions and receptions were the finest I've ever experienced anywhere in the world – they loved theatre and they loved to laugh. I've always said that the further away from London, the greater the reaction – and 12,000 miles is pretty far! Although, one night in Adelaide, one poor chap in the stalls actually died laughing.

I flew from Sydney to Barcelona from where a tiny plane had been laid on to fly me, plus the

386

producer, via Ibiza to Menorca. I'd never been in such a small aircraft. It had one, rather noisy, engine and an ex-RAF pilot for whom the term 'gung ho' might have been invented. However, he oozed confidence and as soon as we were airborne he asked me if I'd like to fly the plane myself. I didn't debate too long; to a man who had passed his advanced driver's test in a 1924 Racing Bentley, flying this little crate would be a doddle. I took the controls and, with Gung Ho beside me, had a marvellous time winging across the azure sea to my favourite island. I asked if I could fly over my *finca* in Santa Eulalia and the pilot told me where to go. We came down low and swooped across my little farmhouse.

I'd let some doubtful people use the house while I was in Australia, which turned out not to have been the wisest move. It seldom is. In Ibiza, it's common knowledge that once people have started enjoying living in your house, their instincts turn all proprietorial. I could see laundry waving in the breeze and, more worryingly, a lorry sticking out of the *cisterna*.

Feeling a bit jittery, I followed the pilot's instructions and we successfully landed the plane. Rather proud of myself, but peeved about what was going on up at my house, we parked the plane, signed the aerodrome documents and went up to find out what had happened. We managed to get the truck out of my water supply and found that, fortunately, not too much damage had been done, although, of course, the driver had no insurance, which was expensive for me. After sorting out a few of the usual and ongoing hassles of foreign ownership – like disposing of unwanted, unpaying tenants – I flew on to Menorca. This island was new to me; its capital, Mahon, seemed an odd blend of English and French, with less Spanish influence, but elegant nonetheless.

Though it was great to see Terry-Thomas again, it soon became clear that there was something not quite right about the whole set-up. Terry didn't seem at all well, and the movie, *Spanish Fly*, seemed to have been cobbled together a little too loosely. But a job's a job and, with filming due to start in about ten days, I moved into a period but rented *finca* and did my best to get ready for the movie.

A week later, a car arrived at my *finca* and in walked Vicki Luke, as if she was expected – she wasn't – followed by a small, sweaty man carrying a mountain of luggage. I wasn't too sure if Vicki turning up was a good thing but, on balance, knowing Vicki, I thought it might be all right. She was certainly good fun and so adventurous she would liven up the shoot. In any case, I wasn't averse to a little risk myself.

She moved in and almost at once tore off all her clothes and leapt straight into the pool. She was a good, strong swimmer and had a super figure so it was a pleasure to watch her. Later I took her for a wonderful dinner in a local restaurant alongside the historic port. From here Nelson had held sway over the Mediterranean in the early nineteenth century, for Mahon's deep harbour made it a haven for large ships.

When we started shooting, I was shocked to

discover that my old mate Terry-Thomas was showing positive signs of being ill. Early-morning conversation, before make-up, was non-existent; he was disoriented and shaky – not a bit like the normal Terry – and shooting wasn't easy.

In spite of all this we managed to finish the film – one always does, somehow – but I was extremely concerned for Terry. He'd always been a tremendous story-teller and raconteur, but in the evenings, there was none of the usual banter and chat. Once it was over we had a few laughs before we all headed back to Ibiza, but I subsequently heard from Terry's other friends on the island that he'd been under a lot of strain for some time. I hoped that things would turn around for him soon.

Vicki took to life in Ibiza and my gorgeous *finca* like a Labrador pup with a loo roll. She loved the untamed freedom of the place. She was great in the kitchen, around the house, in the pool, watering the multitude of exotic shrubs, feeding the growing horde of feral cats, performing in bed like a circus act with attitude – which I apologise for mentioning, but it was one of her more remarkable gifts. With time to spare, I flew to Hong Kong, and pretty much anywhere I felt like in between, but Vicki didn't want to leave Ibiza. I told her I was taking the long way home, but she was welcome to stay on in the *finca*, if that was what she wanted. But no sooner had I set off for Hong Kong than she changed her mind and decided to follow me.

Over the years I've got to know Hong Kong well, and I've always loved the colour and diversity of Chinatown, but we stayed only a short time before heading off for Thailand. I'd always been fascinated by what I'd heard of Thailand and thought Vicki would be the ideal travelling companion, as she was so daring.

Someone recommended a trip up to northern Thailand, near the Burmese border, where the ancient hill tribes still lived the traditional way. To reach the hill country from Chiang Mai, we had to take a boat up-river, then continue on foot through the jungle to the higher ground where the opium poppies grew. It really felt like pioneering stuff and, certainly, very few tourists went up there in those days. Vicki was very excited by the whole trip, but unfortunately she succumbed to a stomach infection – more or less inescapable at some point when travelling in this part of the world – and when she became too weak to walk I had to carry her. This, by the way, was after she'd told me I was far too old to be doing a trip like this at all!

Finally we arrived at a village of bamboo and thatch where our guide had arranged for a cousin of his to put us up, along with all the domestic creatures that wandered in and out of the house. We were wonderfully fed, and after supper the guide asked me, particularly, if I'd like to come with him for something special. I guessed he was inviting me to partake of a few puffs on his opium pipe. I politely declined and quickly fell asleep. I'd never touched anything like that and had no desire to do so.

Later, in bed, my guess was confirmed when I heard the men's voices next door grow more garbled, high pitched and drawn out until, eventually, they relapsed in the stertorous sounds of troubled sleep. Vicki, now recovered, and I woke in the morning to find our guide still practically out of his mind, stumbling around like a zombie. He'd obviously rather gone for it the night before.

Eventually he sobered up – or whatever the equivalent is with opium – and we started on our way back. This time we got a ride in a small open lorry that was plying the tracks, picking up and dropping off local peasants along the way to the river. From there we got the boat to Chiang Mai and made our way back to Bangkok.

We spent a lot of time exploring the beautiful waterways that criss-cross the city. While we were cruising one day, a whopping insect landed on my bare arm and stuck its long hooter into my flesh. I was looking for a way to remove it when Vicki, unfortunately deciding to take the initiative, yanked it off and threw it in the water. At this point I realised the creature's proboscis must have been barbed, as it had left a lot of it behind. The following day, the flesh around the wound began to redden and swell, and I was in a lot of discomfort. We learned, too late, that the way to remove these beasts was to put a burning cigarette end on their rear, which made them release their hold in an instant – as any of us would – and take their proboscis with them.

Despite the pain in my arm, our flight to India the next day was delightful. The English skipper was charming; having realised I was on his flight, he invited us up to the cockpit to watch the approach and landing in Bombay. He invited us to join him and the crew, who were having a turn-around break in the city, at a party in their hotel that evening.

As we waited by the carousel for our luggage, gradually getting used to the intense heat and the unique whiffs of India, I noticed Vicki's expressive face twitching with anxiety as she gazed at the baggage appearing through the hole in the wall.

'What's the matter?' I asked.

'It looks like our luggage isn't here.'

'I'm sure it'll turn up,' I reassured her, but she continued to look very het up. 'Seriously, Vicki, what is the problem?' I asked again, growing suspicious.

'I packed something that didn't clear through Customs in your case,' she admitted reluctantly.

'You did what?' I exploded. I was in no doubt what the 'something' might be and that we were facing the possibility of having our collars felt in no small way. With my reputation, they'd make an example – and a meal – of it.

Vicki obviously thought the same; she was skipping about like a grasshopper, looking more nervous than ever. As calmly as I could, I approached the most senior-looking airport official, a tidy, clerical Indian, and explained that we hadn't got our bags, while everyone else on our flight had.

'Oh gosh! They must have stowed them in the wrong hold. They'll go on to London now, and then we can have them sent straight back.'

'But that'll take days,' Vicki wailed. 'Can't you get them off?'

'I'm afraid that would delay the flight. It's out of the question,' the official said adamantly.

At that moment, the pilot walked through the hall.

'Hello, everything OK?'

'Well, no, actually,' I said, trying not to look too anxious. 'Apparently our luggage was put in the wrong hold and it has to go on to London. This chap says they can't take it out.'

The captain turned to him. 'What are you talking about? Please arrange to have Mr and Mrs Phillips' luggage unloaded from the second hold at once.'

'I can't do that. It would mean holding up the flight.'

There was a gleam of triumph in the skipper's eye. 'There'll be a far bigger delay if I don't sign off my flight. I've got the key, and I'm still captain until I sign the hand-over – and I won't be doing that until those bags are off.'

'You can't do that,' the official gasped, as if the rules were holy writ.

'I can, and I will.'

Ten minutes later we were watching our bags being taken off. Again our friend the skipper took charge. 'Bring them through the crew door – no need to waste time in Customs.'

I was bloody annoyed by what Vicki had done, but I forgave her, because in the end I appreciated that it was this wacky streak in her that had persuaded me to do things I would never have dreamed of otherwise.

Somehow I managed to acquire one of the lovely

colonial rooms at the Taj Hotel in Bombay, and we spent a few days drinking in the extraordinary vitality of that vast, bustling city where Bollywood glamour rubbed shoulders with almost unimaginable poverty.

We then travelled north via Baroda and the wonderful old cities of Rajasthan. In Udaipur, our hotel was a palace shimmering in the middle of a lake between two ranges of russet hills. On the lake shore, below the towering wall of the three palaces of the Maharana of Mewar, the reflections of the colourfully clad women quivered on the water as they beat their washing clean on the smooth old rocks of the embankment. Then it was on to the beautiful pink city of Jaipur before heading for Delhi and Lutyens' magnificent Viceroy's Palace. As usual, I spent most of my time in the old markets, looking for Indian jewellery and gems.

By the time our Indian trip was over, I still had a week or two of exile to use up, and I thought it best to take Vicki back to Ibiza, where she couldn't get into too much trouble – I hoped. She settled right back in there, and would probably still be living there now … if I hadn't rather impulsively decided to take her to London.

14 • Sextet

I came back to London full of energy to find I was a grandfather again – my daughter Claudia and her husband, John, had had a second child – and Andrew was at Kent University doing English. Caroline had moved into the top floor of my house in Maida Vale, and Roger was still living with Penny, but boarding at Mill Hill. Curiously, Perk House seemed to cost as much to run with two in it as it had with six.

In order to pay for this and the growing needs of my married children, I had a few projects lined up, though nothing that excited me much. *The Man Most Likely To...*, which I'd left at the Duke of York's in a healthy condition with Henry Magee in the lead, had suffered the same fate as when Jack Watling stepped into the lead role a few years earlier. A matter of weeks after I left for Australia, bookings fell and the show folded. This inevitably discouraged my possible backers for the movie version and the project was put firmly back on the shelf, where it has lingered ever since.

I had hoped that Stella Richman and David Frost's company might by now have come up with something under the terms of my contract with them. Instead, they claimed my trip to Australia was in breach of our agreement and they moved to terminate the contract.

I went to see the lawyers retained by Equity, who urged me to sue. David Frost had become very powerful in the industry, and they seemed to think my contract was a good one. So we went to court. I asked Carrie if she would testify about the contractual discussions at which she'd been present. She was kind enough to agree, even though while I was in Australia she'd married John Bennett, whom I'd worked with in *Crooks Anonymous* in the early sixties. She told the court I'd made it clear from the start that a tour Down Under was always on the cards, and Frost's people had said that was OK. However, Frost's lawyer was one of the best in the business and we lost with a big roll of drums.

It was irritating to me that, early in the run-up to the case, the Frost/Richman company had offered to pay me something in settlement. It wasn't a great deal, but with hindsight it was madness going to court, and the whole affair was made worse by one of the papers grossly mis-quoting my opinion of him. I had a high regard for David Frost, and still have.

While the court case was going on, I was rehearsing a play called *Roger's Last Stand* with Roy Kinnear. We took it on tour, where it did well enough to come into the Duke of York's Theatre. Here, though, it was not a great success. Worse, in the way these things happen, it led directly to another doubtful venture when I became a member of Lloyds of London, which I regretted almost from day one.

One of the girls in the cast had an uncle who

was involved with various syndicates in this great cockpit they call the Insurance Market. Like a lot of people, I was easily seduced by the idea of not having to put any actual cash into the deal in order to draw a return. One simply had to put up assets to demonstrate that, if the underwriters got their sums wrong, one could put one's hands on the shortfall. Of course, I was told, they never get their sums wrong, so the need will never arise. And it was true that for a few years all went well. Then, lo and behold, a whole lot of risks turned out not to be profitable. I didn't lose any money, but I wasn't making any either, so after a few more years I decided to give it up before my luck ran out, as it had for so many others. There wasn't any obvious cloud in the sky, but I had to wait three years before my release.

On the plus side of *Roger's Last Stand*, I got to work with Roy Kinnear, which was a joy. He was a very likeable chap, always joking, brave as a lion, sound, loyal and solid – physically solid, too, with a body as hard as iron. I had to hit him in the course of the play, and for maximum verisimilitude he urged me to do it with as much strength as I could. It was like hitting a cliff, and he didn't flinch an inch. Even taking into account that I've never been very good at boxing, it was impressive – Roy could take any amount of punishment. In my efforts to hit him hard, I succeeded only in breaking three of my fingers. He was, in all, a lovely man, happily married and coping with great courage and generosity with a disabled child, which led him to devote a lot of time and energy to the benefit of several related charities.

Meanwhile, Vicki had invited some Australian friends over to Ibiza, where she was as happy as a sandlark. We were regularly in touch on the phone; while I paid the bills she made sure the *finca* was well looked after.

The following year it was suggested that I revive a lovely old play and tour it abroad, with me directing. I jumped at the chance. *To Dorothy a Son* was one of my favourite plays, which I'd originally done twenty years before with my ex-wife, Penny. We booked it into Bournemouth in the baking, dry summer of '76, and drove there across the parched, brown desert that much of southern England had become, reminding me of the more arid parts of Morocco.

It's a sweet play, with only three in the cast, and it went down so well in its short stay on the South Coast that we decided to take it to Hong Kong, where audiences always reacted well to traditional English plays. Our confidence was repaid when it proved to be a success there. The whole trip felt like a holiday.

I was on my way home, via Bombay once again, when I got a call from John Gale, my partner in Cyclone Films, and a busy, daring impresario.

'Leslie, thank God I've found you! I've been trying to track you down – the cast list for the new Michael Pertwee play is ready.'

I'd agreed to play the lead in *Sextet* at the Criterion, and had asked for casting approval as well. 'Good. Who have you got in mind for the main girl?'

'Angela Scoular, I thought,' John said. 'And

she's available.'

I'd always had a lot of time for Angie Scoular as an actress – she'd impressed me ten years before when I first saw *The Man Most Likely To...* in Windsor, and again when she'd played a wonderful Bond girl with just the right blend of sophistication and coquetry as she scribbled her phone number on George Lazenby's thigh. She'd been great fun to work with, too, even while pregnant on *Doctor in Trouble*, and we'd always got on well.

'Great!' I said. 'I like her; I've been wanting to work with her again.'

'Excellent. I'll see you in six weeks' time for first rehearsal.'

I could hardly wait to get back and start work on the play.

Sextet felt like a hit from the moment I read it. It was cleverly constructed, unusual and well balanced, with good lines distributed among the parts. Six people on a yacht, hence the title, although perhaps it could have been just as accurately called *Sex at Sea,* or *How to Hump in a Bunk.* One couple had been invited on the cruise so that the boss of an advertising agency can judge whether or not the husband is suitable for an important job in his firm. Mistresses and estranged wives supply the complications – and it all happens at sea, which was to surround us in the theatre.

The play was to be directed by Robin Midgeley, with whom I'd done a television play by Fay Weldon, which he'd insisted on broadcasting live on the grounds that would give it more edge. During the course of our broadcast, all the lights at Pebble Mill went out. By good fortune, the dialogue involved difficulties with builders cocking things up, which allowed me to ad lib into the pitch black (which I thought was being broadcast to the nation), 'And now they've messed up the electricity, too!'

The public never heard it; they were already listening to a continuity person apologising.

Sextet was blessed with a strong opening cast: Julia Lockwood, Peter Blythe, Carol Hawkins, Angela Scoular, me and Julian Fellowes. Julian had a wonderful part, the aspirant employee, and some of the best lines. He thought he was going to walk away with all the notices and was sure the play would lift him right up the ladder. However, it seemed gravity was against him and he didn't quite pull it off. He told me, though, that he was also busy writing; I encouraged him to stick with it – which turned out to be very good advice indeed, in view of his recent Oscar.

Angie was playing the skipper's wife, a slutty and anarchic woman. Told by her husband to wash up, she responds by throwing all the crockery over-board – which Angie enjoyed immensely. She found it more difficult chucking a cream cake into Julia Lockwood's face every night. It was, in fact, a big round bath sponge with a hole gouged in the middle that was filled with double cream; the thing was never properly washed out and so it started to go off, leaving poor Julia with a face full of sour cream every night. That, as they say, is show business!

When I started rehearsals with Angie, I couldn't deny how strongly she interested me. By the time rehearsals were over, Angie and I had become close. But with the long distance between me and Vicki, she had read the writing on the wall, packed up her chillums, kaftans and ethnic baggage, and moved on. I heard that she too had met someone else, and was forwarding her acting career.

Angie had many connections in the theatre through her maternal aunt, Margaret Johnston, who'd been a well-regarded star in British movies during the '50s and played leads at the RSC. When her husband, the famous theatrical agent Al Parker, died, Margaret stopped acting and took over the running of the agency – a task in which she revelled and became notoriously powerful. Angie had grown up knowing a number of her aunt's illustrious clients – I don't doubt, for instance, that at some point in her childhood she'd been dandled on James Mason's knee. I'd met him in Hollywood, of course, when she was about ten.

When the play got to Eastbourne she was invited to stay in the home of another of her aunt's clients, Peggy Cummins, with whom I had shared a lot of laughs and some great moments on the set of *In the Doghouse* almost twenty years earlier. Naturally Peggy asked her house guest if she'd like to bring me up to dinner one evening. It was lovely to see Peggy again, but I could tell she was surprised by my interest in Angie. I was in my early fifties by then, Angie in her early thirties, though it didn't feel like such a terrible gap to me.

When our tour reached Bath, I bought Angie an opal-encrusted scorpion (her birth sign). She said it was the first piece of jewellery she'd ever been given, and there in that lovely Georgian gem of a city we fell in love, finishing the pre-London tour on a great high which, I felt, marked the beginning of a new era for both of us.

Sextet came into London and opened at the Criterion on 13 April 1977. The London critics were not over-kind, although Michael Billington described me as British theatre's favourite phallic symbol; while *Punch,* having knocked the play for its plethora of puns, described me as 'King Leer'.

But despite the critics' best efforts to rubbish the play, it had all the public appeal I'd anticipated. The punters flocked in. It was a fun show to be in and the audiences were all on my side. By this time, Angie and I were living together in Maida Vale. For a number of reasons, I loved doing this play as much as any of the long-runners I've done in the West End.

It was memorable in other ways, too. In one scene, Julian's character loses a contact lens and concludes that it must have fallen into the gin and tonic he just drunk. One of the cast suggests that if he eats some roughage, it will, after an appropriate lapse of time, reappear. So he goes off and gets a large frying pan in which to lay his stool, followed by a funny, quite daring scene in which the lens is recovered.

The frying pan, obviously, was a very important prop. One Saturday matinee, we came in to find the stage management team in a terrible state.

'Where's the frying pan?' someone asked.

'How on earth should I know?' I replied.

'It's disappeared – someone must have taken it.'

'Who'd want to steal a frying pan?' I said, and carried on to my dressing room. To my amazement, the handle of the missing prop was sticking out from underneath my armchair. I went to the door and called the stage manager, who came rushing in with the rest of the crew.

'What's it doing in your room?'

'How the hell should I know?'

One of them pulled it out. We all gasped with horror. In it was a bloody great turd, as described in the script.

We all gazed at it, shocked, until one of the stage management laughed. 'For God's sake,' he said. 'It's one of those rubber joke ones.' And he picked it up.

'Uurgh!!' He dropped it as if it were electrified. It was human and terribly real.

The presence of this object in the prop frying pan in my room was grotesque and inexplicable, but it became more so when other turds kept turning up all over the theatre – on one of the girls' dressing tables, two along the corridors, on the stairs, in the middle of the lavatory floor. Every evening a new batch of turds was dropped around the building. This was rather disturbing and we had no idea who was responsible.

After a few days of this, we called in the police. They said we would have to lock the stage door and everyone must be checked in and come through the front of house. Still the turds kept on coming.

'It's what they call an inside job!' someone joked with the theatre manager, though it certainly wasn't funny any more.

The original old stage doorkeeper had been so stiff and uncommunicative that we often joked that the management of the theatre were saving money by having a waxwork copy placed on the door. Recently, though, he'd been replaced by a new chap. We came to the conclusion that this new chap might be responsible for the faecal plague. He wasn't charged, but the management sacked him. After that, the turds stopped. We heard that he got a job at another theatre, though we never heard of an outbreak there, so the mystery lived on.

The set for the play was novel and elaborate. The boat was set in a tank of water, so it would look as if it were out at sea. When Julian left the production, we decided in a traditional, light-hearted thespian manner to play a farewell trick on him on his last night.

There was a scene in which he had to jump over the far side of the boat into the water. We poured some greasy yellow fluid into the tank, just out of sight of the audience. It looked suspiciously grimy and I left a notice floating on it, 'Goodbye, Julian – we've all anointed it in here.'

I'm not sure poor Julian got the joke, though. In all honesty, I don't think I'd have done either, had I been the victim. When I met him years later in Scotland on *Monarch of the Glen*, just after he'd won an Oscar for his *Gosford Park* screenplay, we had a good laugh at the memory, with masses of congratulations from me for his tremendous success as a writer, reminding him that Tony Hopkins maintained an Oscar was worth more than a knighthood.

In April 1978, a year after it had opened, *Sextet* was renamed *Six of One*, partly for the benefit of provincial ticket agencies whose punters thought the original title might be rude, and partly due to the theatre's geographical position, surrounded by small sex cinemas showing films with titles like *Hard Up!*, *My Swedish Meatball*, and *Truck-Stop Women*. I'd never actually noticed any punters in raincoats looking especially disappointed that ours wasn't a dirty show, and the name-change brought a few minor problems.

Friends who thought I was in a new play came to see me afterwards and said, 'Sorry if this sounds cheeky, but haven't we seen this play before?'

It was a little embarrassing when they thought the new name was just a wheeze for duping people into coming twice.

In November '78, *Six of One* closed nearly two years after it opened. During the run, Angie and I had gone from strength to strength. I admired her as an actress, I adored her, and I loved her company; she was intelligent, observant and very funny. To give ourselves a break after the continuous run of the play, I took her to Ibiza for the first time. Once I'd dealt with the hassles of removing yet another bunch of non-paying tenants, she loved it as much as I thought she would. As always, I was delighted to be there to unwind, and we returned to London refreshed and happy. Like Caesar, taking the tide of affairs at the flood, I suggested that she move into Maida Vale with me. Nearly thirty years later, she's still here! Not bad for a couple of busy actors.

When seven, Angie's son Dan came to live with us both in Maida Vale. While she'd been working throughout the '70s, Angie's mother had looked after Dan's day-to-day needs, and virtually brought him up. Perhaps inevitably, she'd come to view Dan almost as her own. This did cause a few problems. We always tried to accommodate her, but it was difficult; puzzling for Dan and not easy for Angie. Meanwhile, I committed myself to taking responsibility for him and, although I never formally adopted him, I treated him as I did my own two sons.

Later that year my ex-wife Penny, still in her early fifties, suffered a serious and very debilitating stroke. She was with her Russian boyfriend at the time – another actor. She was taken first to the hospital in Burnt Oak, and then to a small hospital not far from where I live in Maida Vale. She underwent an operation there, but sadly it was a deep stroke which made mobility very difficult for her.

Caroline, my eldest daughter, was hugely solicitous and rallied round courageously to attend her mother. She was sure that Penny had been prescribed too many drugs by her doctors in the past. Penny had always been prone to headaches, hay fever, bad backs and all sorts of complaints that required external remedies. Caroline told me about all the jars of pills in Penny's cupboard and I agreed with her that they couldn't have helped.

From time to time Angie and I would fetch her from the hospital and bring her back to my house in Maida Vale for visits, sometimes with the family. Thankfully, she and Angie got on well, but the truth was, as far as I was concerned, in many ways I had never stopped feeling married to her. Certainly I'd continued to take my fatherly duties and the upkeep of Perk House very seriously, and so far hadn't remarried.

When Penny was able to leave hospital, she moved in with Caroline and her husband Mike, but while she was there, she fell and broke her hip. When it was repaired, she was determined to move back to Perk House, which she was able to do only with a lot of support from Caroline, and others, including Roger, who was now up at Cambridge. She did her best to cope, but couldn't do the things she most wanted to, like tending the flowers in her beloved garden, or walking her Labrador (successor to Pippa) in the green fields behind the house in Mill Hill.

Having developed strategies for coping with her mother's great affection for Dan, Angie and I were settling into an enjoyable and fulfilling life together. We decided that we would work together whenever we could.

One of the first suitable projects was a revival of *Canaries Sometimes Sing*, a charming comedy of manners written by Frederick Lonsdale in 1929. In 1930, it had been a hit on Broadway and a movie had been made starring Yvonne Arnaud. It's a sharply observed portrayal of two couples who realise they ought to swap spouses, but have to confront all the doubts, disruption and disapproval this would cause in pre-war England.

Lonsdale, a sophisticated and highly regarded playwright in his time, had created a clever device through which my character – Geoffrey, a commercially successful playwright, downtrodden by his social climbing wife – is able to deliver his asides. He has a pet canary (who lives in a cage which doubles as a metaphor for the Lonsdales' marriage) in whom he confides as he tries to decide whether he should abandon his marriage. Done right, the device works well in revealing his private thoughts which drive the plot.

Frank Hauser, our director, told me he would get a cage with a stuffed canary in it.

'Why can't we have a real one?' I asked.

'God, no! We don't want a live bird fluttering around all over the place.'

'But you do! That's exactly what you want. If I have to talk to the bird, and it just sits there looking ... well ... stuffed, it could be quite boring.'

'But we can't have a real bird.'

'Let's try it!' I begged.

Our live canary was a great success. As we bonded and it became used to me, he would get very excited, fluffing out his feathers when I walked over to talk to him (if it was a 'him' – I never knew). Some nights, he even earned his own applause. He was so helpful to the production, we had to get him an understudy.

We put it on at the Yvonne Arnaud in Guildford

in early '79, with Nyree Dawn Porter playing opposite me. That production didn't make it to the West End, but I knew the play well by this time and, thinking it had a broad appeal, I decided to take it to South Africa, with me directing and starring, and Angie taking over the leading woman's excellent role.

It was great to be back in South Africa, and with Angie for company. The play was a huge success in Cape Town and went down as well as I could have hoped. I soon plunged back into seeking out more of the wonderful stones and African carvings I'd found on my last tour.

When the summer holidays started in England, Dan came out to join us. We'd sent him to Swanbourne House, a good boarding school in Buckinghamshire where he was beginning to settle in. It was lovely for Angie to have him out here with us, and a great excuse for me to revisit all the wonderful places I'd been with Andrew and Roger in the early seventies.

We'd been invited by the Rattrays to visit the MalaMala Game Reserve, a privately owned region of the Kruger National Park, where they ran a beautiful safari lodge. As we had only a couple of days, instead of driving the 500-mile round trip to the Park as I had last time, I hired a small plane to fly us from Johannesburg. It may have been quicker, but it was many times more terrifying. Our pilot, as often seems to be the case in these small aircraft, was very casual, even cavalier about the whole thing. He started by asking if we minded giving a friend of his a lift to somewhere which may or may not have been on the way. Of course, we said we didn't mind, but I was quite concerned when the pilot got lost and had to find his way by flying up the Sand River. When we came to land at the safari lodge in MalaMala, we approached it from the wrong side, and landed out of sight. Since no one had seen us arrive, no one came out to meet us.

The pilot switched off the engine and I looked around in the eerie silence. There was no sign of the lodge or its buildings or the stockade that surrounded it. We were very close to thick bush, and in the open a number of buffalo and other animals were shambling about. The Afrikaner pilot couldn't raise the lodge on his radio and it looked as if we were going to have to walk. I started climbing out, when he stopped me.

'There are wild animals out there, man. You can't just walk around without protection. Listen, I've got a gun; I'll go and we'll come back and get you. Whatever you do, don't leave the plane.'

As if we were likely to!

He pulled a revolver from his locker and jumped down, leaving Angie, Dan and me sitting in the plane in the middle of the open veldt gazing suspiciously at baboons, zebra and grazing buffalo, to name but a few. God knows what other predators were lurking under the cover of the nearby bush. I could only think that, if for some reason our intrepid pilot didn't make it to the lodge, we'd be stranded, defenceless, amid thousands of deadly animals. Eventually, however, he did return with a jeep from the lodge and with great relief we bounced across the dusty landscape and into the lodge compound. We were given a tremendous welcome and made very comfortable, but we were already dreading the return journey.

In the morning, very early, the three of us, along with a Bolivian gold merchant and his wife, piled into a Land Rover driven by a white ranger with a black ranger riding rearguard, and set off into the bush. Once again it was the bird life that impressed me even more than the animals, but I received a sudden surge of adrenaline when we encountered our first lioness.

This was made more alarming by the fact that, early in the day, the white ranger had clumsily dropped his weapon from the vehicle and the stock had broken, making it effectively unusable. I'm not saying that James Bond couldn't have shot someone with it, if it were all he had in a tight spot, but that was clearly beyond the skill of our white ranger. He had, he informed us with a light laugh, also forgotten to bring his regulation revolver. He didn't seem to mind; he was far more interested in taking photos which, no doubt, he was hoping to sell. He had brought with him an elaborate camera in a hefty metal case.

The lioness was lying a few feet from the edge of the track ahead when we first spotted her. We slowed, and the large, rather scruffy animal, peeved at having her snooze interrupted, lurched to her feet yawning like a lazy cat and sauntered off along the track. After a few dozen yards she turned towards a large spreading banyan tree, no doubt to continue her siesta.

Our ranger leapt at the chance to get a close

411

shot of the beast. Fumbling his camera from its case, he let the lid drop back with a sharp bang. Instantly the lioness stopped in her tracks, turned round, gave us a rudely hostile glare and started to stalk back towards us.

With no rifle and no revolver, the ranger was more scared than we were as this gorgeous killing machine strolled slowly towards us with a predatory gleam in her eye. To compound the terror, there was no consensus between the two rangers as to how we should handle it. The black ranger told us to stay calm and still, while the idiot white ranger thought that shouting at her would 'scare her off'.

I opted for quiet and sat stock still; the others thankfully did the same until, abruptly, she lost interest, stopped, yawned and flopped to the ground with her tongue hanging out, clearly not hungry but sleepy.

'Thank God!' I thought. Not only was she not ready for another meal, she was exhausted, hot and needed a kip.

Our white ranger didn't need to be persuaded to get in gear and get out – the other way. We soon met plenty of other beasts: giraffe and small herds of zebra and eland. Grateful to have survived the day, we continued on our way home, hungry and ready to relax as the sun started to drop like a flaming orange over the distant peaks to the west. And then the booby at the wheel drove straight into a gully and broke the Land Rover's axle.

We were now stranded. The white ranger grinned sheepishly at our unappreciative faces; the Bolivian, a practical man, produced a bottle of brandy, while the black ranger tried to get through to the lodge on the radio. Eventually he succeeded and rescue was on its way. However, we were still quite a long way out. Dusk in Africa lasts only a few minutes, and we were soon sitting in the pitch dark. The black ranger took out his lamp and swung it around to discourage the wildlife. We all had a little more brandy to anaesthetise us, or give us courage, if required. But as the ranger swung an arc of light around the vehicle, we saw dozens of pairs of eyes gleaming in the dark. We were surrounded by a herd of bloody buffalo, accompanied by a loud chomping noise and a lot of heavy bovine breathing. I had no idea then how dangerous buffalo could be, but I couldn't have been more sweaty if I'd been Humphrey Bogart in *The African Queen*.

When at last the rescue party reached us and drove the beasts back into the black velvet night, I was told that buffalo, when aroused, can be very dangerous indeed. Back inside the security of Rattray's camp, Dan thought it was the most exciting thing that had ever happened to him. Angie and I, on the other hand, did not and quickly returned to our *rondeval* for a change of underwear and a swim.

We ought to have felt we were avenging our fear that evening when we dined on assorted wild animals that had been culled on the reserve, but the truth is, while I'm quite happy to eat a hunk of beef from some bullock reared on the rich green pastures of England, when it came to chewing my way through ex-members of the herd of wildebeest and buffalo that roamed the plains around us, I wasn't entirely comfortable. However, the great fire, assembled company and unlimited brandy soon put my mind at rest.

The following day, as we were about to set off back to Johannesburg, the pilot staggered out to our aircraft with a vicious hangover, and found the battery in the plane was completely flat. He had to get it going with jump leads from one of the lodge's trucks. This didn't inspire confidence. Nevertheless, we made it back to Johannesburg, shaken but not broken, but I vowed, next time I went on safari, I'd check the firearms and be more careful in my choice of pilots.

Over the next twenty years, travelling with Angie became a regular activity for me. Apart from flights to Ibiza, nearly all my travelling has been connected to my work, in so far as I have always tried to take an interesting route, detouring both ways through as many new places as I can.

When we returned from *Canaries* in South Africa, I was due to play on stage the same role I'd had in the film version of Ray Cooney's *Not Now, Darling*. Ray's plays are always fun, the production was a great success and we had a very good Christmas season at the Savoy Theatre. When Ray asked me if Angie and I would like to go to Australia with this production, it suited us very well. In 1981, we set off on what turned out to be an extended world tour with, variously, David Jason and Andrew Sachs.

On our way to Australia and the Far East, we had time to stop in Sri Lanka, a country I'd wanted to visit for a long time. I'd always heard how beautiful it was, and how sophisticated the people were. We weren't disappointed. The Sri Lankans, like the Indians, are tremendous British movie buffs and they gave me a terrific welcome. Visiting Kandy, where the tooth of the Buddha resides in a beautiful temple, we were about to enter the lift in our hotel when the bellboy dropped all the cases he was carrying and gaped in utter astonishment at seeing me. It turned out that the national TV station had been running a season of British comedy films and I'd been in every one of them. The boy obviously thought that somehow I'd crept into his psyche. I managed to reassure him he wasn't seeing a phantasm, and even proved it by giving him a hefty tip, though he still went on his way in a daze. Although over the years I've grown used to being recognised, this, I think, was the most extreme example.

Our sojourn in the peaceful beauty of Sri Lanka set us up for what was to be quite a gruelling tour, but I was delighted to be back in Australia. As a result of local Equity union rules, the only English actors who were allowed to perform there were me and Andrew Sachs. This gave Angie a nice big lump of free time, although, with a mother born in Australia, we ought to have been able to get her a special card.

It was fun being there with Angie because she was so inquisitive about everything. Although her father was Scottish, her mother's powerful Australian genes seemed to come to the fore. We went and researched her maternal family and looked for the house where her mother had been born in Mossman in southern Sydney. I hadn't really looked at the old colonial districts on my previous tour, and I was struck in areas like Paddington how very elegant and well preserved some of the early Victorian houses were, with their cast-iron 'lacework' around the balconies. There was a great deal I loved about Australia and, for a few weeks of madness, I even became very excited about the possibility of buying an exquisite house in Adelaide. But in the end, I had to remind myself I already had three houses and I couldn't really be sure how much time I would get to spend there.

The play, as I'd expected, was a big hit in Australia. Not for the first time, I observed that the further one is from London, the more appreciative the audiences become. The company was an amiable one and we all got on. I made great friends with Andrew Sachs and his wife, finding him a remarkably versatile actor and an engaging man. Our local implants did well, too; although, as with *The Man Most Likely To...*, we had accent issues, the audiences didn't seem to mind.

We had a wonderful time on the west coast, where we appeared in a lovely theatre in Subiaco, a pretty suburb of Perth on the north shore of the Swan River estuary. Once again Dan came out to visit us, and we took a trip to Rottnest, one of the few islands accessible from Perth, and an extraordinary former penal colony. Rottnest meant 'rat's nest', so called because the island is infested by a unique Antipodean creature called a quokka, a very small sort of wallaby that looks like a rat with excessive hind legs and the capacity to jump very high. All the dwellings were

416

quaintly built on stilts to prevent the little creatures leaping in.

The island is only about four miles by six, and there are no private cars allowed. All visitors hire bicycles, and the lack of motors unquestionably added to the island's charm. It was visits to bizarre places such as Rottnest that made foreign touring such a wonderful experience, and I don't think I'd have done it so willingly without that opportunity.

While we were still in Perth, my daughter Caroline phoned to say that her mother had died in a fire at Perk House. I knew that Penny's condition had been deteriorating, and Caroline had warned me that she feared something like this might happen. My children wanted me to come back to London right away to help deal with the fallout and attend the funeral.

I had to explain that there was nothing I could do about coming back. Obviously, I was devastated by Penny's death – after all, we'd been part of each other's lives for over thirty years, and for a good proportion of that time, happily married – but my coming home wasn't going to bring her back. And there was no way I could simply leave the production – I *was* the show. If I went, they would have to close the production, an awful lot of people would be badly let down, and I would be sued. Leaving was simply not an option.

To this day my family have never really forgiven me for not coming back, and I will always regret that. But I'm sure there's nothing I could have done that they didn't achieve admirably themselves, especially Caroline, with the help of her prosperous and efficient husband, Mike Ludbrook.

I carried on my tour with a heavy heart. Angie understood, of course, how much of a wrench it was for me, in spite of the many difficulties Penny and I had had over the past twenty years. But before I could get back to England we were committed to runs in Hong Kong and Canada.

When finally, towards the end of 1982, I was able to come back to England, the first thing I did was to drive to Horley in Surrey, where Penny was buried in the cemetery of the church closest to where she'd grown up. I could only hope and pray that now, at last, she was at peace.

15 • All Change

Five years after Angie and I first got together, we decided to get married. We'd been wanting to for some time, but with the problems surrounding Penny and, of course, my children, we had chosen to wait. Now, the situation had changed completely; Penny, God bless her, and all her turbulent anxieties were laid to rest, and the children were all grown up. I was moving into a new phase of my life and marrying Angie seemed an integral part of this.

We were able to have a full, traditional wedding in the Queen's Chapel of the Savoy, a serene and beautiful space just off the Strand in the midst of theatreland. I'd known the vicar there for many years and, now that he could legitimately marry me in his church, he was delighted to do it. Through a friendly MP, we held our reception on the terrace of the House of Commons, within whistling distance of the ranting chamber and the corridors of power. Ray Cooney – colleague, travelling companion and close mate – was my best man, and gave a speech as slick and irreverent as any of the long-running farces he had written. He soon got the gathering going, laughing as loudly as any audience at his plays, and largely at my expense, bless him!

Angie and I were both working at the time, so we had to snatch the date from the jaws of a gluttonous diary. We were able to spare only two days for our honeymoon at Wheeler's on the seafront in Brighton. It was cosy and a lovely break, but it wasn't as if we needed to get to know each other. We came back happily to Maida Vale, where normal service was quickly resumed.

After all the recent turbulence in my life, I suddenly had the urge to take another path I'd been keen – though wary – to tread. It was time to take my career in a new direction. I was tired of the kind of roles I was best known for. They had paid handsomely over the years, but I was now firmly stuck in a groove – that's the flip-side of fame. It was risky, but I felt I had to get out and open up my career.

Up until then, I'd had the occasional chance to do things outside that persona, whether as actor, director or producer, but these had all been low

419

key and generally beneath the public radar. I was now fifty-seven and knew that if I was to test myself, to prove I really had it in me to play big, dramatic roles, I couldn't leave the change any longer. And it had to be done firmly and without compromise. For the first time in my career, I had to contemplate doing something I'd never voluntarily done before – TURN WORK DOWN!

All my life I'd been squeezing in almost anything anyone asked me to do, provided the money was there, because I felt that was an actor's function. Now I was preparing to make a complete *volte face*.

NO MORE RUBBISH! was the new cry. TAKE CHANCES! CALL FOR THE CLASSICS! ENJOY YOURSELF!

I talked about it with Angie, and she encouraged me; I told friends, colleagues, agents and producers that any parts involving lecherous twits with suave chat-up lines and dysfunctional trouser braces would not be considered. When I came across friends in the more serious side of the business, I let it be known that I was up for challenging roles in which my undoubted forty years' experience would be useful, and might surprise a few people.

After my impecunious childhood, the urge to grab every opportunity to earn was deeply ingrained and it was quite nerve-wracking to turn away people who wanted to give me money for jobs that I could have done without thinking. But, against the advice of agents and bank managers, I stuck it out until my first reward came through the unlikely portal of actor, producer and friend,

Bill Kenwright.

I hadn't done anything significant for Bill, but he was someone I often saw around, and he had employed many of my colleagues. He was a daring producer with an air of mystery about him. As far as I know he is unique in his field, having sprung from the clutches of a major television soap opera – for years he played Gordon Clegg in *Coronation Street*. By the late seventies he was already established in his secondary role as a theatrical producer, in which he was to become spectacularly successful – to the point where he was able to buy Everton Football Club in 1999, which can't have been cheap.

His new project was a play called *Chapter 17* by Simon Gray, which had already been done at the National under a different name. It was a serious play, tangentially a study of alcoholism and personal breakdown, but the author had now substantially rewritten it to make it more commercial. Unlike other producers at the time, Bill was not swayed or scared by my old cinematic image. He never questioned my ability to handle serious roles and had no qualms about seeing me for the lead in this next production.

I liked the author; I liked the part, and they offered it to me. I was thrilled. At last – a lead in a solid, quality play!

One of the changes that Simon Gray had made meant that my character's father, played in the National production by Michael Redgrave, had become my mother. This character has very little to say and sits silently throughout most of the play. The actress playing the mother in our production resented having to sit around at rehearsals not speaking while I delivered my lines, and she wouldn't stay for them.

That made it hard for me. With Simon's complex lines, it was important to have someone to listen and react. The problem was eased a little, however, when the theatre cat jumped up into her chair.

'Ah, good!' I said. 'Someone for me to talk to.'

Fortuitously, I've always enjoyed talking to cats and, indeed, I've never been without one at home. Or a dog. They make marvellous listeners who, unlike spouses, never contradict one. But I'm wandering.

My role was powerfully written – and based in part, I think, on the author himself, who admitted his problems with alcohol. A good friend gave me some constructive notes on the mindset and physical demeanour of alcoholics, the mild paranoia and the way they walk as if they're treading on soft ground. However, in spite of the wonderful writing and characterisation, there is a serious flaw in the structure of the play. My character, whom Simon sets up brilliantly in the first act, doesn't appear again until towards the end of the second act, when the dynamic drive has gone and it's too late to save it.

This failing wasn't helped by a director who, despite his good reputation, hadn't, I felt, really understood the play. We had a strong cast, though, and the author was present for most of the rehearsals, surreptitiously directing me, giving me notes and help, *en passant*. Simon was, in my view, a wonderful director; I sucked up everything he gave and used it. When I asked him why he didn't just take it over, he simply shook his head. Perhaps he felt it was enough to take responsibility for the lines.

The play kicked off a short tour in Guildford with the aim of a final billet in the West End. Despite its shortcomings, it was a smashing play and did very well on tour. I think perhaps *Chapter 17* was one of the best things I've ever done. Simon seemed delighted with the way I handled it, while I was almost surprised that I'd pulled it off, attributing the success of my performance to some of the most interesting lines I'd ever delivered. My favourite, said when pissed, was, 'I'm a lucky man to have such an unlucky wife.'

Of course, I was disappointed when it didn't come back to London, though I knew it would have needed more work to sort it out beforehand. I don't know if Simon ever tried to repair it; perhaps after one rewrite, he didn't think it worth another. Nevertheless, as first strike in my quest for better roles, I was delighted with this public outing in a serious, intelligent play, and was confident that something similar would soon crop up in another quality play that would take me to the West End.

At home, Angie and I were coping with the constant involvement of her mother and aunts. Inevitably there had been a lingering fallout from Penny's death, particularly for the two children closest to her, Caroline and Roger, and I was still deeply upset she had suffered so much. Roger, only recently up to Cambridge when she'd died, had been so devastated by the tragedy that he was reluctant to carry on with his studies. I went to Cambridge to talk to his tutors, a group of astonishingly erudite and yet practical human beings. Between us we eventually persuaded Roger to resume his studies, though I think perhaps his mother's death and the tragic circumstances of it had left a bigger scar on him, as the youngest, than it had on the others.

Caroline's marriage was running a familiar course, tacking from drama to crisis. She had four children now – Claudia, Gemma, Hannah and James – and loved having a big family, as well as masses of animals. Andrew, who'd set out on life's highway without a map, had become an expert in philately, and was appointed head of Stanley Gibbons' office in Monte Carlo. I've never really seen the pleasure to be gained in stamp collecting; they are not objects of inherent beauty or physical worth, depending only on the esoteric values of rarity and market forces for their desirability. I understand the purpose of speculative investment, but give me a Modigliani or a well-polished opal any time. Nevertheless, I was delighted that Andrew had found a field that engaged him. Once Roger had settled back into university life, heading eventually for a career in law, I enjoyed going up there to see him when I could.

Around this time, Angie arrived home one day with a red cat given to her by one of her aunts who found it at the garage on the M1 where she used to fill up. It was a heavenly, mischievous creature with skewbald markings, who like to steal food from any dish on the table. We named him Prawn, and his genes stayed with us for many years over several generations, establishing the feline domination of the garden for the next twenty-five years, and counting.

I was already reaching an age where close friends were coming to the end of their innings. That summer, the irreverent, outrageous and much-loved Kenneth More died. He was a super actor, as warm and friendly as his public persona, but a lot more wild-tongued and fond of women, right to the end, than his fans may have realised. The day Ken died, I was in a recording studio on a boat in Little Venice with Terry-Thomas, trying to make a commercial in which we played a couple of secondhand car salesmen. This was casting in the old mould, but I didn't mind doing the odd voice-over even if it drew from the earlier career. Terry's Parkinson's disease, presaged by his forgetfulness and disorientation when we were making *Spanish Fly* in Menorca in '75, was now so bad that he simply couldn't do the job at all. However, in order not to hurt his feelings, we went through the motions; the director agreed to shoot it and let him go and then we did it again. It was very sad for me, seeing my old friend in such a state and undoubtedly at the end of his career.

Despite the disappointment that it hadn't quite made the cut and come into the West End, I'd been thrilled to have the chance to do Simon Gray's *Chapter 17*. A lot of people had come down

425

to see it in Guildford, though, and the notices had encouraged me a great deal. I remained hopeful I'd get more parts like this, preferably in the West End or a serious feature film. Then, in a wonderful twirl in the Dance to the Music of Time, my next job took me back to the Haymarket Theatre, where I'd skipped around as call-boy and gofer to Vivien Leigh, Lilli Palmer and other wondrous stars four decades earlier.

Duncan Wheldon was an ambitious producer, and a good friend who had started his theatrical career in Southport in the box office – an experience we had in common. I was chatting to him in his office when Lyndsay Anderson came in to talk about their next production, Chekhov's *The Cherry Orchard*. Duncan introduced us and Lindsay was kind enough to mention things he'd seen me do that he'd enjoyed. It turned out, too, that he hadn't yet cast the part of Gaev. Perhaps I would be interested?

Besides being moving and profound, *The Cherry Orchard* also has moments of great humour. I love the mixture of drama and comedy, and it was exactly the kind of play in which I wanted to be involved. However, I didn't know the part and said I would take it away and read it. I read it and re-read it, and I was thrilled. Here was a strong, beautifully written, meaty and pivotal role in which I could realise my full potential.

I was cast with Joan Plowright, Frank Finlay, Bernard Miles and Bill Fraser. We rehearsed and set up once again at the Yvonne Arnaud in Guildford on the 3 August. There was a pretty hefty set which didn't suit extended touring and, after a week where we had to trim the tall trees in the set in Brighton, we came into the Haymarket.

It was wonderful to be back there, now starring, and in a production of such quality. Lindsay was a truly marvellous director, kind and clever. It was a joy to work with him and the cast. I told Joan Plowright how I'd first met her husband, Laurence Olivier, in these very wings when he came in uniform to watch Vivien Leigh in *The Doctor's Dilemma*. Joan was in the room upstairs, which Vivien had eschewed in favour of the smaller one at stage level, to which she'd fled the night of the great Cusack calamity.

Many times during our *Cherry Orchard*, Olivier sat in the front row to watch; Anthony Hopkins came and told me how much he'd loved my Gaev, and promised we'd work together. Alec Guinness came back afterwards to see Joan, and asked if he might see me too. She sent him up to my top-floor room and I was delighted to receive an accolade from an actor I so admired.

I revelled in this production of *The Cherry Orchard* for the whole of its very successful run. To be part of a play of such sublime dialogue, characterisation and construction was like drinking nectar, especially for an actor who'd survived most of his life on a diet of theatrical roughage. It was this play above all that finally broke the old mould in which I'd been cast, a quarter of a century before, by *Carry on Nurse*, *Doctor in Love* and their successors.

Ray Cooney, besides being a successful writer/ producer of farce and light comedy, also involved himself as a producer of more serious plays. In conjunction with Paul Elliot, he was planning a second production of Peter Nichol's *Passion Play*. It had been done in 1981 with Albert Finney heading a heavyweight cast, on the edge of the West End, and hailed as a masterpiece. I hadn't seen it, but I'd heard that, despite its great reception, the company had not been happy. When Ray Cooney, who knew very well that I was looking for more challenging roles, asked me to consider it, I read it and found it an extraordinary play of great theatrical inventiveness.

Essentially, it is the story of a man and his wife dissecting their marriage and his infidelity. In a brilliant, virtuoso idea, each was played by two actors – one, the actual character; the other, his/her alter ego. Neither pair has any awareness of the existence of the other, so there must be absolutely no reaction or interaction between the 'Actuals' and the 'Alter Egos', which flies in the face of everything any actor is ever taught, and made timing particularly difficult – in itself a potential source of tension between players. The play is constructed so that the first act is strongly comedic and steeped in a wry wit which Nichol can do to pungent effect. A short way into the second act, though, the play switches into a gut-wrenching, powerful drama.

Ray wanted me to play the 'actual' man, a randy picture restorer who has succumbed to the enticements of a provocative young research student. Ray set up a meeting to discuss my involvement with Peter Nichols and his lovely wife, as well as Mike Okrent, who was directing, and another producer, Michael Aukin.

Peter and his wife, undoubtedly still influenced by my movie persona from twenty years before as they hadn't seen any of my more recent work, thought that I couldn't be right for the part. While I might handle the comedy, they wondered whether I would rise to the drama.

In spite of the extra challenge posed by Peter Nichol's staging, I was confident it was right for me, and that I could do it. Ray wanted me, but he couldn't bring the others with him. I desperately wanted to be in the play – to appear in what could reasonably be called a modern classic was the high point of my ambition – and although I was absolutely not in the habit of chasing parts, I was sure if I could persuade them to see *The Cherry Orchard*, they might revise their view.

I sent a joking card and a great bunch of flowers to Michael Aukin and asked him, please, to come with Peter Nichol and his wife to see my Gaev at the Haymarket. Thank God for Chekhov's combination of comedy and profound drama. They came, they relented, I was given the part. When *The Cherry Orchard* came off I started rehearsals for *Passion Play*.

In one of those strange coincidences that fate likes to chuck in our face from time to time, my mother, now ninety-two, was callously mugged in exactly the spot where the V1 fell on Chingford Mount in 1944, narrowing missing me. Mum was walking near the bus stops, carrying her bag containing all the little bits of jewellery I'd bought her over the years. Three black boys, young teenagers, according to witnesses, tried to grab it, but, with her usual determination, she wasn't going to let them take it. In the struggle, they dragged her along the road and broke a lot of her poor old brittle bones. They left her collapsed and crumpled on the pavement and ran off without her bag. Someone called an ambulance and she was taken to Whipps Cross hospital, the first time in her life she'd had to go to hospital.

I was doing a charity performance for the Salvation Army and, in those pre-mobile days, I couldn't be reached. As soon as I heard, I raced down to the hospital and found my lovely sister Doris already there, caring for our mother with the same affection she had shown her for the last sixty years.

I was devastated – I was so used to my mother being strong, self-reliant and very independent in spirit. I drove back to London and resumed rehearsals for *Passion Play* – a pill to learn – which was now due to open in Leicester. We still didn't know for certain that it would come into the West End after that, but the producers were hopeful. I was less confident than I had been about my part; it was difficult to keep the balance right, and relations with other members of the cast weren't easy. My opposite number was Judy Parfitt, who was a fine actress, and there was some great comedy in the first act. It was clear from early in rehearsal that it was in the nature of the play for there to be tension among the cast, as there had been in the previous production. It was an uncomfortable piece, and relations between opposite numbers and our Alter Egos were constantly uneasy. My Alter Ego, Barry Foster – a client of Angie's aunt Margaret, who adored him – was a good actor, talented and a likeable man, but this was not an easy play to get right, which sometimes involved the Alter Egos playing from an upper level – a second storey, as it were. Once, during our turbulent rehearsals, Barry tumbled off the platform on to the stage where I was standing. I felt that this production, like the last, was already cursed and doomed.

As our opening approached, I was in constant touch with Doris and the hospital about my mother's condition. She was showing no signs of recovery and the added depression this caused me didn't help with the play.

Finally we opened and, as our first night progressed, I began to feel that it was all working, despite all the misgivings. I was encouraged by the big appreciative laughter in the first act and the pin-drop silence that descended as the dramatic tension mounted in the second. It seemed as if there couldn't be a single person in the auditorium who wasn't deeply moved or disturbed by what they were watching.

As the final curtain fell, there was a stunned silence, followed by massive applause. I was now back in my dressing room, thanking every deity I could think of, when Peter Nichol banged on the door and burst in having run round from the front of house. He put his arms around me and hugged me with all his strength.

'Leslie,' he gasped, still panting, 'that was fantastic! Great!'

I nearly cried with joy as I realised just how

nervous he'd been about my part, and that I'd vindicated the risk he and his wife had taken in casting me. Peter was utterly genuine in his appreciation and we were all thrilled to learn that we were definitely going into London when the Leicester run was over.

We were to have an instant transfer, closing in Leicester on a Saturday night, and reopening at Wyndham's Theatre on Charing Cross Road the following week. We took our final bows in Leicester and I drove back to London knowing Mum was in a coma, with the hospital asking me to come as soon as I could.

When I reached the hospital on Sunday morning, my mother was still alive. My sister and brother were there too, of course. I was aware that for the last twenty years or so, my mother had rather taken my sister's help for granted. Doris was a gregarious sort who loved to stop and spend a few minutes with people she knew, but if she happened on friends when walking through Chingford with Mum and started chatting, Mum would complain that she wanted to get on. Nevertheless, Doris, always loyal and selfless, was especially bereft at our mother's passing. In a way, without children of her own, she'd made Mum her child.

The three of us surrounded Mum and I held her hand as she breathed her last. For a moment, she opened her eyes wide, as if she'd seen an angel, before she died. It was deeply moving and with aching hearts we left her peaceful and went into the ante-room. I asked the nurse there if she could let me have Mum's large wedding ring, which hadn't left her finger since the day she married. She fetched it and put it in my hand. I passed it to Doris.

My brother Fred pointed out that it was 25 March, exactly fifty-one years to the day since our dad had died in Middleton Avenue, Chingford. We buried Mum alongside him at the beautiful old All Saints' Church on Chingford Mount where, as a boy, I'd sung in the choir. I gazed around at the setting of my childhood, and thought of all the effort and dedication the courageous woman in the coffin had put into seeking the best for me by taking me up to the Italia Conti School all those years before, and how much I had to thank her for.

There's no doubt that the wounds and trauma of the attack inflicted on her by the three boys in Chingford had ended her life, but the culprits were never caught; never, in my view, seriously sought. I subsequently found time to do some detective work of my own. There wasn't much to go on – a twelve-year-old in a yellow shirt – but even when I thought I'd identified one of the boys, there wasn't enough to persuade the police to check it.

Just after my mother left us, *Passion Play* opened at Wyndham's Theatre. We were all nervous, and made more so when at the half – half an hour before curtain up – stage management announced they had problems with the set and automatic cues. It wasn't surprising; they'd had only a day to set up a highly technical set – two-tiered and revolving, so that characters could move from room to room – with synchronised lighting and music cues. For this, the opening night, when all the critics would be there, they would have to do it all manually, which was bound to make it slower and get in the way of the flow. Aspects of the play depended on the technical set and this complication only added to the difficulty of timing in a play where the Actuals could not take cues from their Alter Egos.

In any other circumstances we would have called the production off, but the First Night audience and all the critics were on their way in and, with the play's history, people were expecting something pretty interesting. The audience weren't told about the technical problems and we opened the play on a wing and prayer. I can't think of any worse circumstances in which to present a West End first night, but *Passion Play* wasn't just a hit, it was an enormous hit in my life, and the best play I've ever done.

The reviews were extraordinary, and the play was finally hailed as the masterpiece many already believed it to be. This production of one of the most daring, challenging, agonising plays I've ever read, ran for over a year. I got some of the best notices I've ever had in my career, which brought the American director Sydney Pollack to the show, after which he asked me to play the Governor in *Out Of Africa*, shot in Kenya with Robert Redford and Meryl Streep.

Many friends came to support me in *Passion Play* and were tremendously generous in their praise. Among them, and as generous as any, was Leonard Rossiter, whom I was to see again very shortly afterwards. We'd both been asked to appear on *This is Your Life* for Patrick Macnee. The programme went well, and it turned out to be a bit of a reunion of old chums, as these things often are, rather like a memorial service.

There was to be a bit of a dinner later, but Leonard was appearing in Joe Orton's *Loot* and I walked up to the theatre with him. As he disappeared through the stage door, he said he'd see me later at the restaurant.

He didn't, though. With great sadness we were later to learn that, after his first entrance, he'd gone back to his room; when he failed to appear again, the call-boy was despatched to summon him. He found Leonard lying on the floor. He'd had a heart attack and was already dead – a healthy man, supremely fit and a regular, hard squash player. These things are inexplicable, and he has been missed so much.

During my three recent plays – the Simon Gray, the Chekhov and the Peter Nichol – Angela had been vitally supportive to me, holding the book, encouraging me when doubts set in, helping me with notes and just by being there beside me. Naturally, when she had a job of her own in Edinburgh and said she was having problems, I jumped in to help her.

The Price of Experience was a three-hander, with two black actors. She was playing a smart lawyer, an enormous role with a lot of lines. She rang to tell me she just wasn't comfortable with it; somehow the lines didn't match her portrayal. She wasn't helped by her director who wasn't offering enough. He would only tell her it wasn't right; not what to do to make it right. I rushed up to Edinburgh to watch the dress rehearsal and afterwards we discussed the part.

'This is a clever, self-assured woman,' I suggested, 'being asked to appear in court for two crooks. She doesn't need their approval, she doesn't need to offer herself to them. At the moment, you're sitting in your chair, too anxious, leaning forward, going to them. Lean *back*, right back into your chair, relax and let them come to you – they need you. Deliver the lines like that, quietly sure of yourself, and it'll make more sense of your character.'

I did ask the director if I could give some advice, and he was happy for me to do so. It wasn't a complicated note, but I hoped it might make all the difference – a simple matter of posture and body language. Angie adopted it, and I'm glad to say it changed the entire way in which the character came across – a small repayment from me for all the help she'd given in the past, and Angie went on to give a terrific performance.

I was reminded of Basil Dean years before when I was in *The Diary of a Nobody*, telling me, 'We're almost there, Leslie, but not quite yet. We'll put some scaffolding round it, and get it right.'

It was wonderful to be back in Africa – Kenya, this time – in exotic but deliciously civilised surroundings. The Shaba National Game Reserve took me back to my adventures with Angie and Dan in the Kruger, but fortunately nothing so adrenaline-pumping occurred here. Although mine was a small part, in *Out of Africa* I had some good strong scenes with Meryl Streep, and it was a huge, if unfamiliar pleasure for me to be part of a serious, thoughtful, Oscar-winning movie that was beautifully lit and directed.

The only sour note in the whole shoot occurred when poor Michael Gough was robbed on the beach with his wife by one of the gangs of brazen muggers that operate along that shore.

On the way home, as usual, we managed to make a detour via Ibiza. This time the hassles that confronted me had been a shock created by visitors. The thank you note left said, had a good time, and sorry about the bed that had been broken and some smashed crockery. But that was the least of the damage. What they hadn't realised, as they left for home, was someone had left a tap running. Over a few weeks this had drained the *cisterna* to drying point, forcing me to think long-term about water. I had several bore holes sunk without result before I started looking for someone who could divine a source and save me littering the whole place with holes. I'm now most careful about who I allow to stay there.

In our usual language of signs, facial expressions and pidgin Spanish, I asked my dear old friend Juan, the former owner of my *finca*, if he knew anyone who could do this for us and he produced a diviner, *el bruco*, a short, dark, horny-skinned man. He paced my land, but the 'Y' branch grasped in his small stubby hands finally quivered only after he'd strayed just beyond the property boundary.

'*Aqui!*' he announced triumphantly.

I made a mental note of the spot beneath a dangling eucalyptus and much later bought more land that included it.

I arrived back in England questioning, not for the first time, the wisdom of being a foreign home owner. As always, though, I came to the conclusion that Ibiza had become a part of me, and getting rid of the *finca* would be like severing a precious limb.

In England, life was running on an even keel. At the age of sixty-two, my career still seemed to have plenty of go in it. Since my decision to jettison the old Leslie Phillips roles and any scripts that included the words 'He*llo!!*' or 'Ding Dong', I'd made real progress. People no longer found it odd that I should be considered for serious dramatic roles or classic plays. And I was delighted when my agent told me Steven Spielberg was coming to London and wanted to see me. He was making a movie of J.G. Ballard's Booker short-listed novel of wartime Japan, *The Empire of the Sun*.

I was immediately impressed when I met him. He had done his homework and, unlike most American directors, he knew a lot about me and the work I'd done. Of course, I knew his work, and his supreme virtuoso skills as a movie maker, and I was delighted when he confirmed that he wanted me to play the part of Maxton, a friend of the family whose child is the key character in the book.

He also told me that most of my scenes would

be shot in a Japanese prison camp and I would have to lose at least two stone off my not particularly corpulent frame. I'd never been asked to do this before and, somewhat naïvely, I thought it was simply a matter of eating less. In fact, I lost over two stone and eventually made myself quite ill.

Seven weeks after I'd seen Spielberg, I turned up to join the film for my first day's shooting on location in Virginia Water, where the dense rhododendron gardens of Surrey were doubling as suburban pre-war Shanghai. Spielberg greeted me warmly, evidently impressed with my emaciated body.

'Leslie!' he laughed with his natural warmth. 'Where did you go?'

We were shooting a lavish scene near the beginning of the film in which I'm greeting the guests who arrive in pristine period cars for a big party. J.G. Ballard himself was in the party and I saw him every day for the week we took to shoot the scene. It was wonderfully impressive in the making, and I looked forward to seeing how it would come out.

The following week we shot a scene where, in the course of the party, my character walks out behind the house to find the family's son, Jim, the pivotal character. The boy is playing with his model planes when he discovers a hundred invading Japanese soldiers appearing from among the bushes in the back garden. When we'd shot the scene, Steven came over.

'Oh, Leslie, I want you to put in a couple of new lines.'

I asked him what they were for.

They were, he told me, a link through from an earlier scene, as he'd decided to cut the whole party, which had just taken a week to shoot at a cost that would have kept a small third world country going for a few days – such is the profligacy of the movie industry.

The whole production then moved to Spain, which was to be the location for the city of Shanghai and the prison camp. In the scenes we shot there, it seemed to me that some of the powerful raw material of the novel was greatly changed, though not by Tom Stoppard, who wrote the original screenplay.

With an eye to the very lucrative Japanese market, editing had substantially softened the edges of Ballard's unremittingly brutal Japanese characters, making them rather more acceptable – it's not always possible to be religious about the book. Perhaps Ballard himself accepted that the movie couldn't be quite so overwhelming as the book.

I loved working with Spielberg and watching the way he worked. There's no doubt of his talent. It was and is a classy movie with some wonderful scenes and performances, not least from Christian Bale. It also gave me the chance to get to know the extraordinary John Malkovich, who became a very good friend and who often used to drop in on me in London. And there was a nice moment of contrast during the making of this big serious movie when Gerry Thomas came to visit me on the set in Spain. It was lovely to see him, but it brought home to me what a distance I'd covered, from the early comedies in Pinewood, via Chekhov in the Haymarket, to Spielberg in Spain.

When it came time to say goodbye, Steven lifted his peaked cap and put it on my shaggy head. It was a lovely, spontaneous affectionate gesture from a very special director.

I was presented with another contrast when I arrived back in London. Derek Nimmo was in touch, asking me if I'd like to go on one of his theatre tours around the Middle and Far East. Derek had done a lot of these tours, he knew all the ropes and had the arrangements for them off pat. They were great fun, and surprisingly lucrative. Looking at my diary, I couldn't see anything to stand in the way of what would virtually be a holiday, eating as much as I wanted after my *Empire* diet.

He asked me what play I wanted to do. I'd always made it a rule on foreign tours that I would only do plays I'd done before and knew well, and I thought the dear old *The Man Most Likely To...* might stand another outing. It was, after all, a tried-and-tested hit and still stood up. It was just twenty years since I'd first performed it. Derek agreed. I also pointed out that we needed an *exceptional* girl for the lead.

'So,' he said, 'let's audition!'

Derek arranged for us to look at ten girls for Shirley.

They all came in and read and talked a bit about themselves.

One of them stood out by miles from the moment she walked through the door. Derek and

I watched her very carefully.

She had full curves, all the presence and exuberant sexual magnetism the part demanded.

We asked her what she'd done on stage.

'Nothing,' she said with a shrug. 'But I want to be an actress.'

'What do you do now?'

'I'm a photographic model.'

I gave her the script to look at and said we'd talk to her again. When she'd left the room, Derek asked, 'What have you put in your comments?'

'Just "Wow"!'

Derek laughed. 'But can she act?'

I looked at him. 'Let's call her in and hear her read.'

He nodded.

She came back in and she read Shirley well. And so we offered the twenty-one-year-old Elizabeth Hurley her first job. Elizabeth was sensational. The part might have been written for her, although, in fact, she was about two when I'd first performed the play – but it was better than ever now, thanks to her.

Once the tour started, there were a few tricky moments around Elizabeth. On a beach in Abu Dhabi, some vigilante mullah spotted her swimming without her top on. I wish I'd been there, but sadly I wasn't. Nevertheless, because I was the director, I was deemed to be her boss and answerable for her. I was interviewed and told to keep her under control, or she would be deported. I explained the position to Elizabeth, who apologised.

'It felt so like the Côte d'Azur,' she said, 'I

442

forgot where I was for a moment.'

The management also asked if, on stage, she could dress more modestly. I pointed out that Elizabeth Hurley in an old overcoat a few sizes too big would still look sexy and they could only agree. I also noted that Elizabeth's attire didn't stop even the locals coming to see the show and we were packed out to capacity. Even those who couldn't speak English didn't need an interpreter, as long as they could sit there and just watch.

As far as I was concerned, there was absolutely no doubt that, in her first professional acting job, Elizabeth Hurley was a big hit. I wasn't even remotely surprised by her success in the immediate future. She had become a star, just like that, on tour in the Middle East – even the camels couldn't wait to give her a ride!

16 • Stratford and Tennessee

The Christine Keeler affair of 1963 had been one of the most written about incidents of public misconduct to rock Britain in the last fifty years. It had all the essential ingredients of a first-rate, headline-grabbing scandal: power, politics, sex, espionage, aristocracy – and money. That it had taken twenty-five years for anyone to get around to making a movie about it was astonishing. It was even more remarkable that this brilliant, multi-layered story should have ended up in the lap of Michael Caton-Jones, a still-wet-behind-the-ears film director of twenty-nine. He went on to make a convincing job of it.

In the movie, *Scandal*, I was cast (as, ironically, I so often have been in my later career) in the role of the aristocrat, if indeed the Astors can claim to be true aristos. Lord Astor was a very rich party animal of no more influence than his money allowed. He had a beautiful house, and a taste for fooling around with beautiful girls.

The story centres round a friend of his, 'society osteopath' and part-time artist Stephen Ward, who had connections with a large number of rich and powerful people, who used him for introductions to easy-going, fee-earning, beautiful – or at least sexy-looking – girls. John Hurt plays the complex, charming and ambiguous Ward with his usual intelligence and a wonderfully light touch. Ian McKellen sympathetically plays the unfortunate cabinet minister, John Profumo, a weak man tripped up by his own sense of self-importance and weakness for younger women. Profumo was introduced by Ward to a glamorous call girl named Christine Keeler, played in the movie by my favourite actress, Joanne Whalley.

Ian McKellen's only error was a trichological one. He had made his own arrangements for hairdressing and arrived in the make-up caravan on the first day wearing a cap. When he took it off, there was an incredulous gasp from the rest of the cast. Ian had had his hair done in such a way that he looked, not like John Profumo, but a Mohican who'd been pulled through a hedge after a night on the fire-water. It was astonishing, but for some reason our young director didn't do anything about it. Of course, once they'd shot one scene with Ian, he was stuck with his crazy hair. I'm sure Michael in retrospect must have regretted not taking an early initiative, because Ian looked frankly absurd. No one else said a word openly until the movie was finished, when the press certainly didn't hold back and attacked Ian mercilessly, which was a great pity, as he's such a smashing person to work with and a great actor.

I, on the other hand, had my hair receded to match the character I was playing. I loved making *Scandal* and I was delighted when Lord Astor's daughter came up to me after the premiere and said how closely I'd managed to recreate her father. I especially liked working with John Hurt, who I've never seen turn in a bad performance – and a very likeable man, to boot. John showed his true dramatic commitment, too, in the nude scenes, when he had to strip off. Joanne Whalley's part as Christine Keeler required her to strip off completely beside the swimming pool with me, but she wouldn't for some reason.

John was angry about this, but I was inclined to be sympathetic. I had a feeling her boyfriend might have been unhappy about her doing it – who knows; Val Kilmer, I imagine, could be quite powerful. Joanna was going to marry him soon. For whatever reason, the director had another girl up his sleeve ready to do the job for her. However impressive Joanne's figure was, her stand-in had the most incredible figure I've ever seen – sadly I don't know her name and didn't get her number!

I was rather sorry we couldn't use the Astors' former home, Cliveden, a very elegant Thames-side mansion, a few miles upriver from Maidenhead. Stephen Ward had a cottage in the grounds where, finally, he killed himself when all his rich and powerful friends had turned their backs on him.

The trigger to the whole scandal was Defence Secretary Profumo's affair with Christine Keeler, who was also seeing Eugene Ivanov, a handsome Russian naval attaché. This was seen as a serious risk to national security. And Profumo lied to Parliament about his actions. I wonder what the response would be now to a similar scandal?

In the film, the Russian was played by a Dutchman, Jeroen Krabbé, who was also a talented painter and craftsman. Christine Keeler herself, by now a middle-aged woman with a sour disposition and no hint of her former glamour, came on to the set several times. One morning in the studios, Jeroen, who knew I was interested in jewellery, showed me a marvellous pendant. When I asked where he had bought it, he told me he'd made it himself. I'm more interested in antique jewellery, personally, but I was very impressed. He'd made it specially, he said, to give to Christine Keeler, because he felt she'd suffered a lot and come out of the whole thing so badly. When she next came on the set he greeted her warmly and gave her the piece, but she accepted it very ungraciously. He was puzzled, and a little hurt by her reaction to what was meant as a friendly act.

I kept up with Jeroen after making the film. The son and grandson of Dutch artists, he began to do less acting and more painting. Since then, I have maintained an interest in his work and have been to several of his shows.

Despite my normal reluctance to pre-judge movies before the public have reacted, I was impressed with Michael Caton-Jones' direction of *Scandal*. Before it was released he was clearly nervous and apprehensive about his first big feature.

'Don't worry,' I reassured him. 'You'll be very busy after this.'

The film opened to great acclaim and set Michael on his way to America to make many big movies. I worked with him again, ten years later, on *The Jackal* with Bruce Willis, and more recently, he worked again with John Hurt in *Shooting Dogs*.

That year was marked for me by the death of two special but different actors.

In April 1988, Kenneth Williams was found dead in his flat, thought by many to have committed suicide. Kenneth was an immensely complicated man, who simultaneously lived as two very different personae. The public Kenneth was a performer – loud, caustic, brash, wittily cutting and permanently on show. The inner Ken wasn't a bit like that – thoughtful, gentle, insecure, reflective and highly intelligent. Sexually he was an oxymoron – a promiscuous prude – and his mind must have been a battleground of conflicting needs.

For all that, I personally doubt that he did take his own life, because the one area in which he was utterly unequivocal was his love for his mother, and she was still alive. I simply can't see that it's possible he would have wanted to inflict on her the suffering taking his own life would cause her.

In spite of all his jeering and cutting jibes over the years, his posturing and bullying, which I recognised as only defensive, I was immensely sad when I heard he had died. I was surprised to find how much I missed him – and when I meet mutual friends, they never stop talking about him.

Another super actor – not as close to me as Kenneth had been, but a man I liked and respected enormously – also died that year. Roy Kinnear was killed in a horrible accident in the course of filming. He was in Spain, shooting another of the very successful series of *Musketeers,* when he fell from his horse, sustaining serious damage with very bad internal bleeding. It seems insufficient care was taken of him, and he didn't survive. It was a great loss; he was one of the warmest, most consistently funny men I ever met in the business, brave, kind and noble, too. With his charming wife and the disabled child they adored, he had a very happy marriage.

On the plus side, my great colleague and Ibiza chum Denholm Elliott was awarded a CBE – a source of rejoicing in our corner of the island (though he should have got a 'K'). With his enigmatic charm, which had not dulled with the passing of time, Denholm was as busy as ever, and recognised in Hollywood as one of the great British character actors. Recognition in his native land was well deserved. I could honestly claim Denholm as a best friend.

And in England – Tottenham, to be precise – there was big excitement at White Hart Lane when Spurs paid Newcastle United £2 million for Paul Gascoigne. I'd seen him play several times on visits to the north-east, where my old Durham Light Infantry connections are still held. I was, though, a Spurs supporter, and went often to watch them with a friend of mine who was manager of a big London hotel that maintained a lavish box at White Hart Lane. Now, as a known supporter of the team within the sound of whose ground I had been born, I was invited down to meet the new Geordie wonder boy after his first game. There was a great crowd round him, all wanting to speak to him or get his autograph or just touch him, but when it opened up a little, he spotted me, and called out in that irrepressible Geordie voice – 'Whey, Leslie! Leslie Phillips!' – and pushed his way through to shake my hand.

'It's great to meet you, mon! I've loved all those fillums of yourn since I were a little bairn.'

It turned out he was a genuine fan, albeit of the old Phillips model. He hadn't, for instance, been to see me in *Passion Play* or *The Cherry Orchard*. But I didn't mind; he was such a lavishly warm-hearted chap, I liked him from the start. After that he became a great friend, and still is, whenever we meet!

What an old actor and a young footballer would have in common isn't obvious, but Gazza had an engaging frankness, enthusiasm and passionate zest for life that was really infectious. He came to see Angie and me in Maida Vale with his family, his sister, who was an actress, Jimmy 'Five-Bellies' Gardner and other Newcastle chums, to whom he was consistently and unselfconsciously loyal. I also got to meet his dad, of course.

As a Spurs supporter, I was delighted that over the next four seasons he scored thirty-three goals for us. When he badly damaged his leg in an important match, I made sure that I went to see him in hospital. When he showed me his ghastly wound, I thought he would never kick a ball again. But he did – and how!

In 1989, Angie and I were given a marvellous opportunity to tour together through the Middle and Far East in Alan Ayckbourn's *Taking Steps*. I'd broken my rule of doing only plays I knew on foreign tours, but I discovered in this – the first Ayckbourn I'd done – how playable he was.

It was lovely to be working with Angie again, as she'd been through a rough time. She'd found it hard to deal with her mother and a sense of guilt – totally unjustified in my view – about the conflict over Dan in his early life, although Dan himself had long since settled down and was getting on fine at King's, Canterbury. Nor had Angie been getting the kind of jobs she liked; she was facing the uncomfortable truth that, after a time, roles for women dwindle to a handful and are hard to come by, even for someone as accomplished and smashing looking as she is.

This tour gave us a chance to open our life together, to see and experience foreign places and meet new people. We tacked across the world, starting in Dubai, where we met the irrepressible Mr Bathia, an extraordinary Indian gentleman with fingers in pies on three continents, including, it turned out, an Indian restaurant in Horseferry Road, the Kundon, where we were to become regular customers. At his invitation, I held my seventieth birthday party at the Kundon, with my whole family, which is quite a gathering. It was a magical evening, topped off with the arrival of a gold Cartier watch he'd had sent over from Dubai.

Bathia was a most expansive, generous character, with an insane laugh, and a penchant for decking himself in pearls and diamonds. He was one of those people who always knew, without bullshit, where and how to get anything from anywhere through his complex web of international businesses. He was a great fan of mine and had an encyclopaedic knowledge and library of all the films I'd ever made. Rather quaintly, he had an immense desire to sound like me, and begged me to teach him how to use my phrases and expressions. It was a little bizarre, though quite endearing, to be greeted by this larger-than-life Indian saying, 'Lummy! Hel*lo!*'

He appeared to be very wealthy, with his own jet and sixty or seventy cars, including a gold-plated Rolls. To say he was a one-off would be a serious understatement, though all he wanted from me was to share his company, along with his caviar and Dom Perignon – I think he thought that was what I usually had for breakfast.

But he was a lovely chap, and I was very upset to hear that, driving with his usual exuberance at great speed along a desert road from Dubai, he'd hit a new camel-crossing which sent his Rolls flying into the air, where it turned over and came back to earth upside down. The steering wheel went through his chest and the most extraordinary fan I ever had was killed on the spot. I felt truly bereaved, as if a great light in my life had been put out.

In Oman I was taken at dawn to the Sultan Qaboos' stables to see his horses race on a track around a sumptuous little palace just off the beach. There were some wonderful animals among them but, sadly, no gambling was allowed. From there we went to Guam, Korea and, in particular, to Hong Kong, where we stayed with our friends, the Chief Justice, Sir Dennis Roberts, and his exuberant, madly attractive wife, Fiona.

Fiona was tremendously striking: younger than Dennis, flame-haired, long-legged, glamorous and not afraid who she shocked. She was a barrister working at the Hong Kong bar, and the old guard were horrified when the Chief Justice, in whose court she'd been appearing for the last few years, announced that he was going to marry her. It was a brave move. Effectively, the Chief Justice is deputy to the Governor – a pivotal role in the Far East!

They invited us to stay with them in their house on the Peak and were fabulous hosts. We loved being there, with a chauffeured Rolls to get us around, smiling servants and a butler who was a dignified version of Noel Coward. It was always entertaining; anyone interesting who was passing through or staying in Hong Kong might be invited, and there were some wonderful parties. As a work trip, it would be hard to see how it could have been less arduous.

We went on to Singapore after that, where, as soon as I mentioned that I enjoyed horse racing, an invitation arrived for lunch at the races – or so I thought. We were ushered into a lavish dining room at the race course and given a splendid lunch. As the time for the first race drew near, I was anxious to see a few horses; once I'm there I take my racing seriously. I asked when I could go out and assess the chances.

'Somebody will be around soon with all the odds and take your bets,' I was told.

'But I'd like to see the horses in the parade ring.'

'You can't do that.'

'Why not?' I asked, puzzled.

'There aren't any horses here. They're running on a course up the coast in Malaysia.'

I'd had no idea we were going to the 'virtual' races. But after lunch we all trooped through to the stands, to sit and watch a massive telly screen, like the huge thing they put up at Cheltenham which everybody watches, while the actual horses are galloping in the flesh, much smaller, up the track in front of them. It was very bizarre. The horses might not have been real – at least, not on the spot – but the gambling certainly

453

was. In Hong Kong I'd become used to the incredible fever with which they bet, and it was like that here in Singapore. Oddly enough, once one had got used to the idea that the runners were really over a hundred miles away, it didn't make a lot of difference. Indeed, I know people who go winter racing in England and spend the whole day in a box watching it on telly, often with a bit of Francome and McCririck thrown in, and they seem to enjoy it well enough, while avoiding mud or horse droppings on their footwear.

After our run in Singapore finished, Angie and I hired a car to drive up into Malaysia. I'd been there before (I once performed in Kuala Lumpur at a hotel dinner-theatre and the audiences were fantastically appreciative), but this time I'd have a car and the leisure to explore a little. I'd heard there were interesting things to be bought in some of the old cities. We thought Malaysia was charming, and markedly different from its tiny neighbour. In Singapore, all is tidy and regimented; people are prosperous, everything works, living standards are staggeringly high by any measure. However, in Malaysia, one is liable to come across massive pot-holes in the main roads, or stretches where the road has disintegrated entirely. There is far more obvious poverty and subsistence farming, and the Muslim influence has grown to become extremely evident.

Kuala Lumpur, however, is a brave new world, sprouting sky scrapers like Jack's beanstalk. I thought it probably wasn't an easy place to do business, but a hell of a lot of business was being done. We drove east across the country to

Kuantan, an ancient port on the South China Sea. We were on the trail of the legendary Jim Thompson, looking for antiques and silks. In one shop, rooting among the bric-a-brac, I found a bottle of ridiculously old Rioja, sitting in the sun, but very cheap. I was fond of this Spanish wine and knew a bit about it. I bought the bottle out of interest and we drank it that evening. It was nectar – the most delicious Rioja I'd ever tasted. It seemed amazing to have found it in a Kuantan junk shop, lying out in the hot sun.

We were dining in Kuantan a few days later, in a beautiful restaurant of a hotel overlooking the harbour, when we witnessed the most moving human drama I've ever seen.

As we ate, gazing out across the sea, a small boat, no more than 150 feet long, limped into the harbour, jam-packed with people. As soon as they'd docked, the Malaysian police arrested them all and lodged them in a barricaded compound on the beach. We soon discovered that they were refugees from Vietnam, so called 'boat people', still coming all those years after the end of the war because there was nothing for them at home and stories of riches to be found in other countries had tempted them to sacrifice what little they had for the sake of a fresh start somewhere else. There was, clearly, no fresh start for them here, though. It was incredibly sad to see their disappointment and despair. God knows what became of them.

We went down to see what was happening. It was even more distressing close to. Mothers with babies who must have been born on the ghastly voyage were herded into the pens. Orphan children roamed among them, howling or crouched, catatonic with distress. The scale of human misery was utterly gut-wrenching. It was a salutary experience to see just how much misery people could find themselves exposed to. It was the most moving thing Angie and I ever saw on any of our trips.

In sharp contrast to the rawness of life in the Far East, later that summer we spent a lovely, sybaritic fortnight in Italy, thanks to Carrie's brother-in-law, Colin Rogers. He was the producer of *Summer's Lease*, a television play from John Mortimer's book, in which I had a lovely (though short-lived) part, playing opposite Sir John Gielgud – the first time we'd worked together since *The Barretts of Wimpole Street* in 1957. He was still in great form as an actor and a delightful man.

Soon after we'd started shooting, John, who was over ninety, fell ill and had to go back to London – a hellish problem for the production, but it was decided to keep it on hold with everyone in situ, in the hope that the great old actor would get better quickly. I still had a big scene to do with Sir John, which allowed me and Angie two weeks to wander round the local beauty spots, thanks to the BBC. Sir John was frail when he returned, but by the time he'd got his make-up on, he seemed to find more energy – dear Doctor Greasepaint doing his stuff – and he was able to finish his role in the film.

Back in London, I signed to take part in a much-heralded new television series. I was to co-star with a young actor of whom a lot was expected. *Chancer* was well produced and well written. As a comment on the money-oriented decade that had just passed, it was accurate and relevant. Fast moving, stylish and deceptively sophisticated, it was a big hit, and undoubtedly brought me to an entirely new audience.

It was a challenge and fun to work with an ambitious young actor like Clive Owen. He was, it seemed, very anxious not to be upstaged by a man of sixty-five, and this created a sort of tension between us, on and off screen, that was very productive. I enjoyed my part, James Blake – an upper-crust, conniving, silky-snide shit – and I was given some very good, tailor-made scenes.

The first season ran for thirteen episodes, and the second for seven. The response to the second was as good as the first, and just when a third season looked inevitable, the plug was pulled, and rumours were rampant. All I heard was that somebody had gone to bed with somebody they shouldn't have – and it wasn't me or Clive. End of story. And a bloody shame – we were all very disappointed. *Chancer* certainly launched Clive Owen, but it also showed a lot of producers that this old dog could – and had – learned a few new tricks.

I've never lied about my age, but as they say, 'You know you're getting old when the policemen in the street start to look young.' I'd passed that milestone. Now I'd reached a point in life when

457

not just the policemen but the judges, too, were beginning to look fairly juvenile. This came home to me when I found myself regularly being cast as a judge. In 1990, I presided over two different courtrooms.

In the first, I was Lord Lane in *Who Bombed Birmingham?*, a television reconstruction of the trial of the Birmingham Six. To do this effectively, I looked up my dear friends, Sir Dennis and Lady Roberts, who knew Lord Lane well. Dennis gave me a detailed description of the judge, whose most notable characteristic was a complete lack of visible emotion when delivering a judgement or sending a man down for life, offering it quietly, as if he were asking for another lump of sugar in his tea.

When it came to it, though, the director didn't like the way I was doing it. He felt that these pronouncements would have been made with a large dose of dramatic irony. As he spoke, the producer, who was a bright young woman, leapt into the battle.

'The way Leslie's doing it is *exactly* right,' she said. 'Don't alter it; it's perfect, and chilling!'

Primary research, you see. It was one of the parts I was really pleased with.

My next judge was more fun to do – Justice Michael Argyle in the *Trials of Oz*. This was a wonderful, funny and revealing reconstruction of the historic trial for obscenity brought against Richard Neville, the editor, and Felix Dennis, the publisher, of the magazine *Oz – Schoolkids Issue* in the early '70s. In real life they'd been represented by John Mortimer, now played by Simon Callow; the prosecutor was played by Nigel Hawthorne, while Neville was played by Hugh Grant.

Hugh was a charming young chap, who confided in me that he wasn't really an actor, but a writer. However, although his take on Neville's Australian accent was barely detectable, I recognised that he was very good looking and had tremendous presence on screen, like his girlfriend Elizabeth Hurley, whom I'd directed. They joined me for lunch one day at the BBC White City, and were both very happy and in love.

To get my Justice Argyle right, I once again consulted Dennis Roberts, who had known the man and marked my card for me so that I was able to reproduce all the mannerisms of this stern, old-fashioned arbiter of justice who still believed in the death penalty. In a clear instance of life imitating art, I fell fast asleep on the set and someone took a photo – they knew I wasn't acting at the time, but it fitted the part.

It seems astonishing now, but by misdirecting the jury Argyle got the *Oz* Three convicted and banged them up, until they appealed and were let out again – on the proviso they must stop working for *Oz*. Our television version earned some wonderful notices, and I've gone on to play several more judges since. It seems to me that, the older I get, the more interesting parts I'm being offered.

Angie's mother, Helen, who'd been suffering Alzheimer's, died in 1991. Angie had always been made to feel that she had let her mother and her aunts down, and now she felt it was too late to do anything about it. Thank God, though, a job which she had piloted and done two seasons the previous year, as Lady Agatha in *You Rang, M'Lord*, was confirmed for another two seasons, which kept her busy during what was a tricky time for her – tricky for me, too, trying to help her keep it all together.

It was a well-written sitcom, a kind of comedy version of *Upstairs Downstairs*. There was a good, jovial cast, with some wonderful moments, and the public loved it. Even at a time when terrestrial programmes were beginning to lose out to satellite, it did very well, with Angie appearing in some twenty of the twenty-six episodes. She looked marvellous, she was absolutely right for the part, and it was great for her to be sharing the limelight while I was going through a quiet patch after my second season of *Chancer*. However, when the series finished Angie sank into a delayed and potentially dangerous depression which worried me a lot. I wasn't surprised, as nobody knew better than me what she'd suffered in many different directions.

Meanwhile down at Tottenham, another sufferer, Paul Gascoigne, despite the attentions of several eminent orthopaedic surgeons, still had a dodgy knee. But it had been suddenly announced that the Roman club Lazio had bought him on spec from Spurs, who had money troubles at the time. Paul left for Rome, almost miraculously the knee recovered, and the Italian club soon started getting their money's worth.

460

I was so busy, as usual, that I never got out there to see him play, but I'd introduced him to my hotelier friend. He loved football and went several times to see Gazza in Rome, as they had become good mates, and they both enjoyed partying. On one occasion, he flew over to watch a game just before he was due to get married, not for the first time. He and Gazza went out after the match for a pre-nuptial piss-up and rather overdid it. They went back to Gazza's luxury flat, where my friend instantly fell fast asleep and was out for the count until noon the following day.

He woke, he told me, feeling Roman rough, as if some small animal had crawled into his mouth during the night, crapped and died there. He staggered to the bathroom where, glancing in the mirror, ready to flinch, he saw with unimaginable shock that, where he normally sported a goodish crop of thick, dark hair, he was now totally bald. On closer inspection, he discovered that his eyebrows were missing too, nor was there a hair left on his body – anywhere. And he was getting married in less than a week's time!

While he'd been asleep, Gazza, for a giggle – he told me – had shaved him from head to toe with an open razor. He was lucky, his friends thought, not to have lost a testicle or two as well. Through my theatrical contacts we fixed him up with a pretty unconvincing wig, and he went off to get married looking very sorry for himself, though probably not as sorry as his future bride would be. It was, I believe, the end of the friendship between him and Gazza, and I was frankly relieved that I never made it to watch Lazio playing at home!

461

To please my friend Gerald Thomas, I'd allowed myself to be talked into a 'pre-change' role in *Columbus*, the first *Carry On* film I'd made for over thirty years. I played the King of Spain, with June Whitfield as my queen, which, of course, was fun, though the finished movie probably should never have been let out of the bag. Peter Rogers was still producing, although nearly eighty. He must have mellowed, because I was paid properly this time, though I'd only done the film for Gerry. I was always fond of him and his family, and I was stunned when he died the following year.

My next trip to Ibiza after we'd shot *Columbus* was filled with sadness. Denholm Elliott, my dearest friend, was dying, tragically, of AIDS. He had always been a sexual adventurer, and sometimes indiscriminate about where he trod. That was his business, but it was heart-rending to see this brilliant, charming, wickedly witty man slowly disintegrating.

When Denholm wasn't working in Hollywood he was nearly always in Ibiza, where he absolutely loved the Mediterranean life. He would swim slowly across his pool with a happy grin on his face, saying, 'This is it, Leslie. This is what it's all about!' He'd been one of the main reasons I'd originally bought my *finca* there.

He was a kind and genuine friend to me for years. When he was very close to death, I saw Sue in the village and she told me Denholm wanted me to go up and see him. This was unexpected, as I was by now quite used to people, including close friends, not wanting to see one when death was near.

'Are you sure?' I asked.

'Oh yes. He specifically said, and made it clear he only wanted to see you.'

Of course, I went straight up to his house, where I found Denholm lying on a day bed. Later I discovered it was true I was the only person he saw. As I left him, he put his arms around me, hugged and kissed me. I walked down to my car, but I couldn't drive, I was crying so much, and didn't move for half an hour. I thought it very likely that would be the last time I would see him alive, as I had to return to London next day to start another TV series in Nottingham. Sure enough, his death was announced on the radio as I checked into my hotel room a few days later. I felt very bereft.

Not long before he'd become seriously ill, he'd given me a lovely plant, a Morning Glory, for my garden. After he died, I took great care of it and have cherished it ever since, in his memory. Although he died many years ago, I still miss his company every time I go to Ibiza.

Fond as I am of beautiful motors, I've always rather liked trains, too – perhaps more so now that driving, on the whole, has become such an interminable bore in this country and the south-east of England has become one great traffic jam. I quite envied Clement Freud his arrangements for his seventieth birthday party. He somehow managed to hire his own train, which took hundreds of his friends from Paddington to

Newbury for a day at the races and entertainment en route.

It was an immensely civilised and congenial way to do it, with drinks and food on the train both ways, and the race course station at Newbury but a short, exhilarating walk from the stands, where another sumptuous repast awaited us, as well as some racing.

His guests were an extraordinary gathering of people from politics, television, films, journalism, the racing world and the aristocracy. It seemed there was hardly anyone with whom Clement hadn't come into contact at one time or another in his eclectic career. Even I'd been on to his food show at one point, and there, in the seat opposite me, beaming away like a Cox's Orange Pippin, sat Michael Winner. I'd barely seen him since I made *You Must Be Joking* for him in '65.

By now he'd relaxed as a film director and reverted to his earlier calling, in journalism. When I'd first met him, he was a cub reporter on the *Finchley Clarion*; now he was the restaurant reviewer for the *Sunday Times*, putting the fear of God into chefs the length and breadth of the Thames Valley. There are few aspiring Michelin Star holders who haven't come in for a pen-lashing in his forthright column. Of course, since then, Michael has also become a star of television commercials, too. Is there no end to his talent?

I made another railway connection when I starred in a short TV series called *Love on a Branch Line*, a cosy, period comedy written by *Reginald Perrin*'s brilliant creator, David Nobbs, and directed by Martyn Friend, for whom I have

464

great regard. It was an enchanting time-warp of a confection, co-starring the elegant and lovely Maria Aitken, another Ibiza friend, and served up with a large helping of nostalgia sauce. I loved my part as Maria's husband, an unusual old man who'd lost both his legs in an accident and whose main hobby was playing the drums. It was very well written, great fun to play and a notable success.

A second series was commissioned and written, again by the clever David Nobbs, but somewhere along the way the dear old BBC had apparently rather carelessly mislaid £50 million that year, and the *Branch Line*, like Dr Beeching's victims of the early '60s, had to be cut. However, this sad story had a happy, if unconnected ending when my favourite actor, Anthony Hopkins, came into the frame.

Tony had first hinted that we might do something together when he'd seen me in *The Cherry Orchard* some ten years earlier and had come backstage specifically to tell me how much he'd liked my Gaev. Now, he said, he had a project for me. Another Chekhov – a film *and* a play back to back.

Granada Films were funding him to make a movie of *Uncle Vanya*, reset in Wales, while the Welsh Arts Council were sponsoring the transfer of the same piece on the stage at the Theatre Hafod in Mold, North Wales and afterwards in Cardiff. The film would come first, on the grounds that it was more realistic for the actors to raise their game from film to stage, than to lower it *vice versa*.

Renamed *August*, it was an original and interesting idea. Tony had adapted the original text, characters and setting from Russia to Victorian North Wales. He was playing Vanya himself, as well as composing the score for the film, and directing both the movie and the stage versions. Although an experienced theatre director, this was Tony's debut as a film director. He'd given me the second lead, Professor Blathwaite, a wide-ranging part with Chekhov's subtle, whimsical humour.

The cast in the play was the same as for the film, apart from Kate Burton (American, though with strong Welsh connections through her father, Richard Burton), who, sadly, could only do the film not the play before she had to return to the States. We filmed for the most part on location in the Lleyn Peninsula, a long finger of land drooping into the Irish Sea, where not much can have changed in the last hundred years.

We staged the play in Cardiff and in Mold, where we were accessible to people from large chunks of central England. To my delight, among those who made the journey into Wales was Ronnie Barker, accompanied by his wife Joy. He rang and told me he was coming, and said they'd like to have dinner with me and Tony, too. Tony said he'd come for an hour, as it would be after the show and very late. I arranged for a table at a very good restaurant, and we all met up there, Ronnie claiming that they couldn't stay too late either.

At three o'clock in the morning, Ronnie and Tony were still there. It was magical to hear those two great natural raconteurs swapping tale after tale and laughing their heads off until all sense of time was lost in one of my most memorable evenings in recent years. I reminded Joy of this evening when I wrote to her after Ronnie's death – it was just one more example of how missed he is.

Any actor who does not own up to the thrill of being asked to do a season with the Royal Shakespeare Company is being, I would suggest, rather disingenuous. It is not a particularly big thrill for one's bank manager, but for any serious stage actor, a season or two with the RSC would be the apotheosis of their career. To receive the summons, finally, in my seventy-second year, was very life-affirming. I felt that this justified all the effort and risk involved in trying to redirect my career, to prove to myself and to anyone else who cared that there was more to Leslie Phillips than 'Ding Dong'. To be asked to act Shakespeare's greatest humorous character made it all the better. Shakespeare generally used Sir John Falstaff to provide sporadic comic relief in the historical dramas. But in *The Merry Wives of Windsor,* he was the star.

Of course, I had to fatten up a little – I should say a lot, actually – and the trim bum and slender legs of which I'd always been quite proud were now a distinct disadvantage. In other respects, too, I think Ian Judge, who directed, wanted a fresh take on Sir John, dressing me in the blazer and waistcoat of a saloon-bar lecher, with Elizabethan ruff. I enjoyed myself enormously; I

467

love Shakespeare's sparkling, razor wit that's still so sharp after four hundred years. It was a great joy, too, to work with a company whose constitution is such that no compromise need be made, and everything is of the best.

I think I mentioned, when discussing my experience with Clive Owen in *Chancer,* that a little enmity between players can be a good thing when it reflects the stance of the on-screen characters. So it was on stage between Falstaff and Ford in *The Merry Wives;* and between Edward Petherbridge, who played Ford, and me.

Edward Petherbridge was a classy actor who'd had many innings at the National and the RSC and no doubt felt he was in his rightful home. Whatever the reason, he seemed to harbour towards me a palpable grudge. I didn't mind; as I say, it helped on stage, because Ford thinks his wife fancies Falstaff and is very jealous of the boozy old knight.

There was no doubt in that season at the RSC that there was quite a bit of public interest in how I would get on, and the attendance at Stratford confirmed that a lot of people who had enjoyed my lighter work were encouraged to have a go at the Bard, because I was there – quite gratifying, really.

We took off with Ian Judge's production on tour around the various RSC staging posts. It was going down well and pulling good houses, but in Newcastle, we had an accident. There is a scene in the play where I have been stuffed into a large laundry basket with a view to being dunked in the River Thames. At one point, the servants

468

carrying the basket, with me in it, have to lower it to the stage floor.

In this performance, something went wrong; one of them lost their hold, and they dropped it straight on to the ground. It was probably only a couple of feet and, for my age, I was in reasonably good shape, but it was quite a shock and it did hurt rather. I make no apologies for uttering a sharp, clearly audible grunt of pain.

Just as audible on the stage, from outside the basket, I heard someone utter the unscripted ejaculation: 'Cunt!' I couldn't be sure from within the basket who it was, and whether they were angry at their own mistake, but I gathered from many observers that the audience heard it too, and maybe the less well-versed ones were surprised at the ripeness of the Bard's language.

In the same RSC season, I also played Gutman in Steven Pimlott's excellent production of Tennessee Williams' extraordinary play *Camino Real* at the Swan. I had another enjoyable bird encounter in this play, recalling the great success of my feathered confidant in *Canaries Sometimes Sing*. This time my avian co-star was a parakeet, and again, a live one. I know that some actors dislike the distraction of live, undisciplined creatures on stage with them, but I love the edge it can give – the positive experience of something different in every performance. I can confirm this as the understatement of the RSC season, as the bird usually perched on my shoulder and gave me a traditional greeting – all over my jacket! It was the only bit I didn't appreciate.

Doing two plays with the RSC to the highest

possible standard, sporadically performed over an extended period in a variety of venues, was very demanding, but for me it represented a pinnacle. I'd come a long way since my mother had timidly brought me from Chingford on the 38 bus to meet the formidable Miss Italia Conti, nearly sixty years before.

In the gaps between my periods of performance for the RSC, Angie and I spent more time in Ibiza. I was not looking forward, even reluctantly, to a time when I might become what most people would call 'retired'. I've always had the feeling that retirement for an actor is a kind of capitulation to age and its concomitant sloth, and potentially a terrible bore. I don't suppose I'll ever submit voluntarily to that state as long as the scripts keep dropping on the doormat at Maida Vale, which, thank God, they still do. However, thinking that I should be prepared, just in case, it seemed sensible to start making my Ibiza shack a serious, grown-up home.

After my *cisterna* had inadvertently been drained a few years earlier, I'd asked Juan my builder to go down on the end of a rope, like Jack and Jill's bucket, to see what had happened. When we tugged him up, he was very excited. The incredibly neat brickwork further down, he said, looked very ancient indeed. He went back down with a camera and we discovered that the reservoir had been sunk and beautifully lined possibly two thousand years ago, in Roman times. He also found that the roots of the trees that I had encouraged had finally broken through the lining of the tank in that inexorable way they have in their search for refreshment, which was why it no longer retained water as it should.

Since then, we'd had it repaired and it continues to be served by its source. While this may have been enough for a peasant farmhouse, where jacuzzis and swimming pools didn't feature, after I'd bought the place from dear old Juan Plannel, and his family had built tennis courts, with facilities, on some of their remaining land at the bottom of the hill below my *finca*, and the granddaughter had started up her nursery school, it was clearly going to be worked hard. Both establishments shared the water source with me. The original spring and its holding well, on their own, just weren't up to the job. It had been clear to me for some time that there would be no point upgrading the house unless we could find a more robust source of water. I promised Angie that, if we found what we needed, I was happy to spend some serious money doing up the place: roads, gardens, pool, sewage and so on, though I wanted to retain the traditional Spanish feel of it all.

A few years before, I'd been down to see my lawyer in Santa Eulalia and quietly bought a little more land from the Planell family, including the spot by the tree where *el bruco* had identified a water source. I was able to tell the man who came to drill our new bore hole exactly where to start. He didn't question it and started drilling. He hadn't gone very far before he struck an aquifer, just as the old diviner had said. The water came spouting up like a geyser, everyone from the village came to shout and cheer, and it's been flowing ever since.

Four days later I started work on the property. Not only was I going to renovate, but also expand the whole place from a loveable shack into an elegant home. The ground was traditionally terraced, like hillsides all over the island, and we allocated one broad terrace to accommodate a new swimming pool. For the house we began to accumulate antique fittings, furniture and material from mainland Spain. After a while I felt we had gathered all we could and I vowed that I wouldn't be getting any more, but one day I was driving down to the village when I came across a Spaniard who had brought a lorry-load of architectural antiques over from the mainland. I couldn't resist a quick look.

Angie spotted the lorry coming up the hill towards the *finca* with me following behind, and gasped as we proceeded to unload every item the man had brought – great terracotta Ali Baba pots, doors, carved stone architraves, earthenware sinks, old wrought-iron door latches – the lot. This was impulse buying on a grand scale. It seemed my collecting habit and weakness for a bargain had got the better of me again, and now, if ever I try to urge restraint on Angie, she reminds me of how I fell in love with a Spanish lorry and its contents.

We also expanded the garden, where I enjoyed growing vegetables, while Angie was keen on herbs and flowers. To help with trees, I had a wonderful old friend I'd known almost since arriving on the island when he'd done a few jobs for me and I'd caught him in the village paper shop, reading a magazine with nothing but pictures of naked women with oversized breasts. We'd had a chuckle about that, bought each other a drink or two and, despite our lack of a fluent common tongue, became great friends. Sometimes this only amounted to sitting side by side in my *jardin*, saying little, as we gazed across the valley and supped a jug of Ibizan wine, strong and violet, but it could be very companionable in small doses.

At the time of the great planting he was a tremendous help, cycling ponderously up the hill to plant, prune and generally look after the plethora of trees that now went in – pines, sabinas, olives, various fruits, eucalyptus, grapes and a mass of indigenous shrubs. The date palm I'd planted was now huge, thanks to his careful management of the lower leaves.

Ten years since we started, the house and garden are more or less done, in so far as these things are ever complete. The house is a palace that will sleep sixteen people – my whole family, if I were brave enough. It seems to have been an awful lot of work, but I anticipate spending more leisure time (whatever that is) there one day. However, I won't ever live there full time. In the end, I'm a Londoner through and through.

One day flying alone from Barcelona to Ibiza, the plane suddenly dived, heading straight down for the sea. I couldn't understand what was going on, but I didn't panic. I was more worried about a young Spanish couple with a small child sitting in front of me. It was quite extraordinary – I've never experienced such inner peace before.

'If this is it,' I thought, 'so be it.'

I was quite happy to meditate quietly while all around me were terrified. As we were almost skimming the waves, I thought, 'Perhaps it won't hurt.'

The next moment, the plane straightened up, hauled itself back into the air, and we flew on to Ibiza, unscathed. It was reassuring to know that Death, when it does knock on the door, isn't all that scary.

17 • Four Score Years Onwards

Ten years have passed since the end of my season with the RSC and the sharp reminder of my mortality over the Mediterranean. Any thoughts that either event might have heralded my retirement have proved false. There have been a couple more stage plays – one as a judge; the other a single hander which an actor of any age would have found demanding – a couple of dozen parts in television dramas, from Agatha Christie to Evelyn Waugh, and more movies. Some retirement!

The truth is, I love the work; I can still learn the lines and refuse to succumb to idiot boards. It's marvellous that there are parts around for men of my age, and I'm relieved to say that it's a while since I've been sent a script which required me to say 'Hel*lo*...' while pouting at Joan Sims (not that it wasn't always a great pleasure to pout at Joan, of course!).

What was tremendously pleasing – and caused me a few lip-quivering moments – was being honoured, first in 1997 by my peers, with an *Evening Standard* Lifetime Achievement Award, and the following year by Her Majesty, with an OBE.

At the *Evening Standard* ceremony, with one of my favourite actresses and friends, Jane Asher, presiding, Joan Plowright kindly made the presentation, taking me back to our outing together in *The Cherry Orchard*. Accepting the award, I could only think of some of my dear friends who were no longer with us and who I would have loved to have been there – Bill Travers, Kay Kendall and especially Denholm Elliott.

In 1997, my career was a mere sixty years long; now, as Pinewood Studio approaches its seventieth anniversary, I find I'm about the only man left who made movies there when it first opened.

Ironically, the year after me, my old adversary Roy Boulting was given the Lifetime Achievement Award by the *Standard*. I'm ashamed to say, I found none of my old animosity had worn off since the ghastly tussle at Elstree Studios, while making *Brothers-in-Law* in 1956. I warned Jane Asher that, once she'd given him the platform, she'd never get him off. By that stage, Roy had fallen on difficult times, living modestly near Reading and writing his own memoirs, which might have been fascinating, if he'd ever finished them.

Sure enough, on the evening of the awards

ceremony, which is televised live with no leeway in the schedule, after Roy had received his award, he launched into his life history and wouldn't stop. Sadly – or not – they had to pull the plug on him, mid-torrent. It was extraordinary to think what a great force he and his brother had been in the British movie industry a quarter of a century and more earlier.

The day I was due to receive my OBE from the Queen, my youngest son, Roger, brought his eldest daughter Charlotte with him and drove me and Angela to Buckingham Palace. It was, needless to say, one of the proudest days of my life, as a fervent patriot and monarchist, to feel that my tiny contribution to the total sum of British cultural influence was being rewarded.

It looked at one point as if I was going to be arrested for attempted treason before I even made it inside the Palace. Roger had swung the car into the inner courtyard and nearly run slap into a contingent of bear-skinned guardsmen marching crisply across the archway. I fear they were required to break ranks to save their skins – both their own and the bears'. Fortunately, no more was heard about it by me or Roger. At the investiture, Her Majesty was as charming and witty as she'd been on the several occasions I'd met her at film premieres and functions for the Royal Theatrical Fund, with which I've been involved for over fifty years. I left the Palace feeling very grateful for this recognition, hoping that it marked a high point – not a full stop – in my career.

Fortunately, the career continued with a trip to the Isle of Man in the company of Trevor Eve. Trevor told me how, for a while, at the start of his own career, he'd lived in a room in the house next door to mine in Maida Vale. He had often seen me sitting in the garden, poring over scripts, and he'd wondered if one day he would be as busy as I appeared to be!

With a super director, Beeban Kidron, he was producing a new version of *Cinderella* for television. There was a strong cast, including the redoubtable Kathleen Turner and, unexpectedly, Jane Birkin. Jane was lovely and very good company; I'm delighted to say, she was kind enough to seek me out for dinner a few times and told me a lovely story about her mother, the actress Judy Campbell.

Judy was appearing with Noel Coward in a play in Scotland – in a cold theatre in the middle of winter. At a point where Noel was required to engage in a clinch with his leading lady, he put his hand deep into her cleavage and left it there as long as the clinch lasted. Judy was flattered and wondered to herself if she was the woman who was going to 'turn' Noel back to the straight path.

As the curtain came down, the great man turned to her, impeccably polite as ever. 'I'm sorry, darling, forgive me! My hand was frozen and I simply had to warm it up before it went completely numb.'

My next job was one of the more fun movies I've made over the last ten years: *Saving Grace* with Brenda Blethyn. Brenda already had two

Academy Award nominations to her credit; I liked her and admired her work very much – who wouldn't? The film had a charming, very English sort of script and, I felt very comfortable playing a vicar for the first time since *Our Man at St Mark's*. We filmed on location around the quaint Cornish village of Port Isaac. Our producer's mother lived nearby and we were stunned by her beautiful house, which sat atop a cliff with the sea crashing on the rocks below.

It was a happy film with a good cast and a first-rate director, Nigel Cole. The screenplay had largely been written by Craig Ferguson, a likeable Scots actor, comedian and writer who was also the leading man – a hippy gardener trying to grow cannabis to get some money together to look after his pregnant girl. Brenda's character, Grace Tre-vethyn, had been widowed, and left unexpectedly penniless, with her house mortgaged to the hilt. She, too, needed money. Her only skill was in growing plants, so she and the gardener get together to grow a massive cash crop of cannabis, with the encouragement of a sympathetic village.

I was also preparing for a one-man show I would be doing at the Edinburgh Festival. I would be on stage on my own for over an hour, so I had a massive amount of learning to do, and when Brenda wasn't filming herself, she offered to listen to my lines and help me with them – immensely kind. She was great fun to work with, too, and a lovely, warm individual.

I heard that Craig's wife was coming over from the States where he'd been working very success-fully on television. I assumed she was American, and as I'd never felt particularly comfortable with American women, finding them a little strident and assertive for my taste, I didn't give a lot of thought to what she might be like. But when Sascha turned up, I took one look at her and thought, 'You're absolutely gorgeous!'

It was the instinctive reaction of any red-blooded man to a stunningly beautiful girl who was also supremely fit, charming, very sym-pathetic – not American but, I think, French. We got on wonderfully from the start. Craig always seemed to have things to do and, when Brenda was busy, Sascha took over listening to my lines for me.

The few weeks in Cornwall passed very enjoy-ably, Angie came down to visit, the film was obviously going well, and the only blot was a minor upset with Cornwall's most famous restaurant. Rick Stein, like several TV chefs, has accumulated a lot of money and, it seems, a large chunk of North Cornwall. I rang his main restaurant to book a table, explaining we were the cast of a film being made locally, and perhaps we might meet the chef and owner, but I was told they couldn't find a table for us for three months.

That put me in my place, but I said we were rather hungry and couldn't wait that long as the film would be finished and cut by then. They offered us a table in another place, also owned by Rick Stein, but it wasn't quite the same. It's a shame Michael Winner wasn't there with us that evening – I'm sure he'd have done better!

While we were still filming, Sascha rang me to

say she was coming over from the States and wouldn't it be nice to have lunch. She was bringing a girlfriend from LA. In the end we actually had dinner, and it was lovely to see her again; she was thrilled too, because she was pregnant. Craig couldn't make it, but I was delighted to have made these new friendships.

The next time I met up with Brenda socially, she and some of the others in *Saving Grace* came to see my one-man show when it came down from the Edinburgh Festival to the Hampstead Theatre. It was a success in both places. We all went off to have dinner together in a restaurant in Camden Town. Everything was going well until, towards the end of the meal, I felt as if I'd suddenly been plunged into a vat of dry ice by something Brenda said, suggesting I'd seen Sascha rather too much in Cornwall.

I was completely flabbergasted and numbed.

I couldn't think what she was talking about. The gathering round the table went silent. I would have been flattering myself if I'd thought Sascha was interested in me. I'd simply derived great pleasure from her company, and it was clearly mutual. Whenever she came to London she'd ring me, and I'd ask after Craig. She had met my wife, Angie, and there were no problems there. I make no apologies for having found Sascha fun to be with. Craig certainly didn't seem worried; when Sascha had her baby, she invited me to their London hotel to come and see him. I'm glad to say I've seen Brenda briefly since, and things seemed to be OK between us. And, of course, we were all very chuffed when

Saving Grace won the Audience Award at the Sundance Film Festival.

The one-man show I'd been rehearsing while I was in Cornwall was based on a broadcast script by Peter Tinniswood called *On the Whole, It's Been Jolly Good*. It was the reminiscences of an old Tory Member of Parliament from the Shires as he approaches retirement, written with all the inventiveness, observation and wit that Tinniswood showed for years in the dozens of plays and sketches he wrote for radio and television. I'd adapted it as a stage show which ran for just over an hour.

It was booked to open at the 1999 Edinburgh Festival where, I was told, there would not be a prompter. Before I went up to Edinburgh, I ran into David Jason at Ronnie and Joy Barker's annual party and mentioned how scared I was about delivering such a long monologue. Twenty years before, David and I had toured all over the world with *Not Now, Darling* and nothing bonds actors like a foreign tour. He was quick to come up with a solution.

'What's the set?' he asked.

'My office in the House of Commons.'

'Is there a phone on the desk?'

'Yes.'

'Do you have a diary and some kind of desk chair?'

'I do.'

'OK, then. Disguise the script as a diary, so if you do dry, you can say to the audience, "Goodness me! I've forgotten to ring so and so and I

481

promised him I would." Go over to the desk, sit down in the chair, open the diary and leaf through it to find his number – and your place in the script.' Clever!

When I got up to Edinburgh, I rented a charming flat at the other end of the Royal Mile from the theatre. Each evening I would slowly walk the whole way, going through the complete script in my head. I would arrive at the theatre in time for the 'half' and then go on and do it, with no prompter and a full house every performance.

Generally, I was able to pull it off, but I'll admit to the occasional lapse of memory. When I did dry up, following David's advice, I sat down and looked through the diary to pick up my line. Of course, if I did it more than once in one night, the audience twigged, but they didn't mind and laughed as if it were part of the show. I also added a lot of dialogue and ideas to Peter Tinniswood's superb writing, which he was quite happy about. All in all it was a tremendous success and got some great notices.

Harking back much further in my history, I was visited by the family of Captain McLean of the Black Watch, whom I'd befriended during his short stay in Chadacre before he went off to fight in France. I'd mentioned my connection with the Scottish regiments in an interview with an Edinburgh paper, hoping someone might pick up on it and come in to remind me of that strange but rewarding period in my army career.

The war was brought back to me again when I played Crouchback Senior in the television adaptation of Evelyn Waugh's *Sword of Honour* trilogy. The part was another pleasing departure for me – a deep, thoughtful and complex man, stoically facing his forebodings of the future. His son, Guy Crouchback, was played by a sparkling young actor, Daniel Craig, whose mother, in a strange piece of serendipity, turned out to be a good friend of my daughter, Claudia, in the Wirral. Daniel's a fine actor, his performance in this series and subsequent movies have impressed me a lot – his recent film, *The Mother*, was so good. Now he is the new James Bond, and I wish him the best with it.

I met up with Daniel Craig again when we were working on *Tomb Raider*, with Angelina Jolie – a lovely girl with whom it was a pleasure to work. She's not just a stunner, but also charming and very professional. When I'd finished working on the film she gave me a gorgeous photo with a wonderful, warm inscription. *Tomb Raider* was one of several recent outings in children's movies which I've loved doing, and which my post-bag tells me have created an awareness of my existence among a whole new generation.

Most important of these was a bizarre, but gratifyingly memorable role as the Sorting Hat at Hogwarts in the first two *Harry Potter* films. I went to the studios in Hertfordshire to meet Christopher Columbus, who was directing. He was an enchanting man with a great track record and a feel for the material he was handling. We talked and he told me that I was exactly what he wanted for the hat.

I had never played a hat before, and this wasn't

just a voicing job. The technology which the cinematographers used to mould my moving mouth into the fabric of the Sorting Hat was extraordinary. I spent only one day at the studios for each of the two films, and since the American actor's union went on strike for a fairer deal, Warner Bros were now paying residuals. The films were such massive hits that those two days' work turned out to be highly lucrative. It was great to be part of two of the most successful movies of all time. Unfortunately, the 'hat' hasn't been doffed since.

In early 2001, my most recent live theatrical production – John Mortimer's *Naked Justice* – opened in Leeds. *Naked Justice* was the first of John's stage plays in which I'd appeared, although I'd worked on *Summer's Lease* and *Rumpole* on television and liked a lot of his other work. I found him tremendously stimulating to work with.

Duncan Wheldon was producing this latest piece and when I was asked if I wanted the lead – a judge, again – I jumped at it. The play featured two judges who disliked each other and were in fierce competition, with the older man being edged out by the younger one, played beautifully later in the production by Simon Ward. They are on circuit, staying in judges' lodgings, vying with each other to establish their superiority. Simon substantially improved his part and brought a lot more to the second act, giving it great strength. It was riveting and as well written and incisive as any of John's plays, though it suffered from one debilitating flaw.

It's an important element of the play, as John wrote it, that the first act was played by a group of characters who are ambiguous and obscure, deliberately misleading the audience into thinking they could be a gathering of criminals. The problem was that people who came to see it knew that John wrote about legal people and, on the posters outside, we were shown in our judges' robes, so any possible element of mystery and surprise is nullified. We worked on it and John rewrote somewhat, but, in the end, it was not quite enough. The second act, though, was wonderful – John at his best, drawing his audience right into the story. We did tremendous business in Leeds and Birmingham, and the following year, on a second tour, in Bath and Malvern. But the events of 9/11 cast a gloom on theatreland, so it never came in, but it was a wonderful part and I'd still like another chance to do it again.

Although I still seemed to be pretty busy, I had hoped that life at home might become more mellow. In some ways, of course, it had, but I've discovered that in the role of father, the extent of one's responsibilities doesn't diminish as offspring become older; one must still be on hand to listen and dispense advice, which is occasionally followed. Three of my children followed me in having four of their own, and now with fifteen grandchildren, a new crop arises. I'm even getting prepared for the arrival of more great-grandchildren (two to date).

On top of human responsibilities, there are one's commitments to the animal world. While it's been a long time since I've kept a dog, there are still a lot of felines in my life. I was away doing the Mortimer play when Angie was asked if she would like to take on a pair of Burmese cats – one of moderate parentage, the other, we were told, a positive prince among his breed. By the time I came home, one had already gone walkabout and was nowhere to be found. Angie was desperately anxious and, being a lover of cats myself, even ones to whom I've never been introduced, with snow on the ground, I knew how vital it was to find him.

We put ads in the local shops and newspapers asking for help and offering rewards, but he'd been missing a couple of months by the time we received a phone call from an Irishman, a builder who lived in a house about a mile away, near Warwick Avenue. He said he'd found a cat fitting the description of the missing one, covered in mud and looking a bit rough. He agreed to keep him in the warm until Angie and I could get down there. We went as soon as we could, and sure enough, there was Angie's Mr Big. I fell in love with both the Burmese right away and they've been the greatest friends ever since, in a way I'm sure anyone who has ever had a Burmese cat will confirm.

Sadly, Mischa is now blind and poor old Mr Big has developed a frightening thing called Lupus disease – a wasting condition which plays havoc with a cat, in spite of outrageously expensive veterinary care. I would do anything for these two wonderful creatures who are so loyal, and so ready to listen, especially when I look back at the great feline companions I've had since I first acquired Smaxie, against my mother's wishes, seventy years ago. There's something especially independent about cats that sets them apart from other household pets. They don't, it seems to me, make many concessions to their masters; they aren't prepared to be told what to do – they tell you, and in doing so, they present a permanently intriguing challenge and strong friendship.

I had also half hoped I might have more time to spend in Ibiza where, after ten years of labour (and expense), the reconstruction and refurbishment of my house was finally all but finished. The offers, however, have kept on coming, and I can't break the habit of a lifetime and turn them down.

One job I didn't turn down was an invitation to present one of the British Comedy Awards in 2003 with the ubiquitous Katie Price – aka Jordan. I've never lost any of my appreciation for a well-made female figure, in the same way that I still like a sip or two of good champagne, so to find myself co-presenting the award with this voluptuous woman was a surprising treat. She was charming, almost demure, and I can imagine in former, more gallant days, young men, instead of scrambling all over each other to photograph her breasts, would have written sonnets to them. As it was, the event exposed me to a barrage of paparazzi and my face was splashed over every tabloid paper in the country next morning, simply because I was standing and associating with an enormous pair. Ah well – whatever turns them on! Personally, I'm not sure I'd know what to do with them.

Another job led to a nice reunion with Geraldine McEwan, who'd starred with me in *For Better For Worse* at the Comedy Theatre fifty years before. We were making a *Miss Marple* television drama, in which the first assistant was my old friend David Tomlinson's son, Henry. He kindly gave me a copy of his father's autobiography, bringing back some great memories. The cast included several other old friends such as Charles Dance and June Whitfield, who'd also recently celebrated her eightieth birthday.

My greatest sadness, though, was saying goodbye to Ronnie Barker. Ronnie and I first met in 1959, in *The Navy Lark*, and we'd kept up our friendship ever since. I was a great fan of his work, and loved appearing with him in the BBC series *Foreign Affairs*. Why he was never honoured with a knighthood, I simply can't fathom, particularly when one considers the enormous amount of joy he gave and the warmth with which he was regarded by the British public. However, I'm glad that he *was* honoured with a major memorial service at Westminster Abbey. Apart from Ronnie's talent, which was prodigious, he was without doubt one of the nicest, most genuine people I've ever met in this crazy business, and I miss him hugely. Fortunately, we will still be able to see his talents on the many repeats of his shows.

I hadn't worked with Peter O'Toole since 1991, in *King Ralph*, a big movie about an American succeeding to the English throne, which went down very well in the States but, predictably, not quite so well here. I'm delighted that my next outing with him was tremendously rewarding, though, as I write, it has yet to be seen in public.

I first heard about the project in 2005, just after I got back from a brief, busy week in Ibiza (fraught with the very last stages of rebuilding the *finca* and landscaping the gardens). Roger Michell (the director of *Notting Hill*) rang out of the blue and invited me to pop round for a chat with him, producer Kevin Loader and writer Hanif Kureishi, at a Covent Garden hotel. I hadn't met either of them before, although, of course, I knew their reputations. Their last collaboration had been an unusual movie called *The Mother*, about a sixty-year-old widow rediscovering her sexuality with her daughter's lover, a young builder sensitively portrayed by Daniel Craig, and they'd worked together more than ten years before on *The Buddha of Suburbia* – a clever picture that was very well received.

As soon as I saw Hanif Kureishi's screenplay for *Venus*, I thought it something very special and wanted to be involved. It was beautifully written, with lines that just lifted themselves from the page. The story revolves initially around the friendship of three old actors, and I loved the part they were proposing for me. Fortunately, I got on well with the writer and director and they rang the very next day and asked me if I wanted to do it.

The other actors were being played by Peter O'Toole and Richard Griffiths – I couldn't have cast better myself – and Vanessa Redgrave was to play Peter's ex-wife, making a potentially heavenly combination. My character, Ian, who's living on his own, has a feisty young great-niece, Jessie, foisted on him by his family, to look after him. Peter's character, Maurice, is a man always open to inappropriate infatuation, following wherever his phallus leads. Despite a fifty-year age gap, he falls for Jessie – the *Venus* of the title. She is played by a lovely young actress, last year's Gold Medal Graduate from the Guildhall drama school, Jodie Whittaker. She milks the old fool for all she can, while Ian looks on in disgust as the relationship develops and disintegrates.

Roger Michell has encouraged an amazing performance from Jodie, whose seductive body perfectly conveys the girl's youthful selfishness. Jodie looks right, she sounds right, and I imagine she'll be up and away after this.

Roger's background as a theatrical director is obvious, too, in his use of wider shots, not endless close-ups to make up for under-acting. Vanessa, as Maurice's ex-wife, is as superb as she's ever been in a part that makes no concessions to an actress's vanity in a part that doesn't require her to be remotely beautiful, but she is a joy to watch.

We filmed for eight weeks around London and at Ealing Studios (where, nearly fifty years before, Kenny Williams had held up the traffic while we were making *Carry On Constable* – and I can truly say it didn't feel anything like so long ago). We did a few weeks before Christmas 2005 and were scheduled to start again in the New Year. I was enjoying the movie, feeling I was working on something pretty special and looking forward to getting on with it when, a few days after Christmas,

Kevin Loader the producer rang to tell me Peter had had an accident. On Boxing Day he'd tripped over a pile of clothes and broken his hip. At my age, and even for a youngster like Peter, hip-breaking is a risky business – so is surgery. The whole production was in jeopardy and had to be put on hold for four weeks.

I hoped and prayed for Peter's sake – and mine – that they would be able to sort him out in time for us to carry on. For a short while, the prospects weren't encouraging, and I think there was a real fear that this potentially first-rate movie wouldn't be completed. However, with a magnificent effort, Peter was back at work four weeks later, in considerable discomfort, but in fine acting form. There are scenes where the poor man has to crawl around on the floor – not easy with a freshly broken hip, but he didn't allow a hint of it to mar his performance.

Peter's Maurice is a *tour de force*. Like me, he loved his lines and, with Richard Griffiths, we found ourselves, three old actors playing three old actors, sparking wonderfully. Peter and I have a lovely scene in the Actors' Church in Covent Garden, where a group of musicians is rehearsing and we dance together – a pair of long-standing, very close friends, old actors who may have worked together for fifty years and are still wondering what new jobs there may be lurking around the corner. One never knows – one can only hope that there are still corners.

There is an unusual and very moving end to *Venus* – a strong finish to a poignant, funny and deeply perceptive movie that deserves to do very well indeed. Certainly it has some of the best lines I've ever had to deliver and, sparring with the always challenging O'Toole, I felt as close to the top of my game as I ever have. But, as I may have told you, I don't like to prognosticate, and how the public takes to it remains to be seen.

In between acting jobs, I find I have also become a writer, a far more arduous calling than I imagined. Of course, having set out to reflect on the last eighty years, with seventy of them in theatre, films, radio and television, was perhaps more ambitious than I realised. In these memoirs, which are already longer than ordered by my publishers, there are inevitably a large number of important people and events I haven't mentioned. I've tried to give a balanced view, warts and all, of my experiences in a career that has had some tremendous highs, and several of the opposite. Whether there are any lessons, good or bad, to be learned, I leave the reader to judge. Most of all, I wanted to make clear the great difference between an actor's public image and the private person hiding behind it, always trying to emerge and surprise.

I have without question had moments of luck and, like the chap in Shakespeare, taken life's tide at the flood, but I was always encouraged and emboldened by the women in my life – my mother, who started it all; my first wife, Penny, with whom I grew into the business; my long-time lover, Caroline Mortimer, who urged me towards more challenging work; and my present wife of nearly twenty-five years, Angie, who encouraged me to make the great change in my career that led to the most exciting work I've ever done. I'm particularly thankful too, to Penny for producing with me such an enormous band of children.

And, above all, I'm eternally grateful to the public who have followed my career with such loyalty over the many, many years, and supported me with special warmth and affection. I've always considered them the missing members of the cast. Bless you all! Or should one close this unique part of my experience with a last Ding Dong or goodbye and not Hello?

The publishers hope that this book has given you enjoyable reading. Large Print Books are especially designed to be as easy to see and hold as possible. If you wish a complete list of our books please ask at your local library or write directly to:

Magna Large Print Books
Magna House, Long Preston,
Skipton, North Yorkshire.
BD23 4ND

This Large Print Book for the partially sighted, who cannot read normal print, is published under the auspices of

THE ULVERSCROFT FOUNDATION